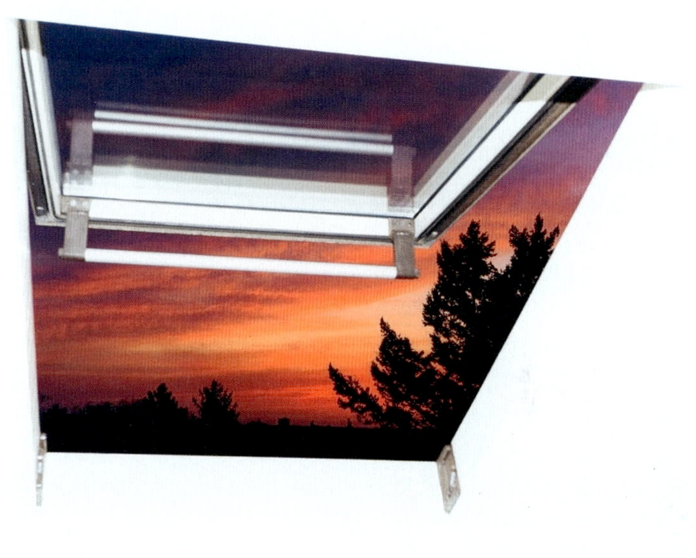

AF473688

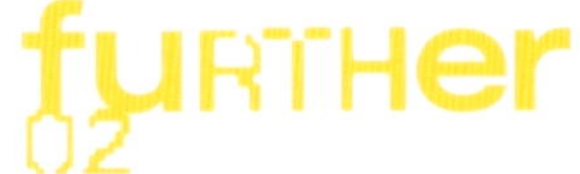
further
02

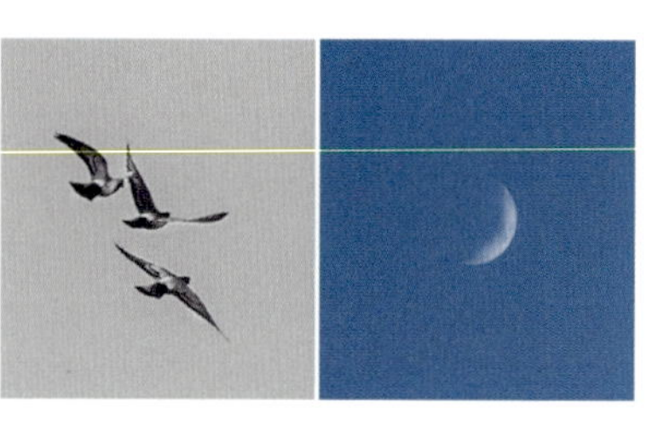

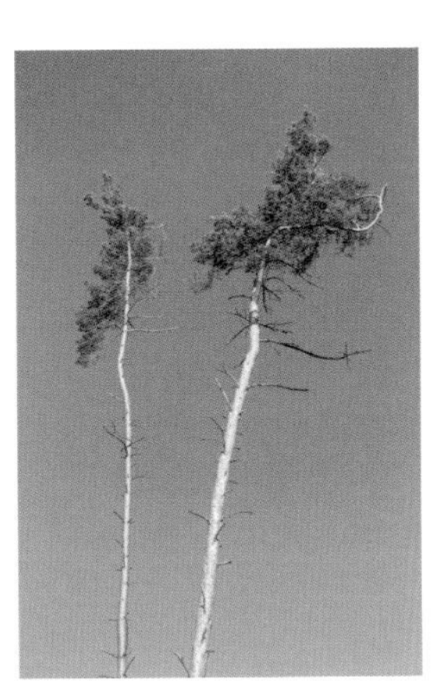

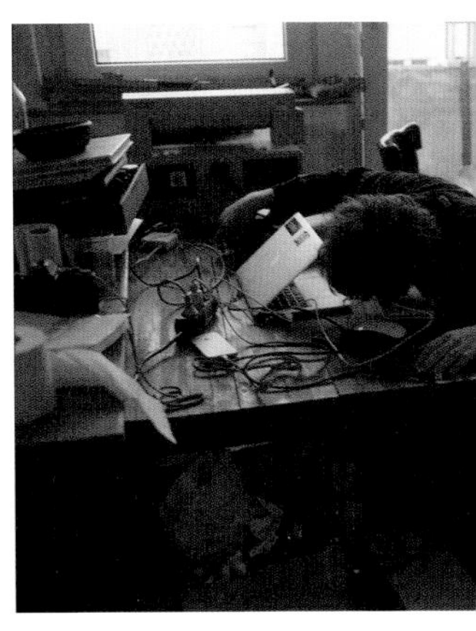

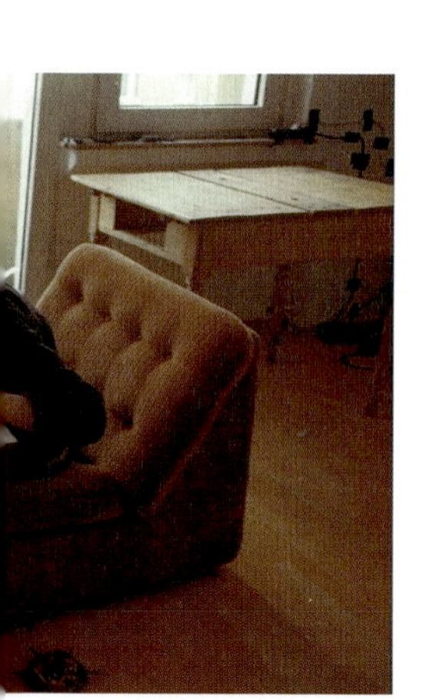

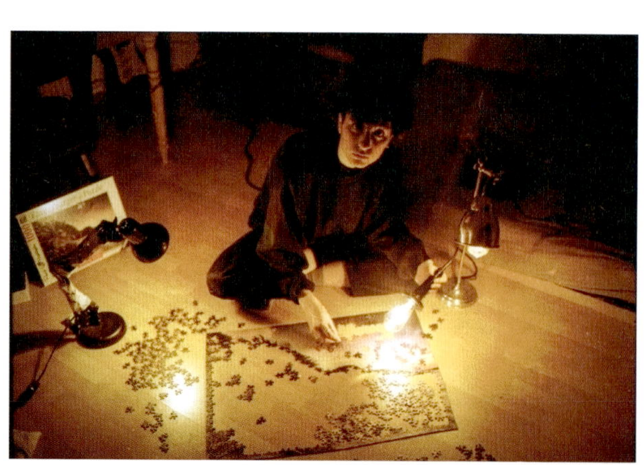

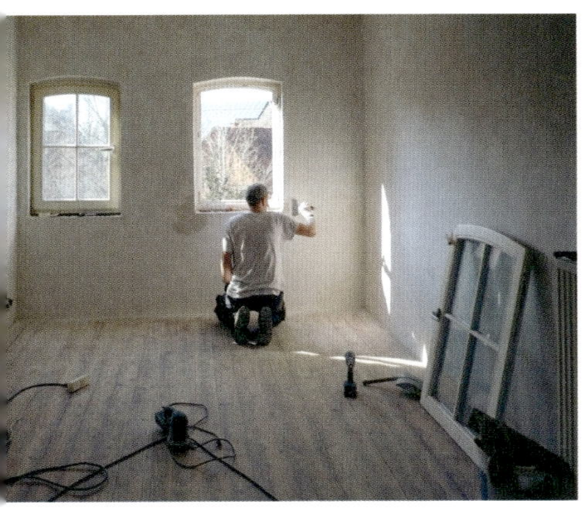
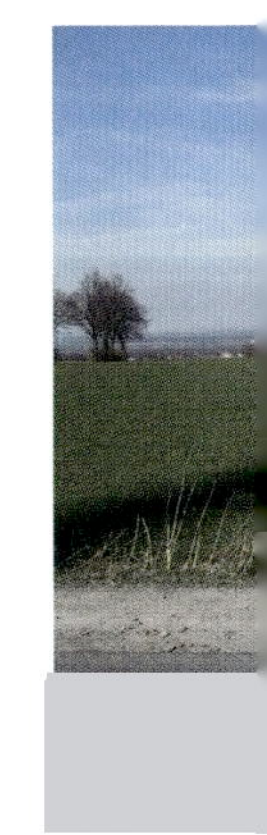
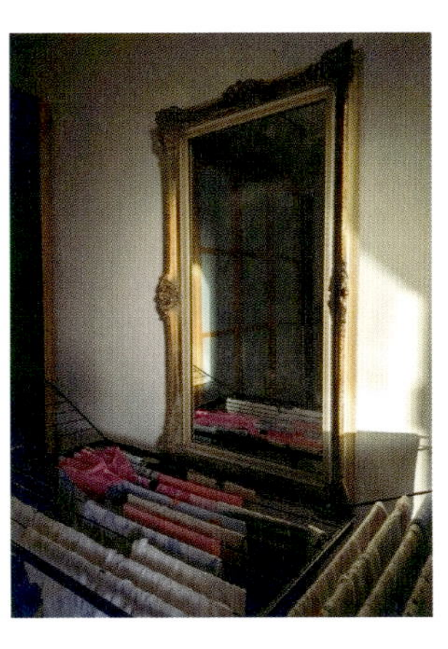
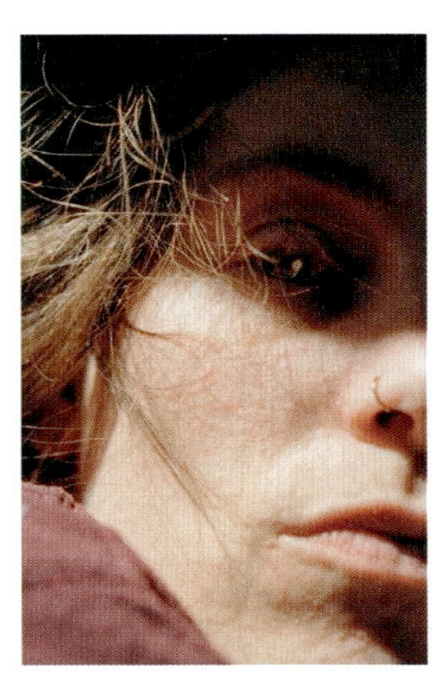
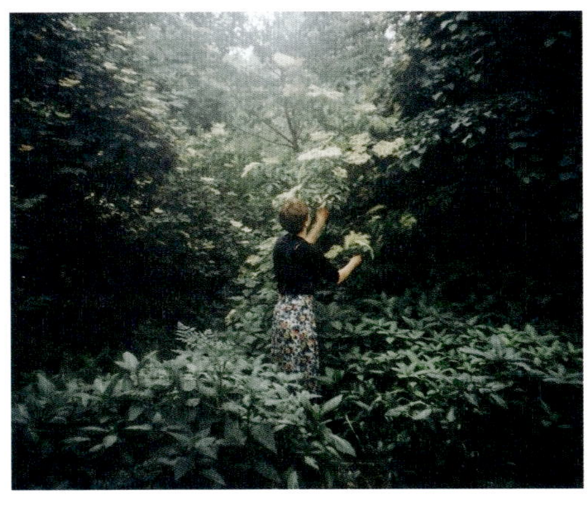
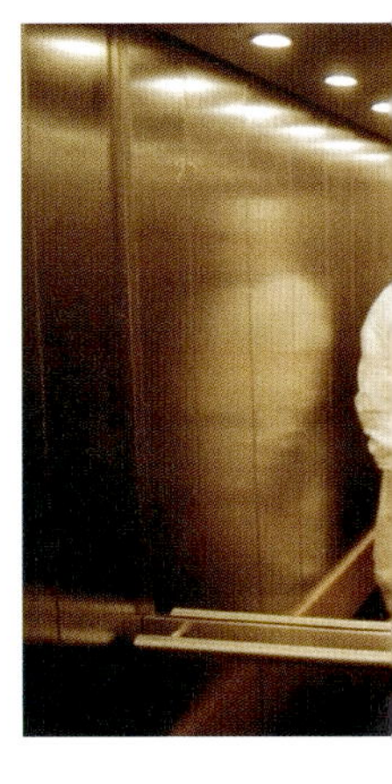

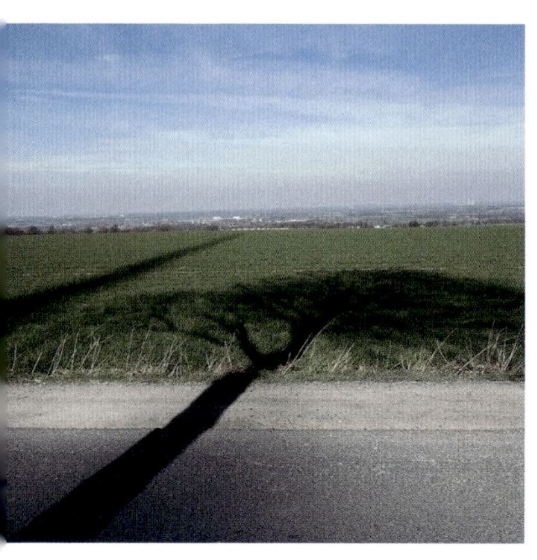
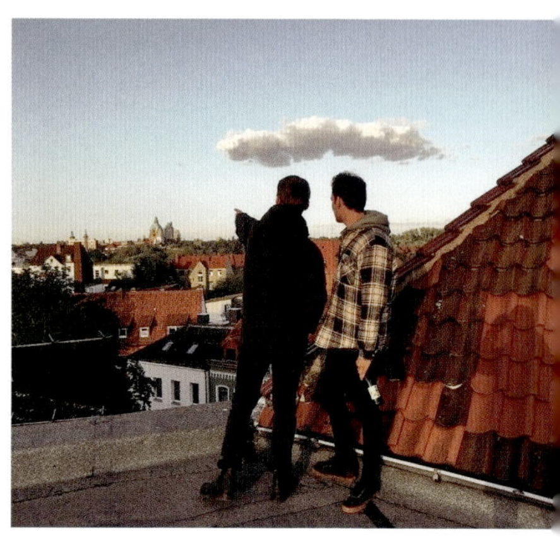
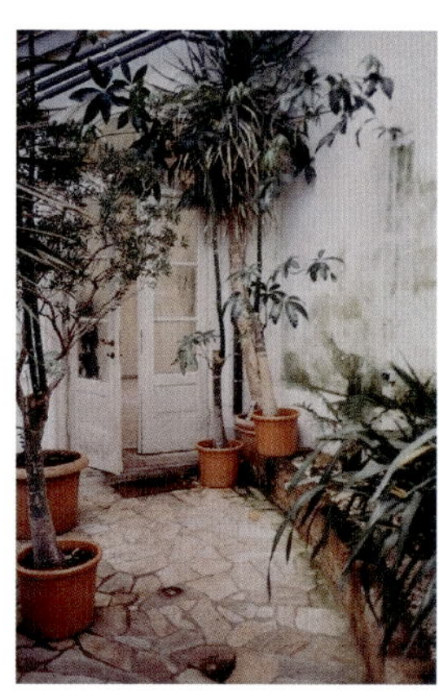
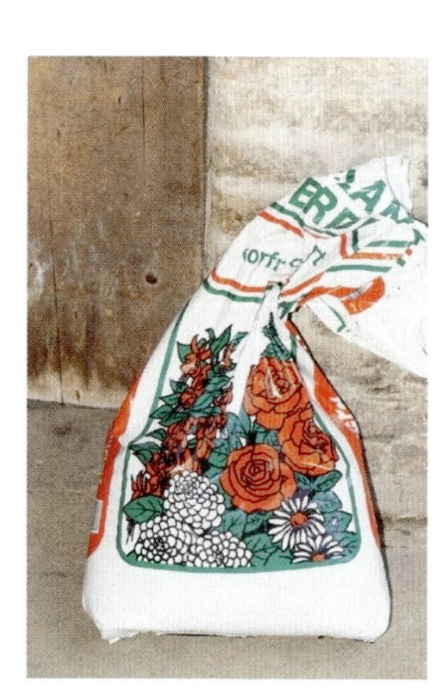
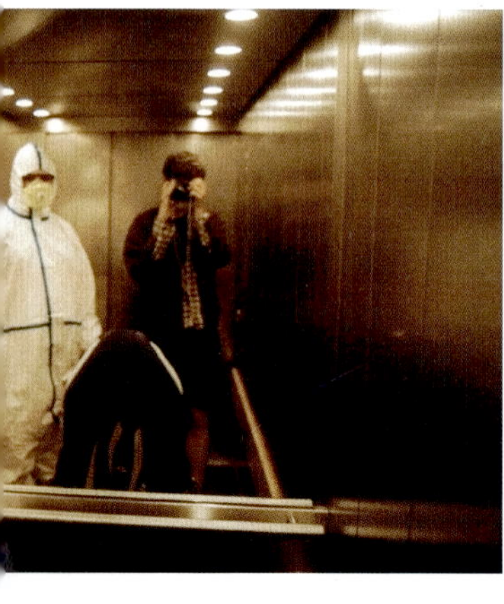

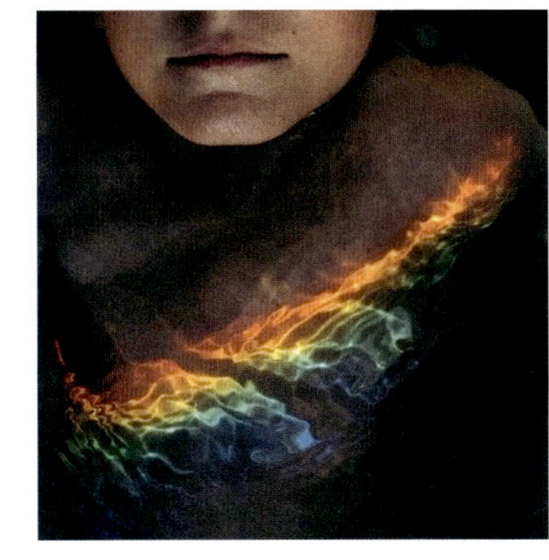

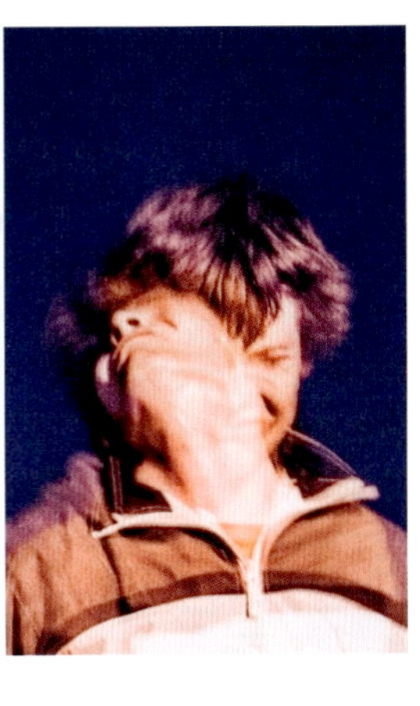

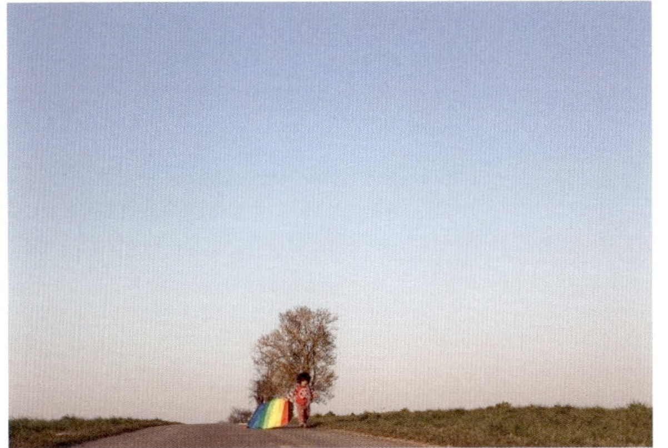

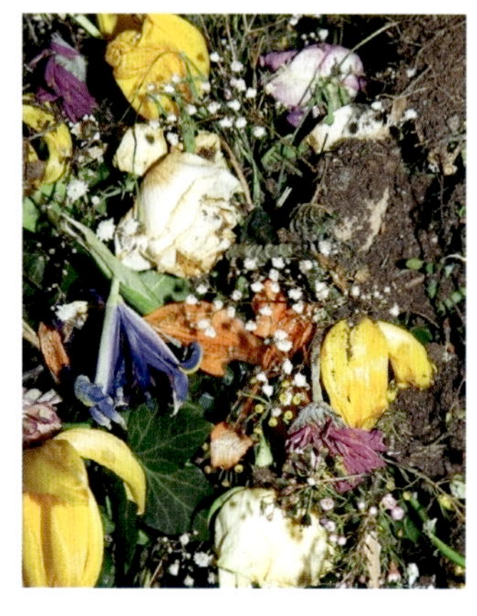

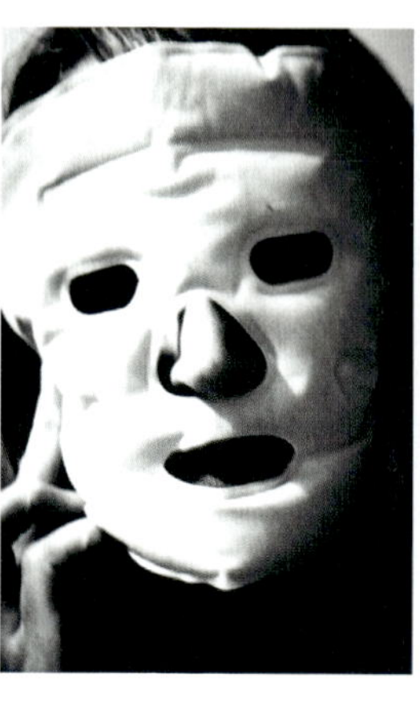

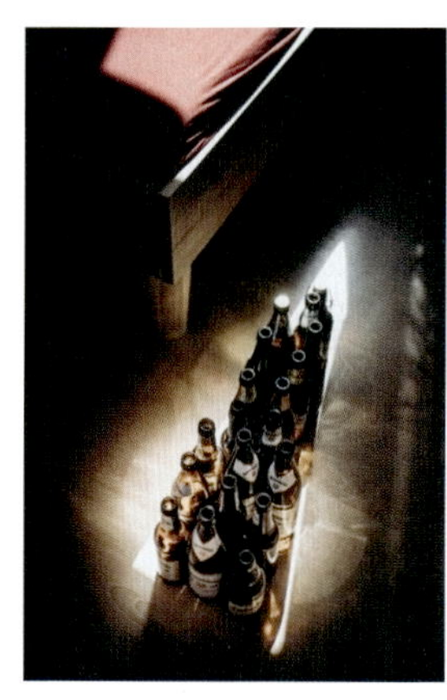

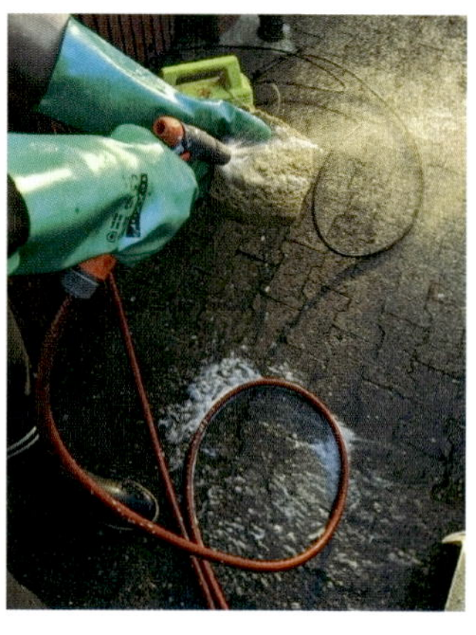

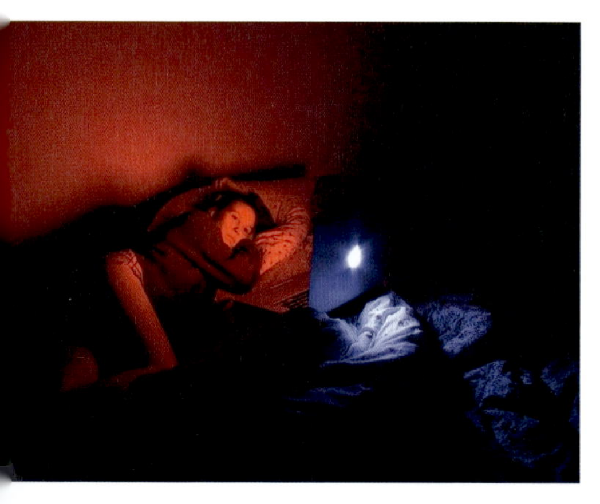

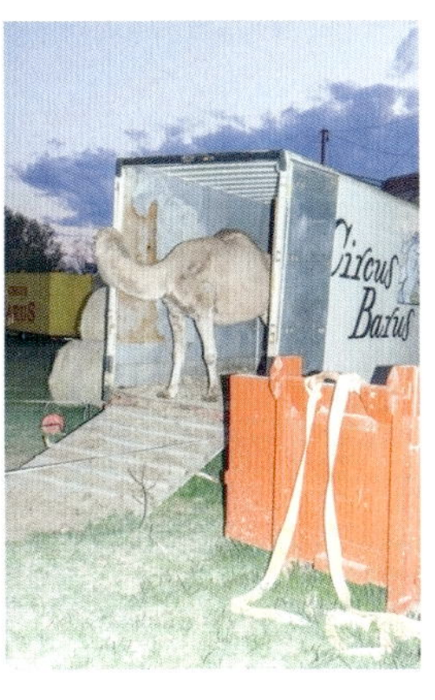
Circus
Barus

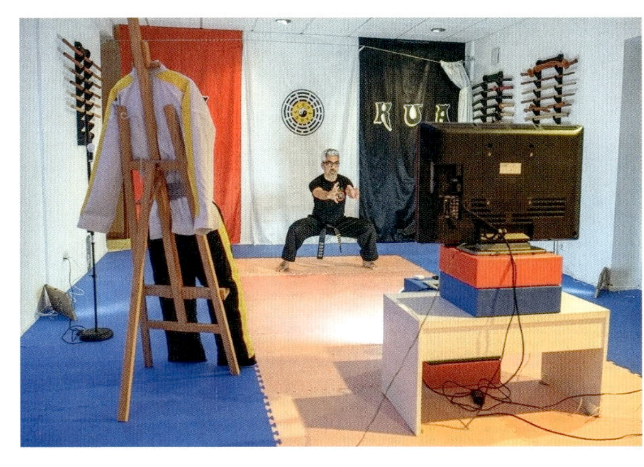

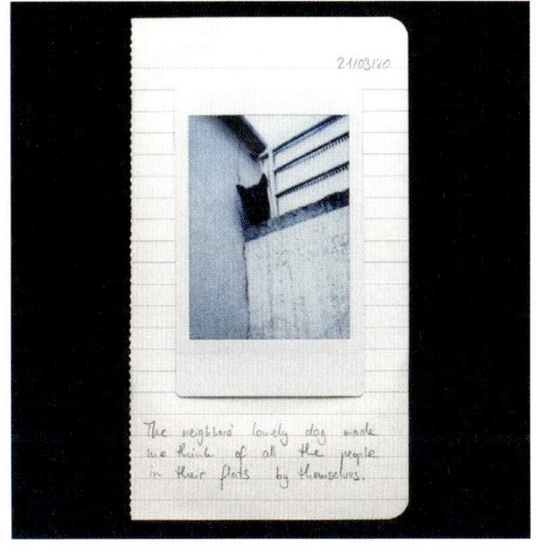
21/03/20
The neighbors' lonely dog made
me think of all the people
in their flats by themselves.

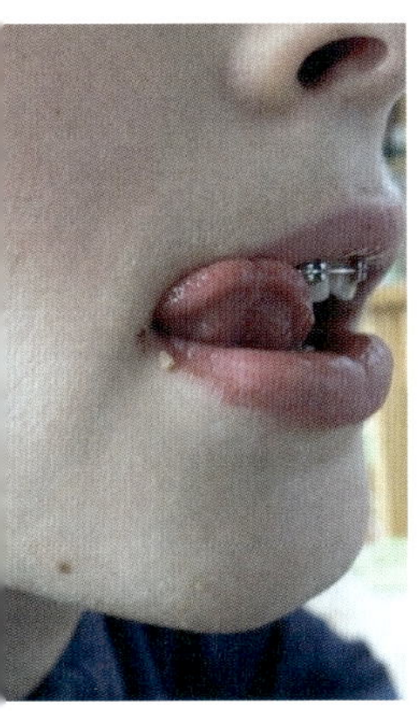

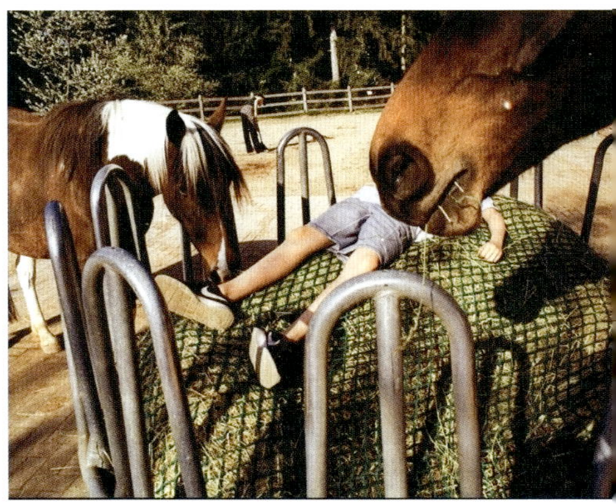

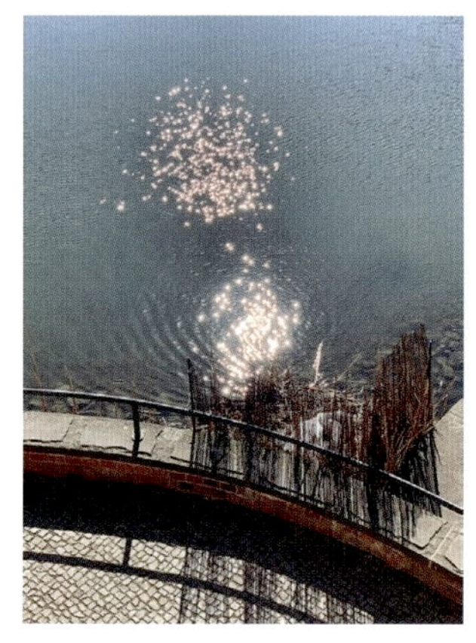
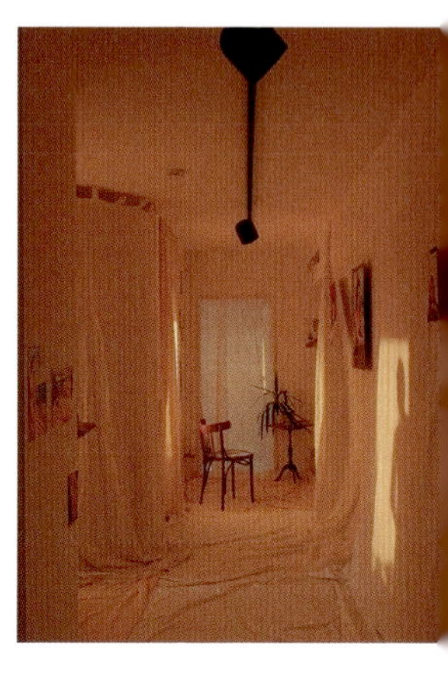
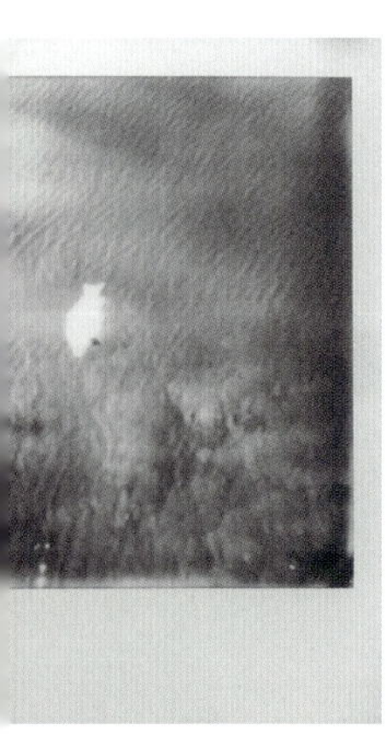
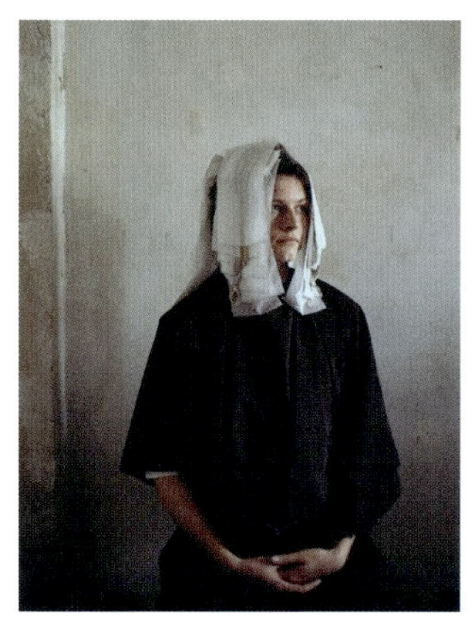
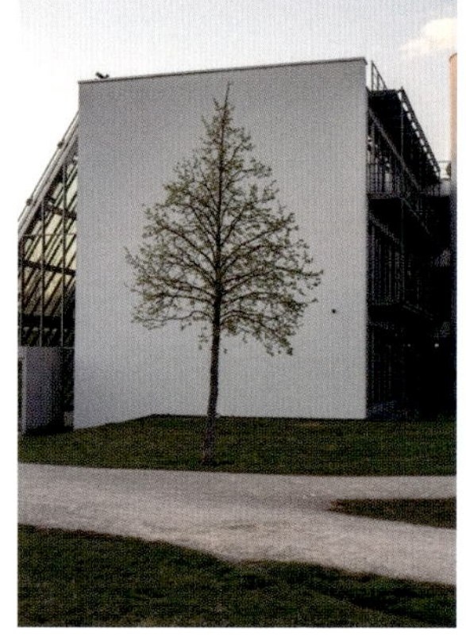
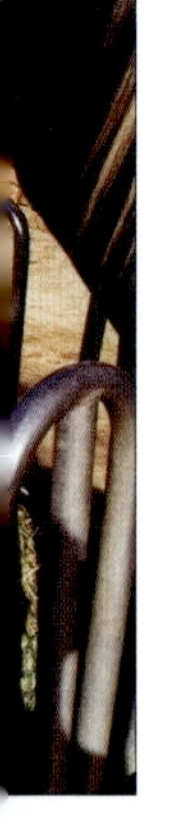
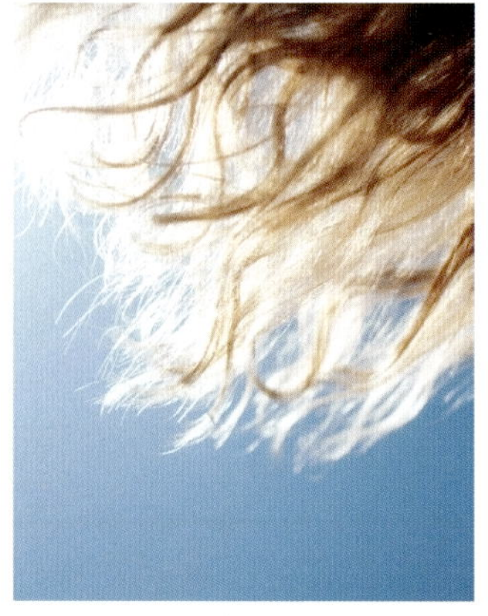

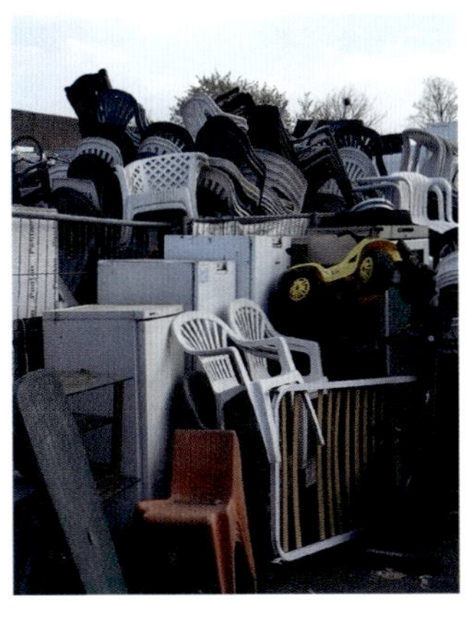
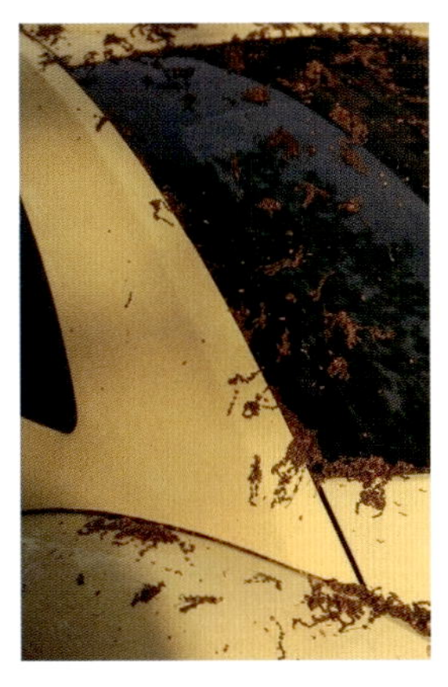
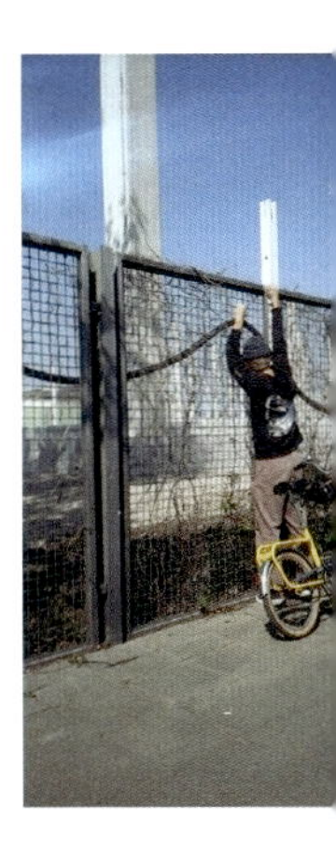
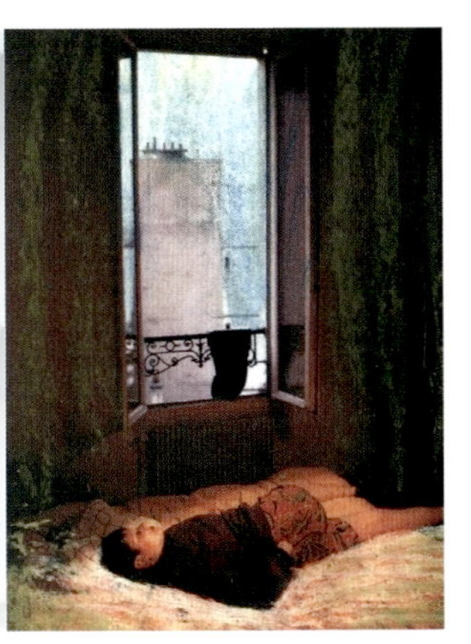
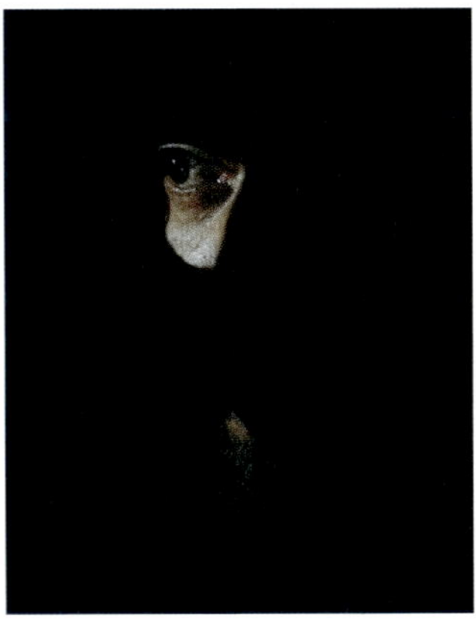
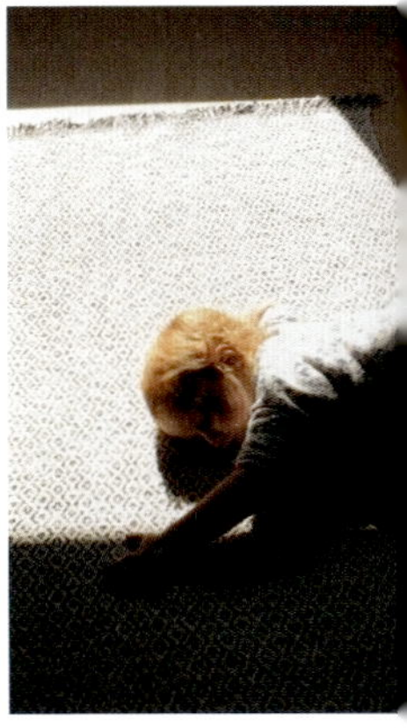

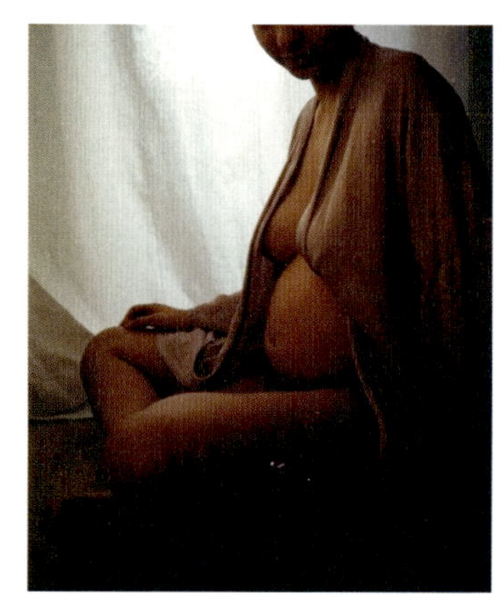
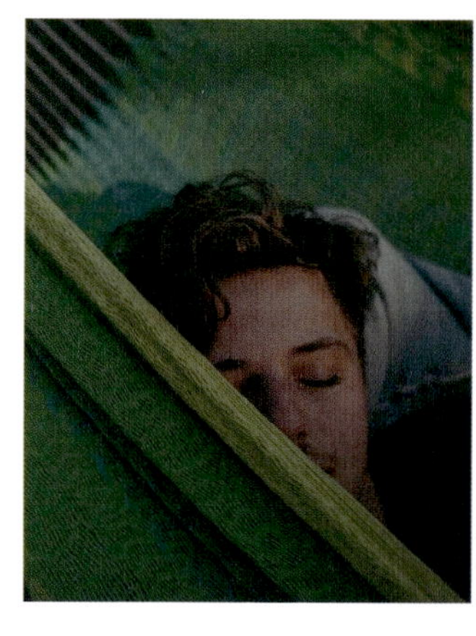
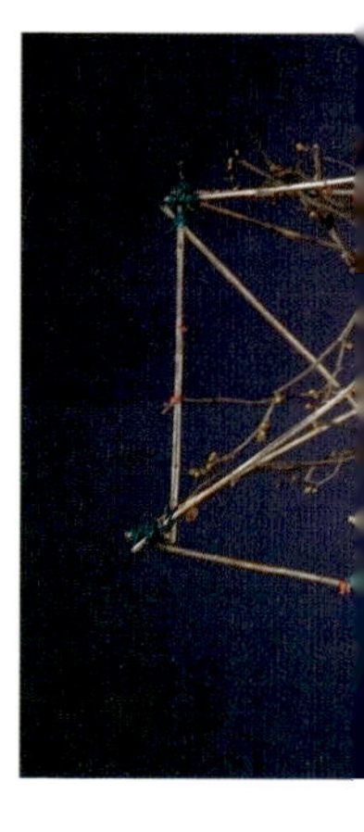
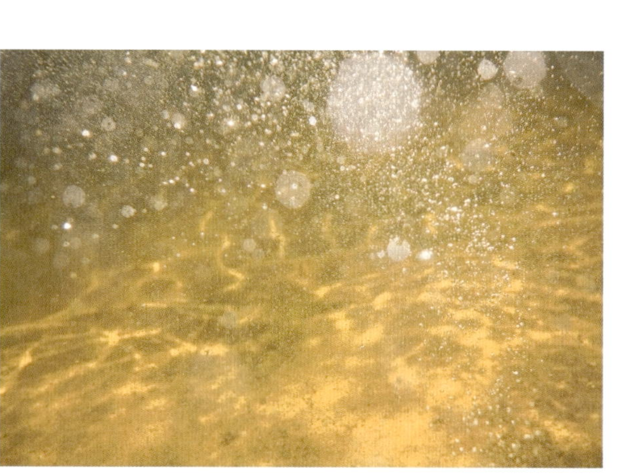

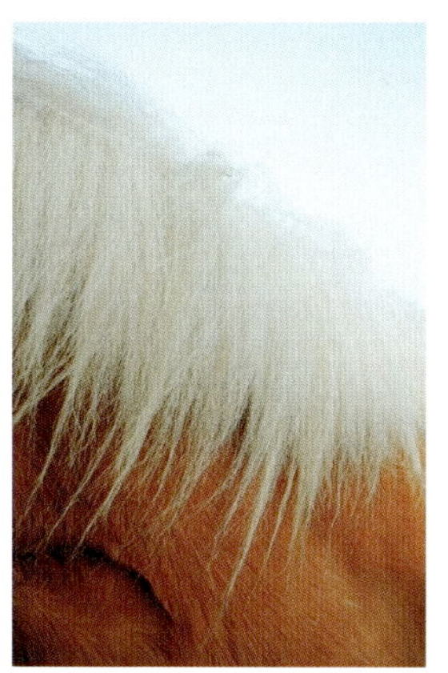
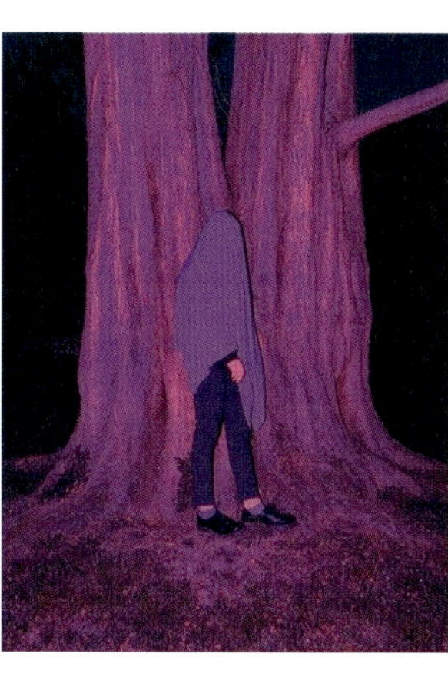
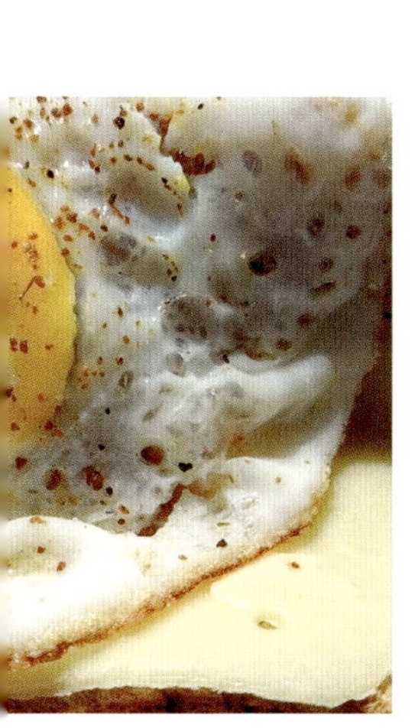
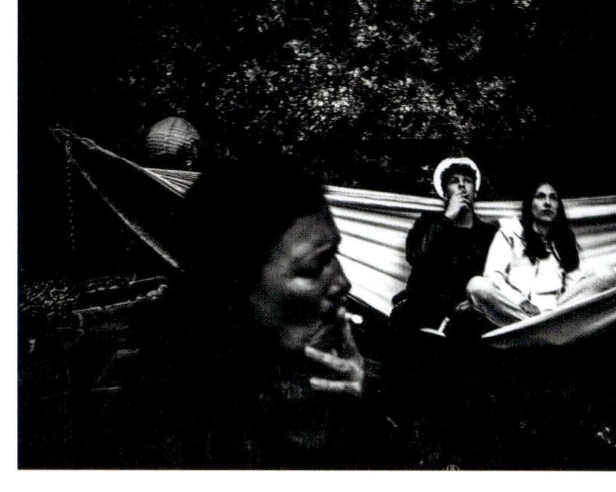
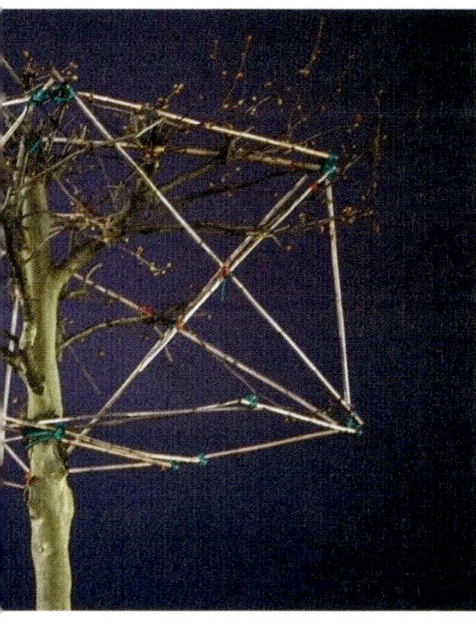

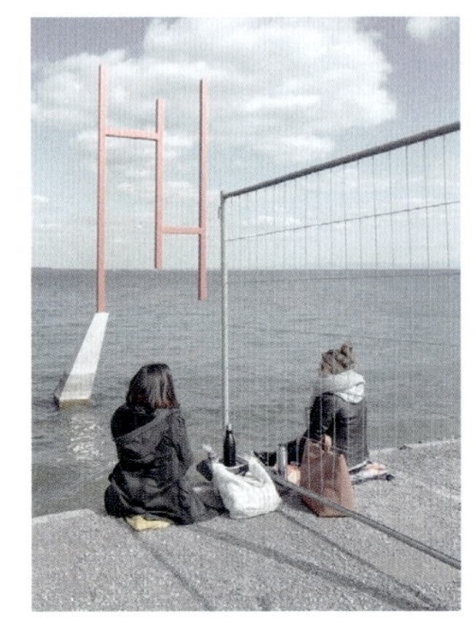

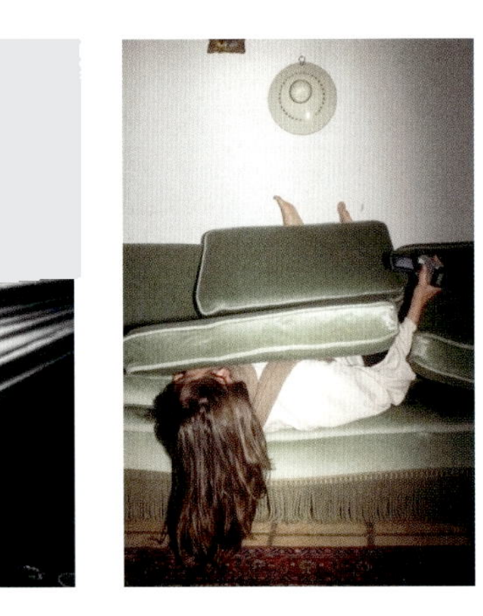

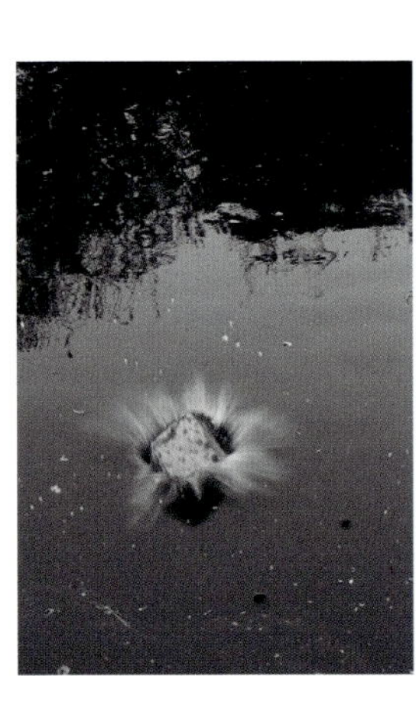

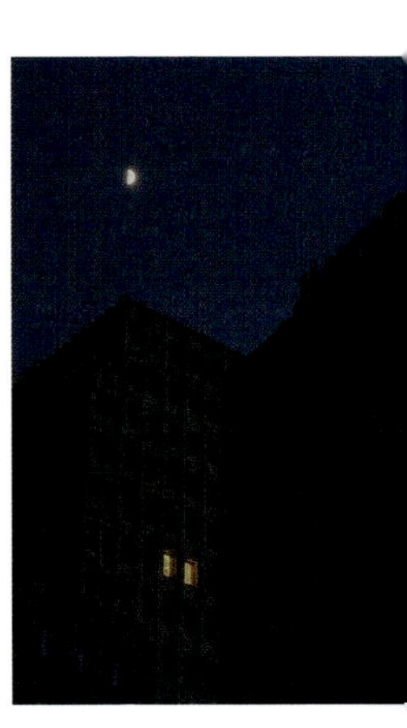

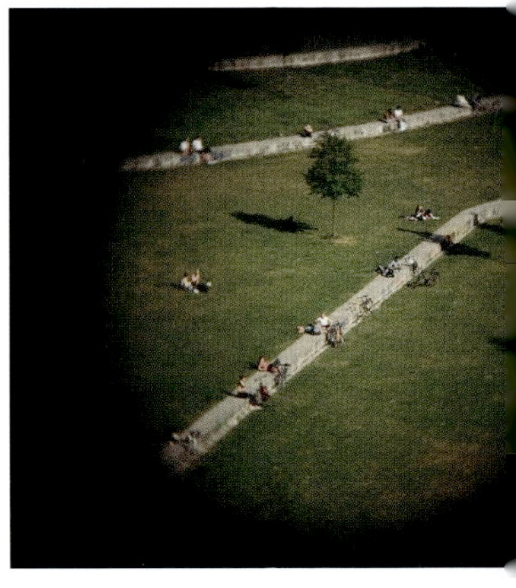

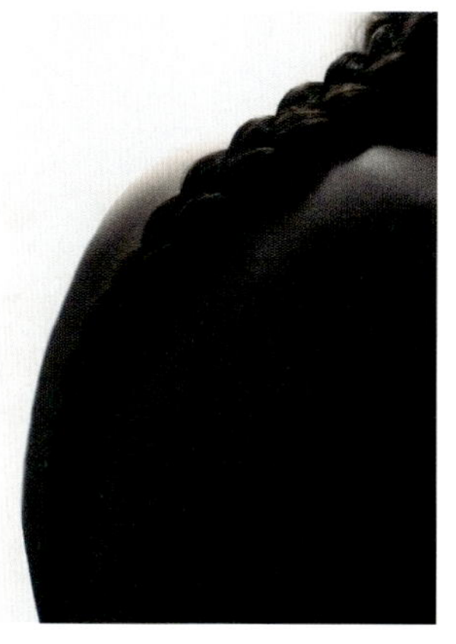
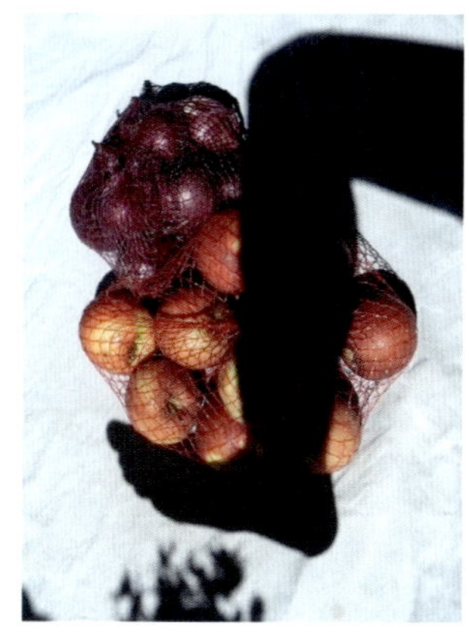
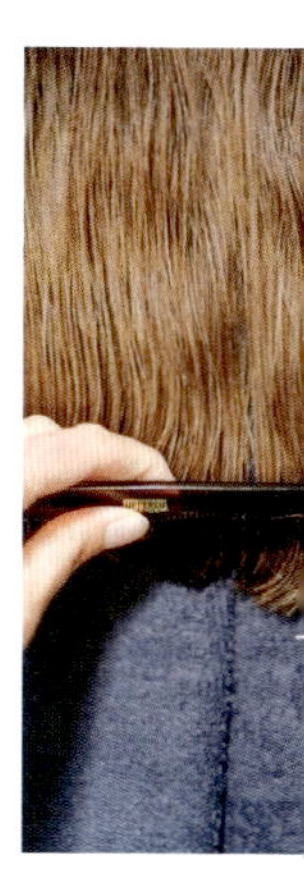
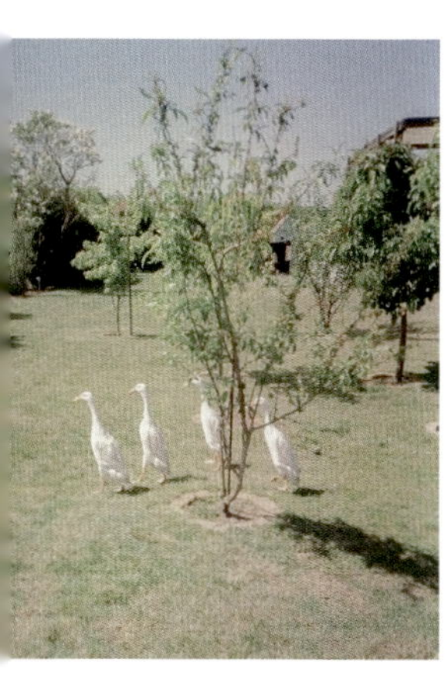
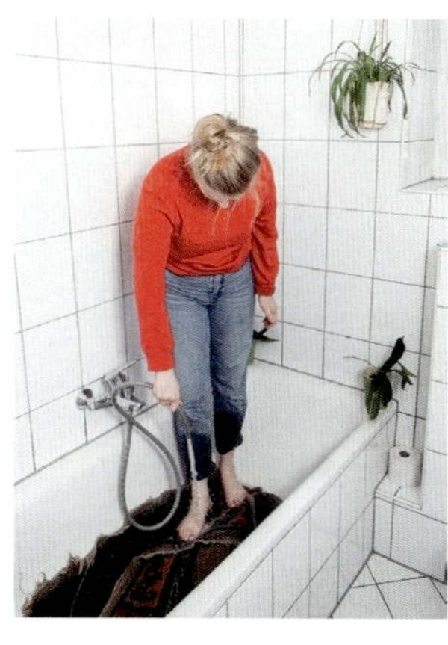
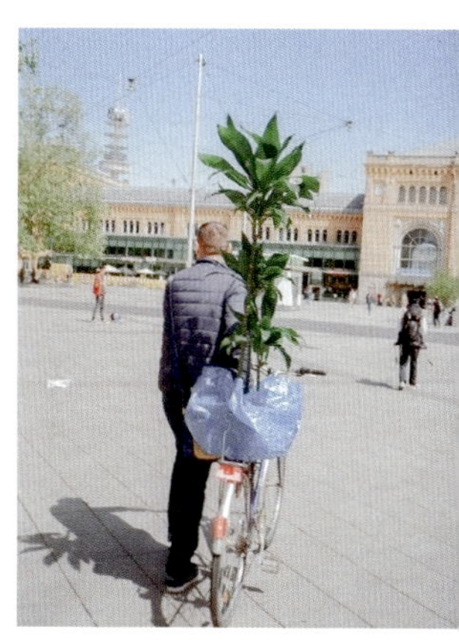
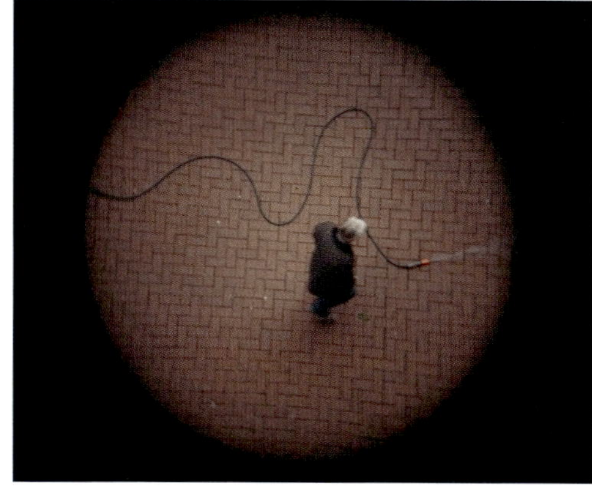

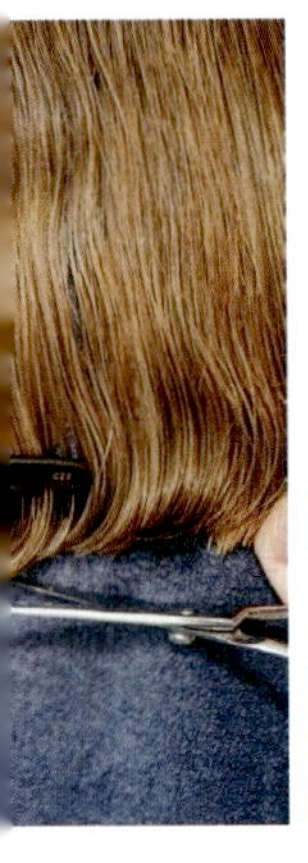
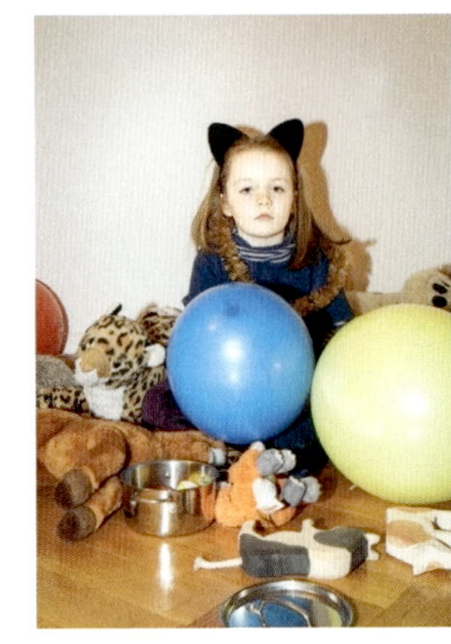
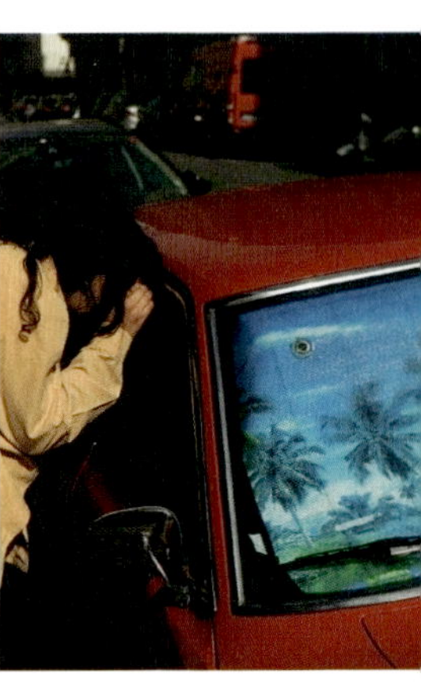
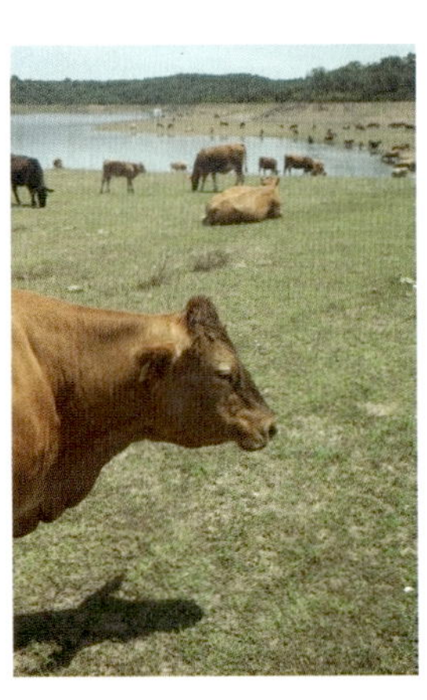
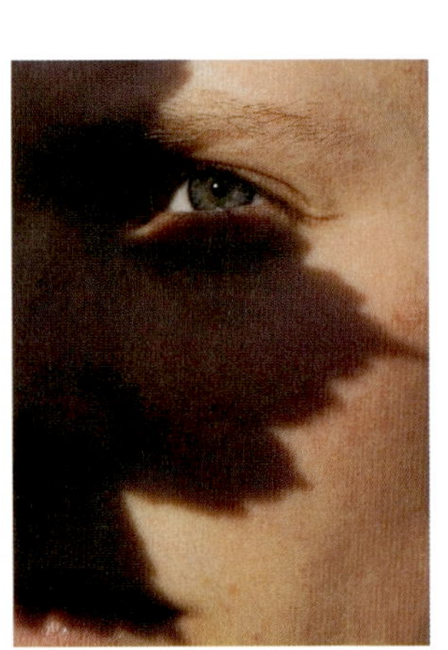
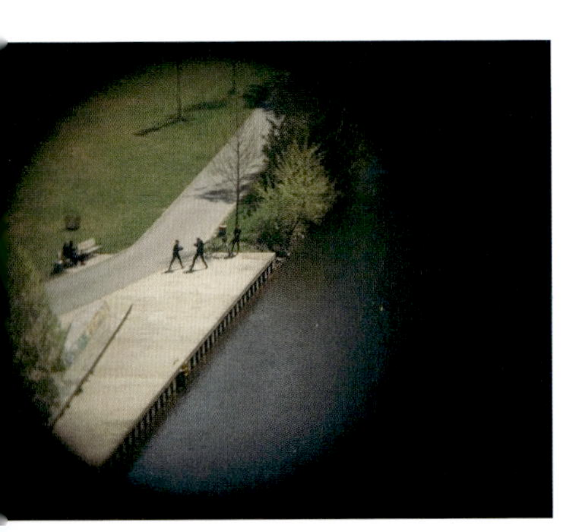
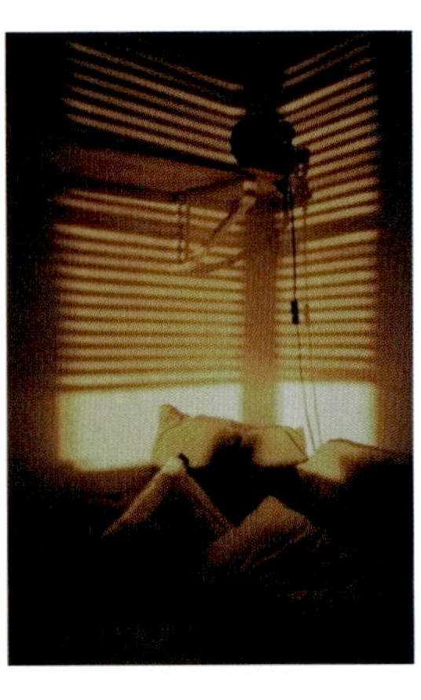

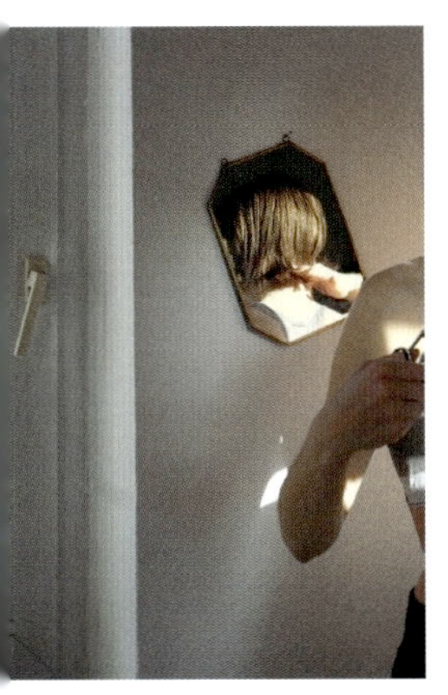

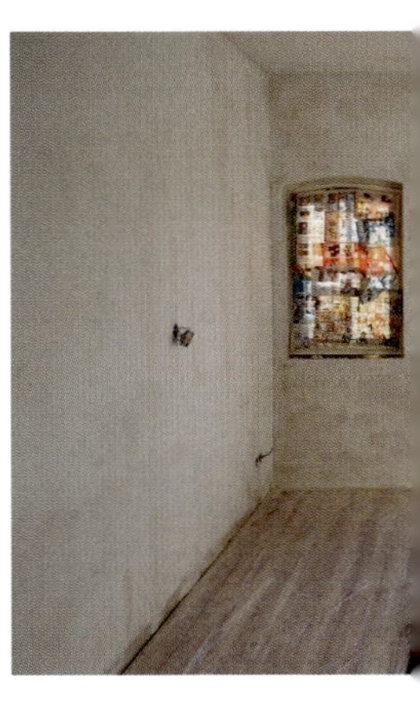

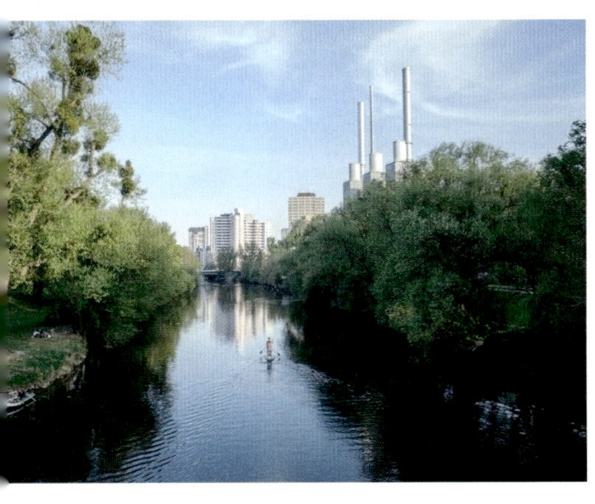

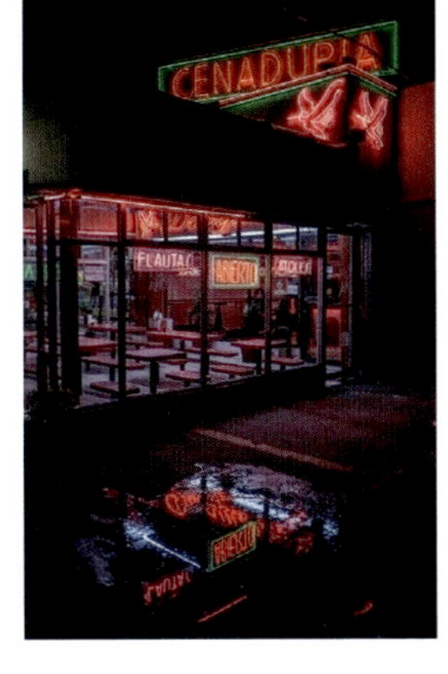

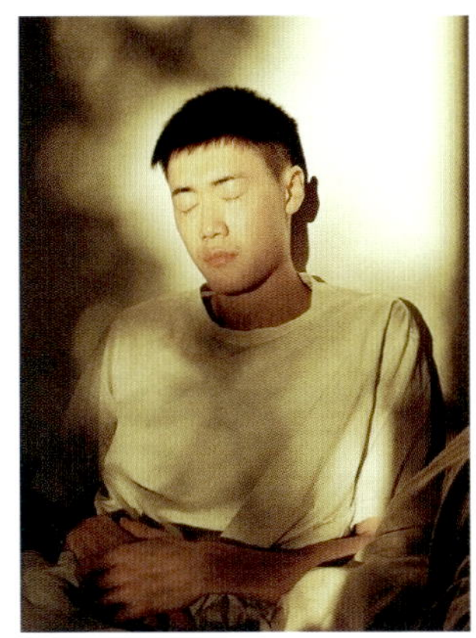

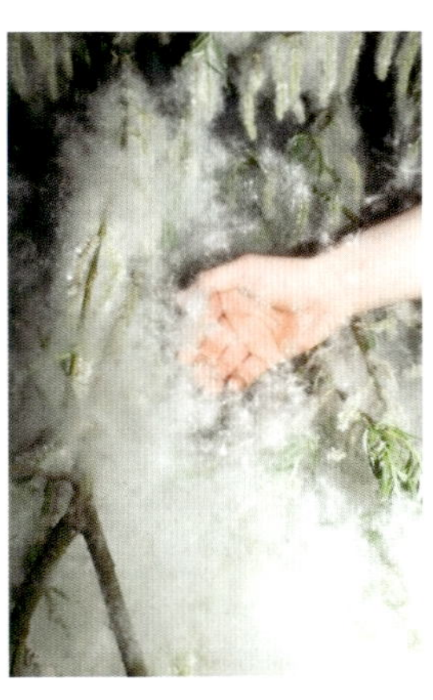

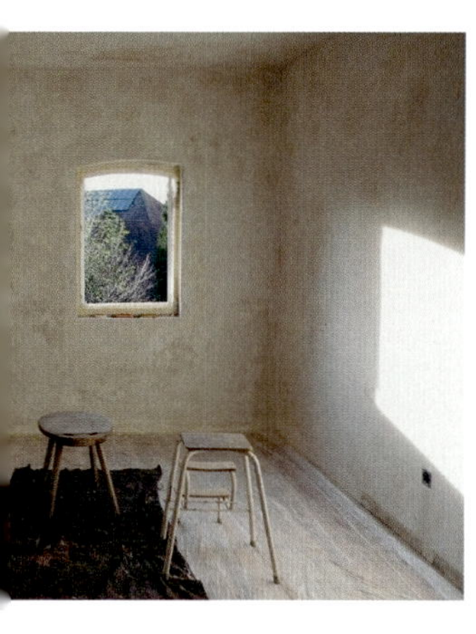
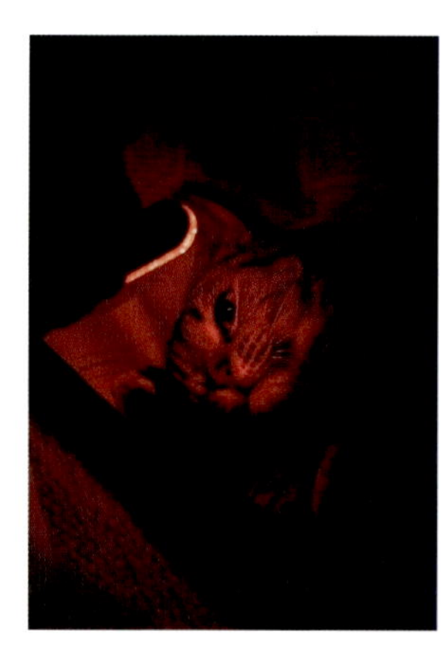
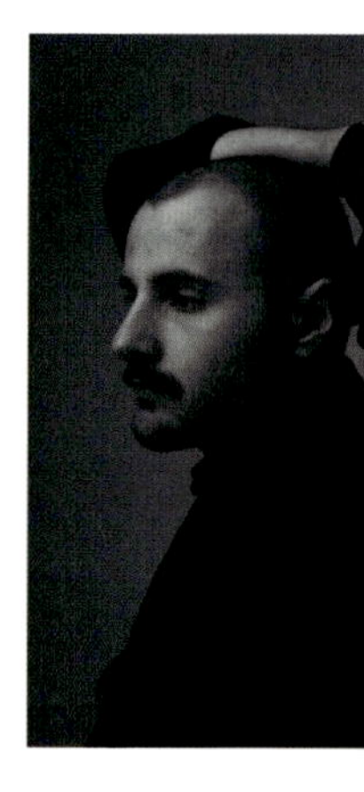
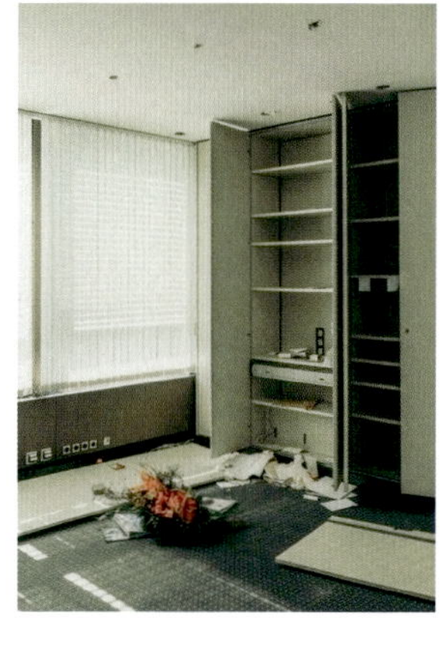
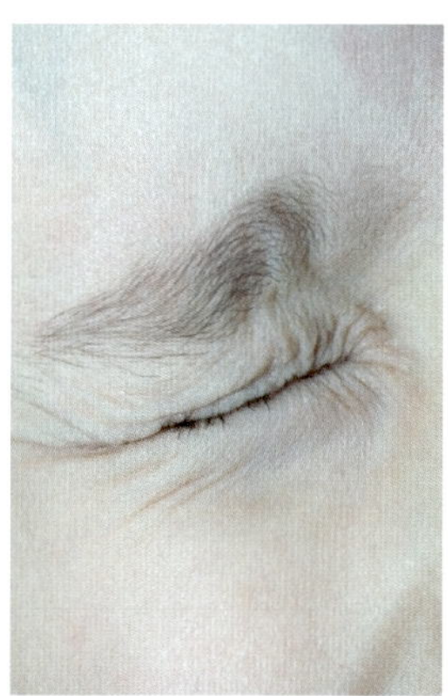
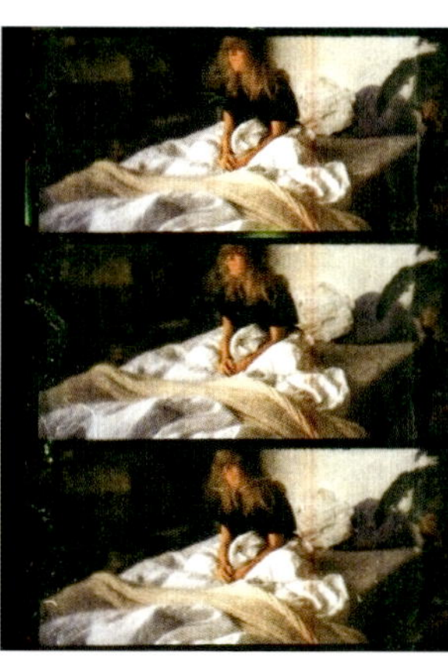

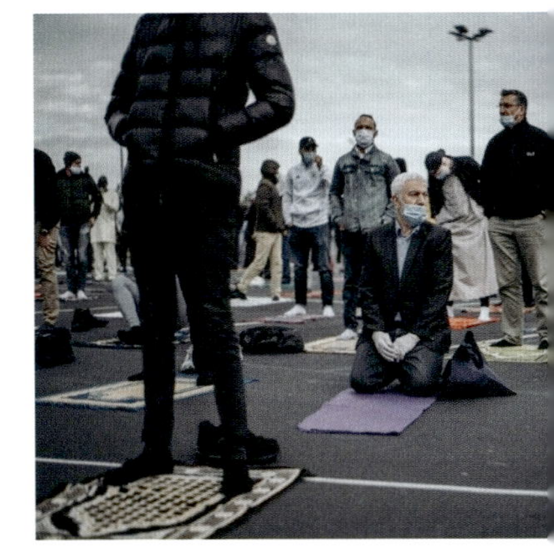

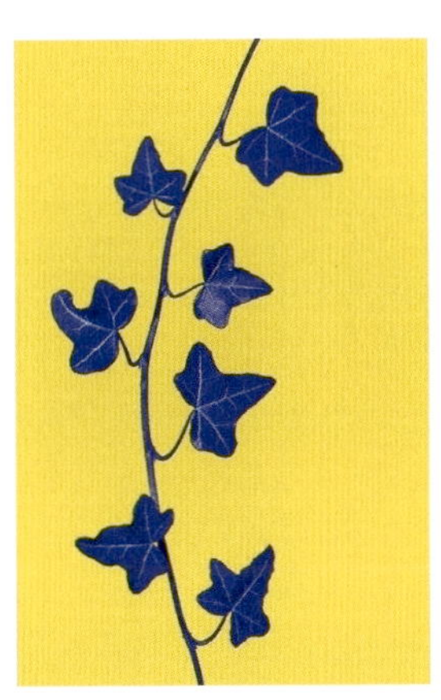

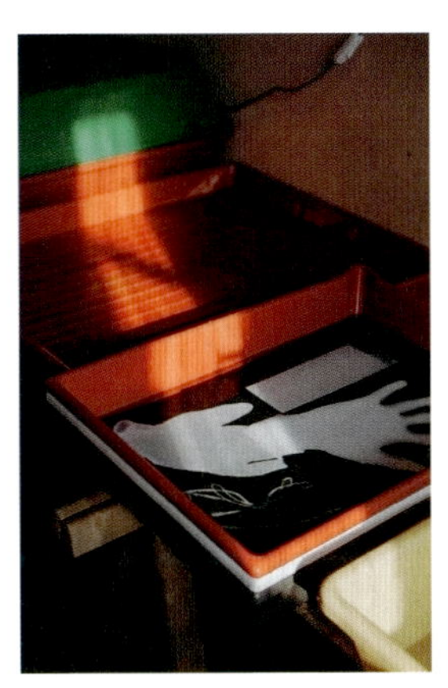

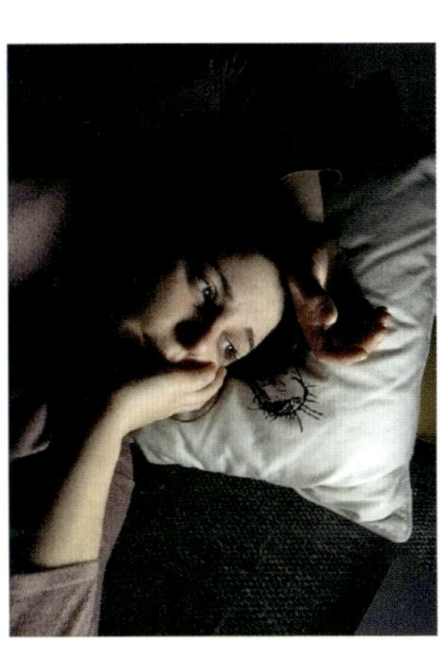

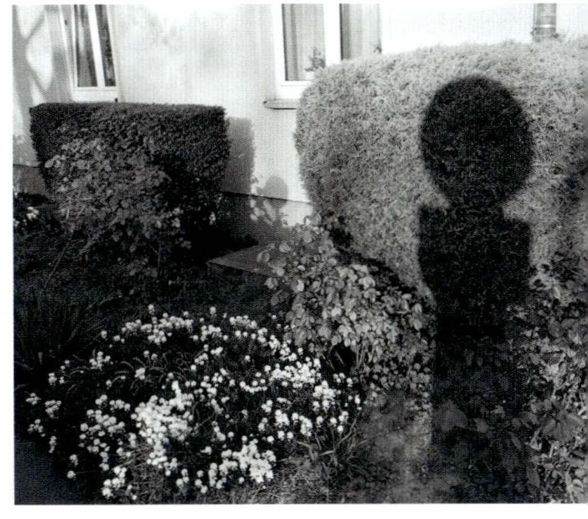

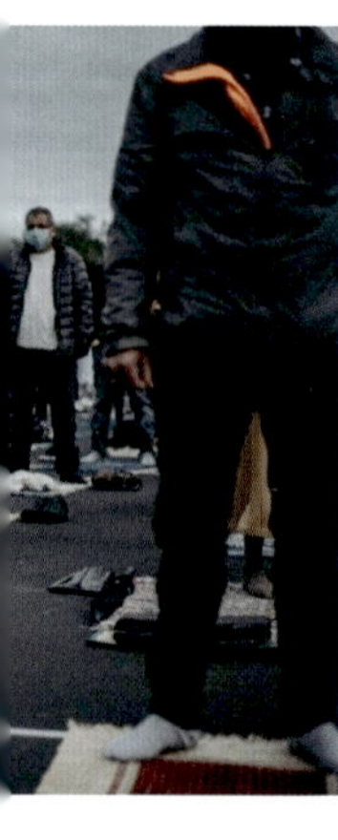

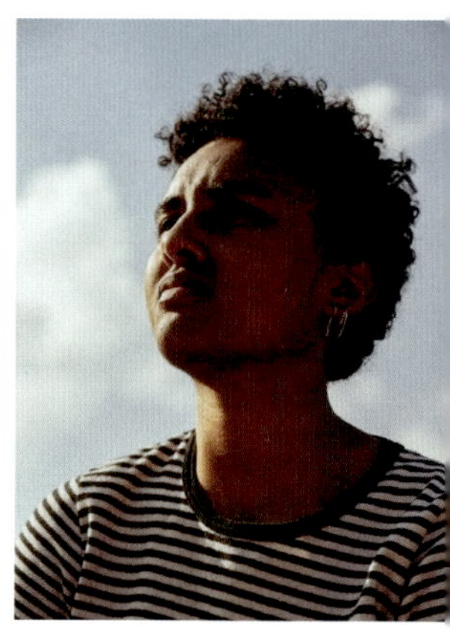

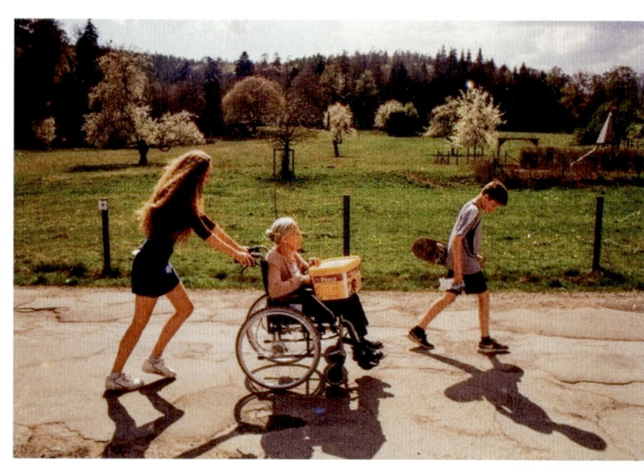

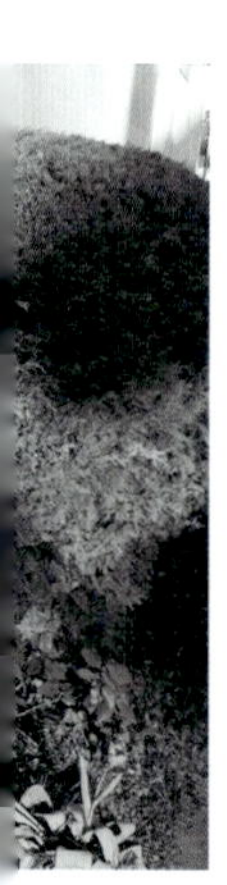

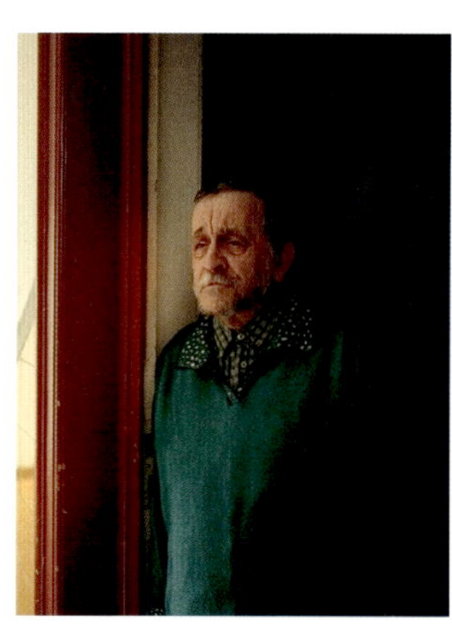

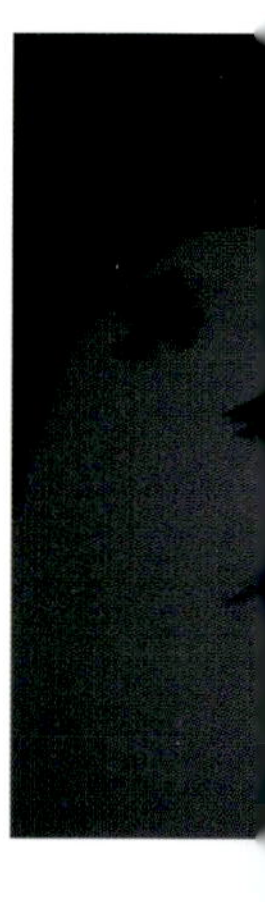

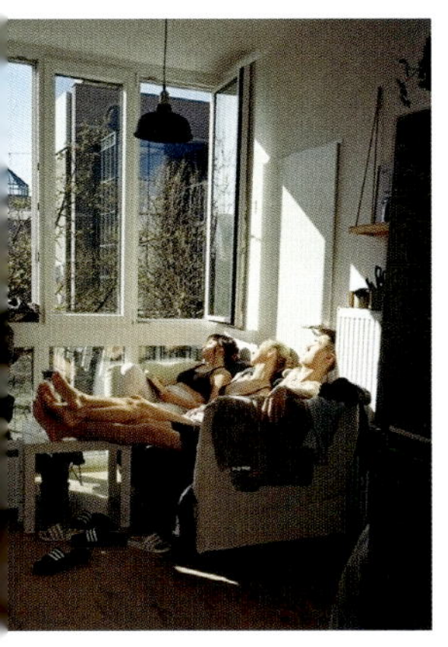

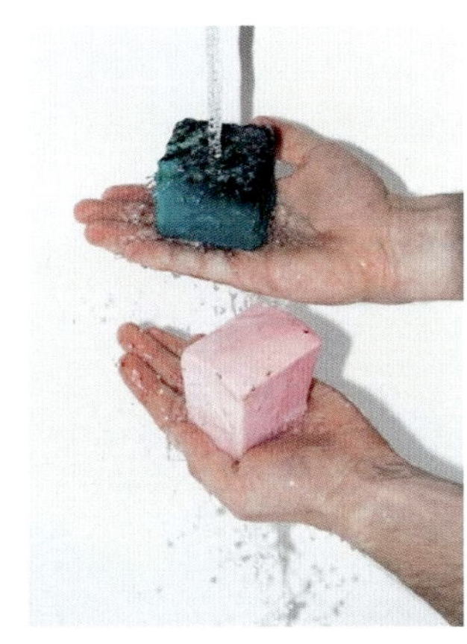

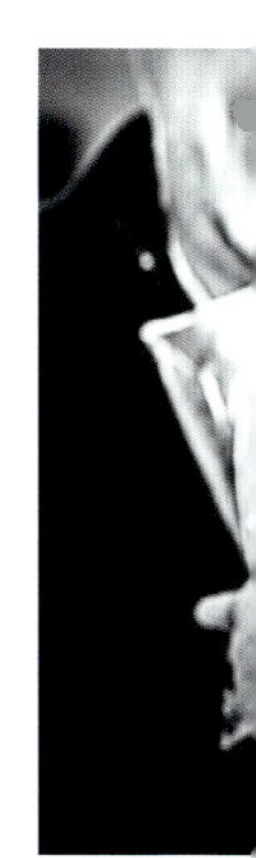

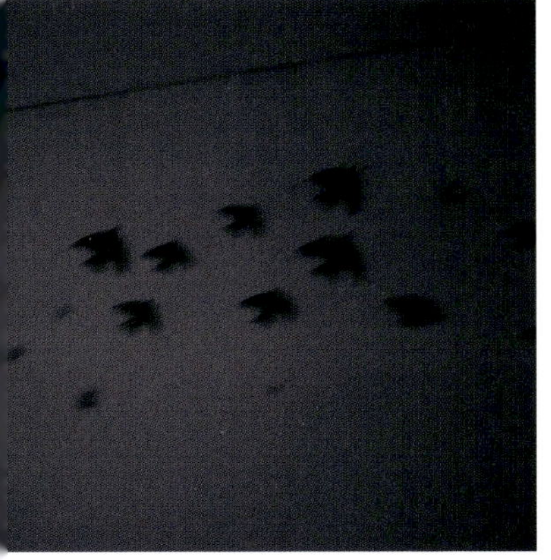

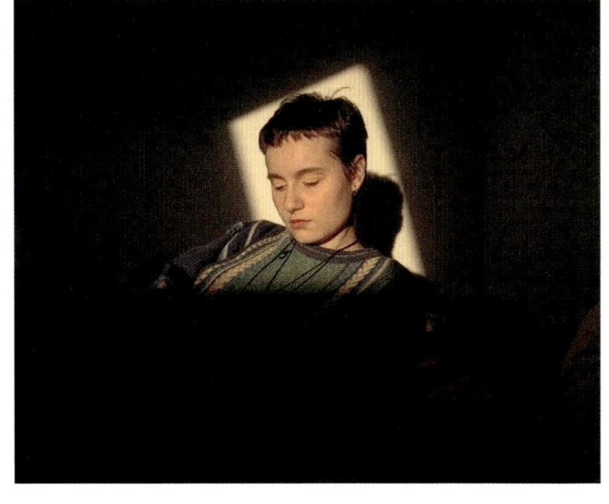

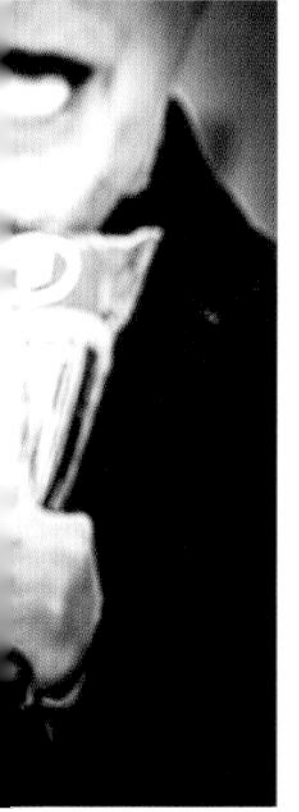

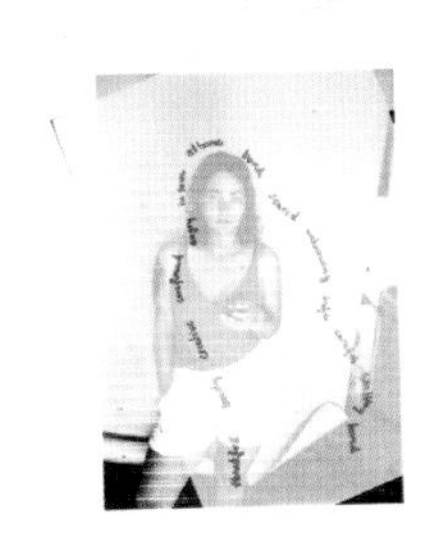

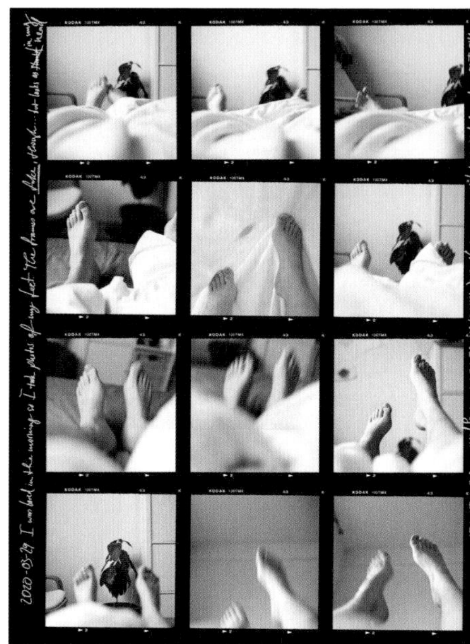

2020-05-29 I was bored in the morning so I took photos of my feet. The frames are fake, though... but looks as in my head

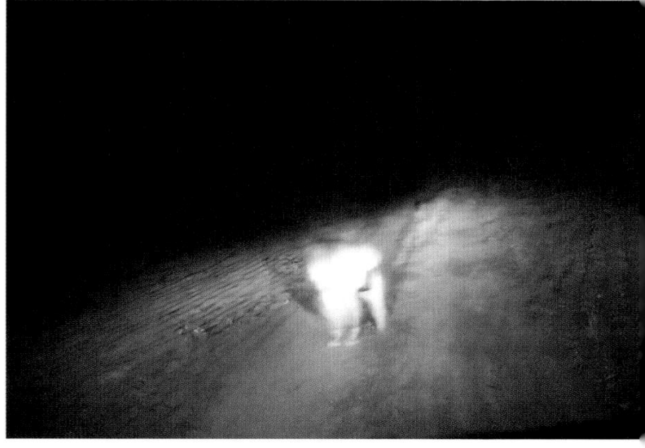

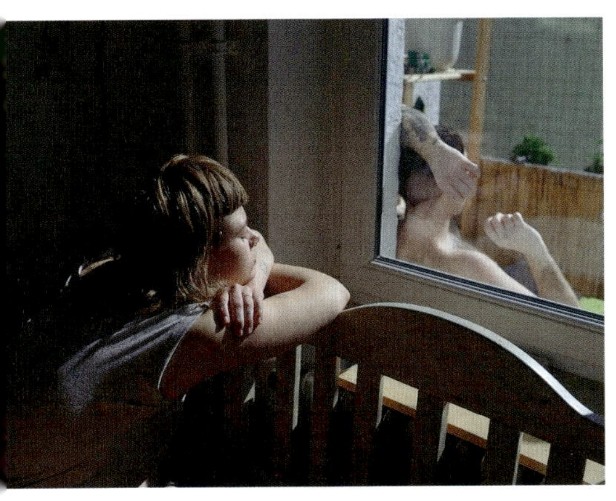

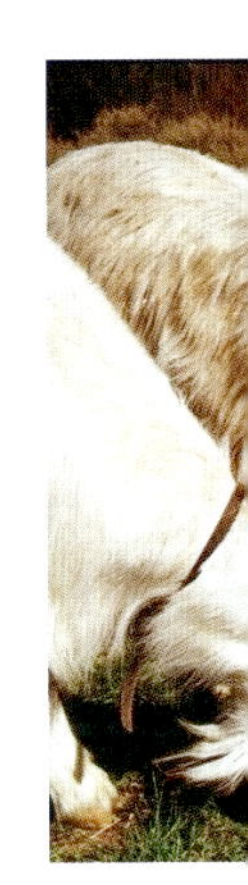

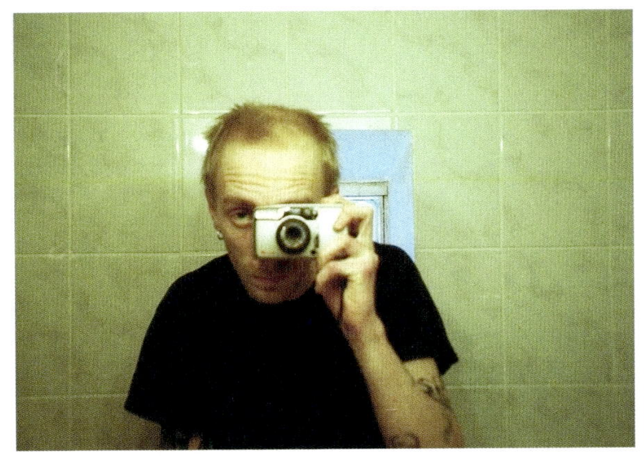

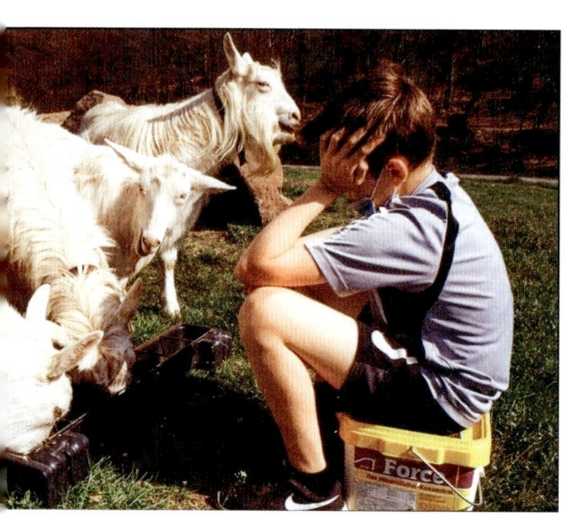
Force

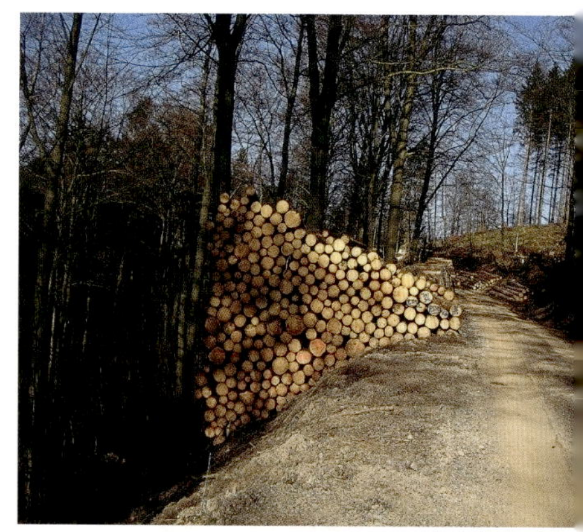

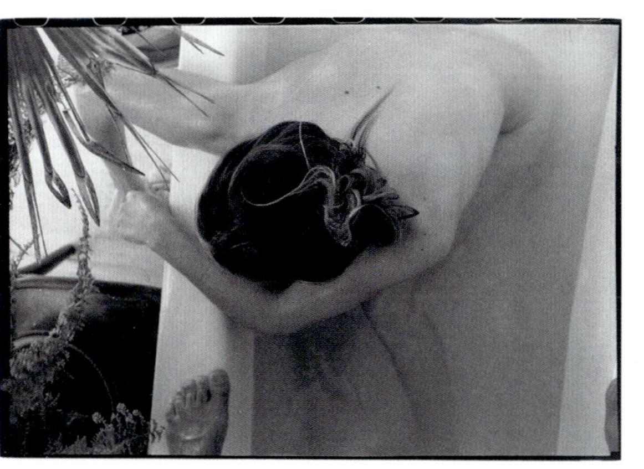

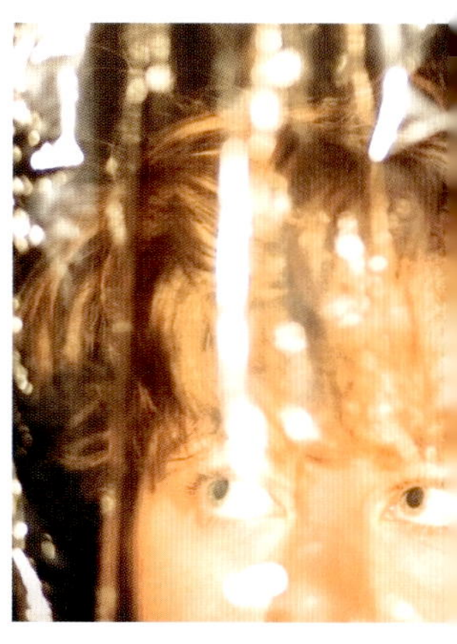

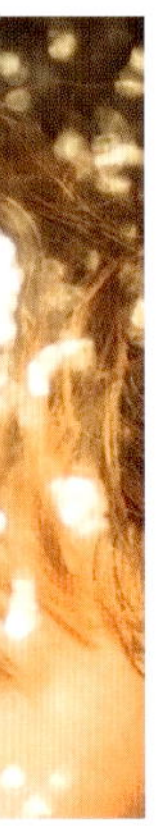

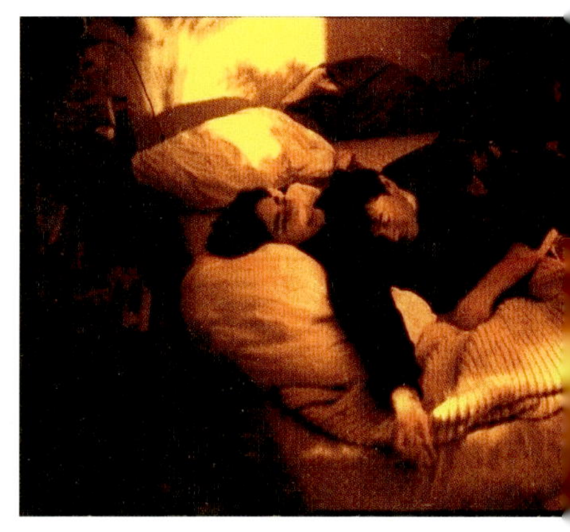

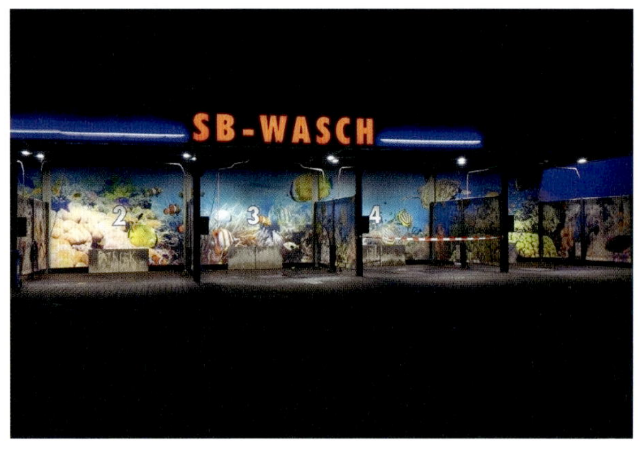
SB-WASCH
2
3
4

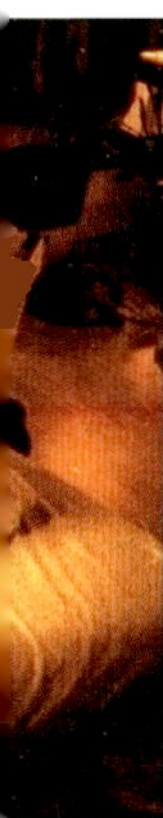

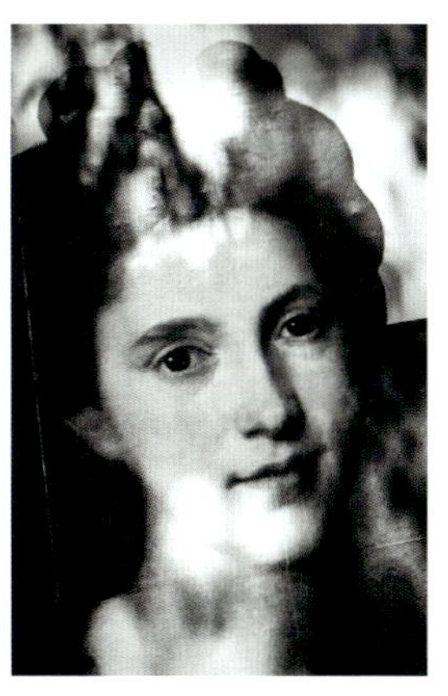

HeY!

We are the fotobus society. This is the second issue of further—our annual publication. The book was made during the 2020 pandemic, a year that turned everything upside down and made the journeys with our beloved blue bus almost impossible. As we realized that more and more photography festivals got cancelled and workshops and conferences in person wouldn't be possible, we had to find other ways to keep our little photo school running. And somehow a lot has happened over the past few months: besides many caring e-mails by our dear bus driver and fotobus initiator Christoph Bangert and a constantly growing number of members up to almost 700 people, a podcast project was born and we could celebrate the release of our first fotobus podcast episode this summer.

On top of that, our members took pictures during the early phases of lockdown to find a little security in these uncertain times and to be able to share their experiences with others. Some of these pictures make up this book's intro, a lot more can be seen on our Instagram @fotobus_society.

further 02 was made almost entirely online. Our weekly meetings, the book making process and the creative exchanges gave us a little stability and were a small callback to a time that was considered normal just weeks before. When we asked all of our student members to send us their personal projects for consideration, almost 200 of them trusted us with their stories and pictures. The range and versatility were incredible and we want to thank everyone for participating. After weeks of discussion, we agreed on 34 submissions that share themes of uncertainty, hope, hardship, authenticity and love. These stories offer glimpses into lives and fates from all around the world, either by documenting humans, the spaces they inhabit or the ideas and concepts they believe in. They aim to show what we chose to do with our time on earth, how we treat ourselves, others and our planet—or they show realities where there doesn't seem to be a choice at all. The authors of these pictures went out into the world to find these stories, facing the difficulties of producing their works. They did it out of curiosity, on their own account to share their discoveries with others. We are proud and humbled to be able to offer them a platform to do so with further 02.

Thank you for supporting the fotobus and our activities by picking up this copy. It is you, our sponsors and our supporting members who make it possible for our photo school on wheels to exist.

CELINE YASEMIN

01

21 GRAMS

The search for identity is central to younger generations, especially in the LGBTQ+ culture, where lifestyles, the concept of gender, sexuality and relationship patterns differ greatly from established norms of society. Celine met young people from all over Europe and took portraits of people who do not want to attribute themselves with this norm, aiming to live a self-determined life with diverging experiences, interests and ideas of life.

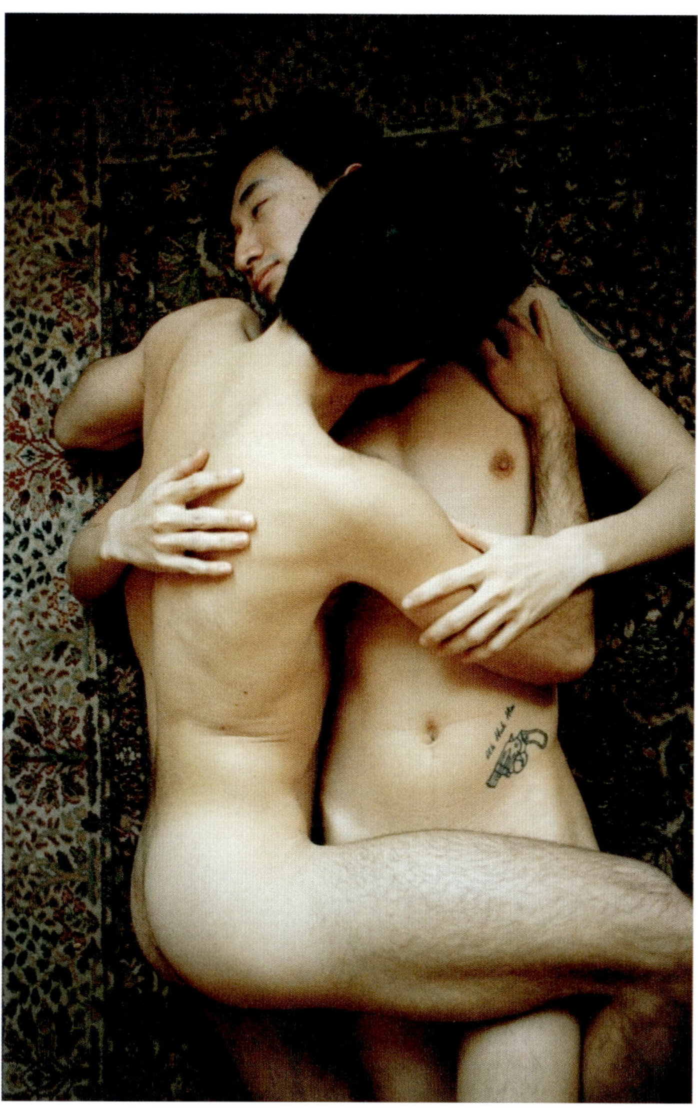

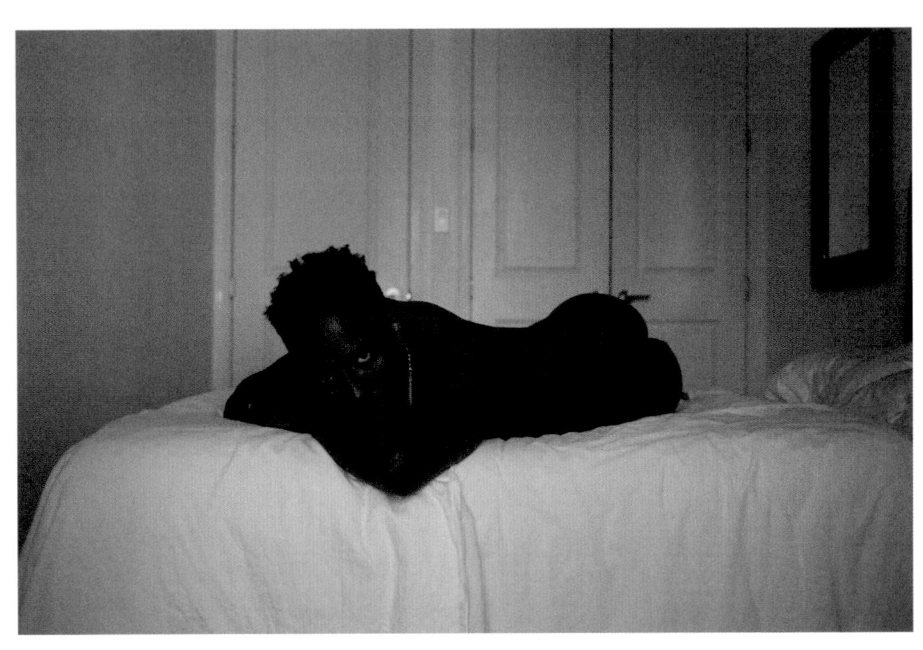

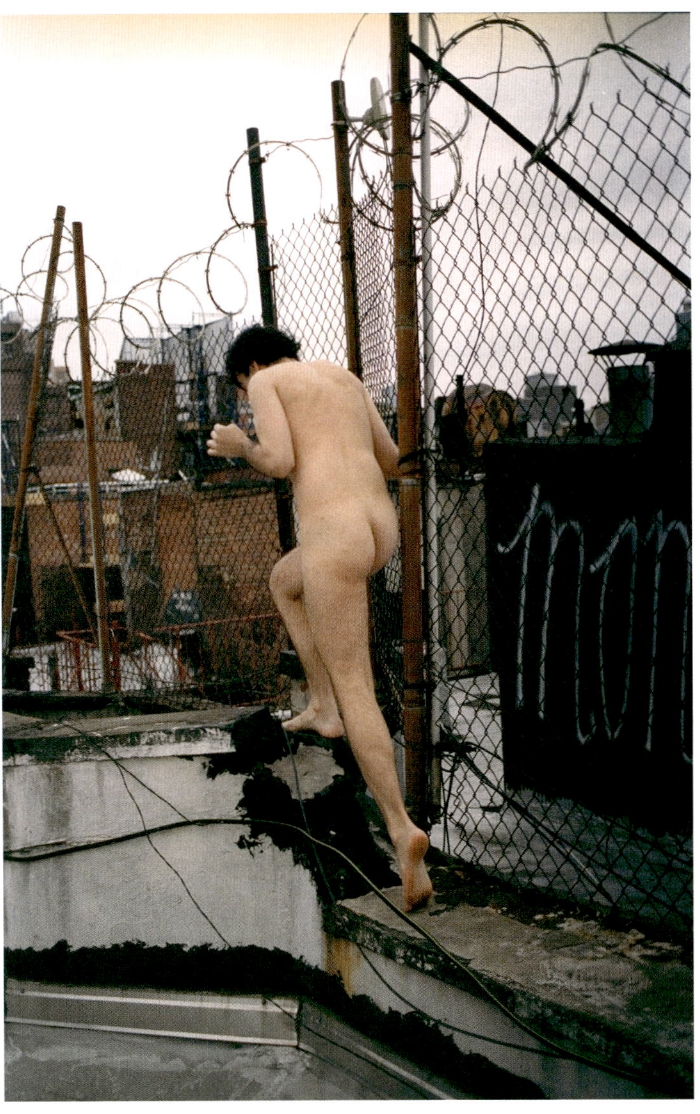

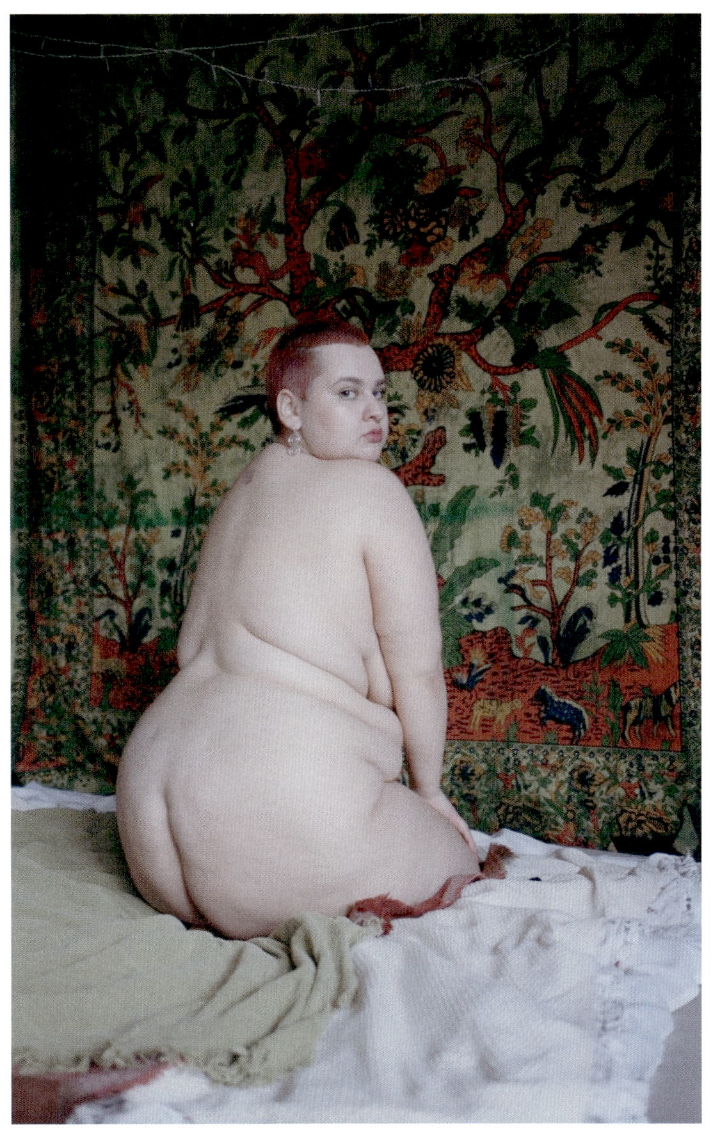

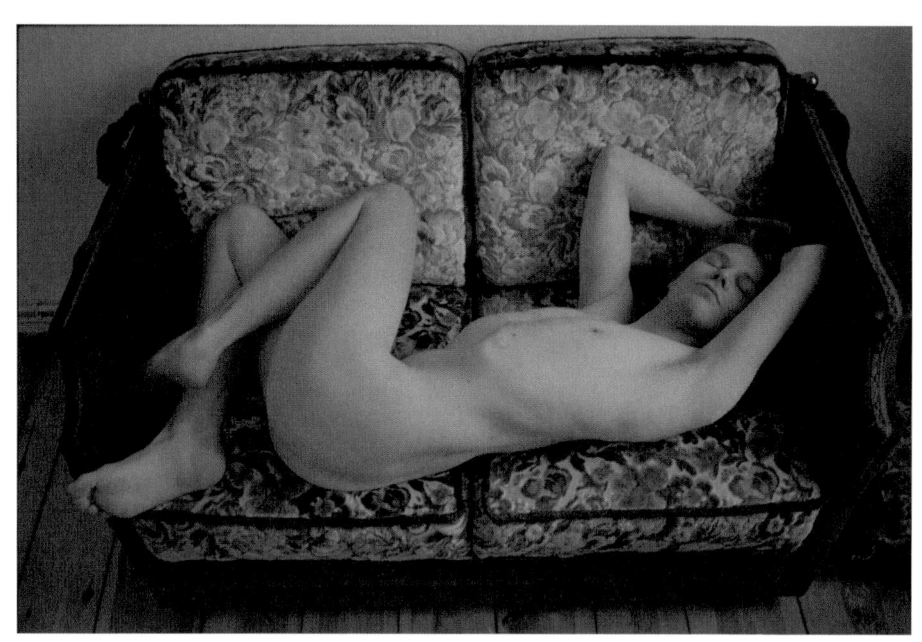

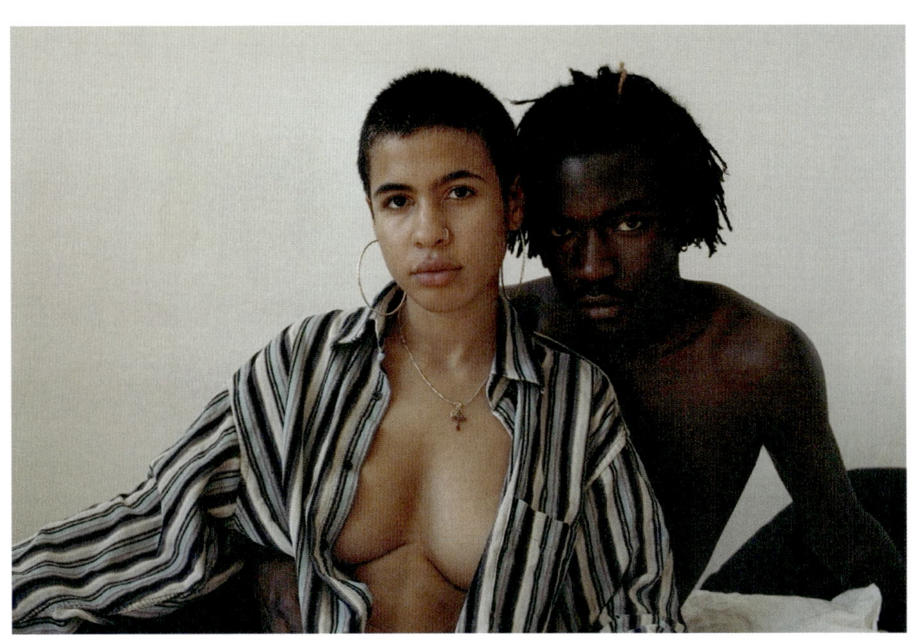

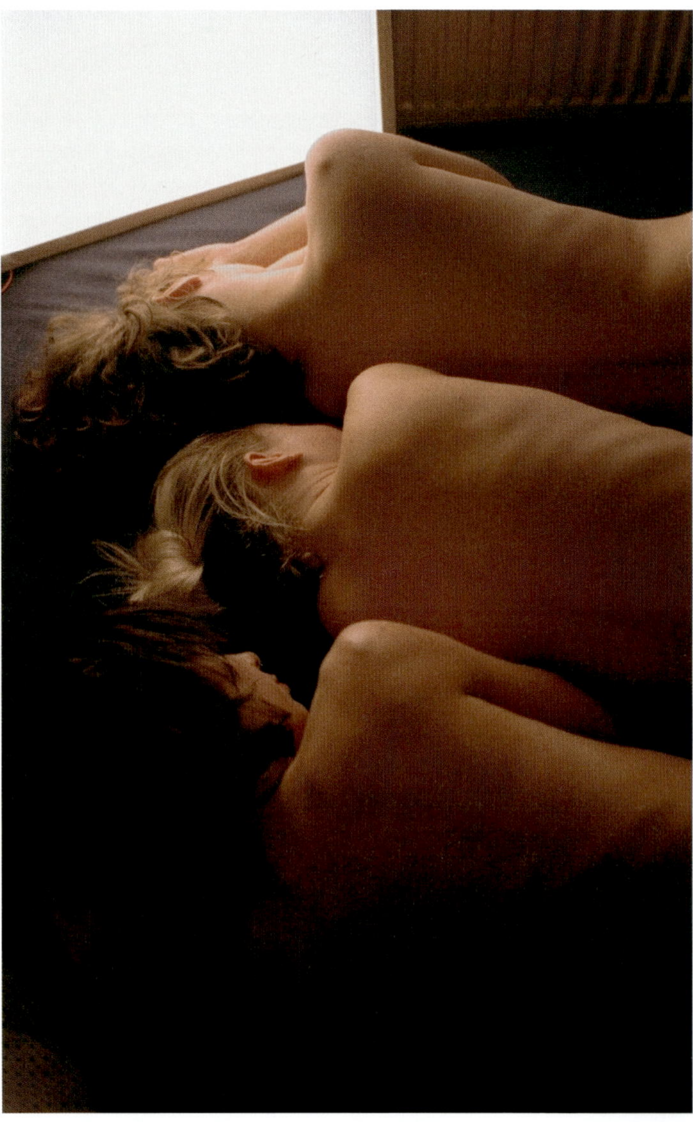

ALIONA KARDASH

B A B U

02

Aliona's grandmother Maria Antonovna Olkhovskaya turned 90 last August. She has three daughters, six grandchildren and eleven great-grandchildren. She was born into a family of old believers in a small hamlet in the Siberian taiga and lived her entire life in a village. At the age of 88, after a serious sickness, she had to move to the city Tomsk with roughly 500,000 inhabitants, in order to be closer to her family and proper medical care.

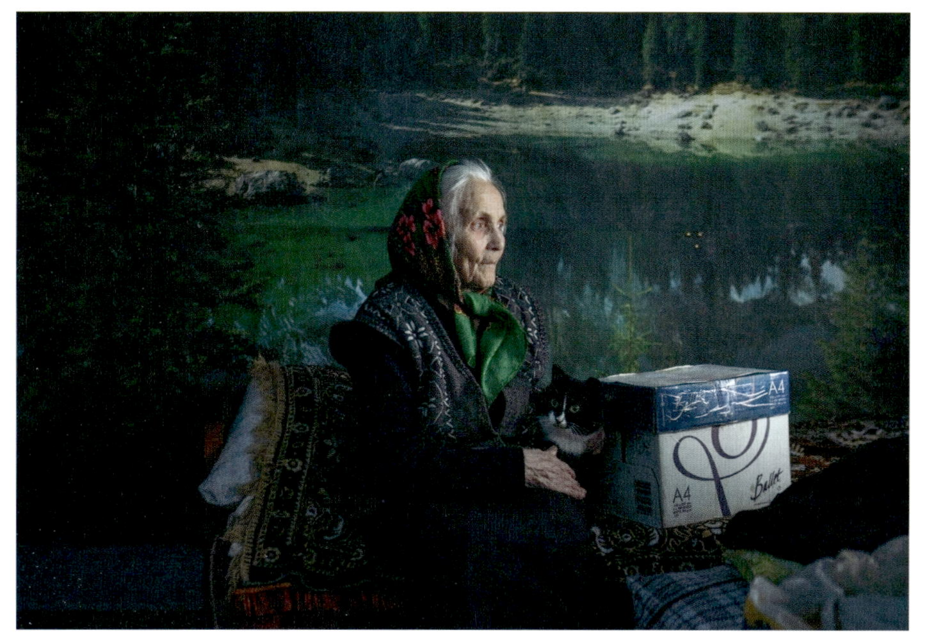

S H K A

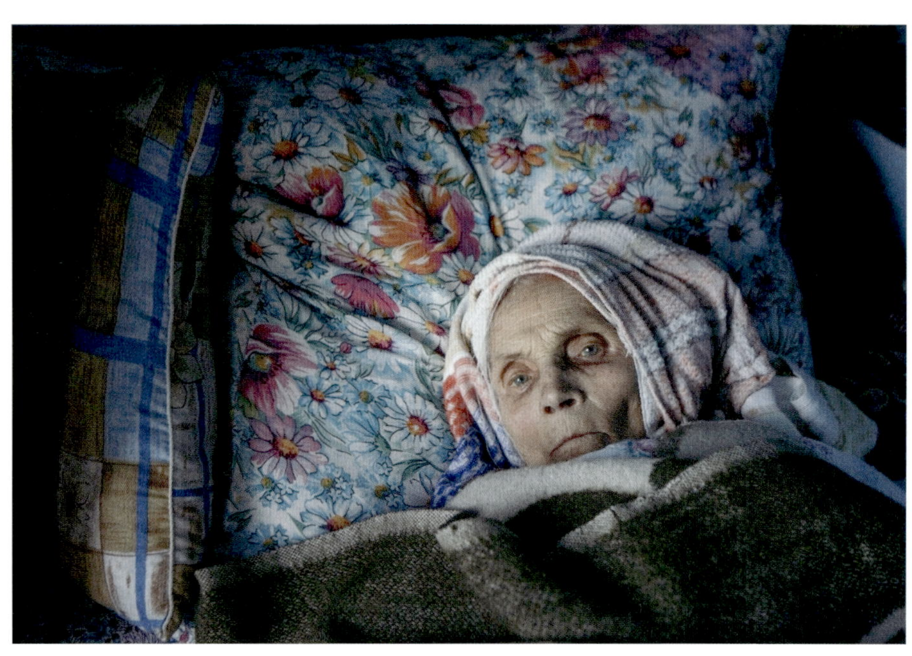

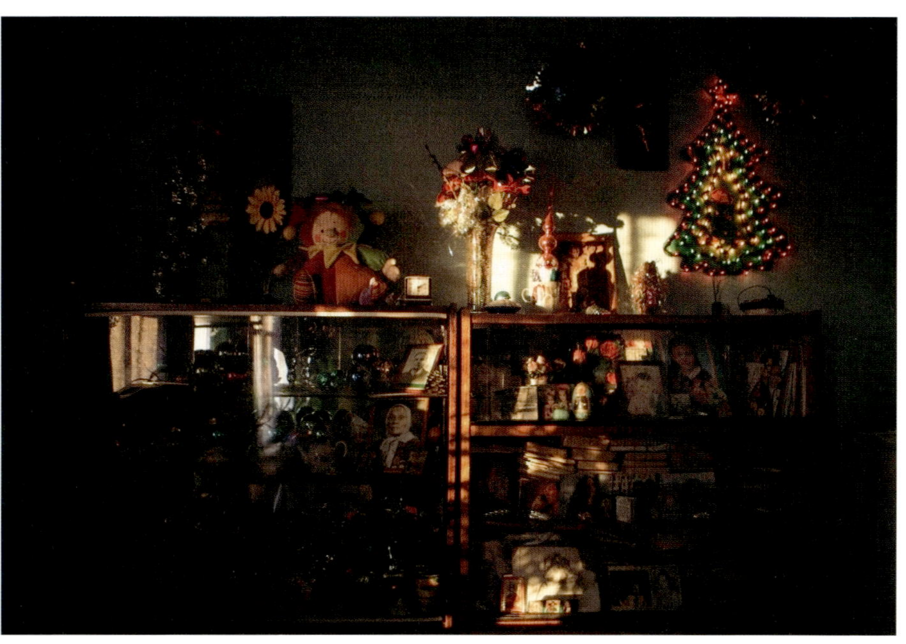

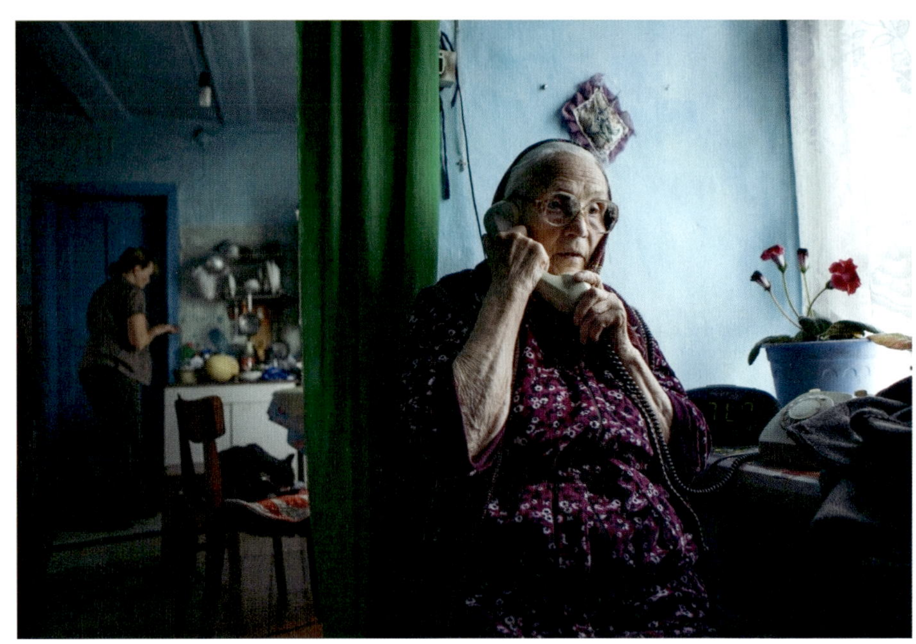

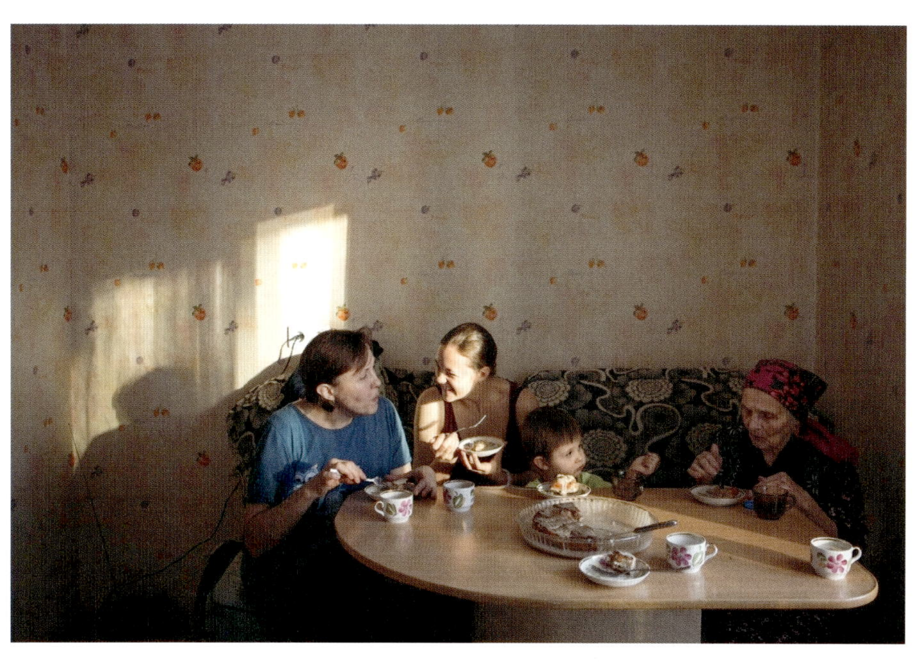

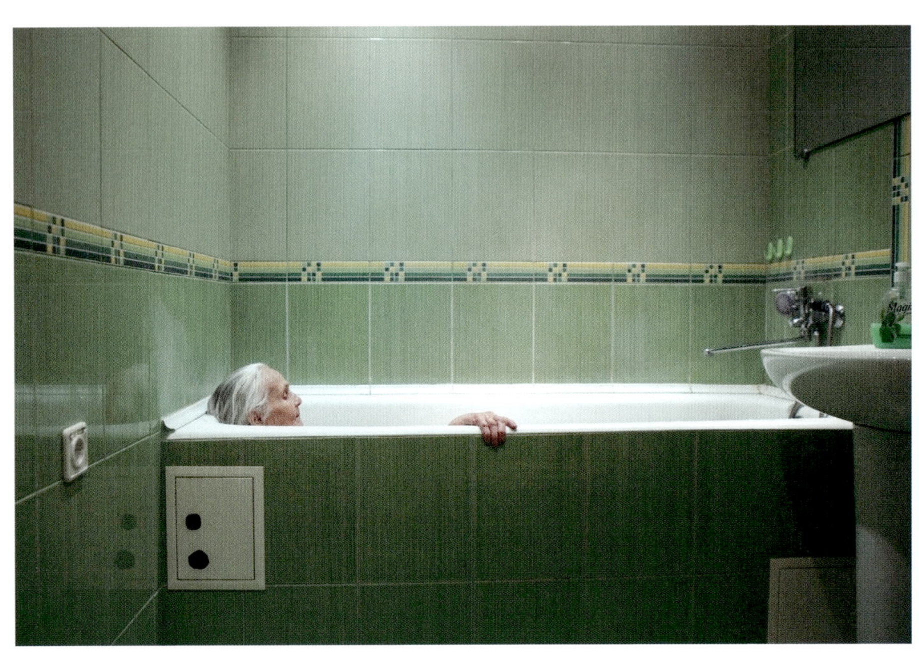

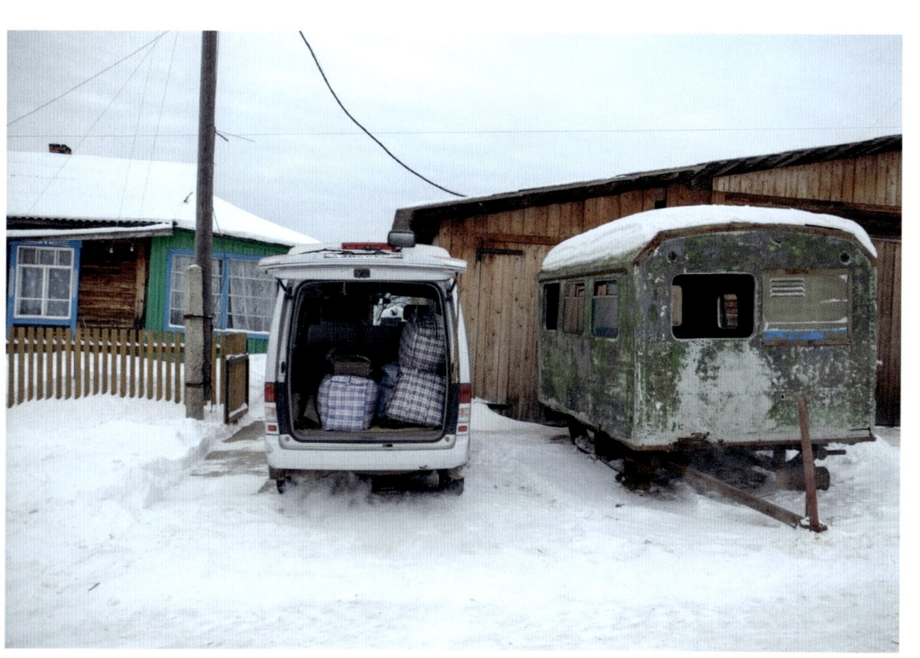

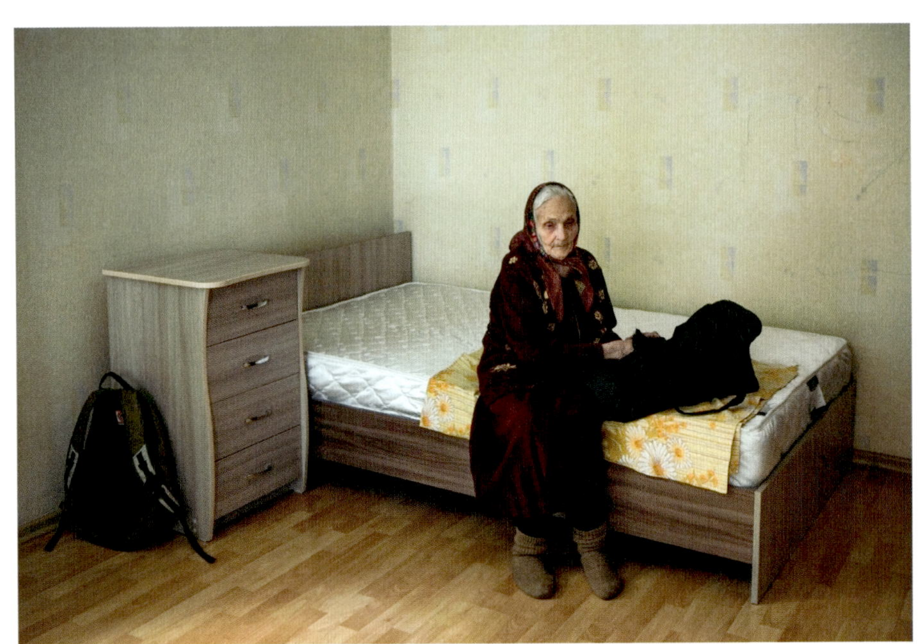

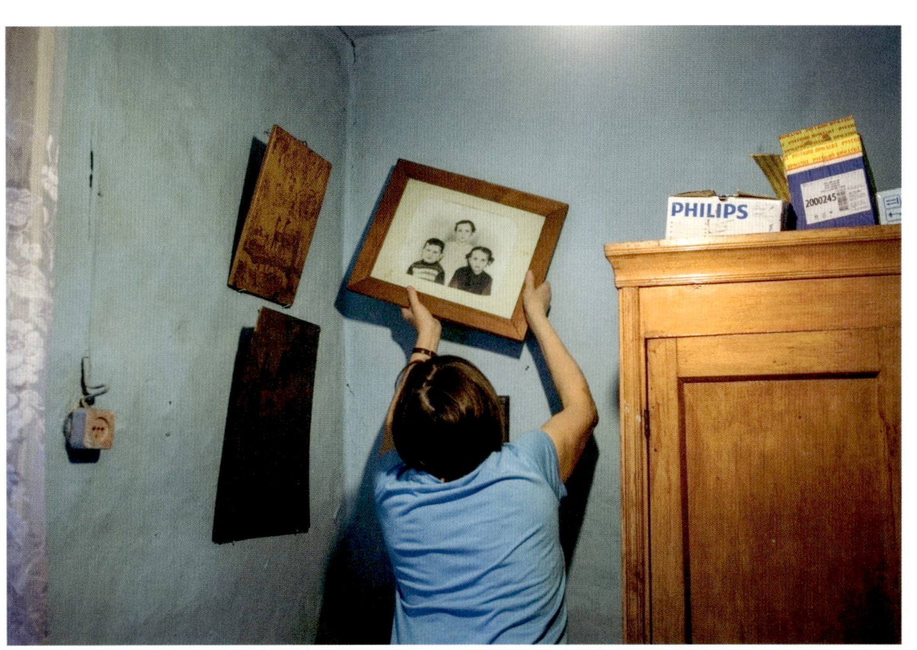
PHILIPS
2000245

FELIX KLEYMANN

03

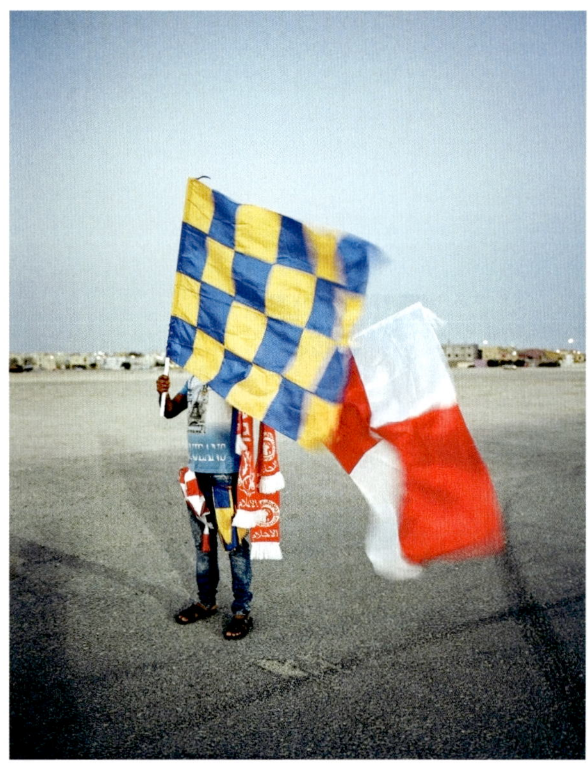

Felix traveled to Qatar, a land between tradition and modernity that, according to its gross domestic product, is considered to be the most wealthy country in the world. The money is being spent with foresight, as the state is investing heavily in diverse infrastructure projects and aims to free itself from a dependence on oil and gas income—leading to massive contraction sites with around 2 million foreign workers in a country with 300,000 citizens.

Improving RealiTY

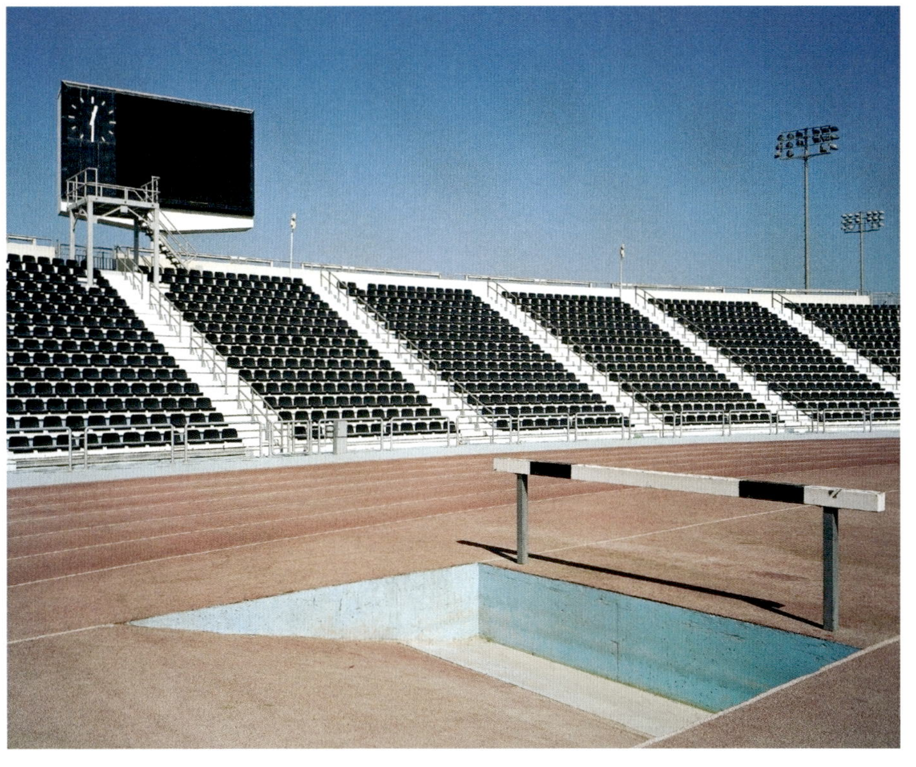

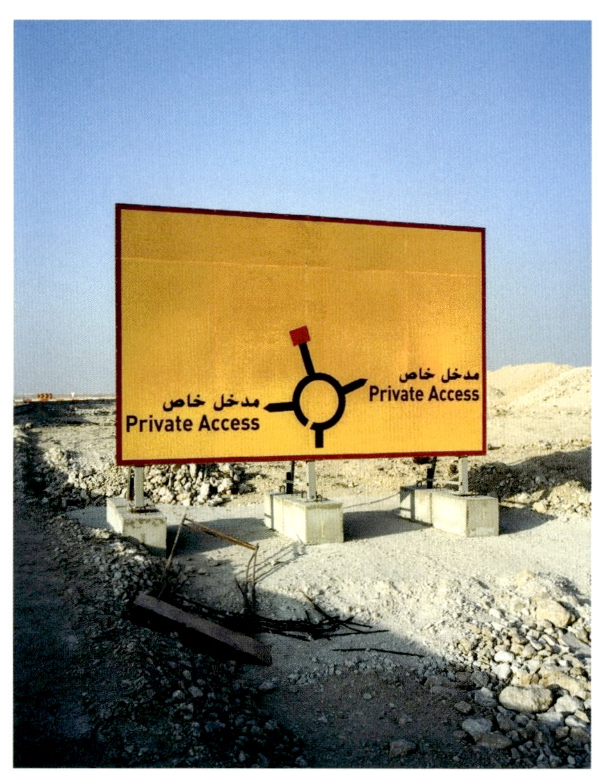
مدخل خاص
Private Access
مدخل خاص
Private Access

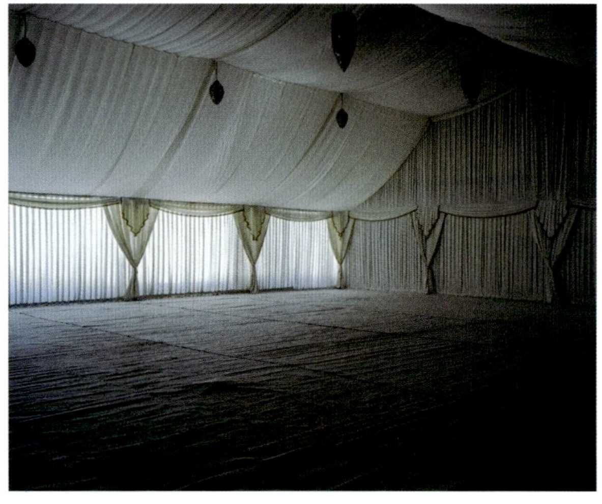

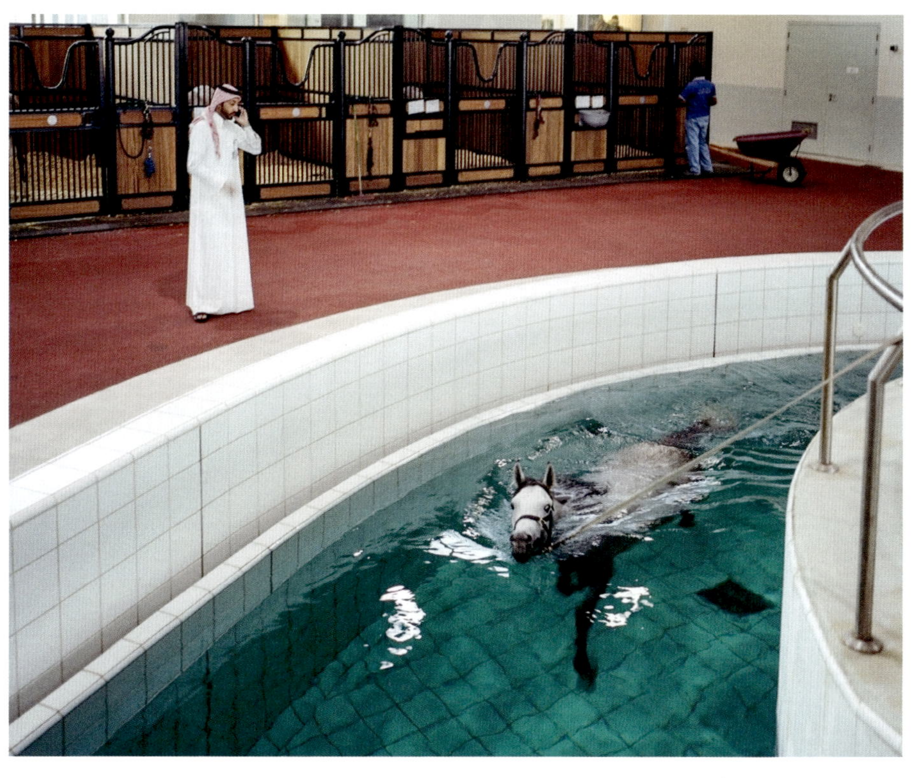

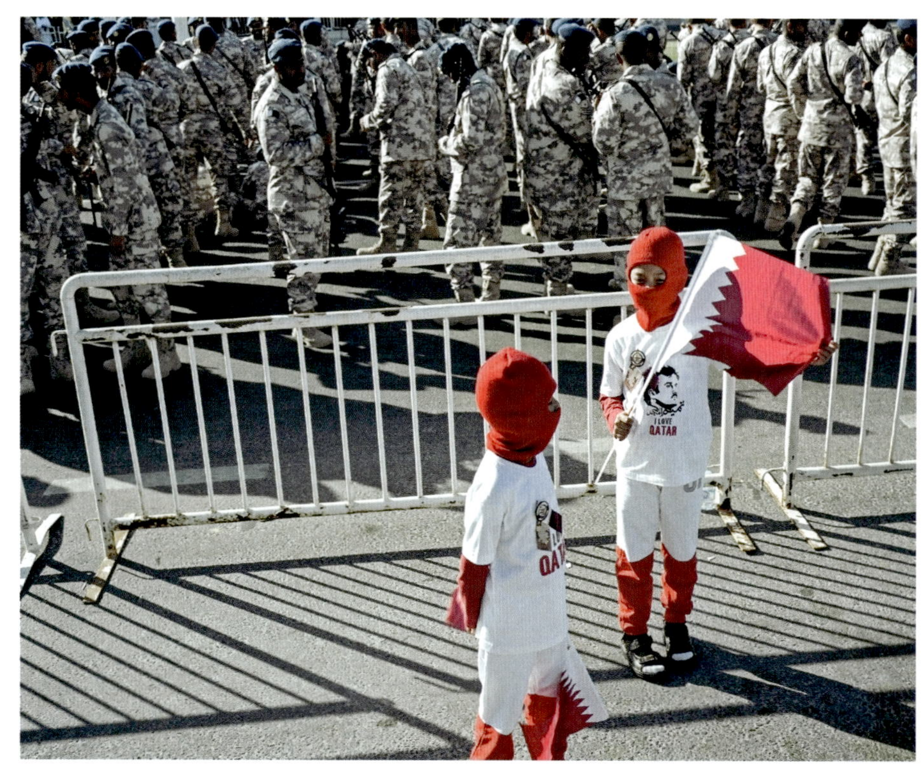
I LOVE
QATAR

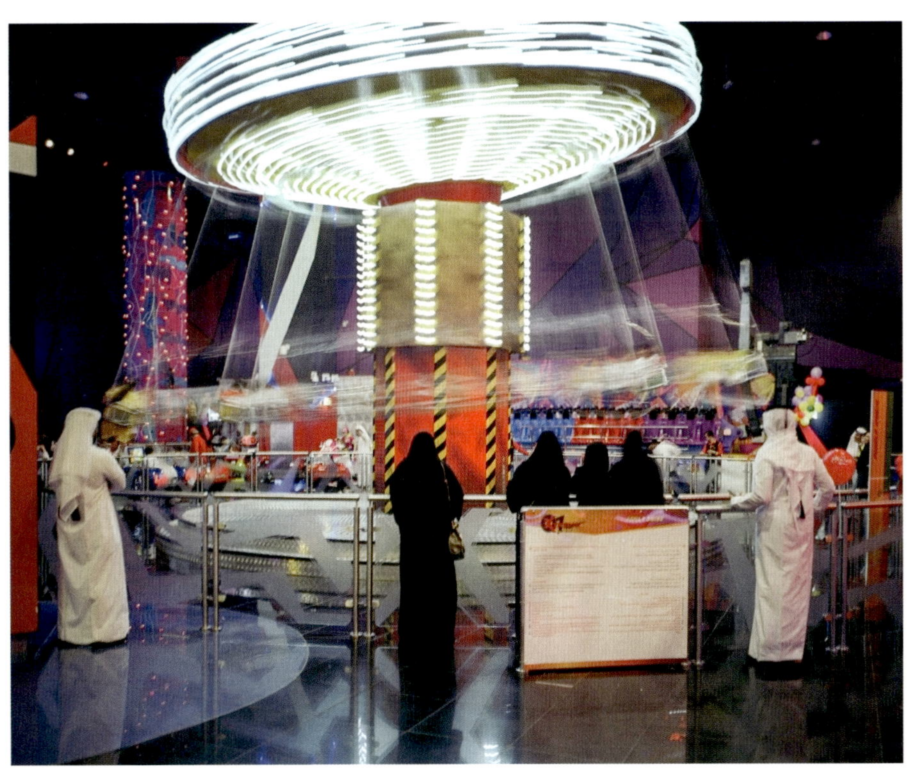

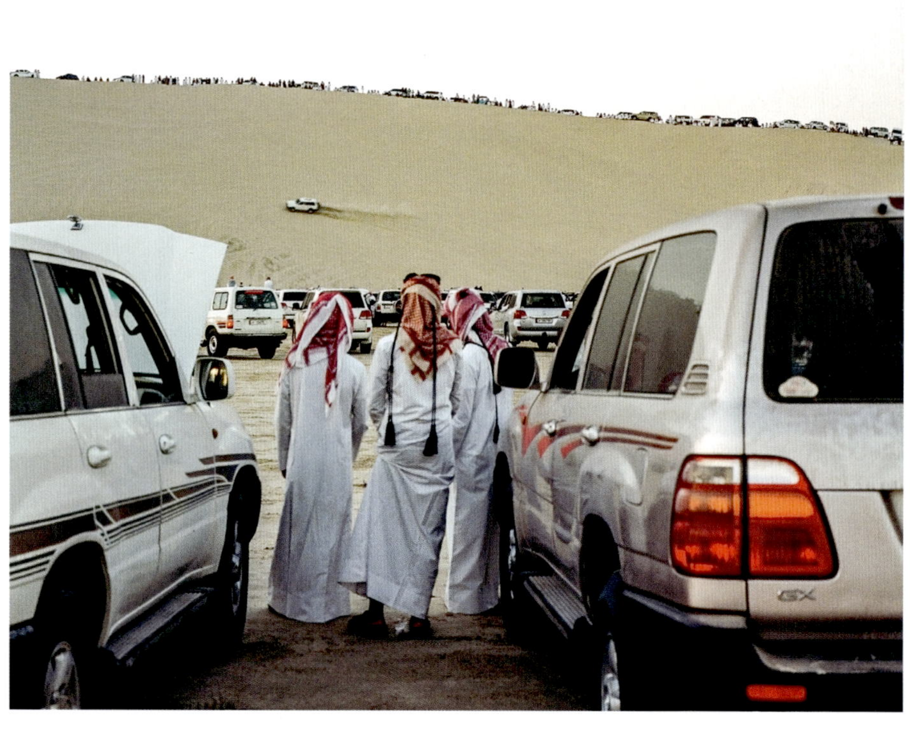
GX

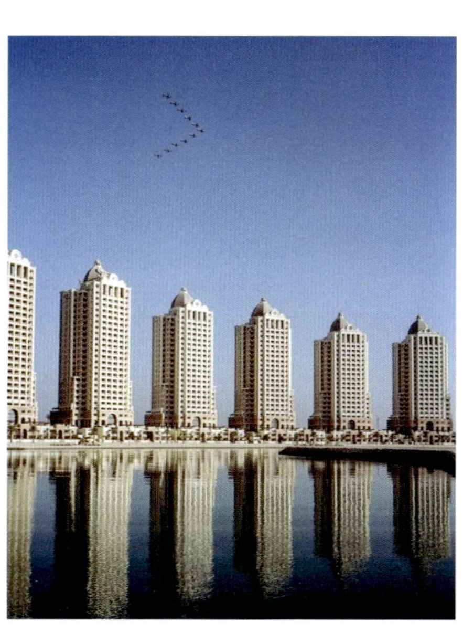

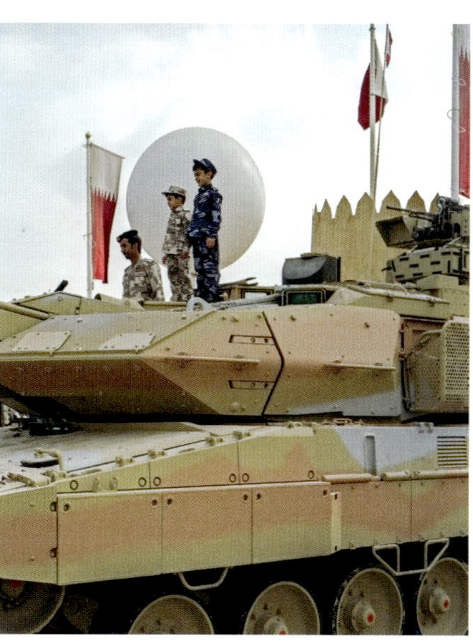

FABiAN SCHWARZE

04

Hey Dad

“I will write you a detailed letter soon...” was the answer Fabian received from his father to the question “Who are you?” He never got an answer, nor did he get one after the many letters he had sent before. The last time he had seen his father was at age 2. Now at age 24, he turned to photography to document his search for his father in an attempt to deal with his fatherlessness.

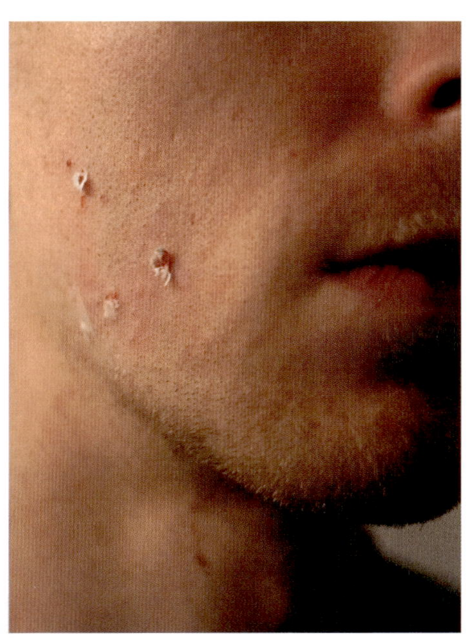

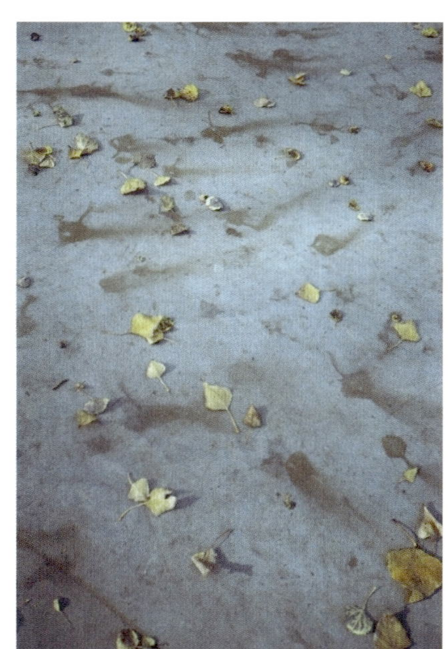

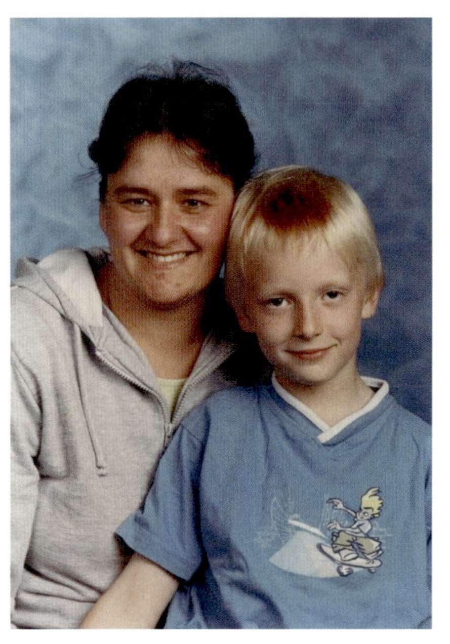

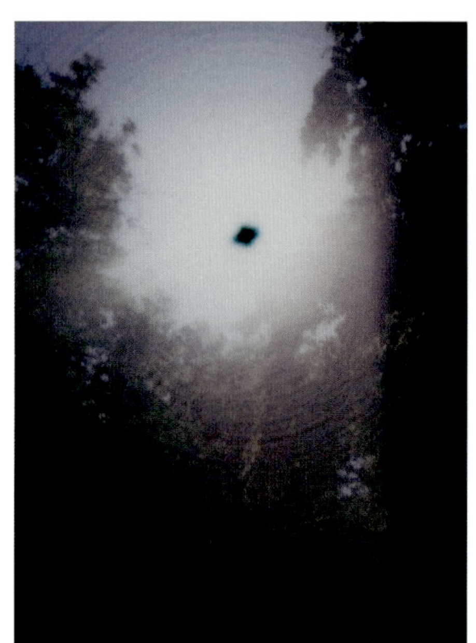

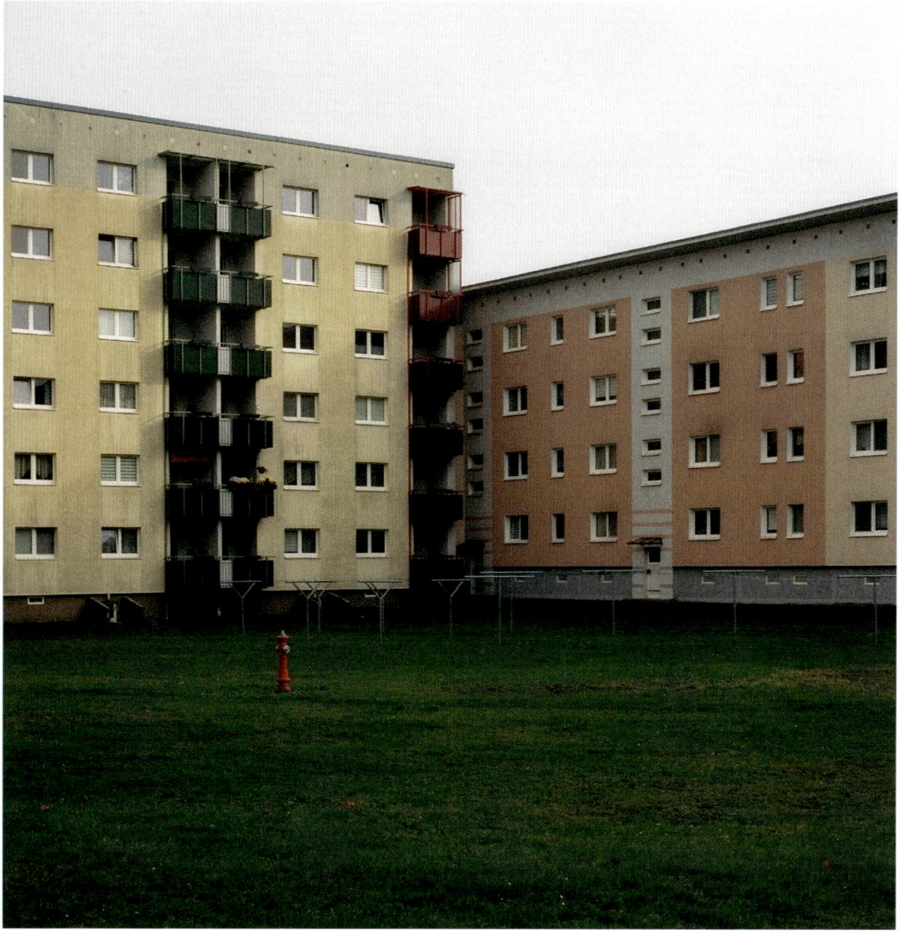

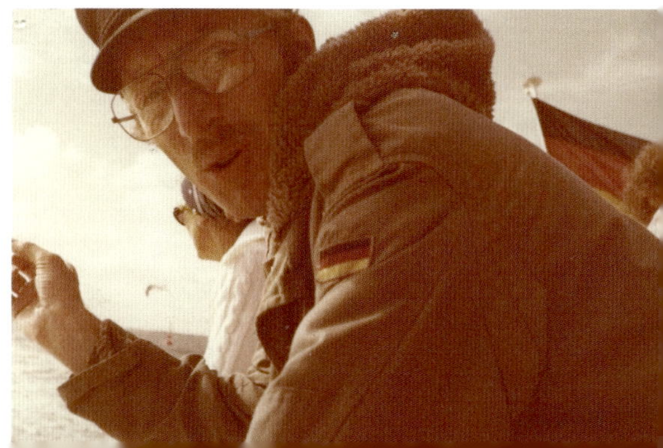

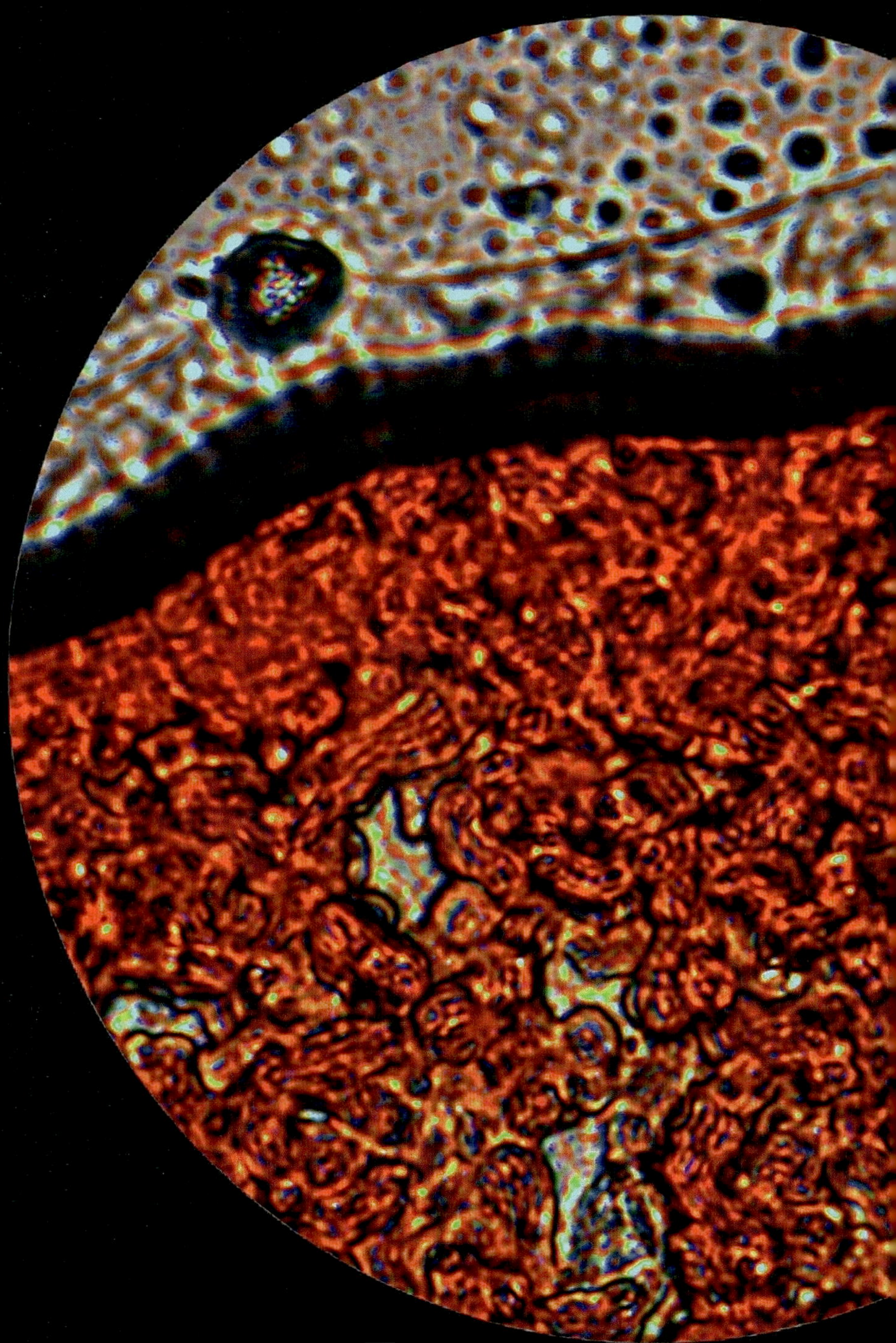

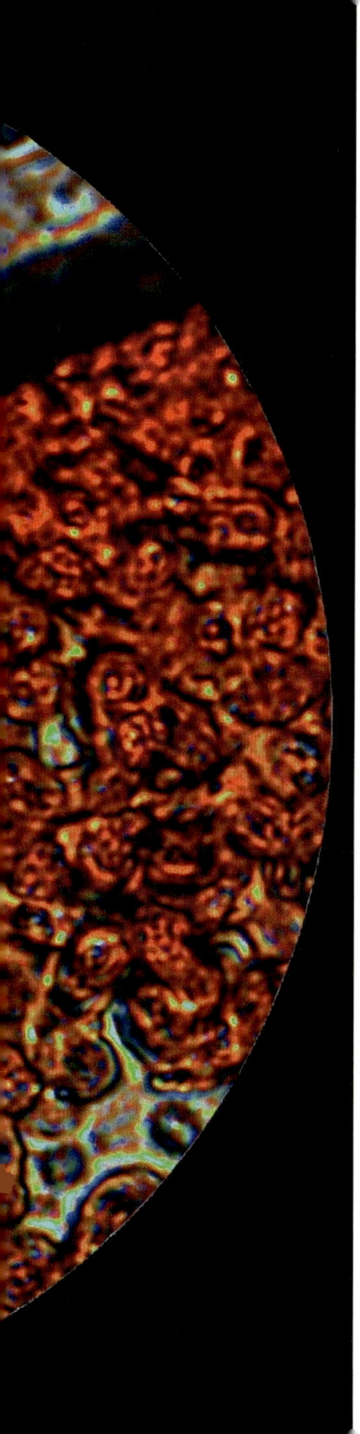

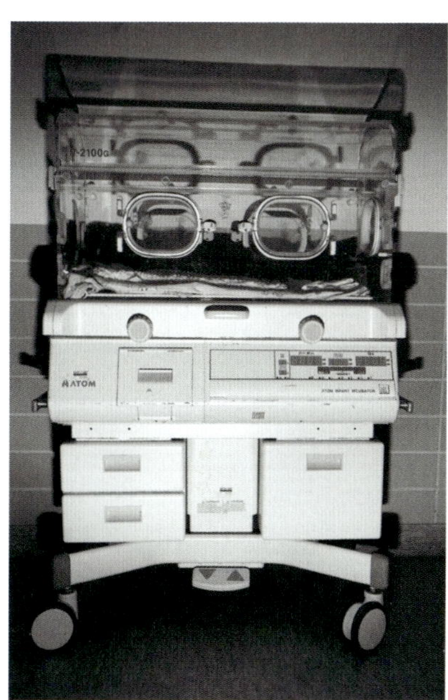
2100G
ATOM

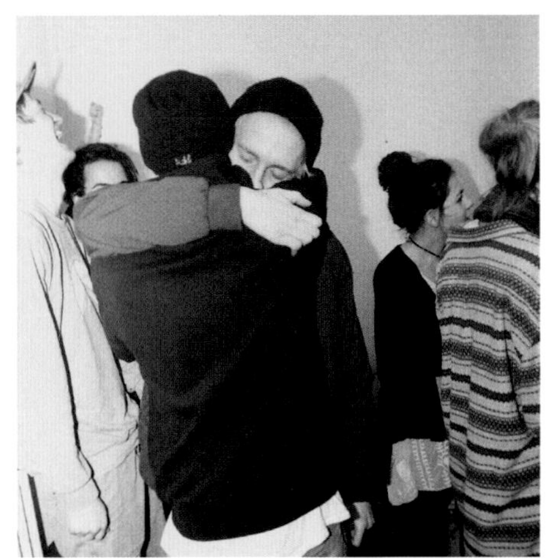

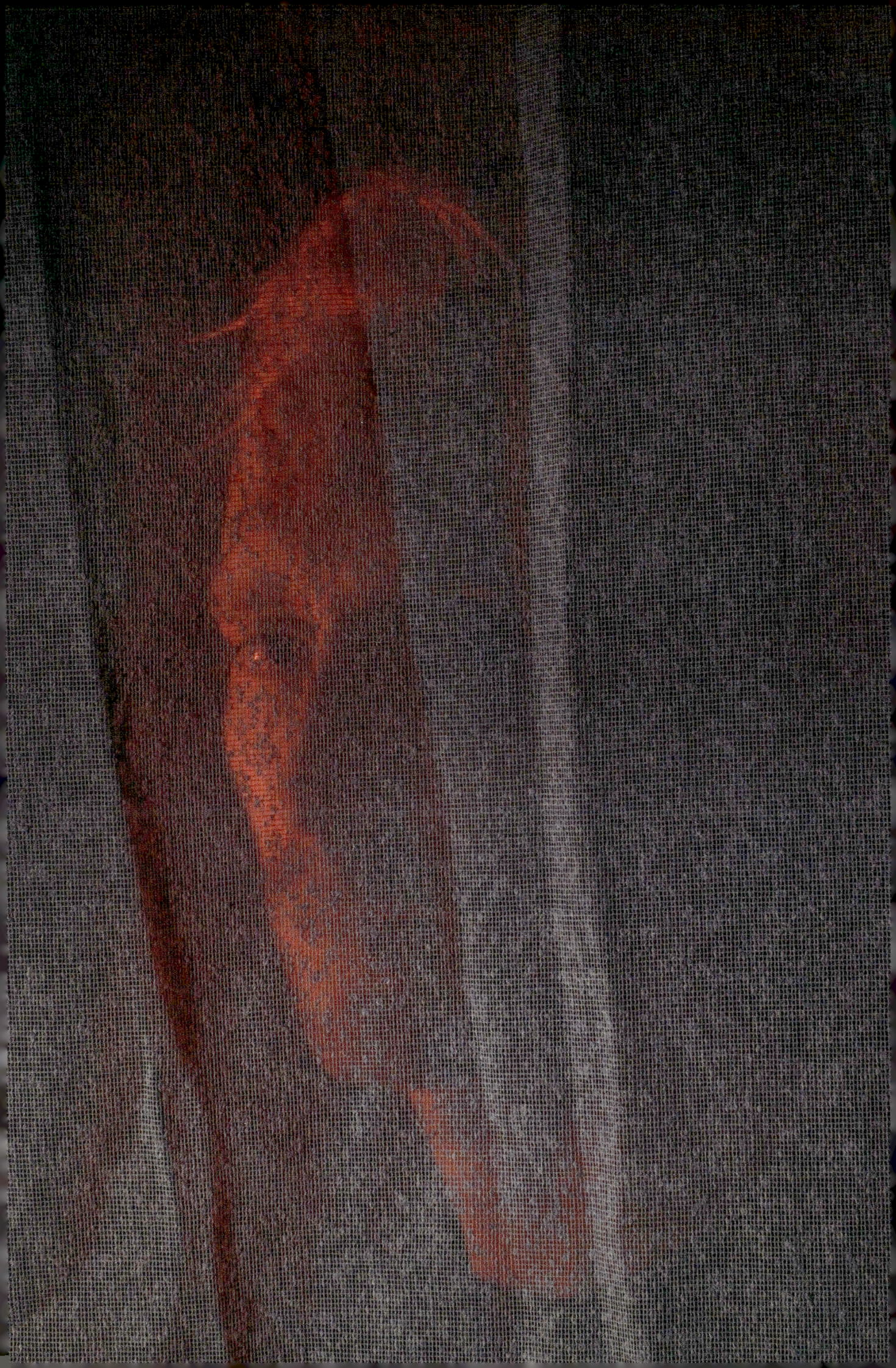

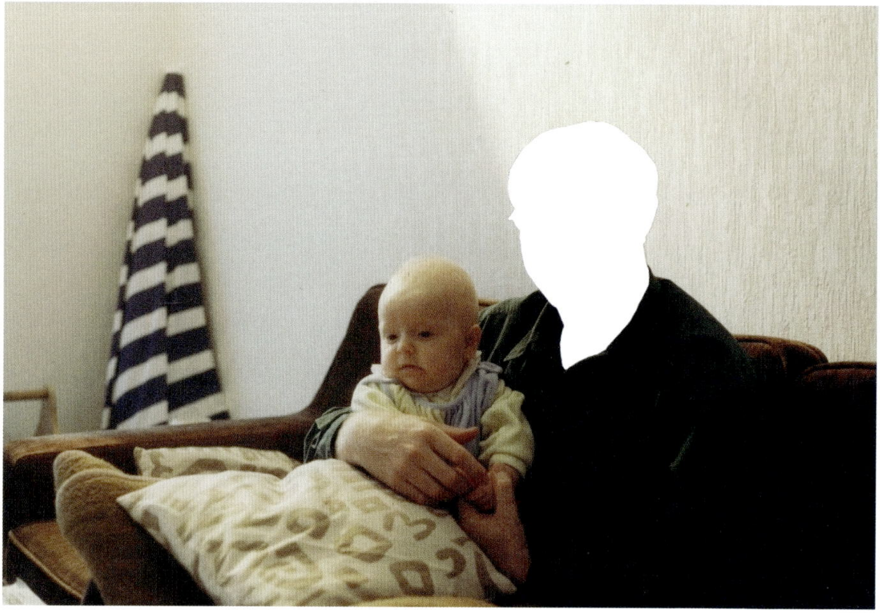

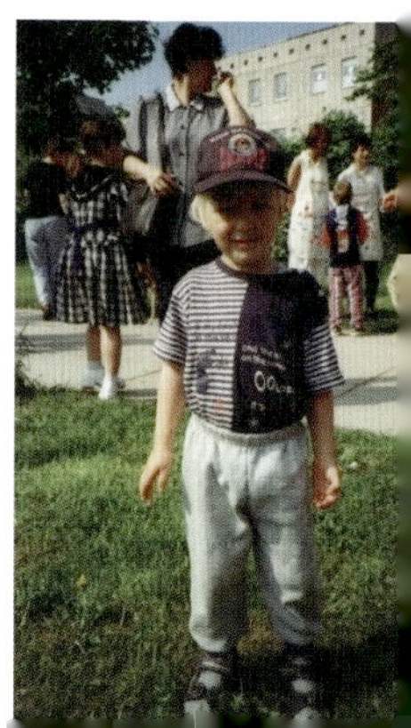

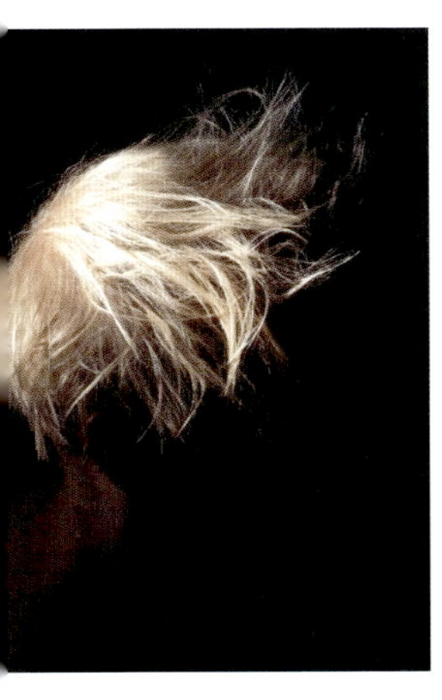

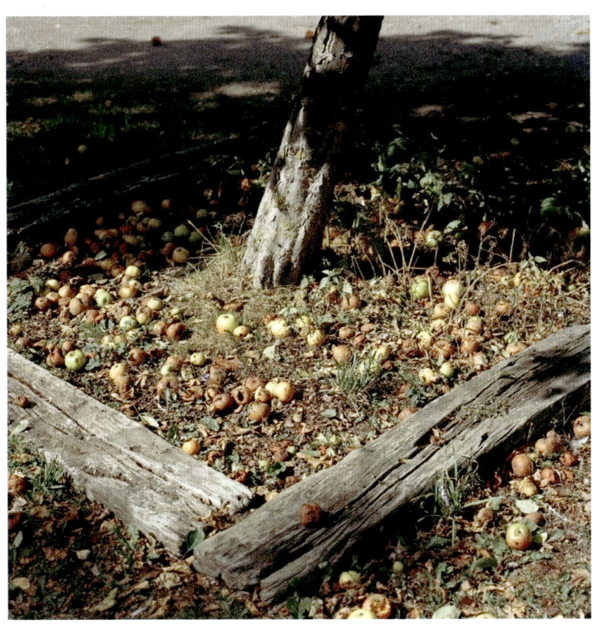

JAN RiCHARD HEINICKE

05

Melting Point

The Arctic suffers greatly from rising global temperatures. A collapse of the Greenland ice sheet could lead to a massive rise in global sea levels; the melting and erosion of the coastal glaciers could severely influence the world's water circulation—including the Gulf Stream that brings a moderate climate to Europe. Richard joined a team of young oceanographers for an expedition to get a better understanding of the situation and to see just how much water is already leaving the fjords.

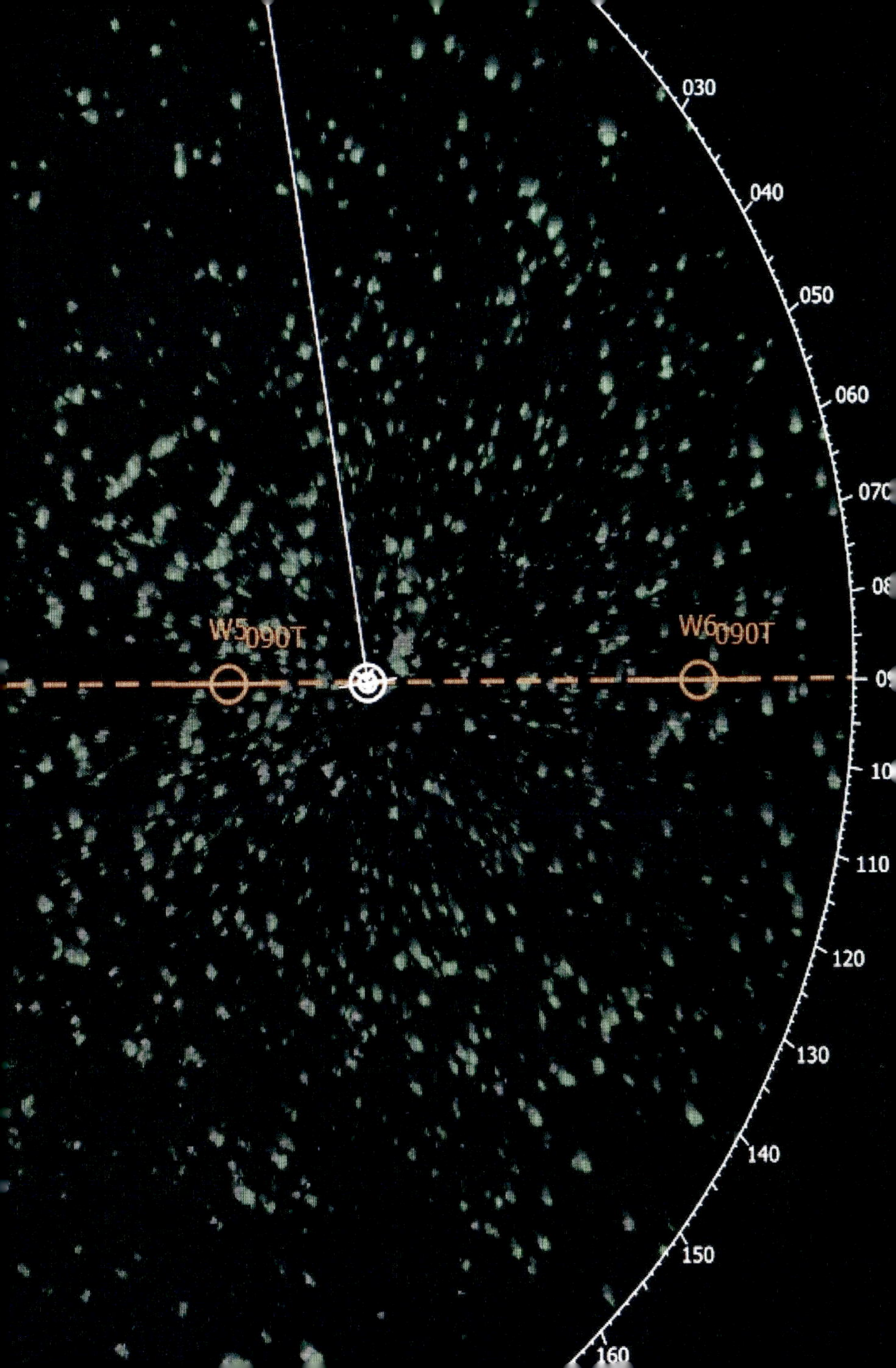
030
040
050
060
W5 090T
W6 090T
110
120
130
140
150
160

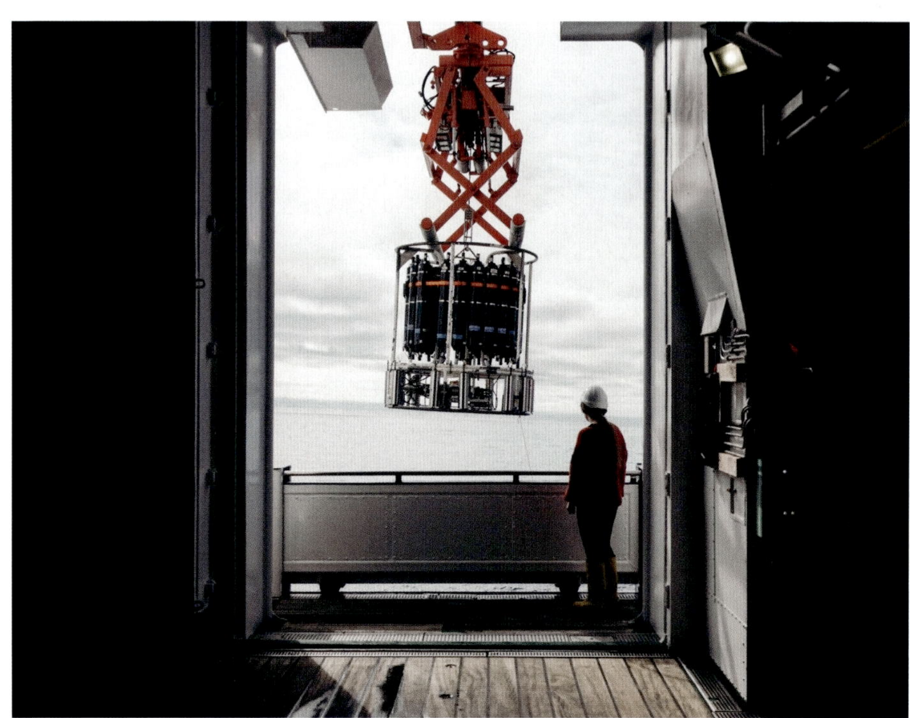

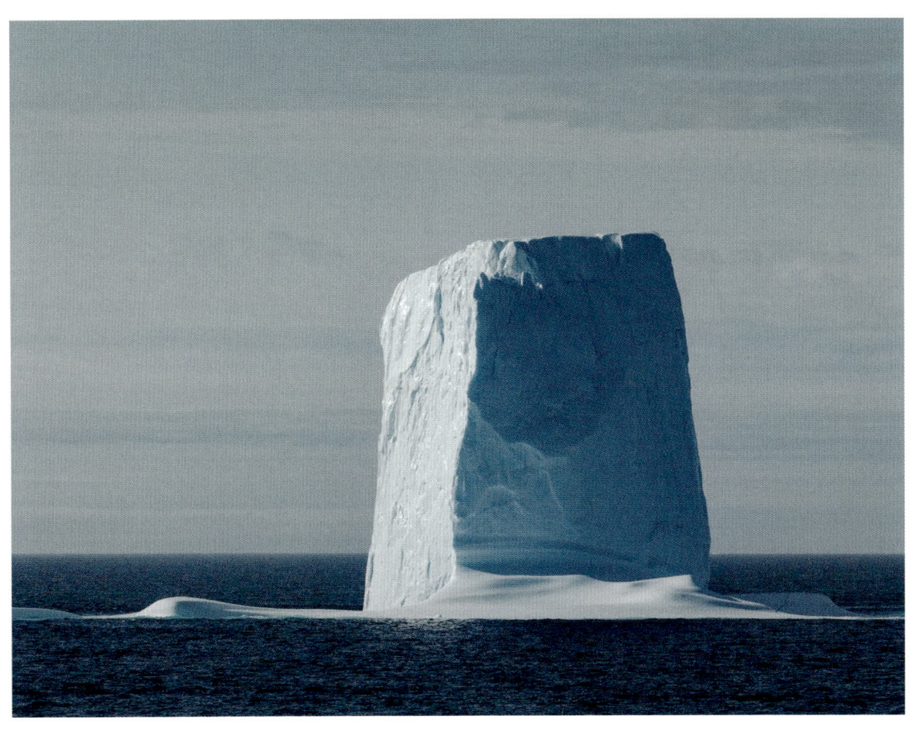

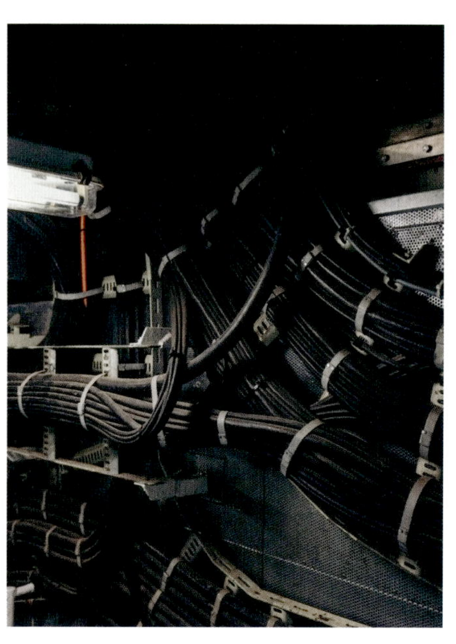

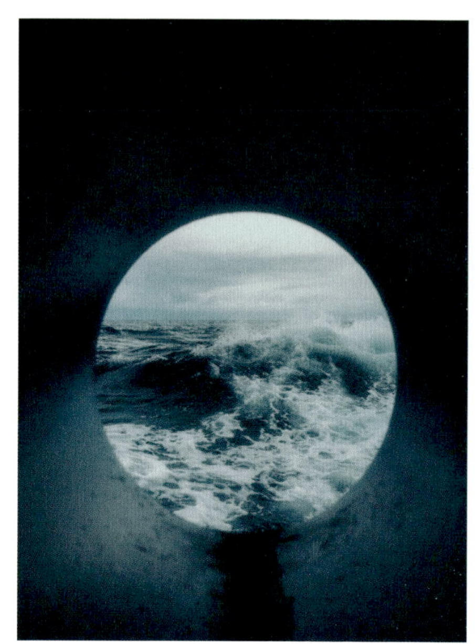

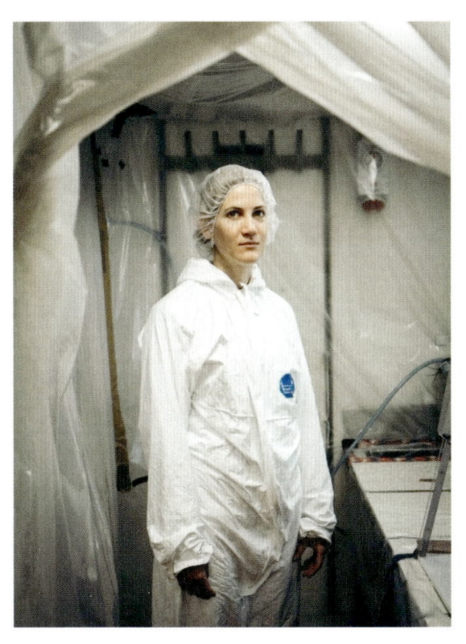

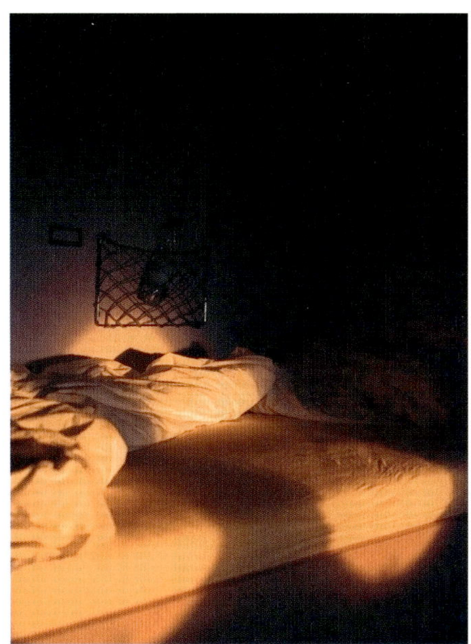

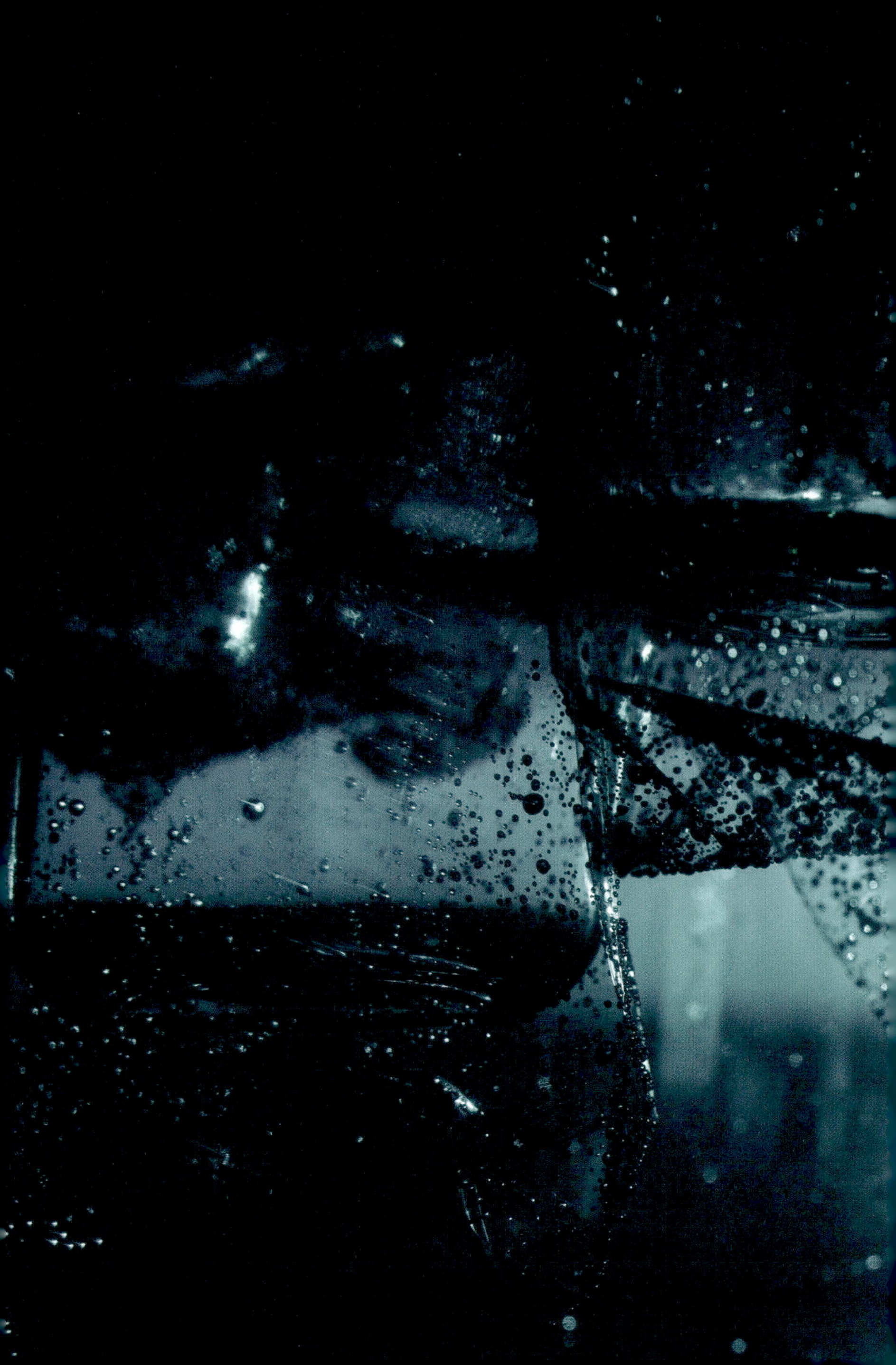

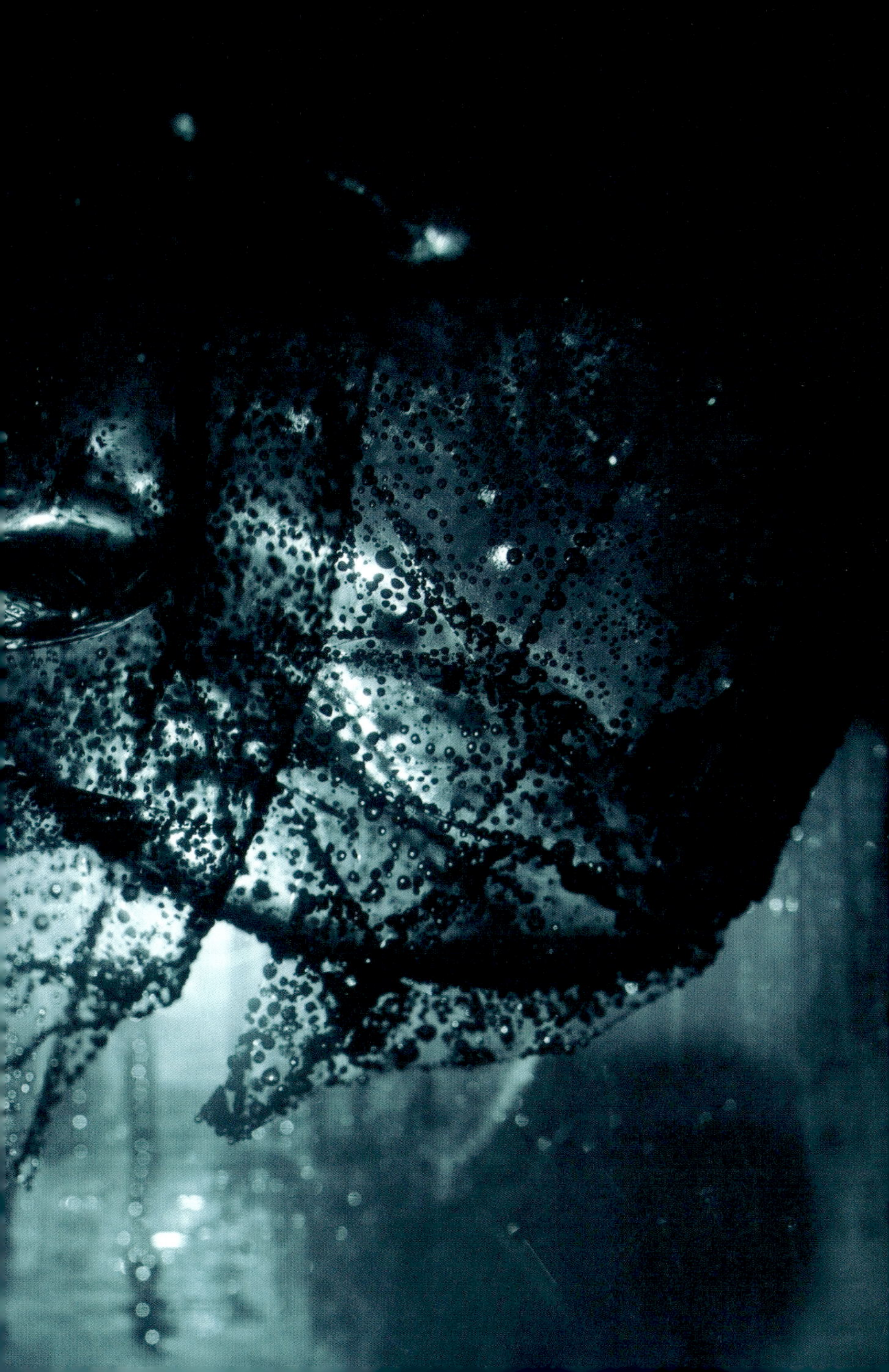

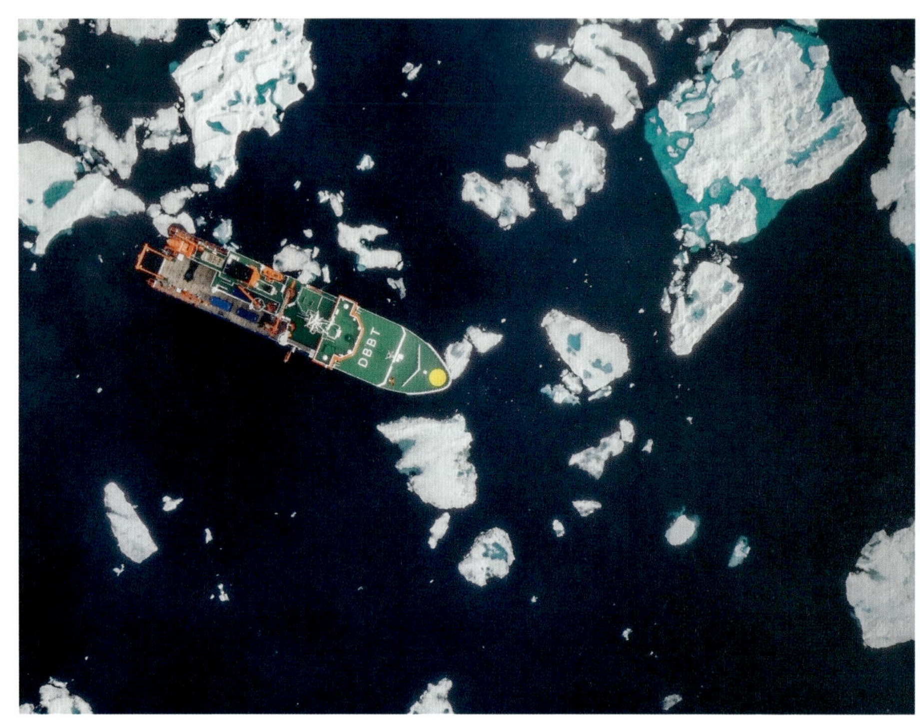
DBBT

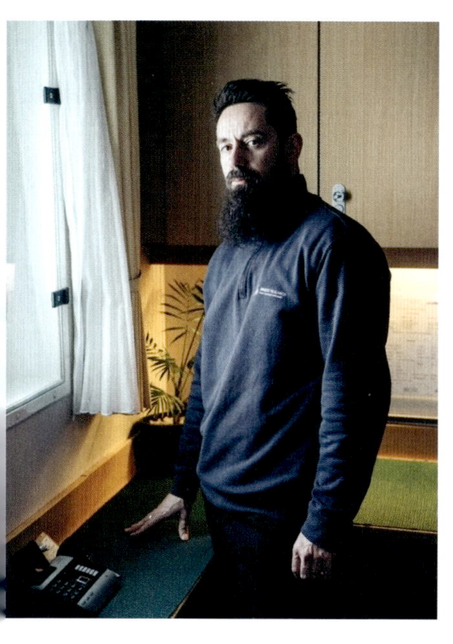

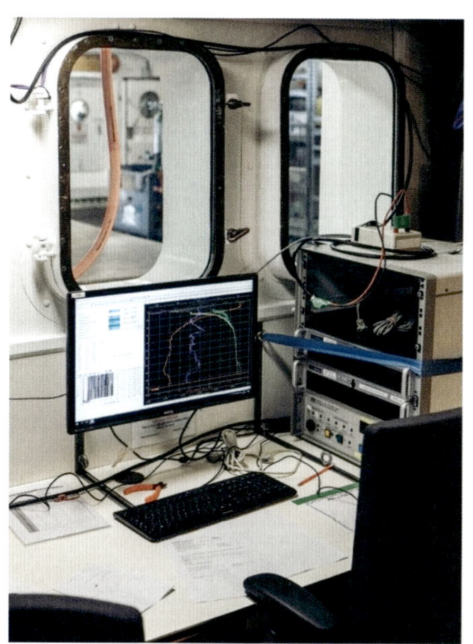

VICTORIA JUNG

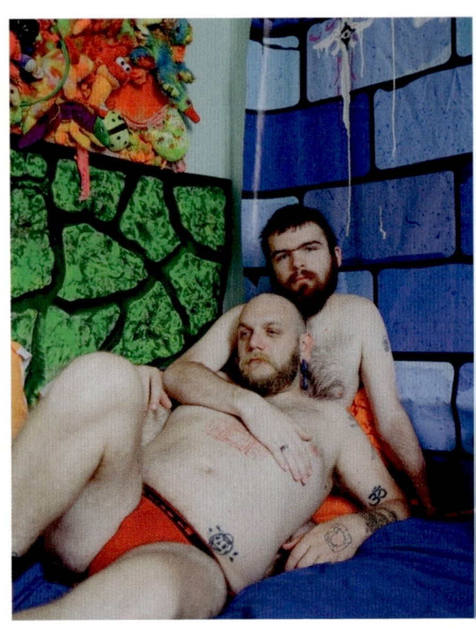

Birds

06

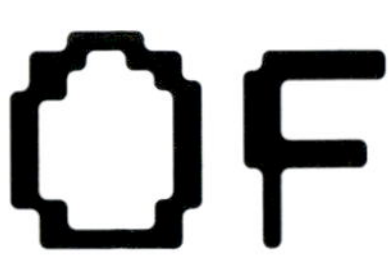

Since the catastrophe that occurred with Hurricane Katrina 15 years ago, New Orleans has been in a state of instability. With sea levels expected to rise and the land under the city gradually sinking below sea level, the next disaster is already impending. Maybe that's why people who don't fit into the system anywhere else find a home there. Birds of passage in search of inspiration and fulfilment. All their energy and productivity flows into the here and now. In doing so, they create an unruly subculture that Victoria sought out to document.

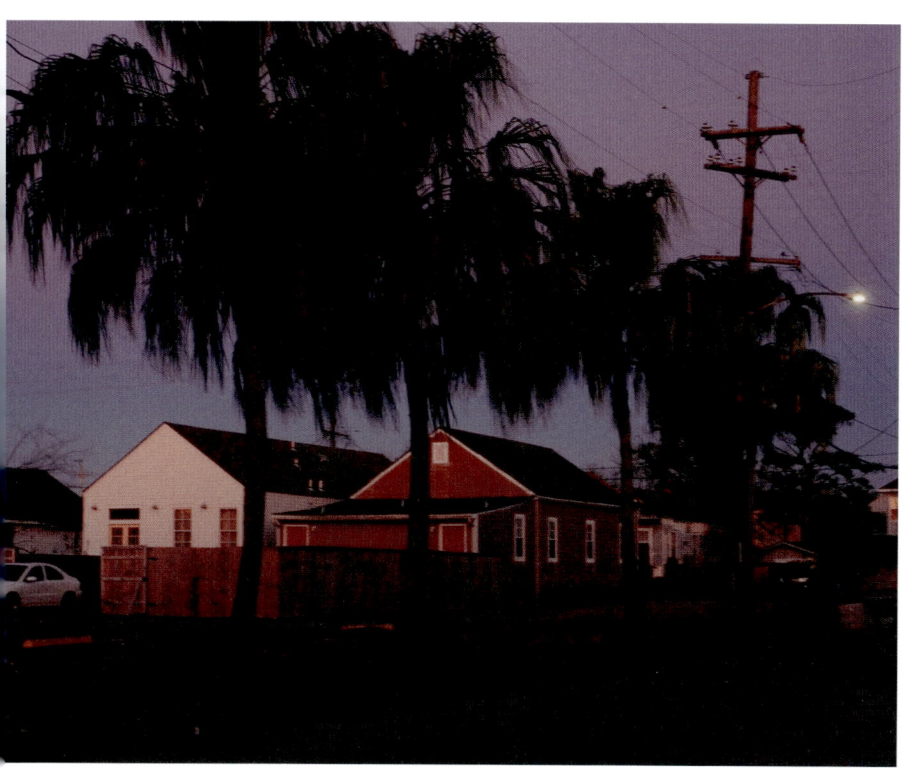

passage

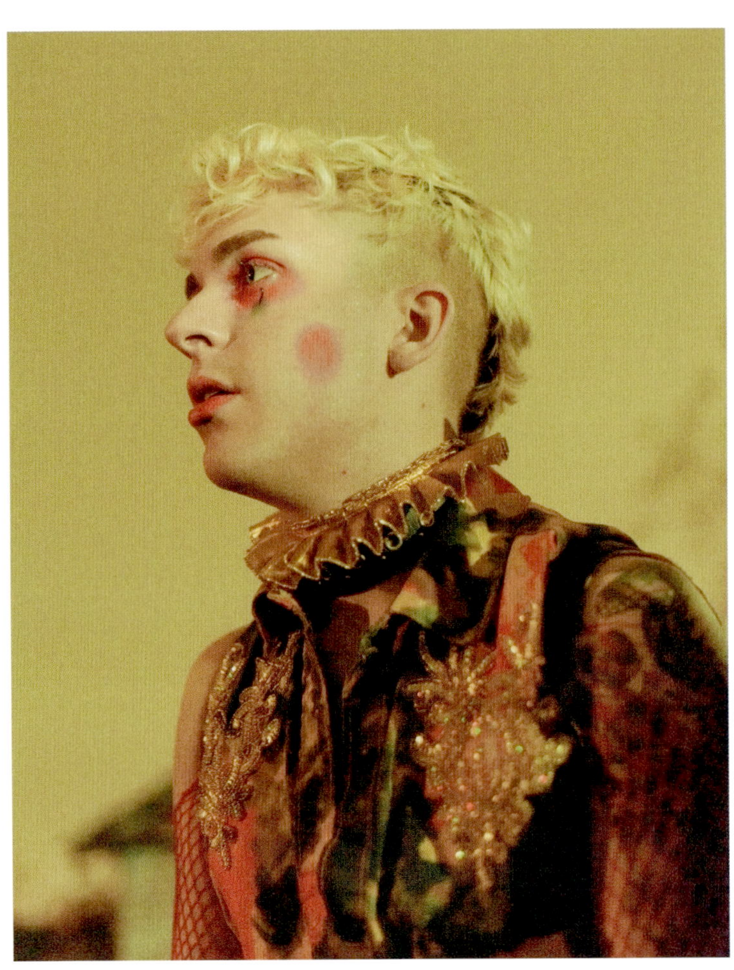

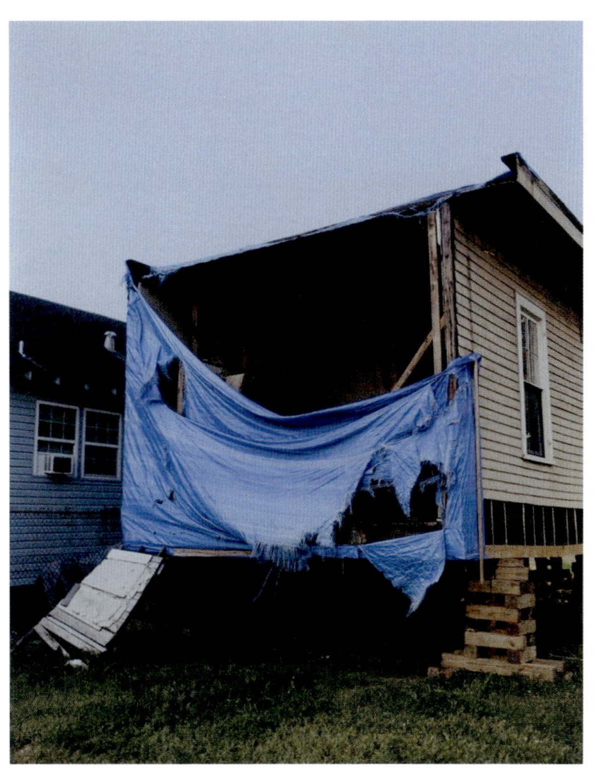

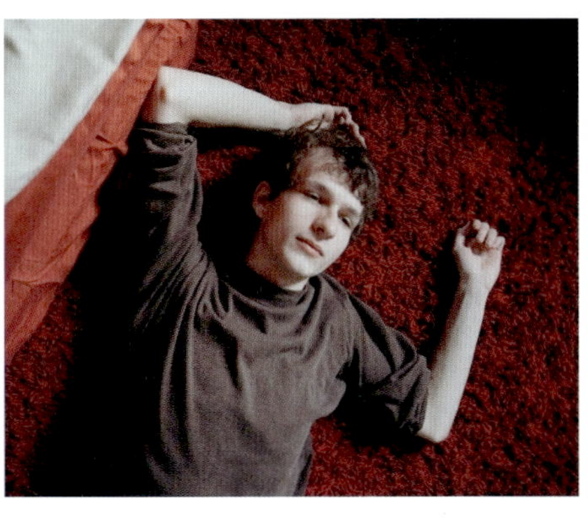

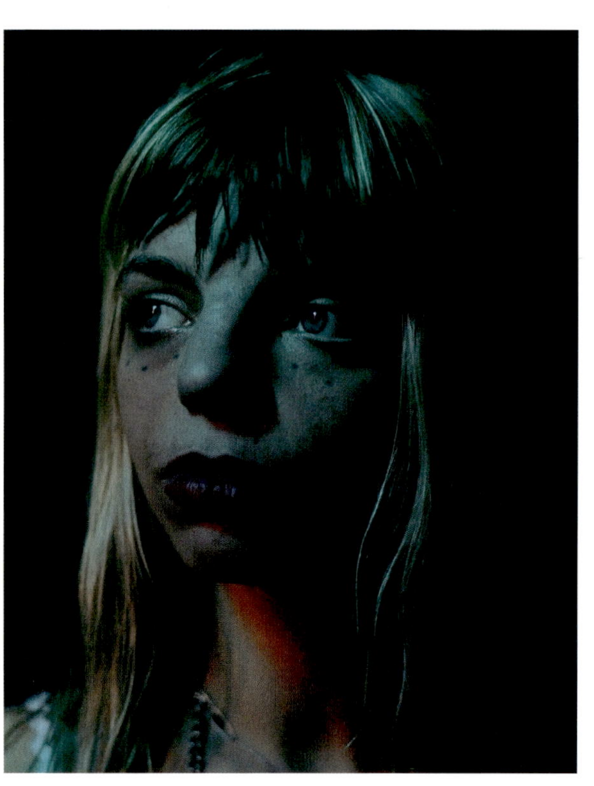

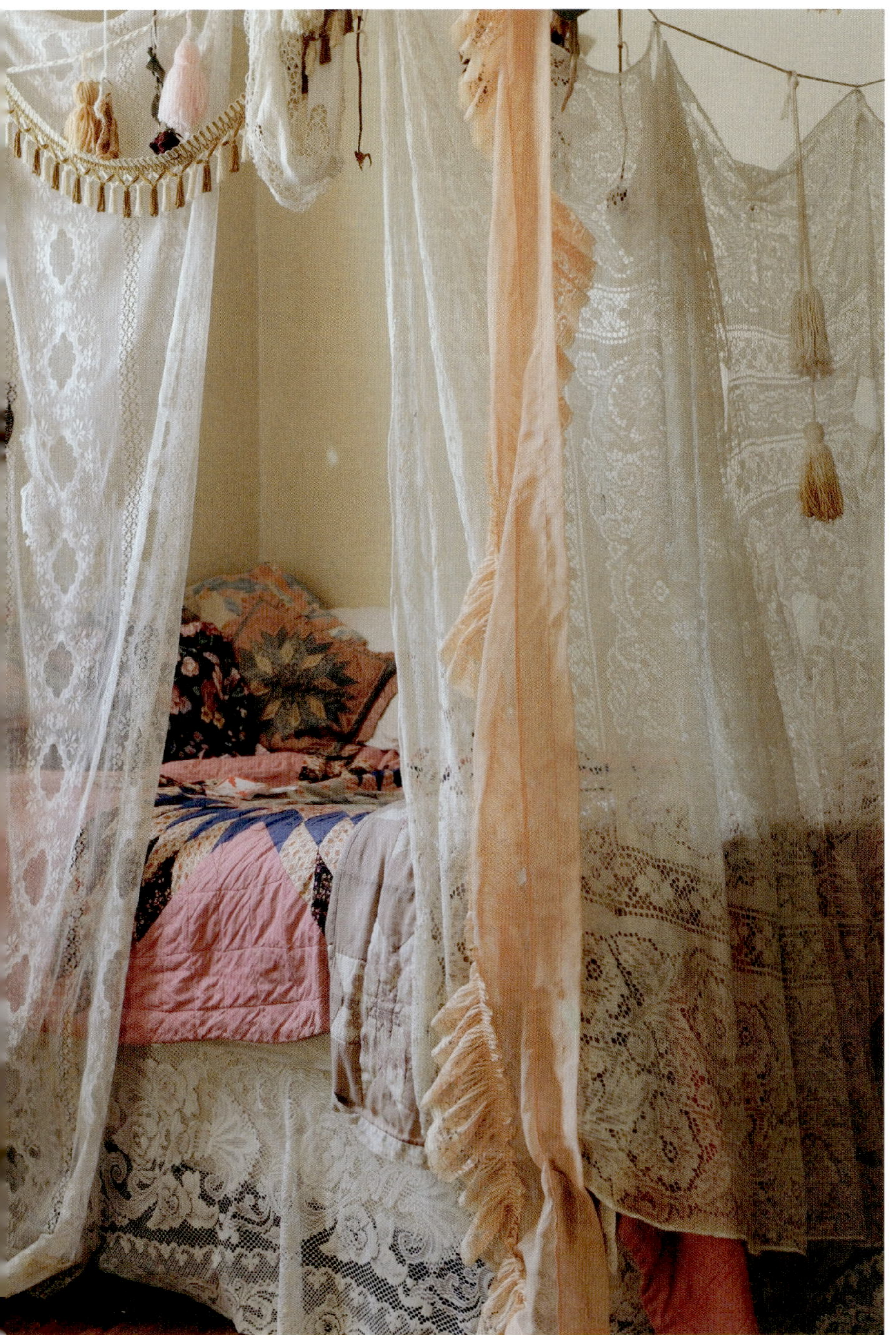

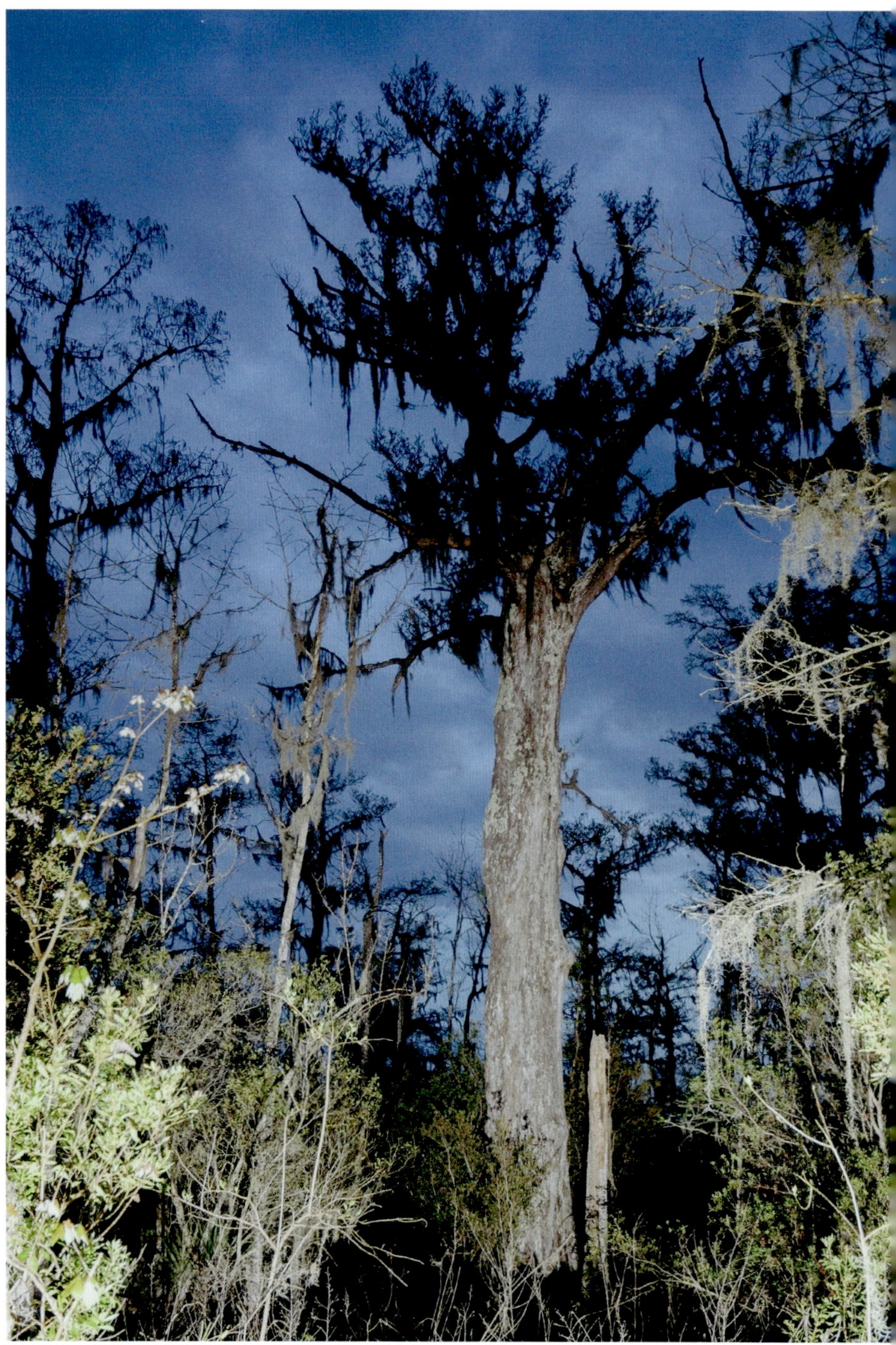

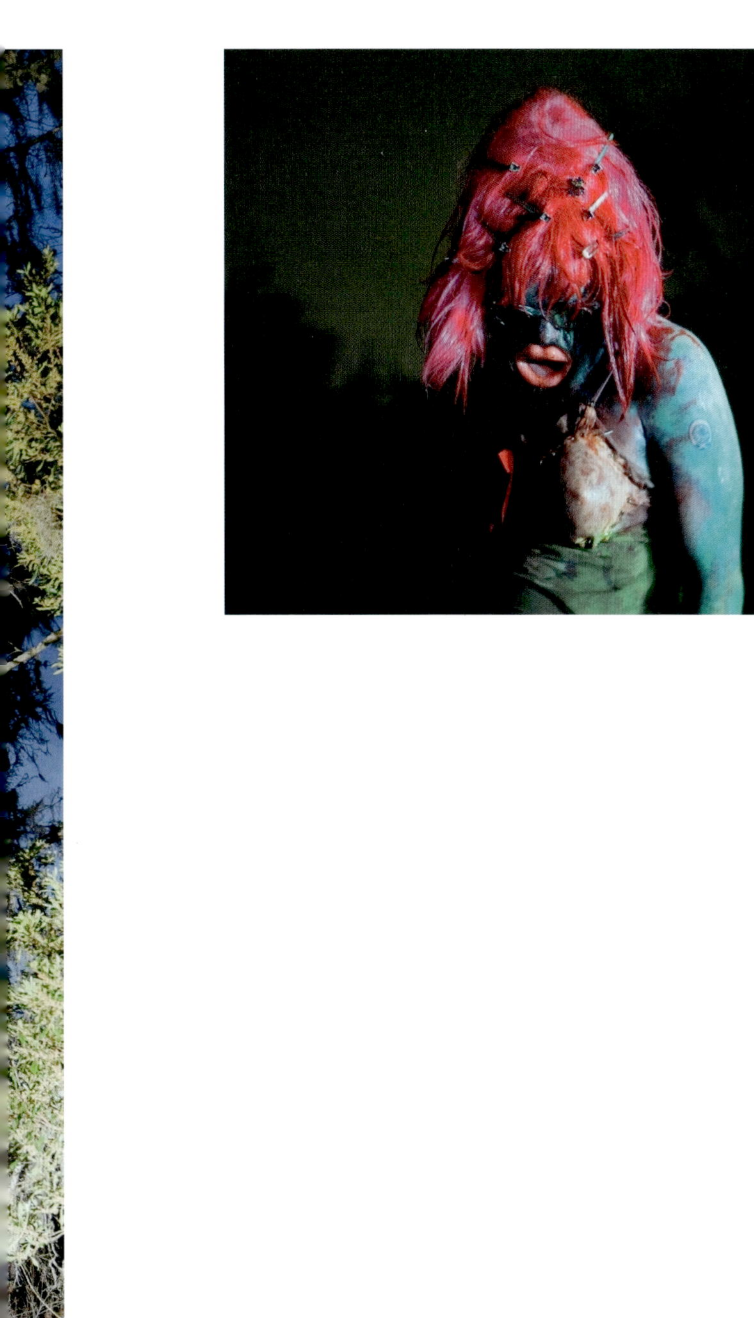

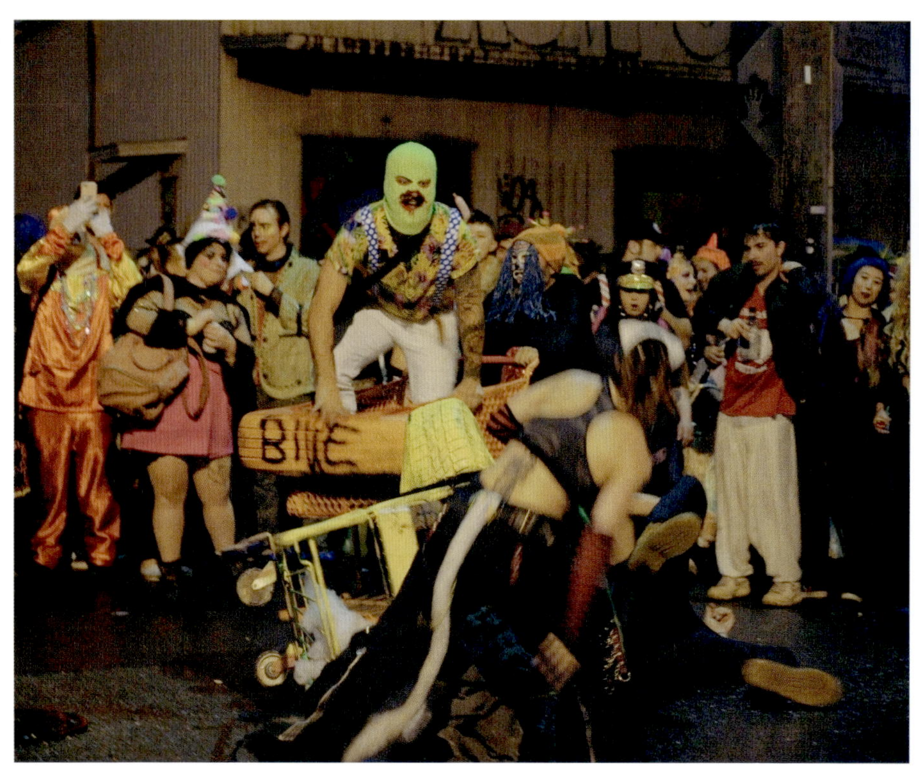

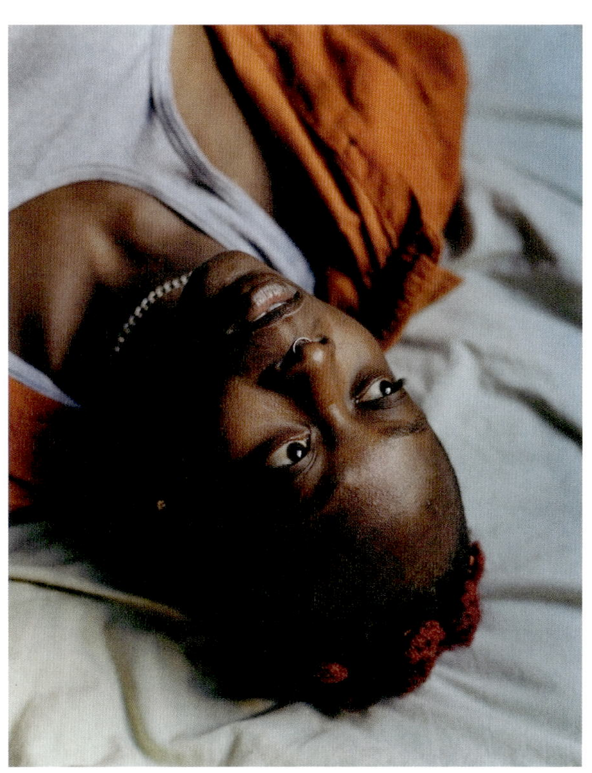

MARGARITA VALDIVIESO

07

*I see the way you looked at me–

*Celeste, I should have gotten your number- m4w

Celeste was the gentle breeze bracing my face on a cool winter day; further stimulating cerebral neurons to serve up childhood memories of past. Hypnotized by the breezes serenade of songs, the treetops sway in synchronized rhythmic. The same breeze re-hydrates life back into the fallen snow into a swirling celebration of dance. Celeste, like the breeze, dissipates into the forest abyss of a seemingly random universe. But the moment will never be lost in memory!

Missed Connections was a popular website on the internet, giving people a platform to post anonymous messages to strangers they had met on the street, hoping to reconnect with them. Margarita took pictures of the places pointed out in these online messages, putting the culture of online dating and US urban landscapes into dialogue. After the board was shut down due to a congress bill, outrage sparked from the queer community, sex workers and love seekers around the country.

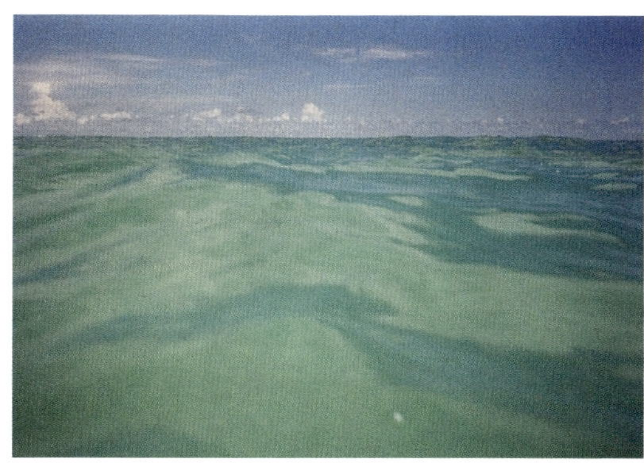

*David-w4m
I told you that your hands are really nice. I have thought of you every day since..All I know is you do real estate.
David is 6'3 black with light caramel complexion. someone please find him for me!

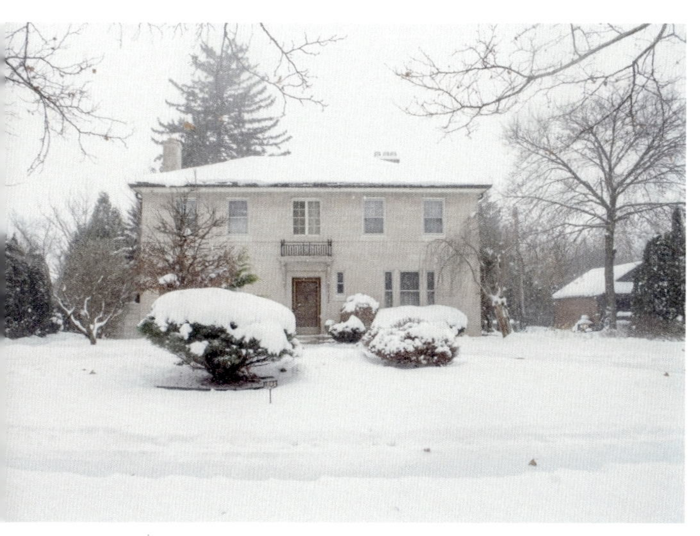

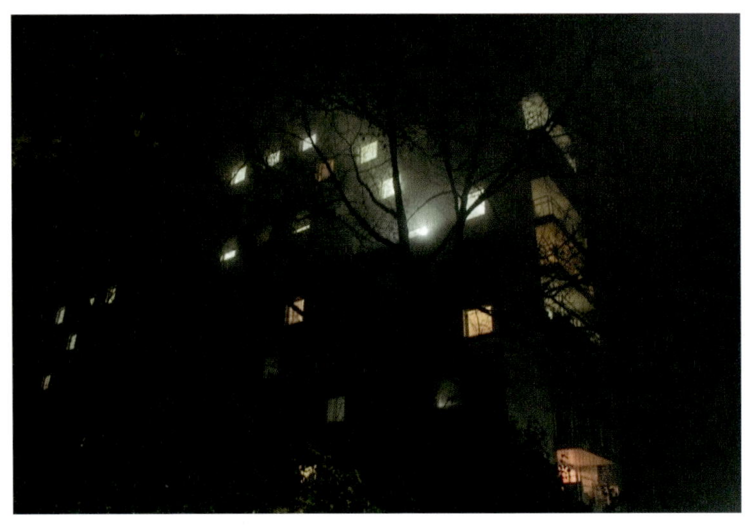

I SEE THE WAY YOU LOOK AT ME-W4M
WHERE YOU WORK? REPLY ME- SENT YOU LOT OF REPLIES...CONTACT ME ON IM, EVERYDAY I LOOK AT YOU WHEN YOU GET IN.

*MI ADORADO TORMENTO-M4W

CADA VEZ QUE PIENSO QUE YA TE SAQUE DE MI CORAZON, VIENES TU Y ME MIRAS CON ESOS OJITOS QUE DICEN TANTAS COSAS, O ME LLAMAS CON ESA VOZ TAN PECULIAR Y QUE ME ESTREMECE DE PELO A PIE, O SENCILLAMENTE PASAS POR DELANTE DE MI PUERTA CON ESOS PASOS TAN TUYOS Y ENTONCES ME DESORDENAS UNA VEZ MAS MI VIDA TAN ORGANIZADA Y APACIBLE.

¿QUE VOY A HACER CONTIGO?
HE TRATADO TODOS LOS ARDILES DE MI BOLSA DE TRUCOS PERO NADA FUNCIONA.

UN DIA DE ESTOS TE VOY A DECIR LO LINDA QUE ESTAS Y ENTONCES VENDRA LA HECATOMBE.

*K...AT WALLMART-M4W

YOU CAUGHT MY STARE WITH YOUR LONGING EYES

...YOU CAPTURED MY HEART

WITH YOUR SMILE.

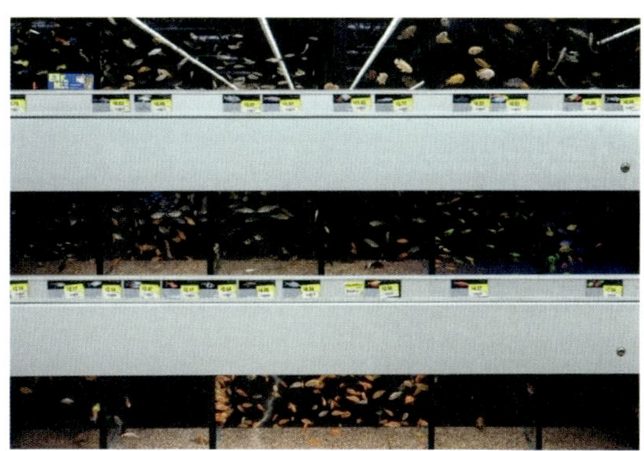

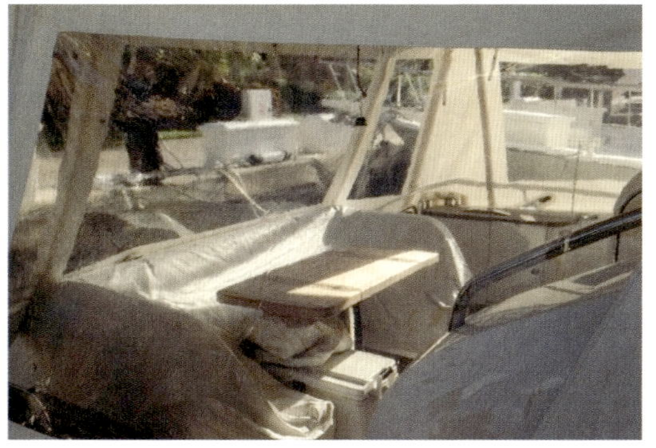

*WEST PALM BEACH-M4W

I WAS EATING DINNER WHEN YOU WALKED IN, YOU TOOK MY BREATH AWAY, YOU WERE SO BEAUTIFUL. CROSSING MY FINGERS I'M HOPING YOU SEE THIS.

I WANT MY HEART TO RACE AGAIN.

WALKING BEHIND YOU-m4w

I KNOW YOU DID
SAY HI...

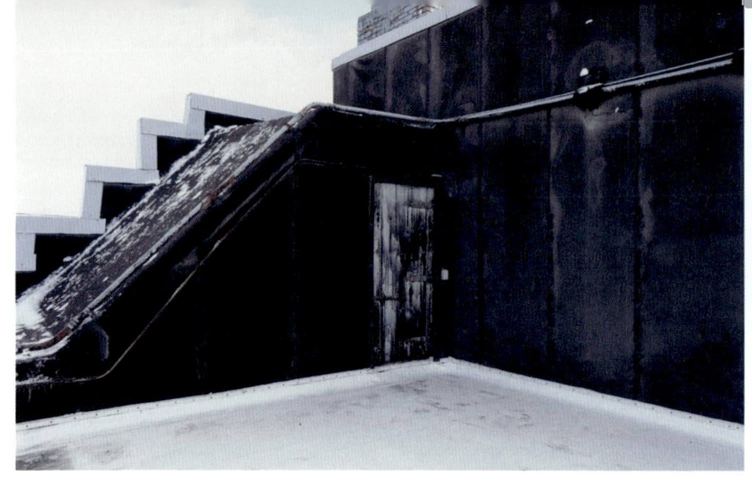

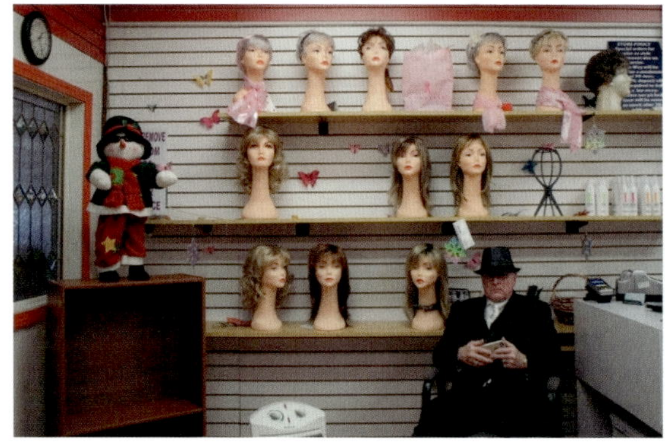

*FRUM MAN LOOKING FOR A FRUM WOMAN-M4W

I AM A FRUM MARRIED MAN, VERY PHISICALLY ATTRACTIVE, IN GREAT SHAPE. NOT SOMEONE YOU WOULD EXPECT TO FIND HERE. I´M LOOKING FOR A NICE FRIENDSHIP WITH A FRUM WOMAN. I AM A BBIG BELIEVER IN THE BASICS. FRIENDSHIP, CHEMISTRY, PHYSICAL ATTRACTION.

*NYC-W4CITY
HOW CAN I
BE POSSIBLY
WRONG ABOUT
YOU?

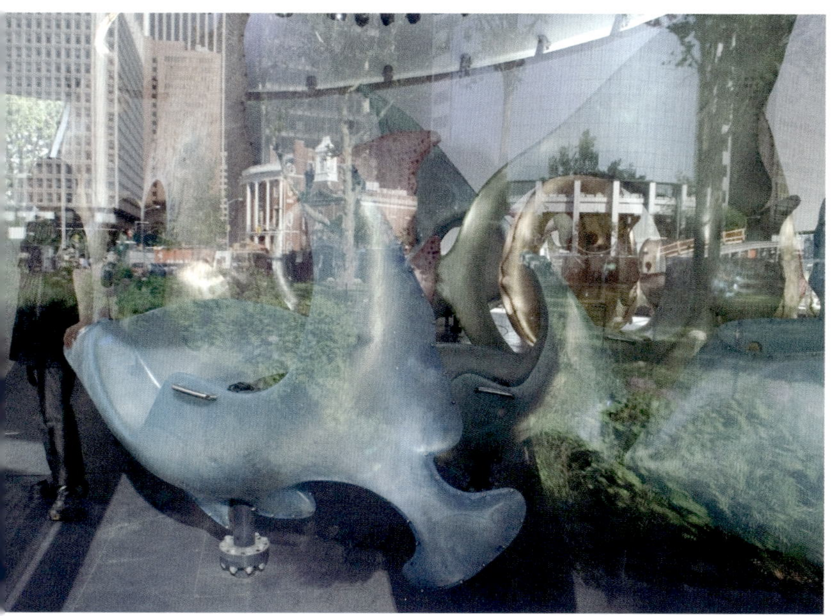

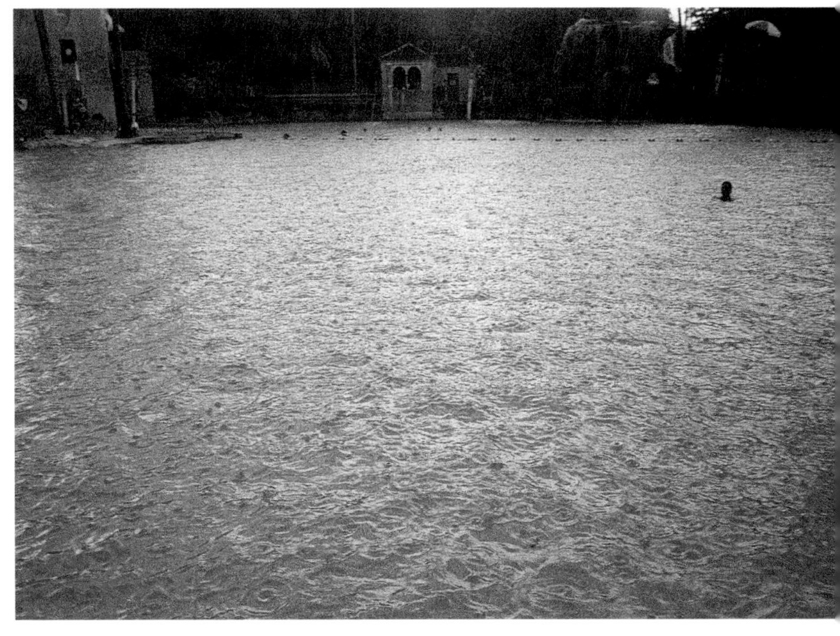

*...WERE YOU EVEN REAL?? W4M

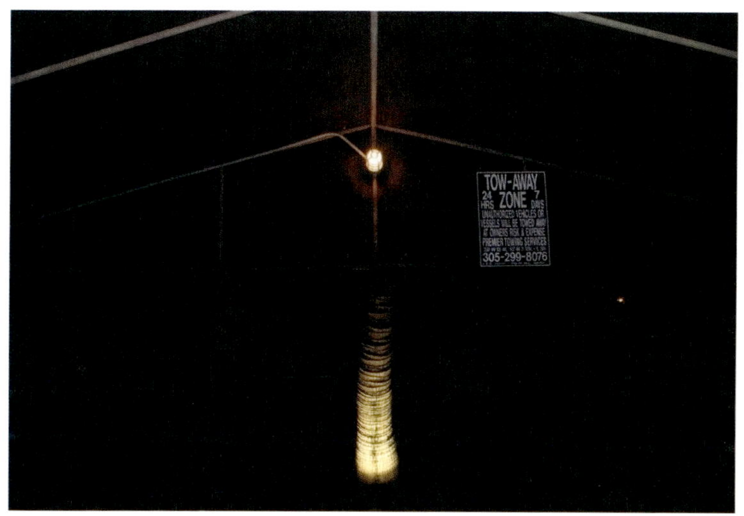

*Vizcaya Masquerade. w4m

1am. White limousine.
You, silver Venetian long nose mask and
black tux, left at Space alone and
I, red sequin gown and gold feather mask,
stayed on for Belle Isle Key.
You are my light.

JULE WILD

Ka$htan

08

You seem to grow up faster in the Ukraine. Jule visited a fascinating country that faces a lot of frustration and injustice, often finding itself between western and eastern interests and influences. And yet there is its youth with its euphoria and hope, and maybe even the chance to change it all.

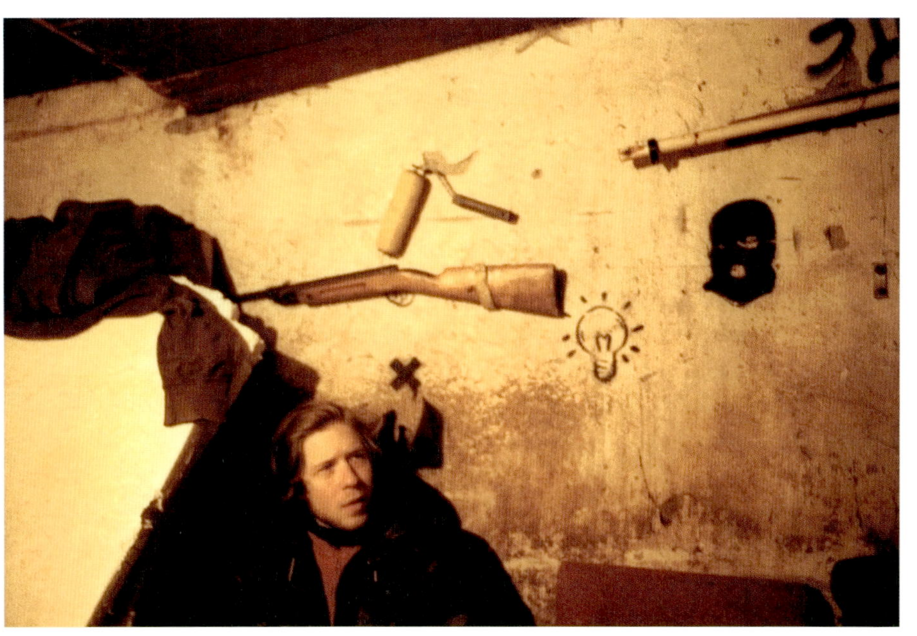

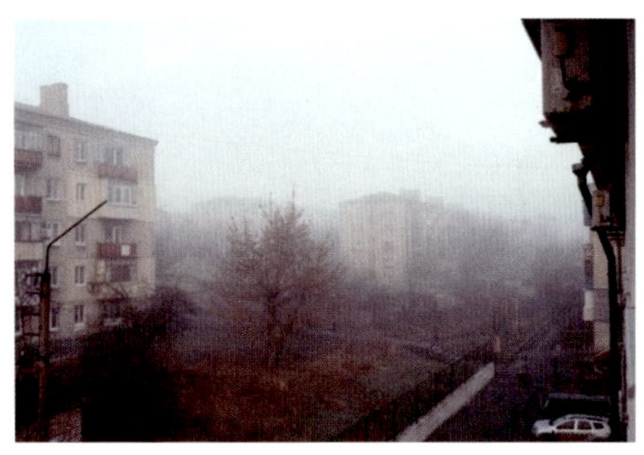

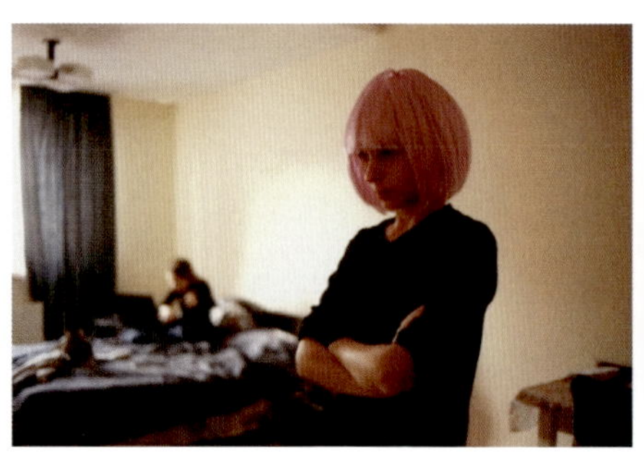

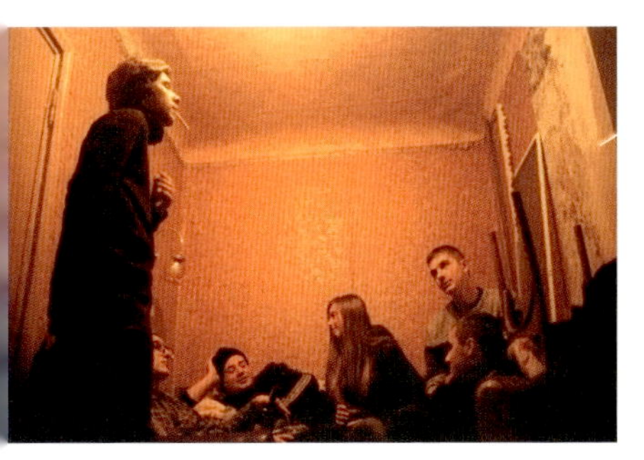

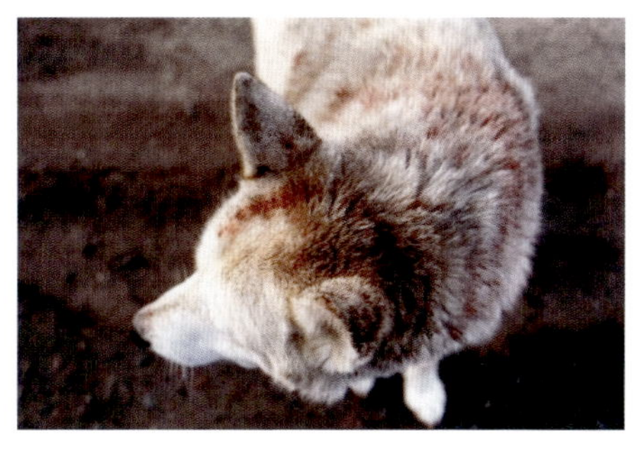

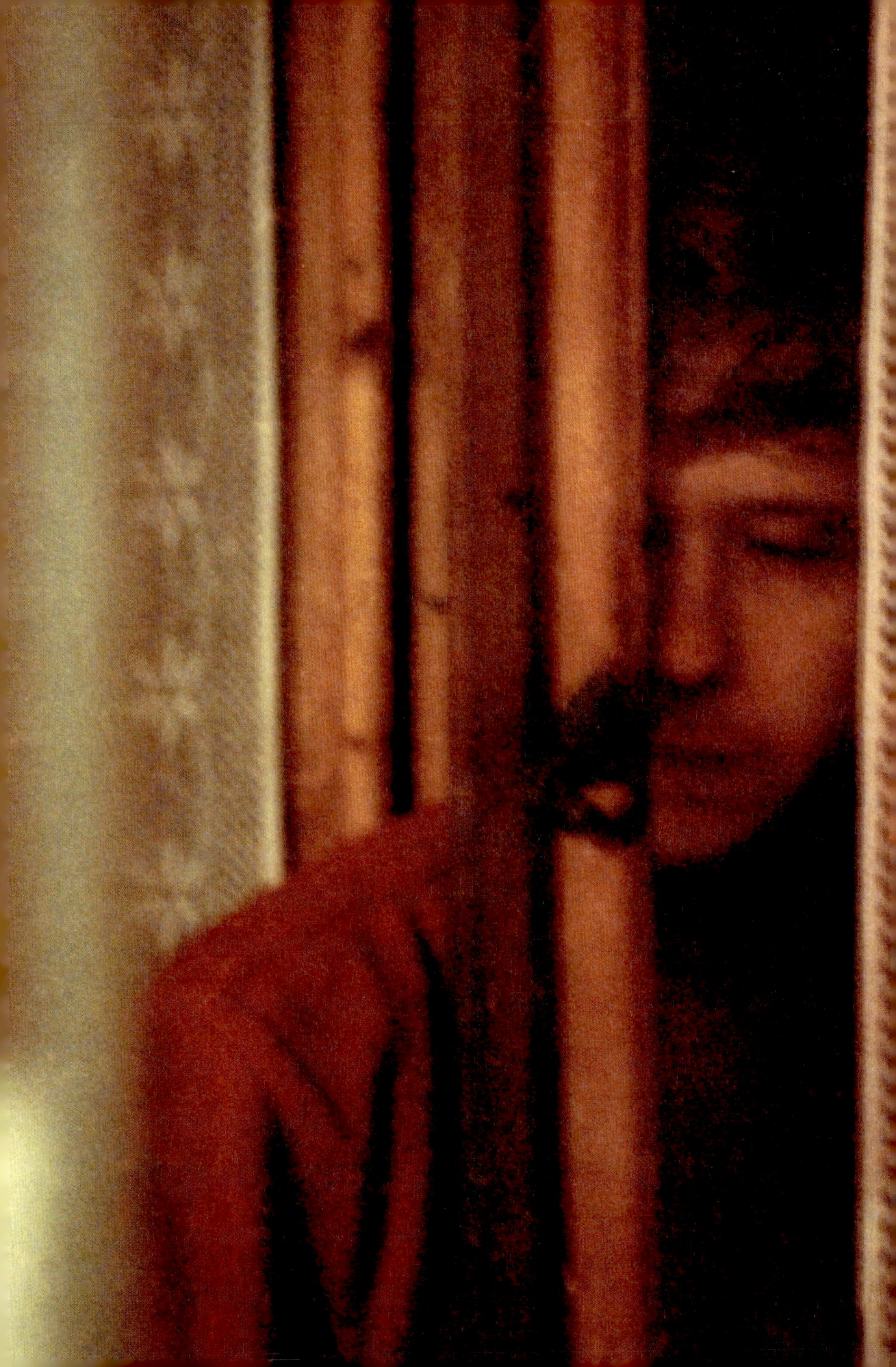

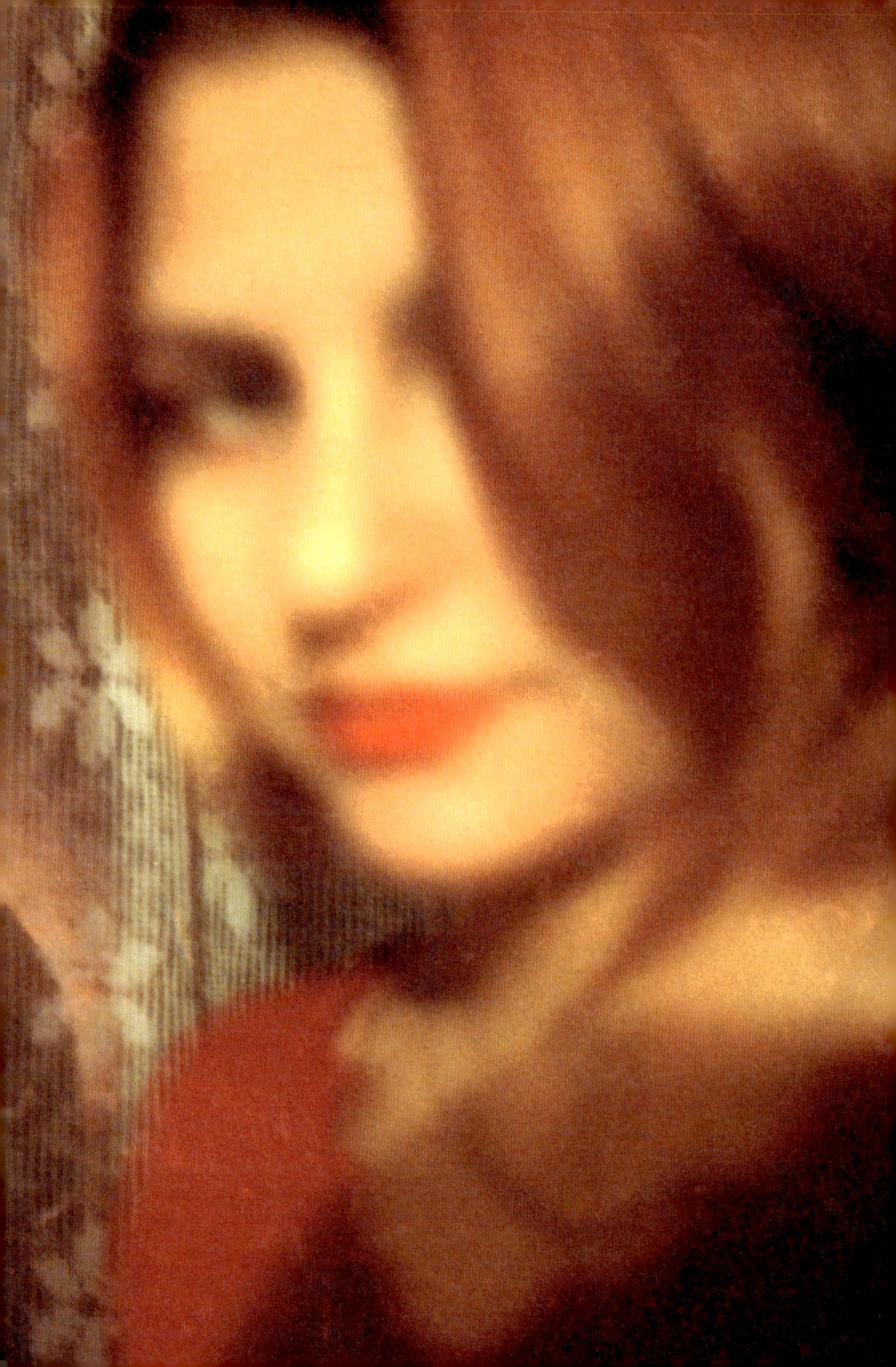

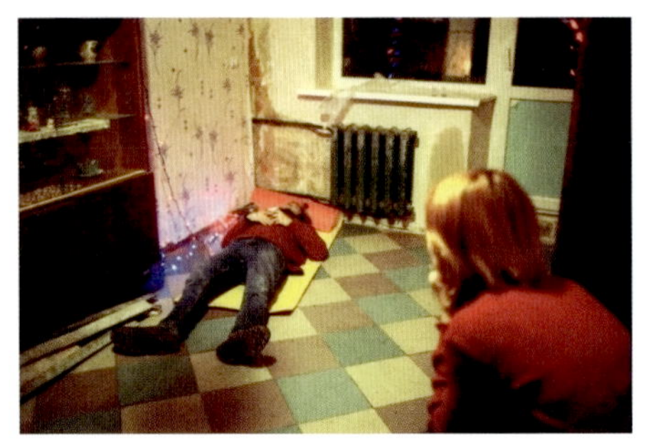

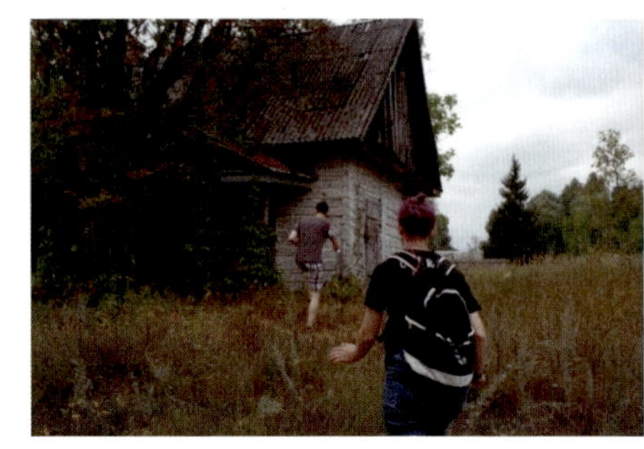

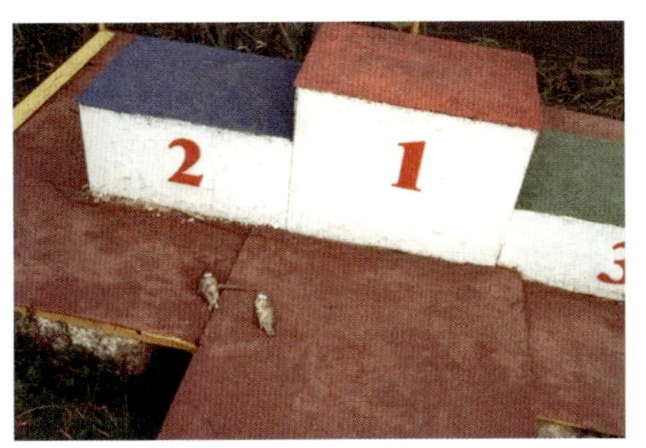
2
1
3

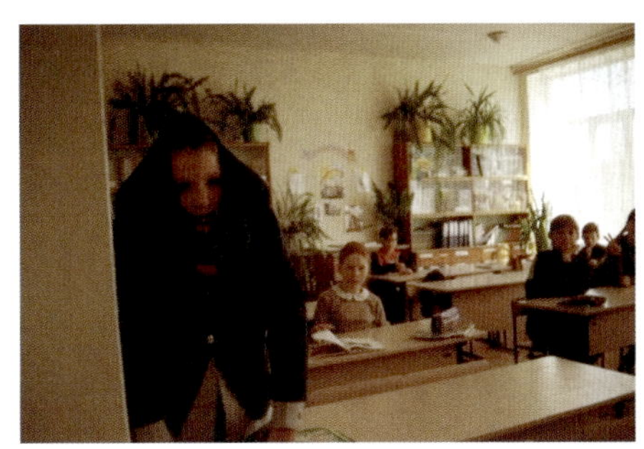

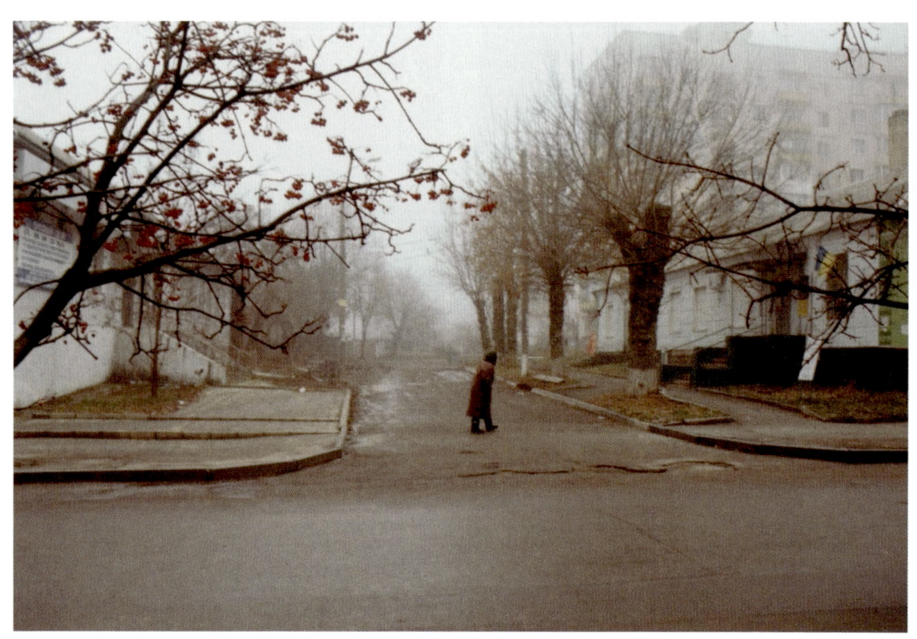

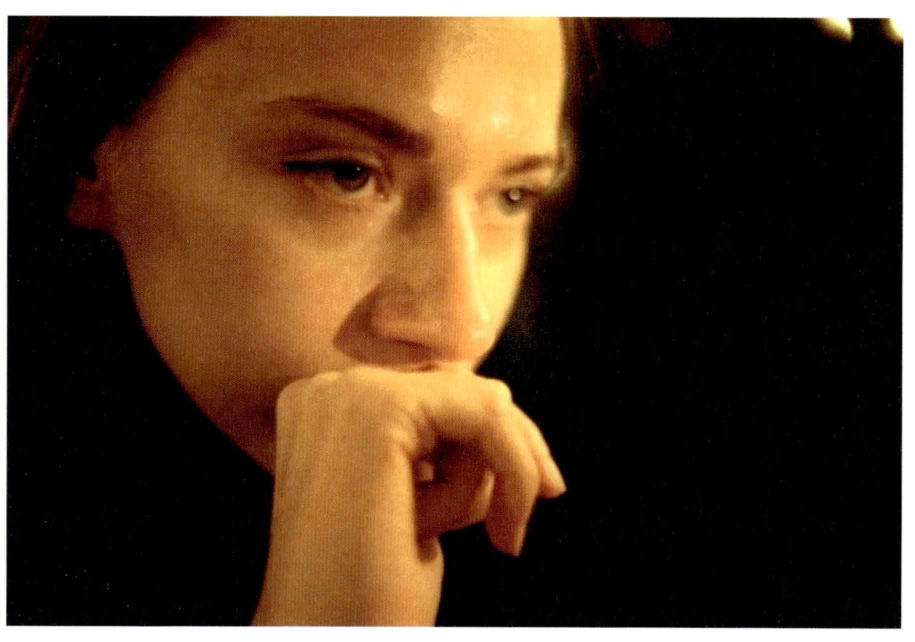

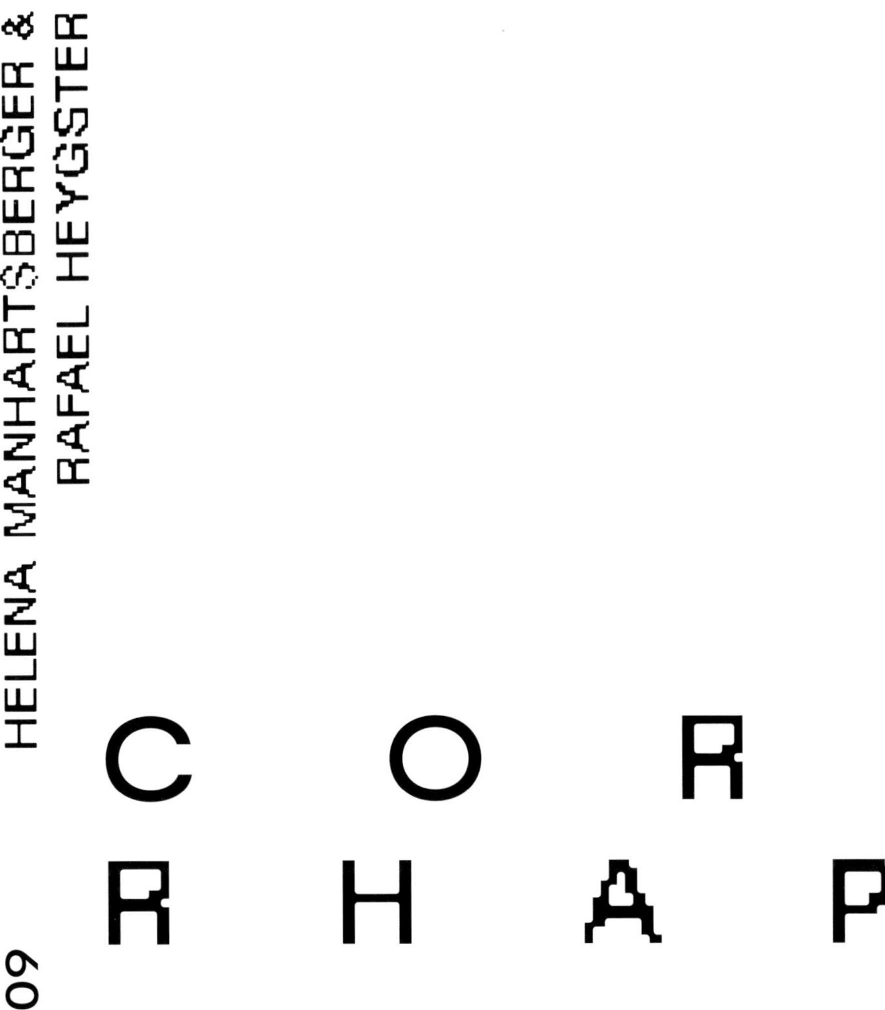

Helena and Rafael documented Germany during the first wave of the Corona outbreak, photographing the infrastructural changes and public life, as it slowly established a "new normality". They felt like being trapped in a mediocre apocalypse movie or a surreal dream. They worked as a team and aimed to depict their feelings by illuminating the situations they encountered.

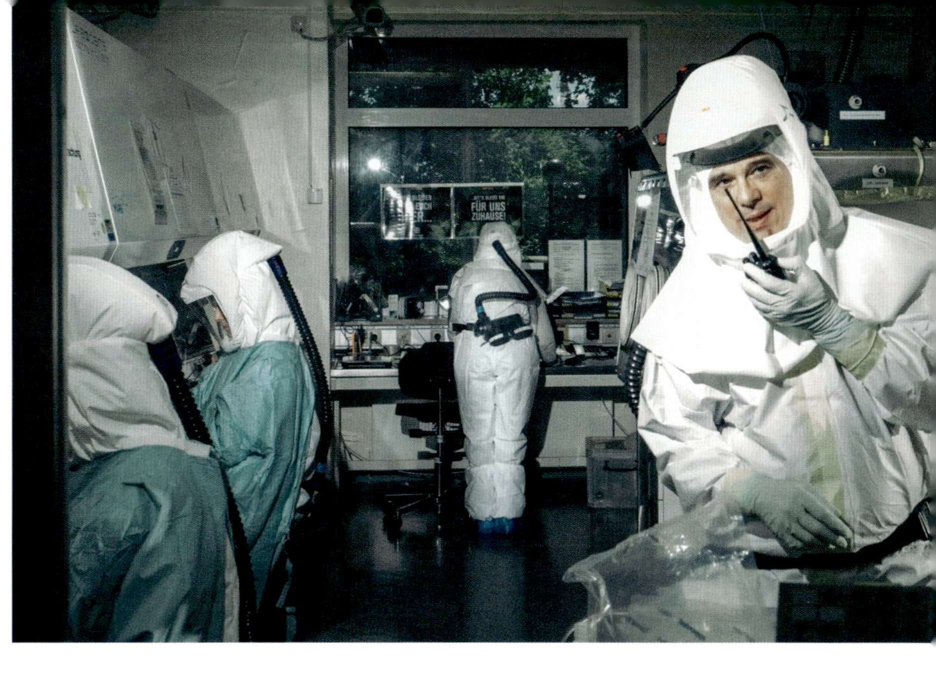

O N A

S O D Y

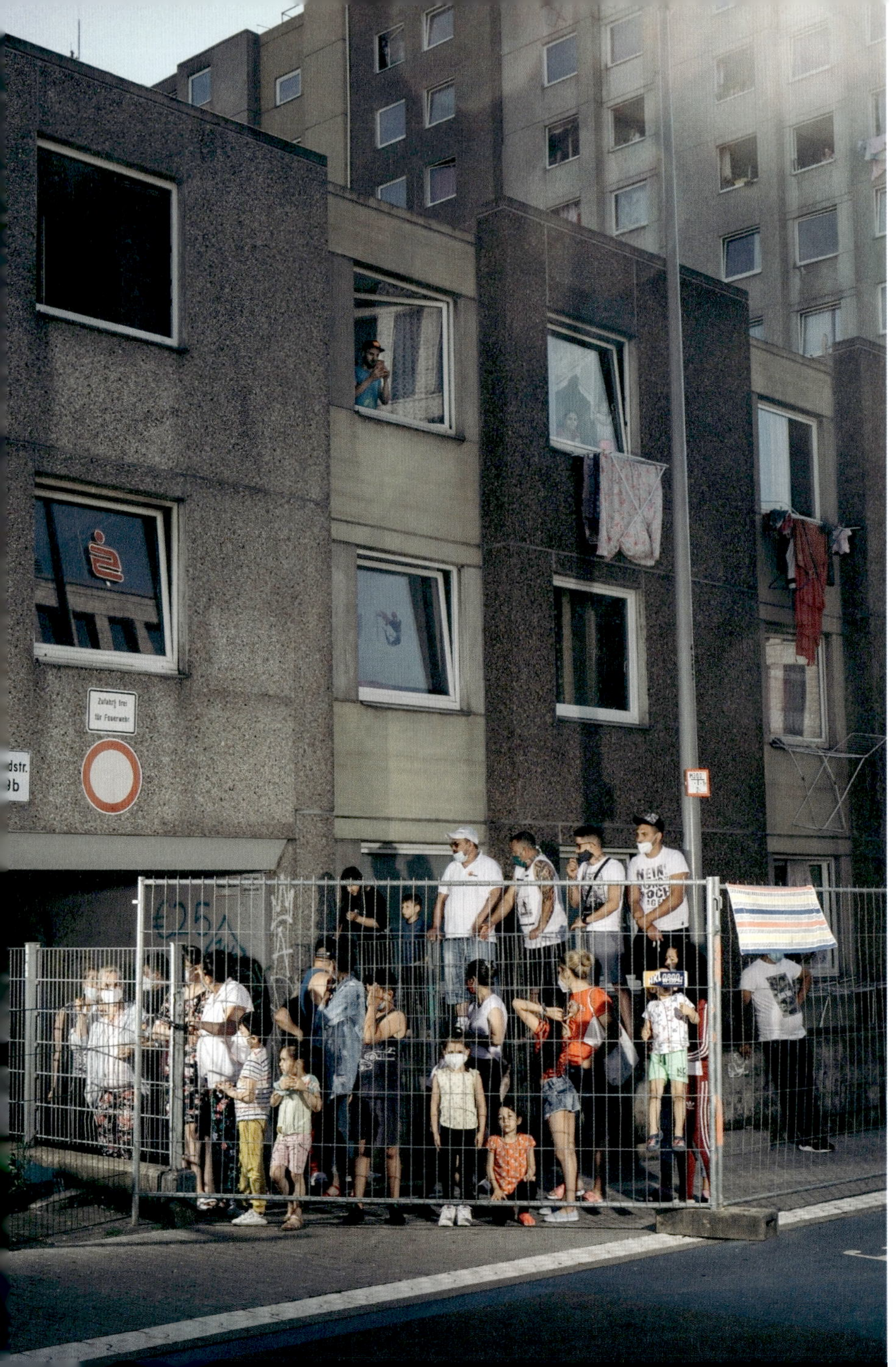
Zufahrt frei
für Feuerwehr
dstr.
9b
NEIN!

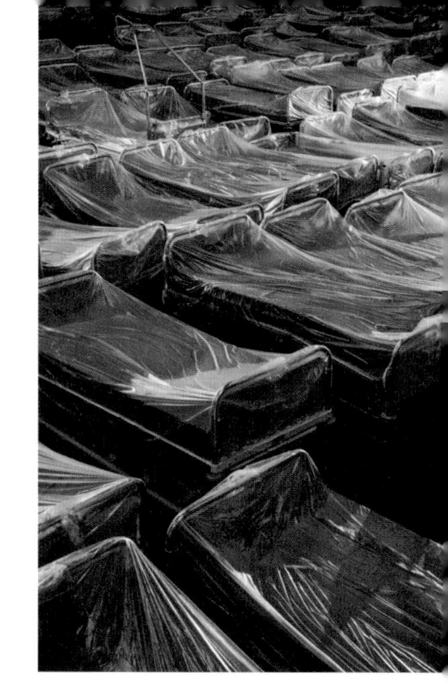

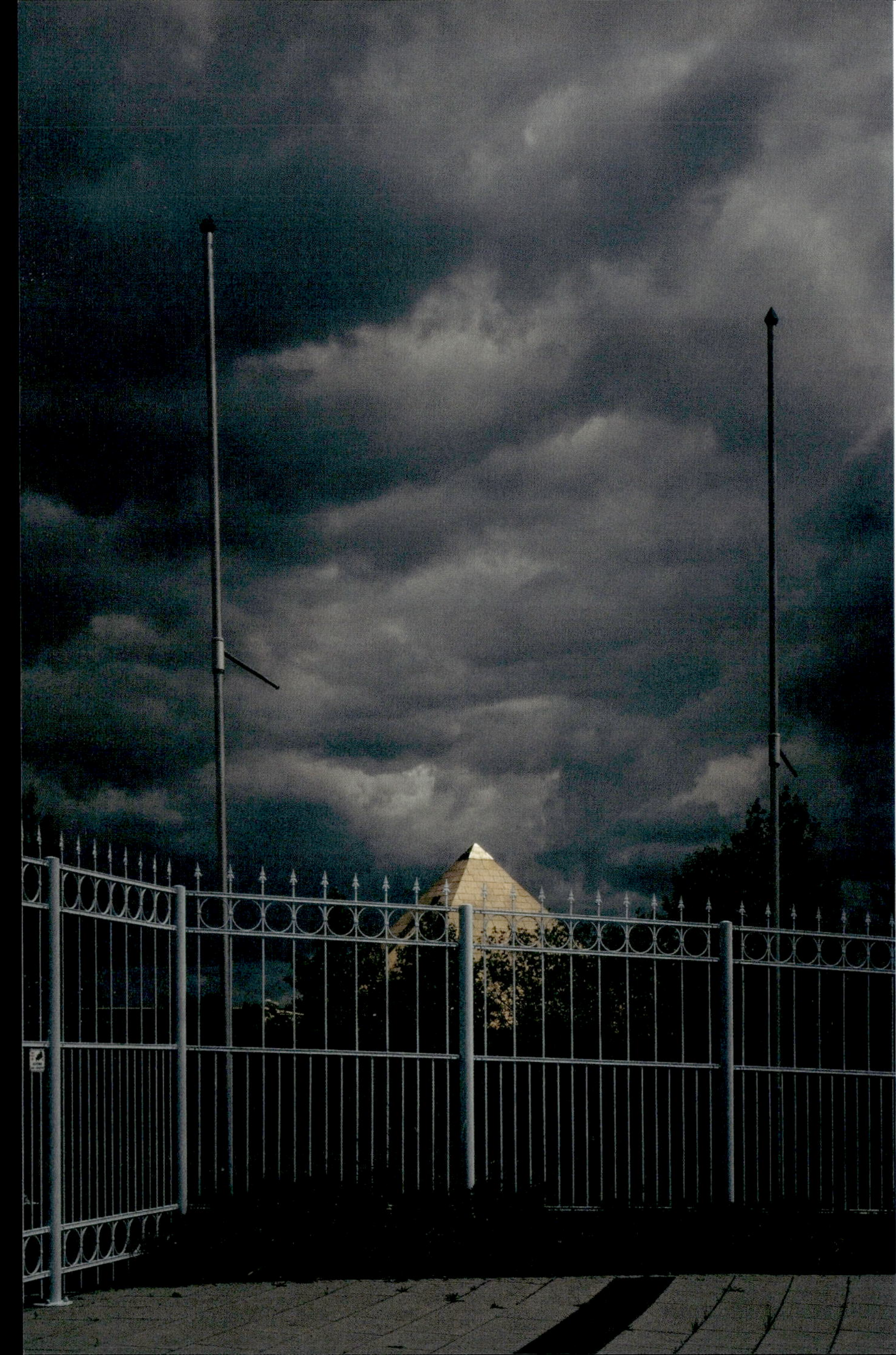

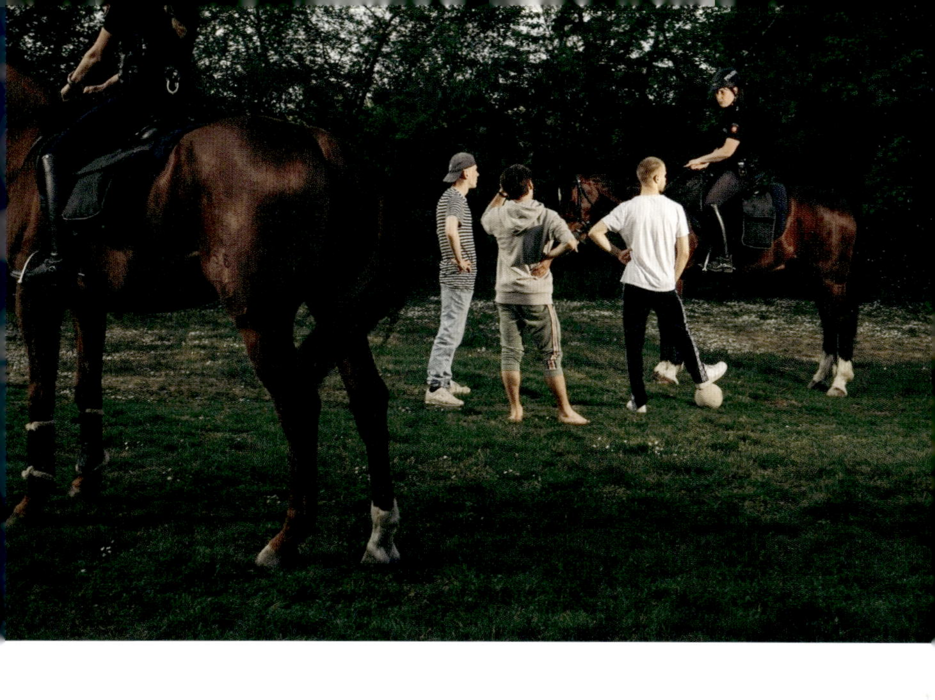

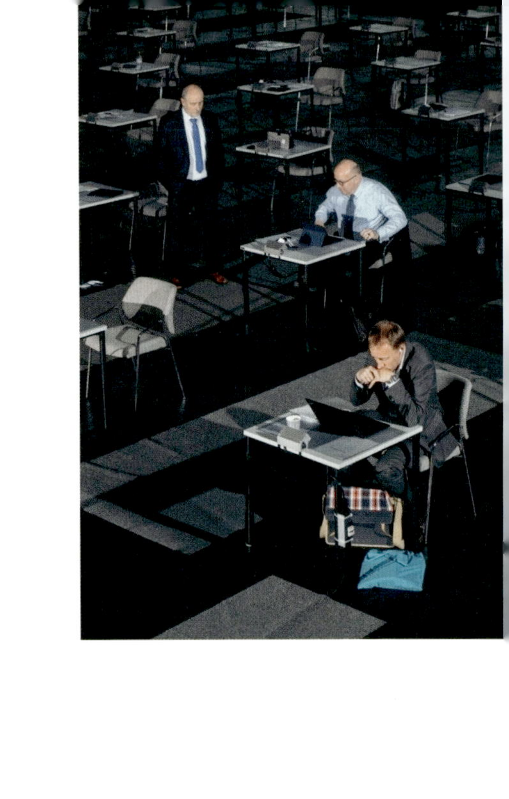

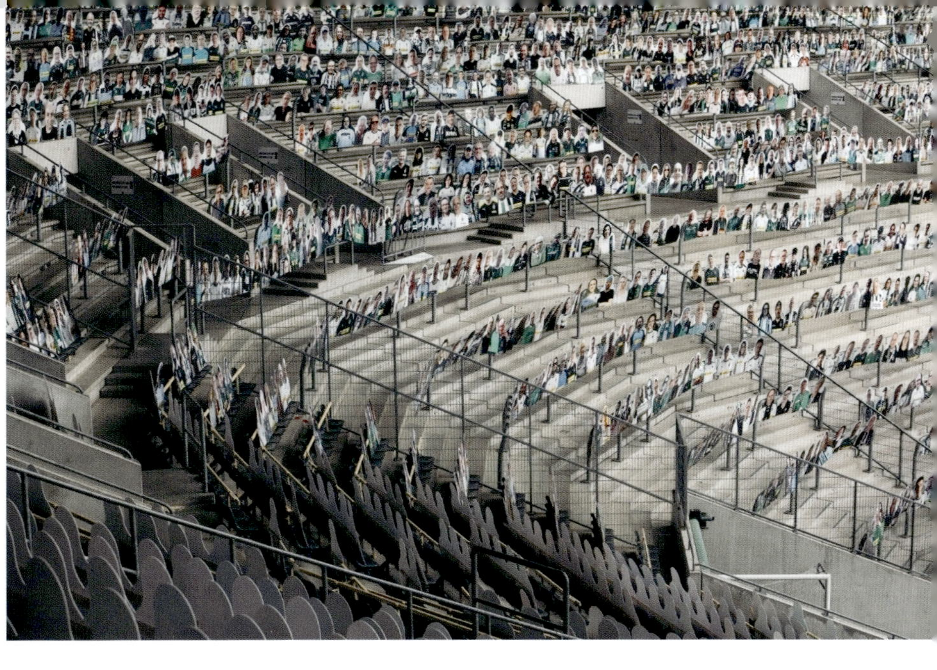

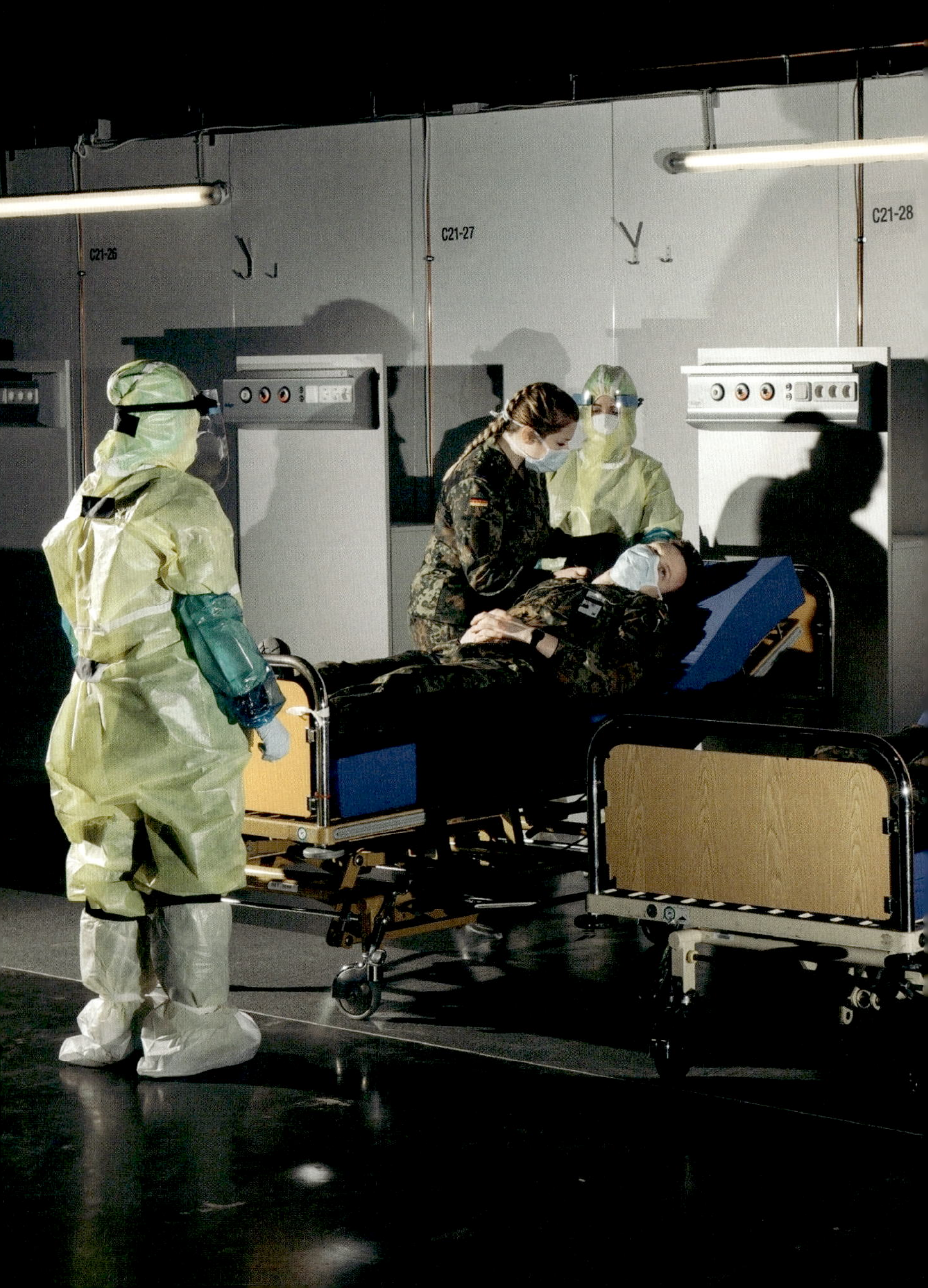
C21-26
C21-27
C21-28

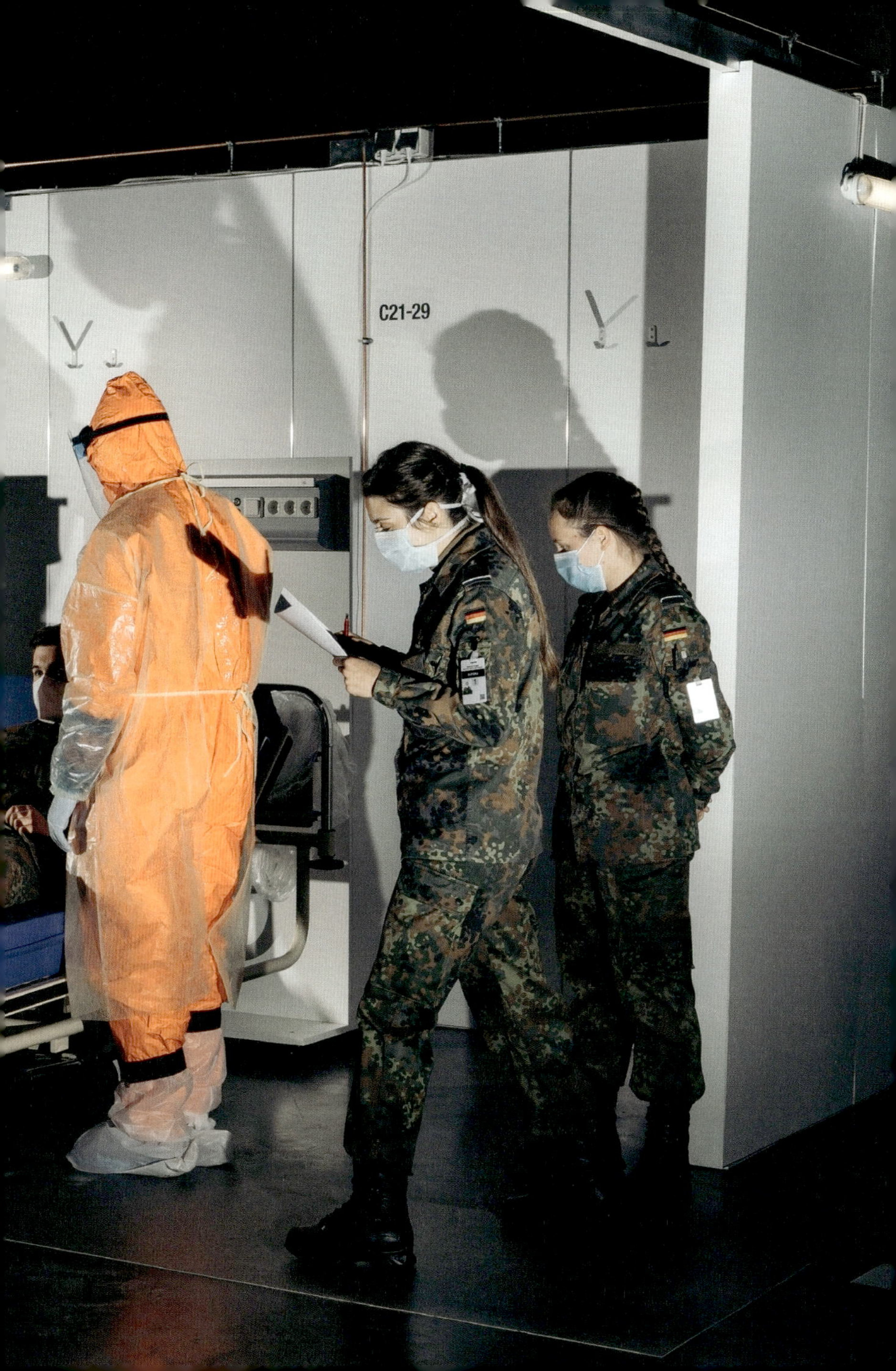
C21-29

LAILA SCHUBERT

10

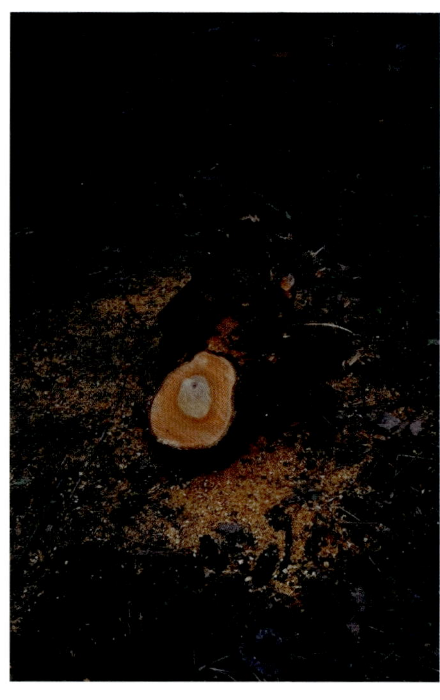

rauschen

Drug addiction is emerging throughout society. Yet the socio-political treatment of addicts is still exclusionary and marginalizing. Laila shows places in public and institutional space, where the abstract term "addiction“ takes on concrete form.

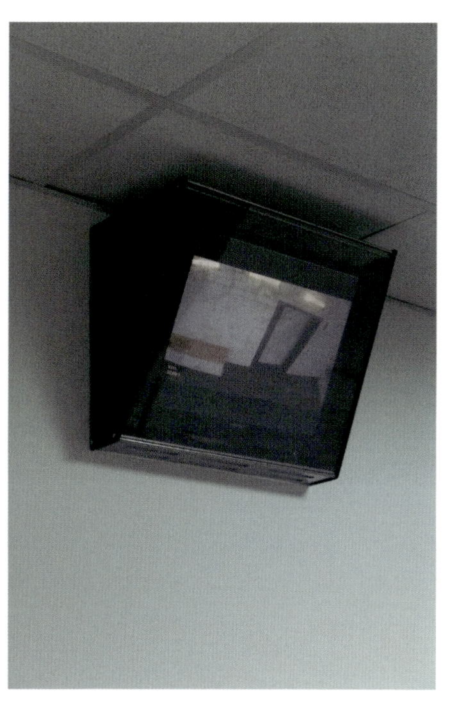
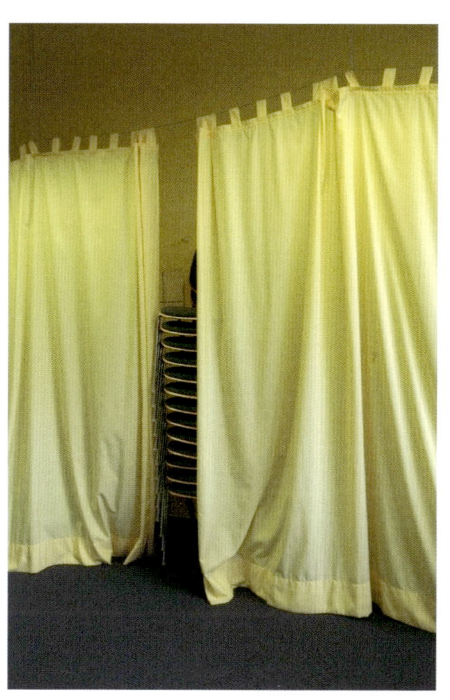

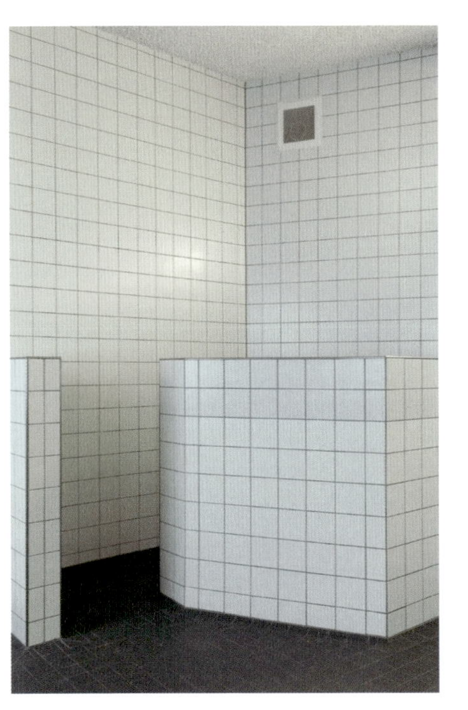

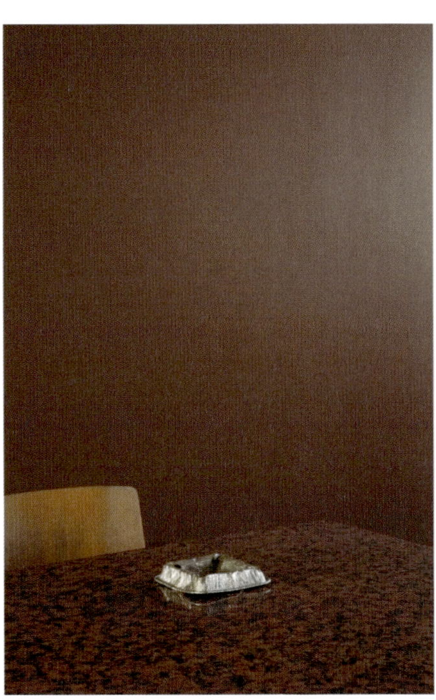

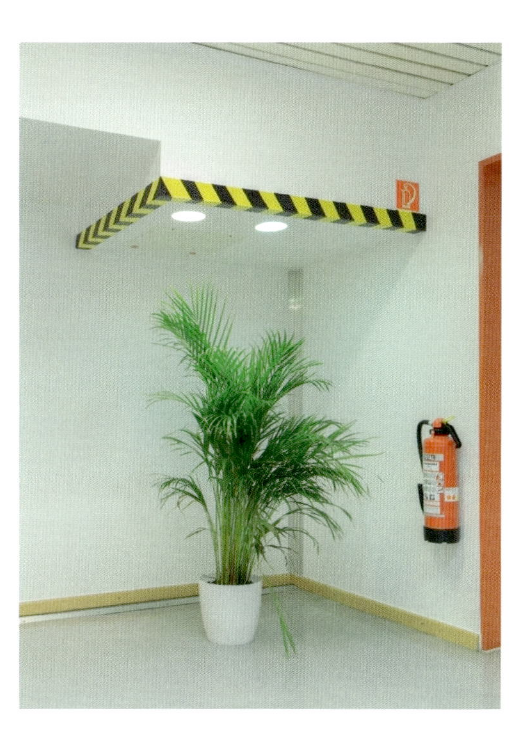

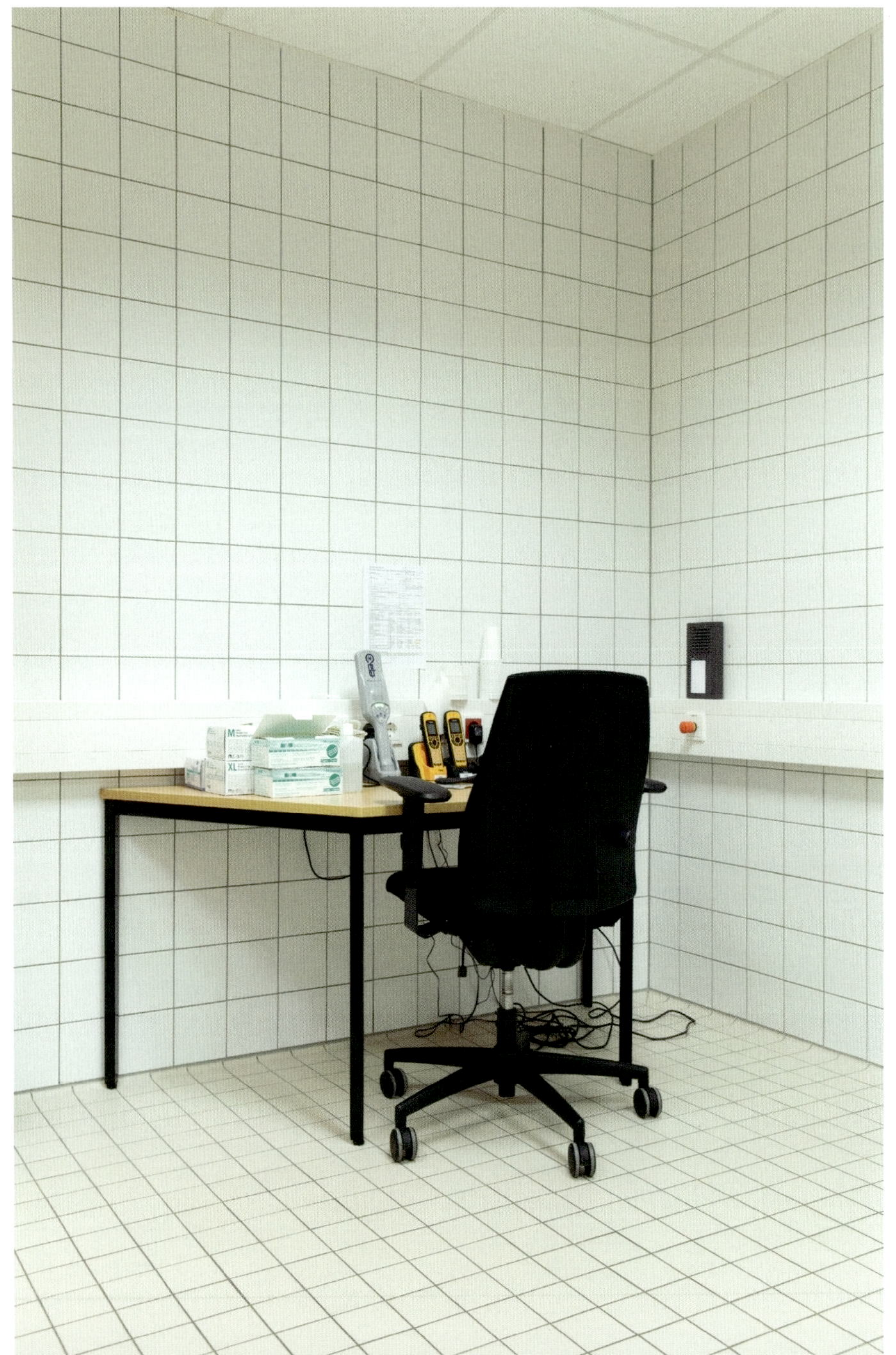
M
XL

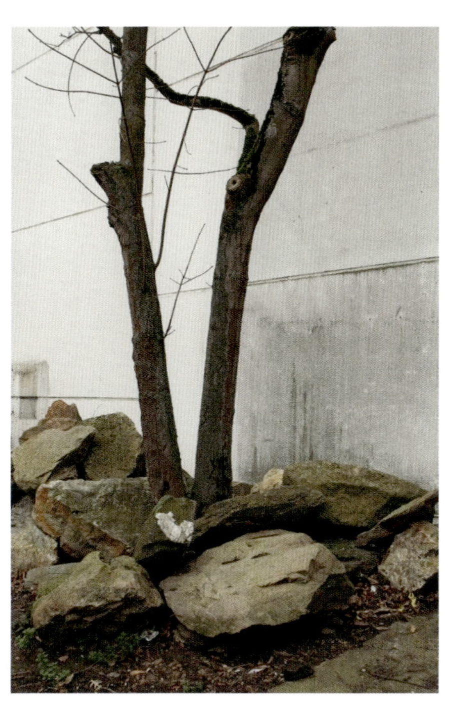

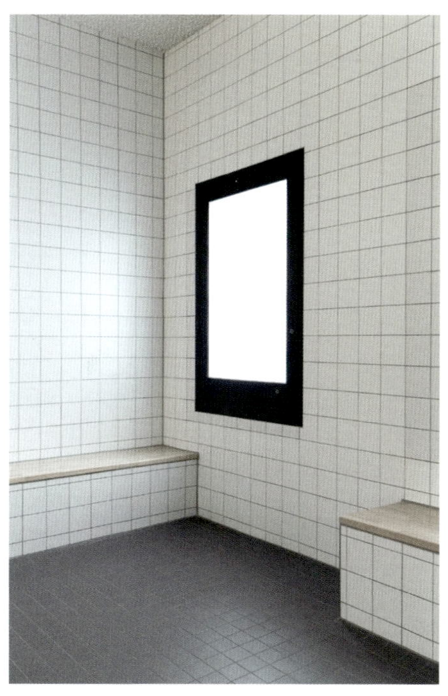

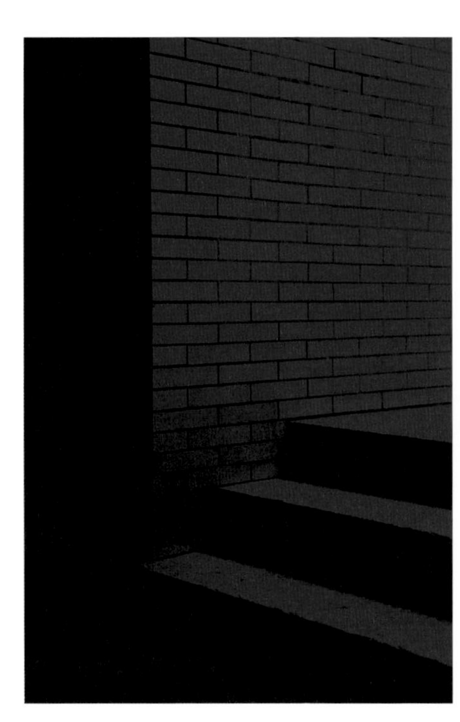

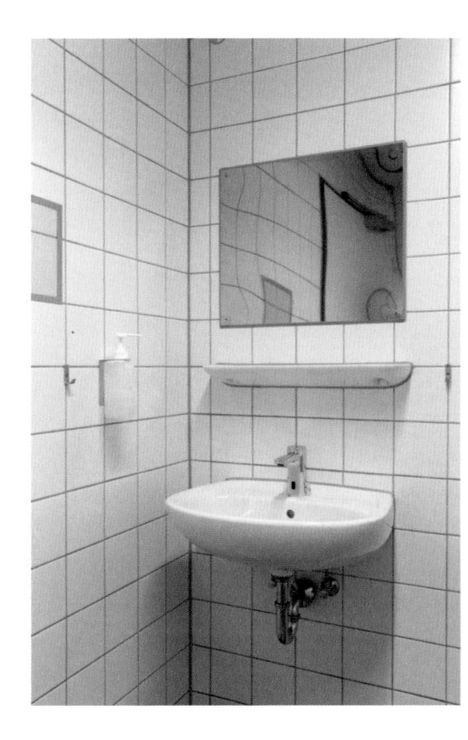

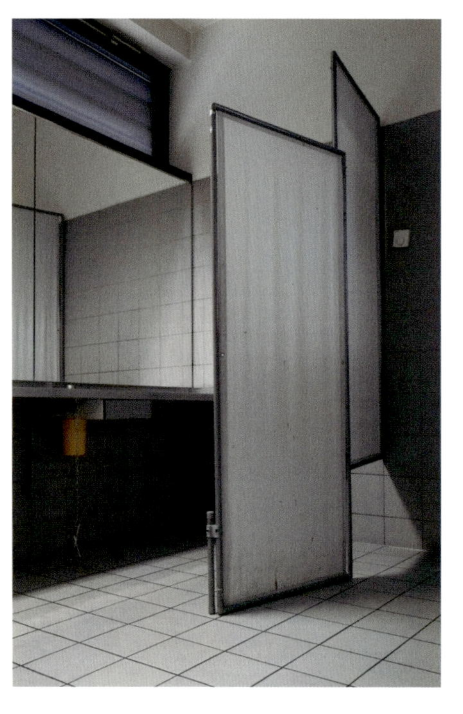

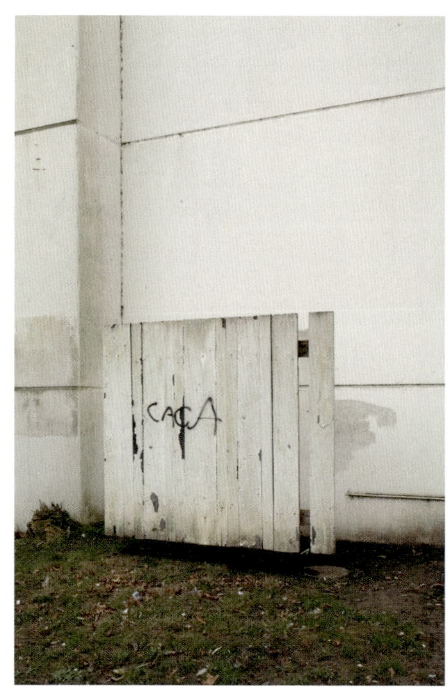
CACA

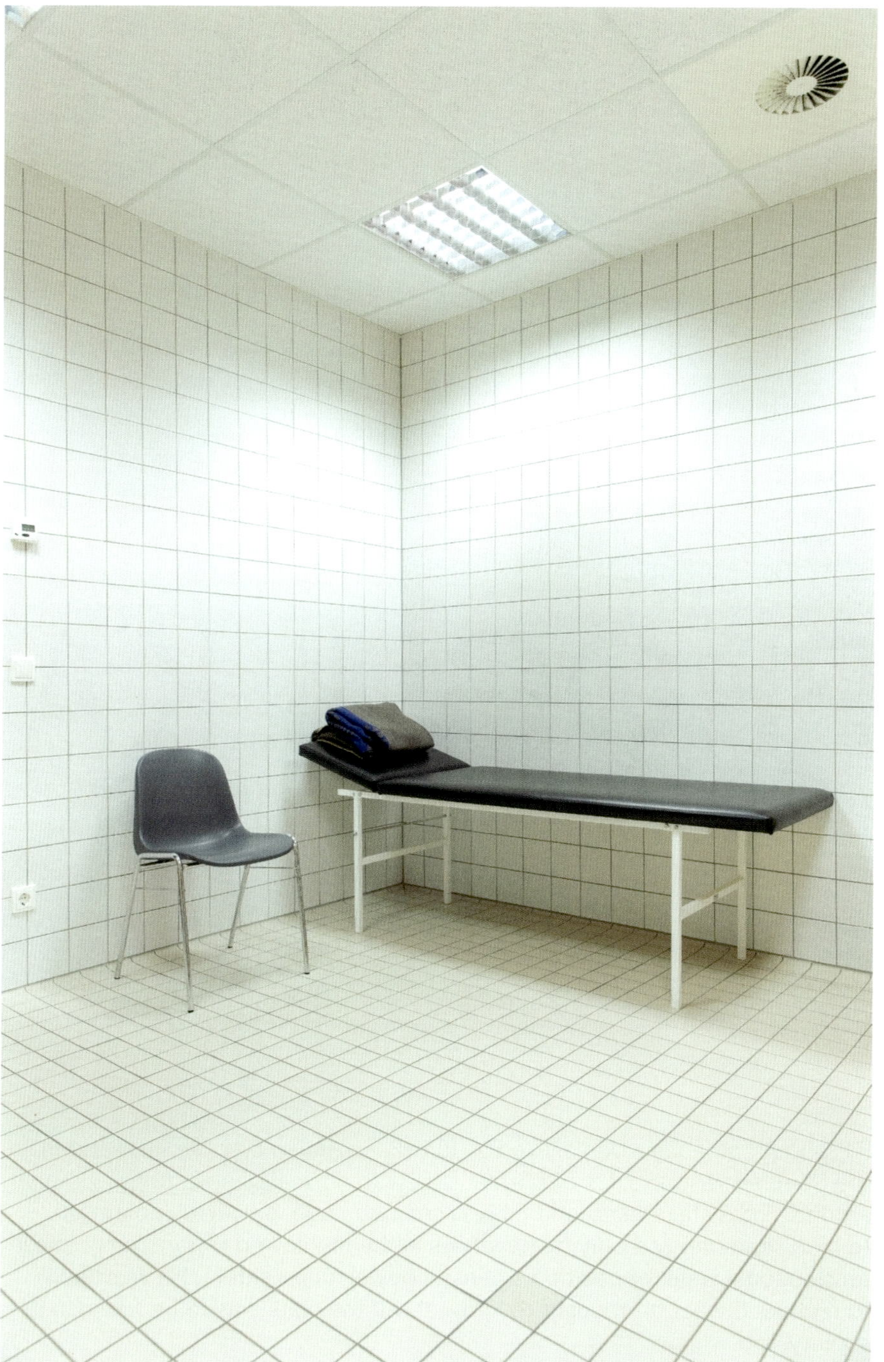

DANIEL CHATARD

PROGULKA

11

For about half a year Daniel lived in Tomsk, Russia—a city like an island in the Siberian vastness. It's of normal size, with normal people, nothing much around. From afar, Russia and Siberia seemed huge, powerful, unfamiliar to him, characterized only by headlines in the media and reports on political tension, on a weak opposition against a powerful president. He was keen to find out if what he thought to know about the state was to be found in its society, too.

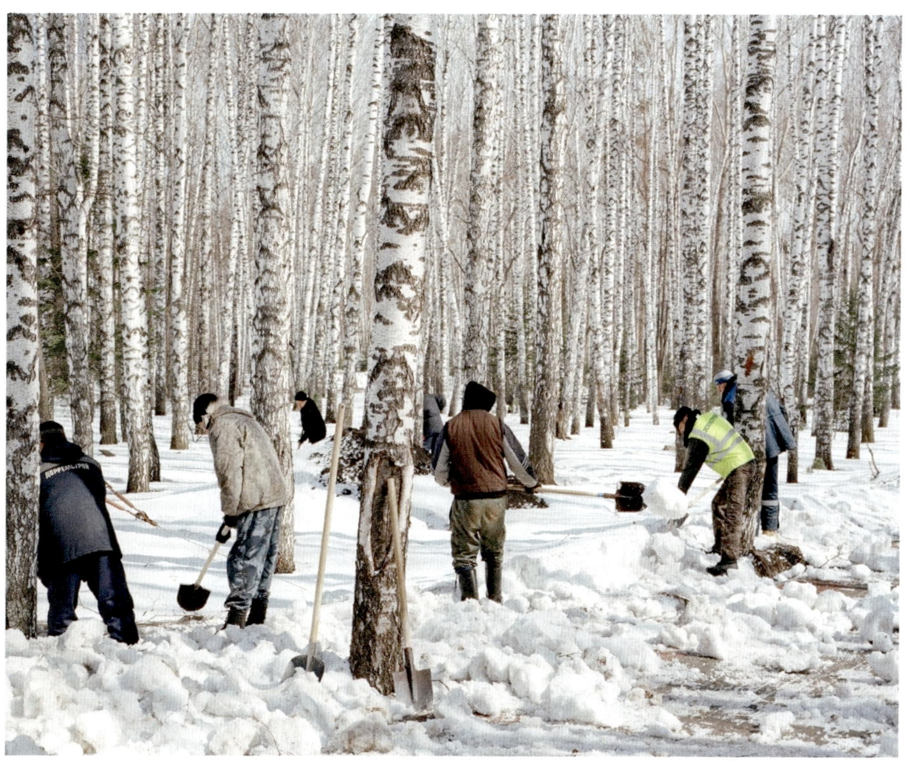

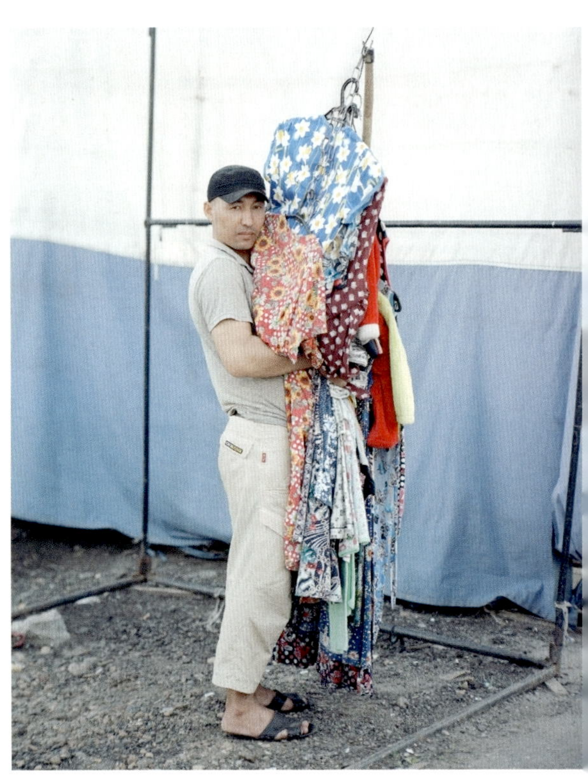

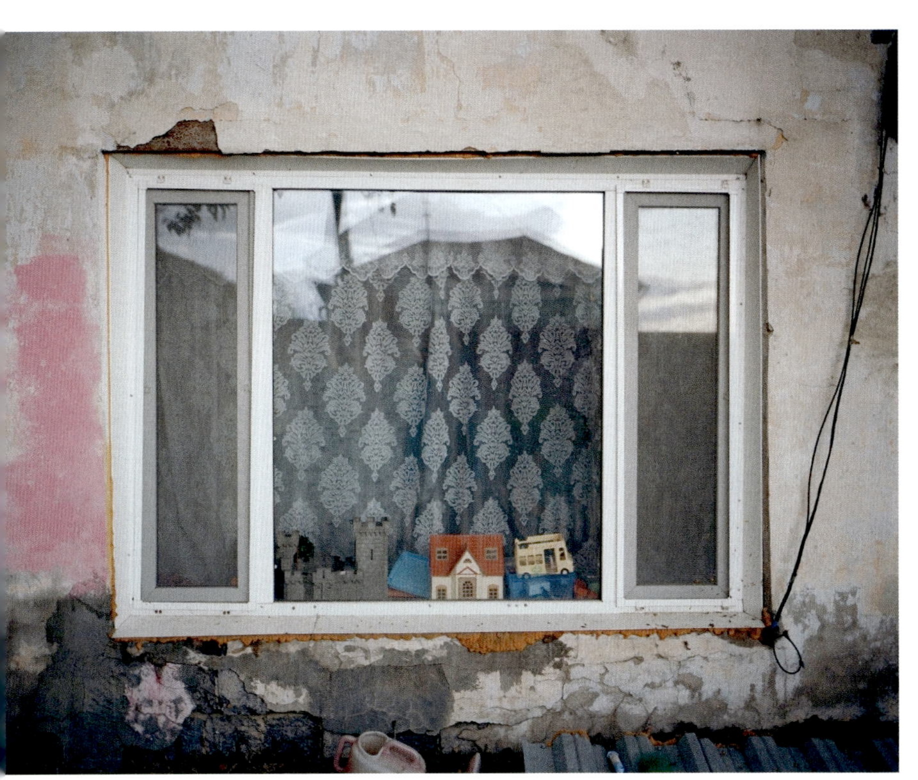

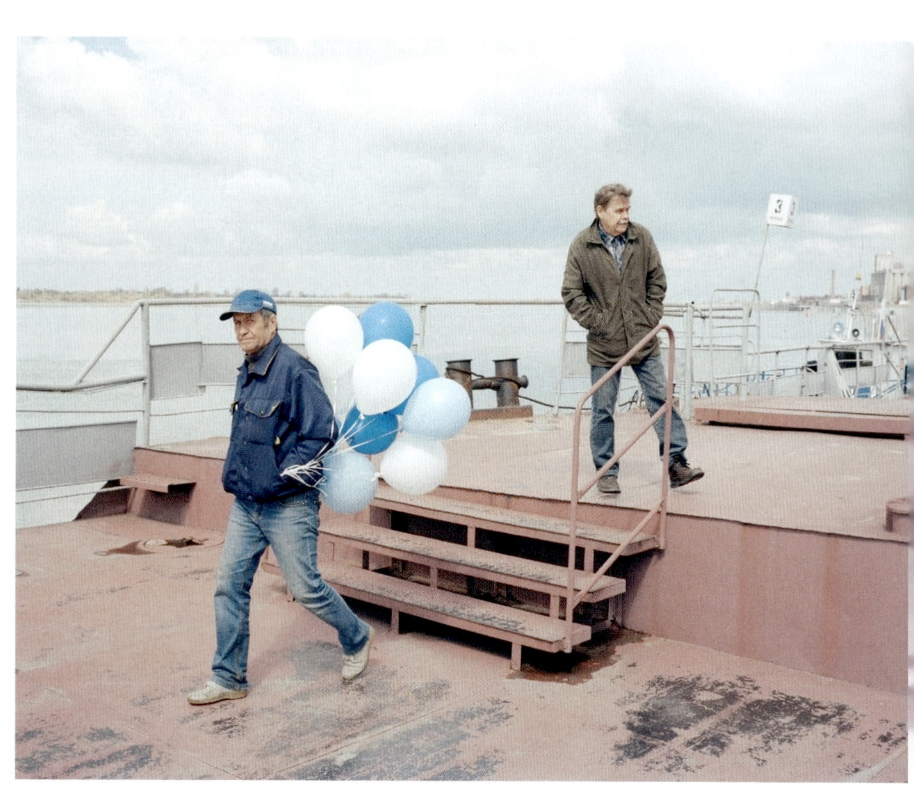

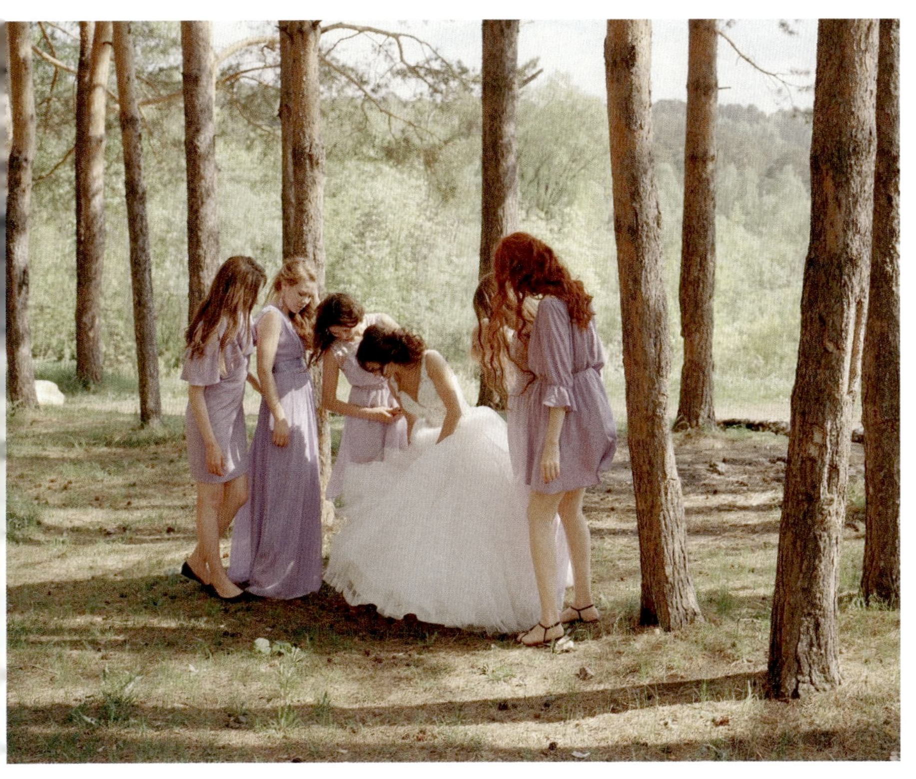

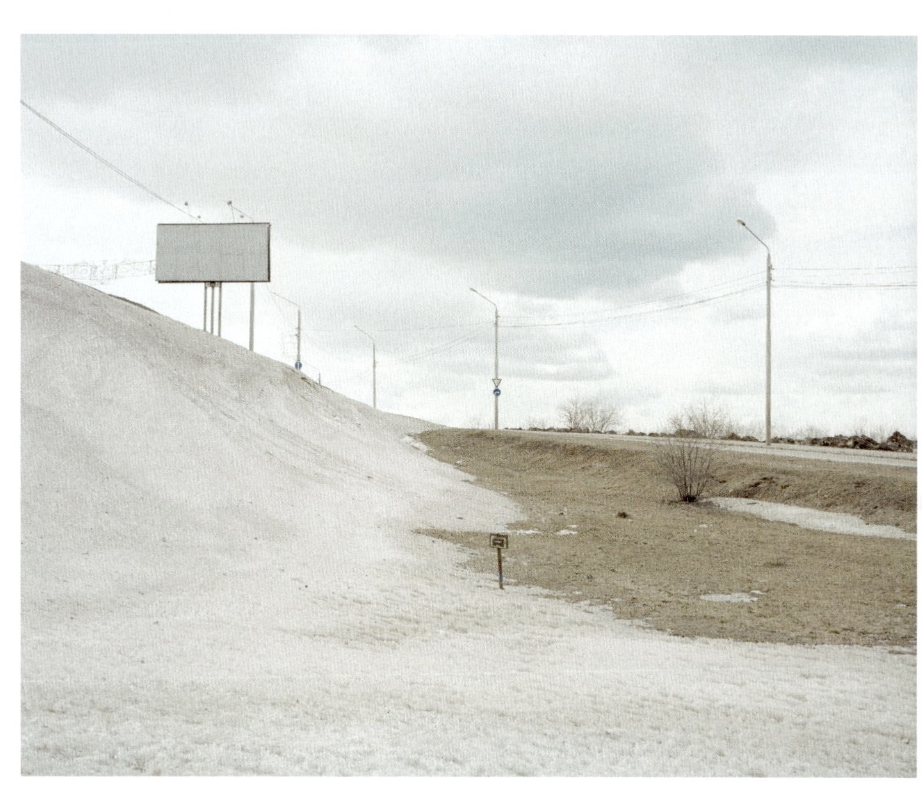

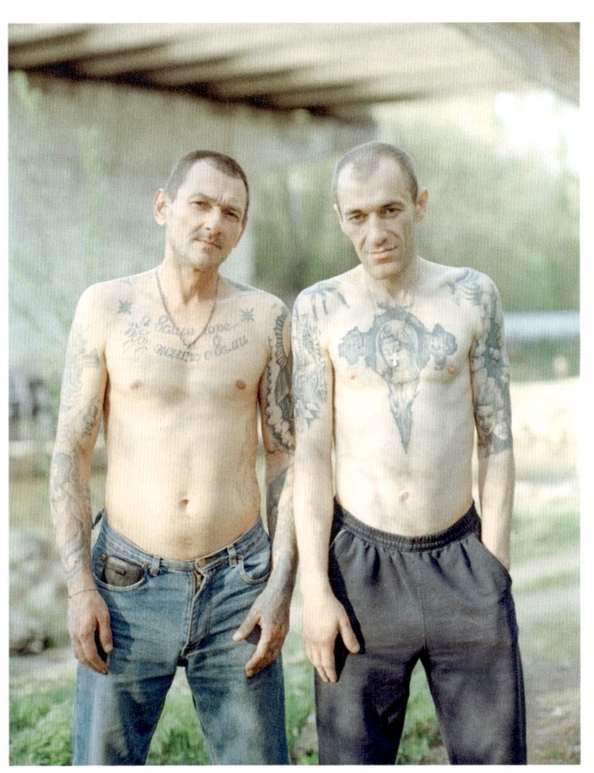

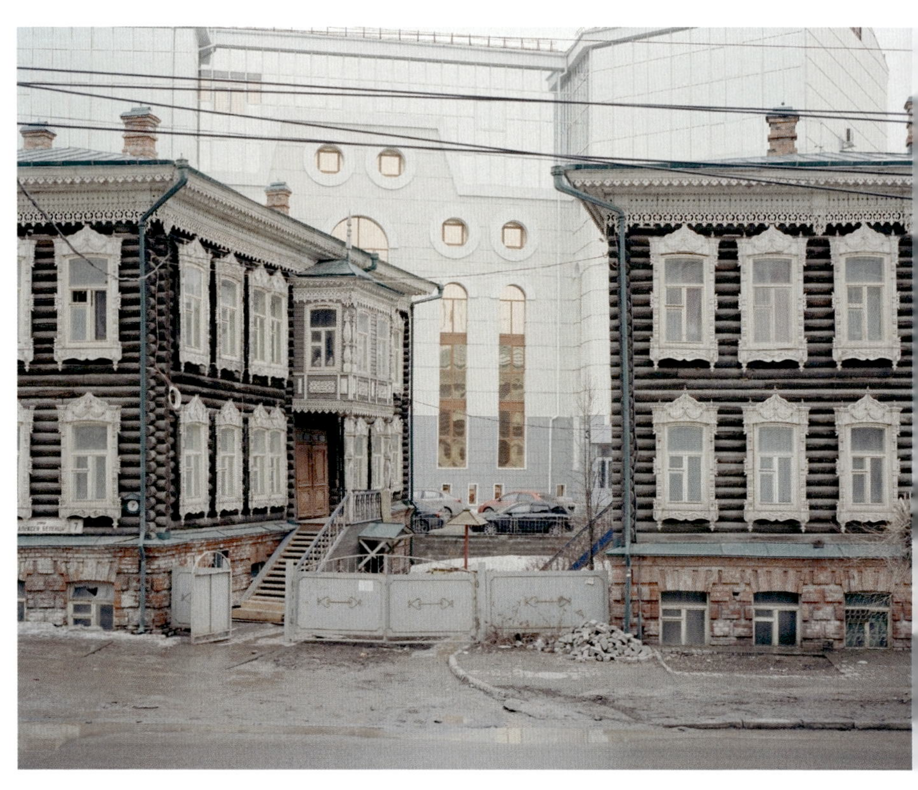
7

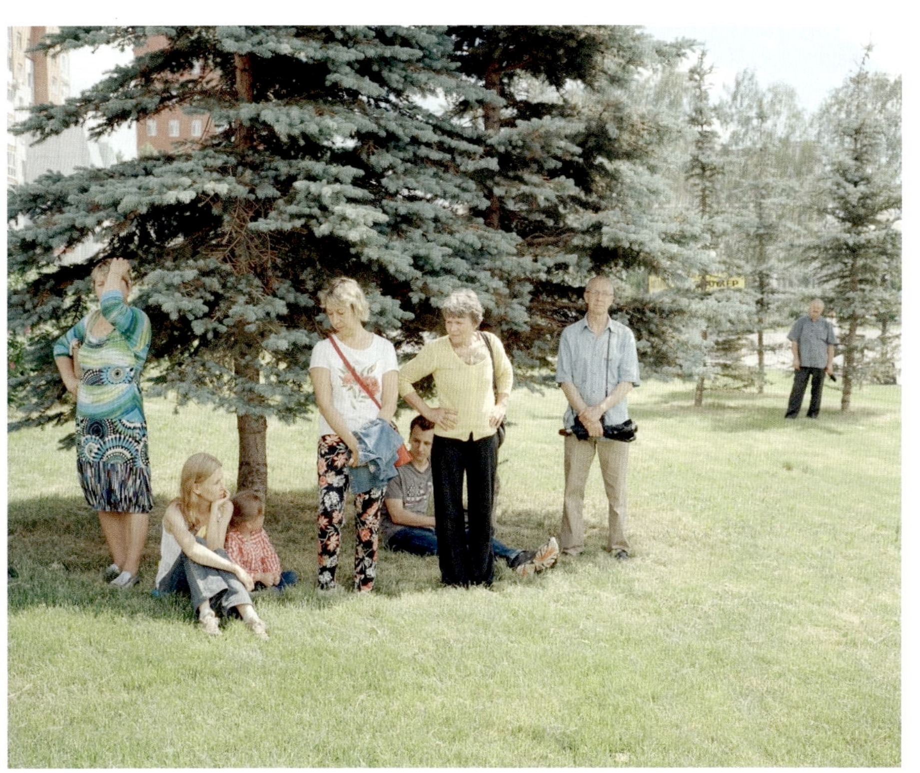

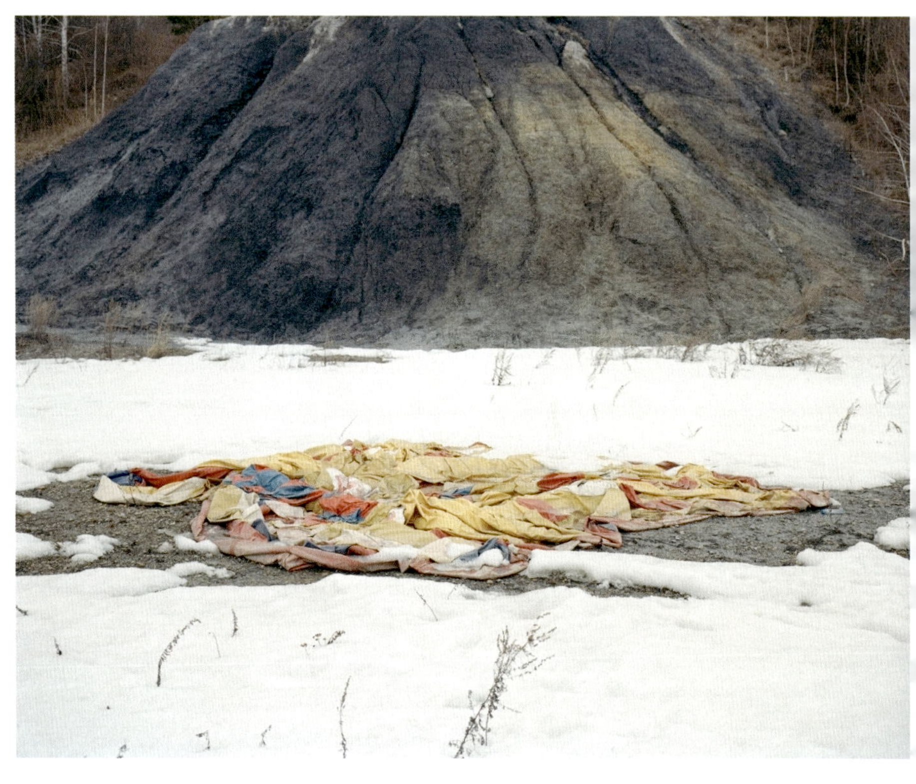

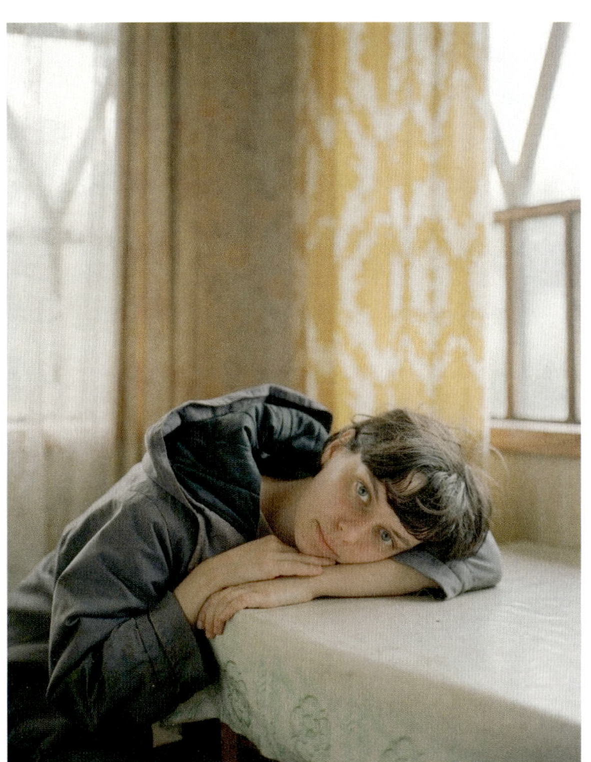

NILS HECK

12

Es geht so weiter

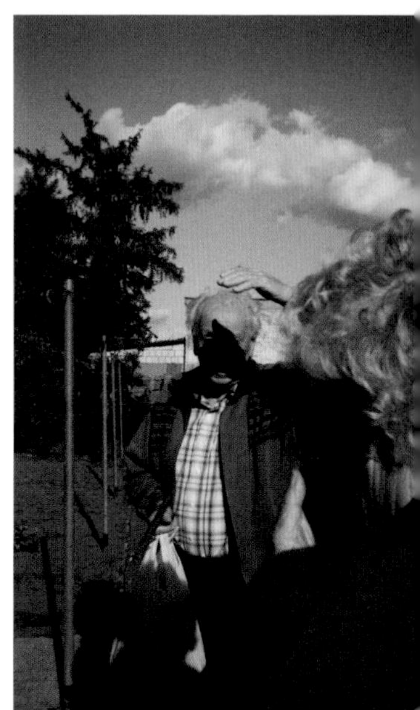

Whenever Nils visits his grandparents to see how they are doing, his grandfather always gives the same answer: “It goes on like this”. Both his grandparents are 93 years old, they still live independently and in love with each other. They have been married for 68 years.

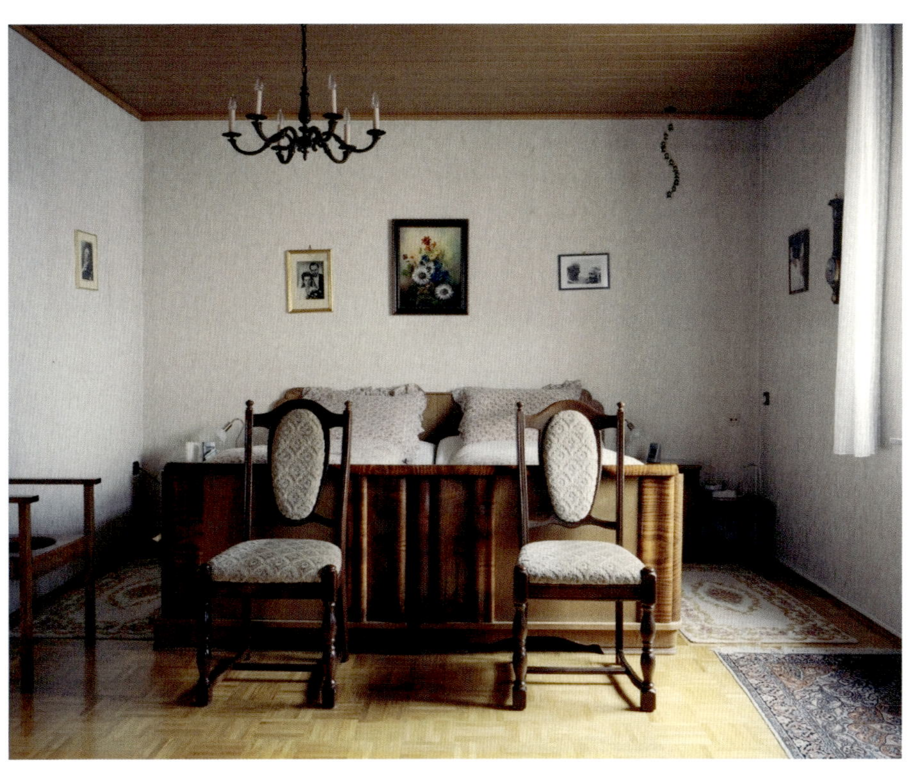

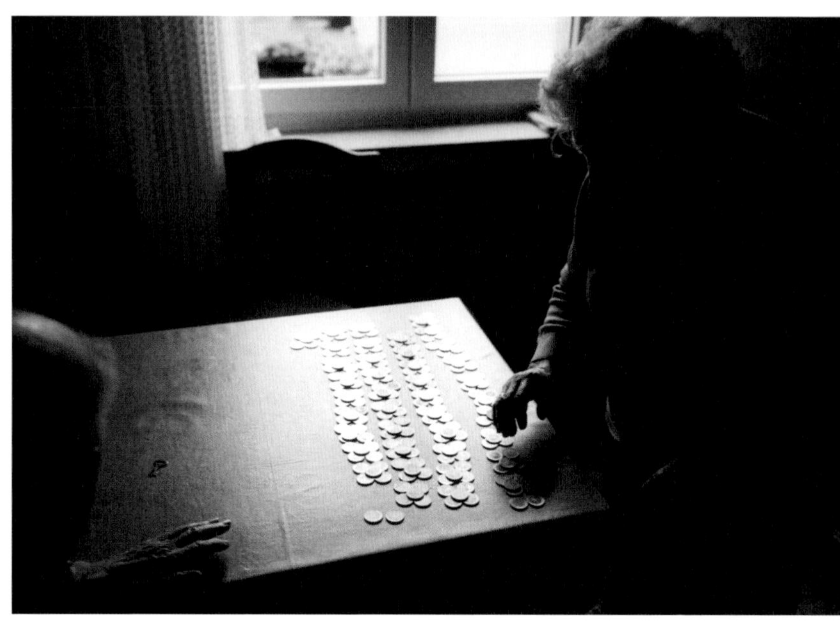

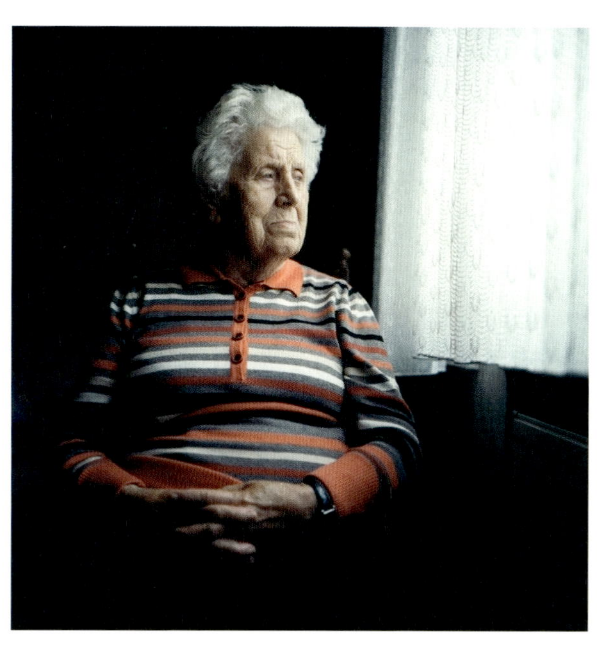

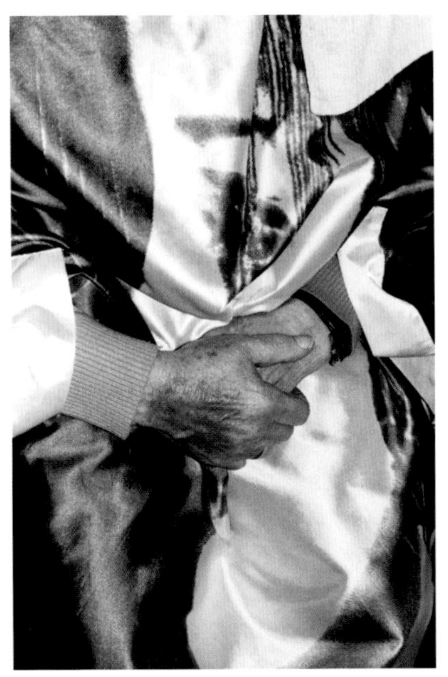

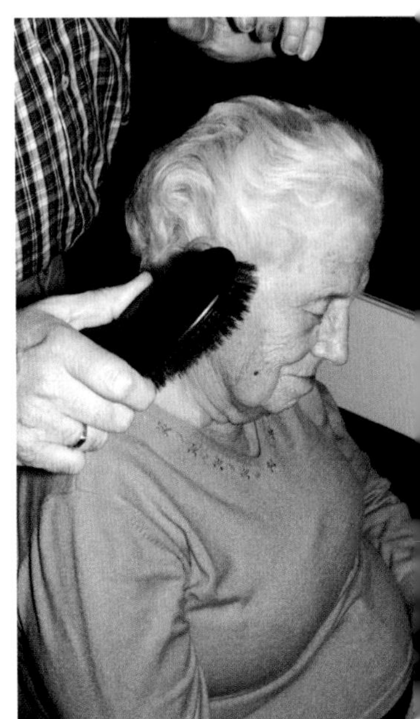

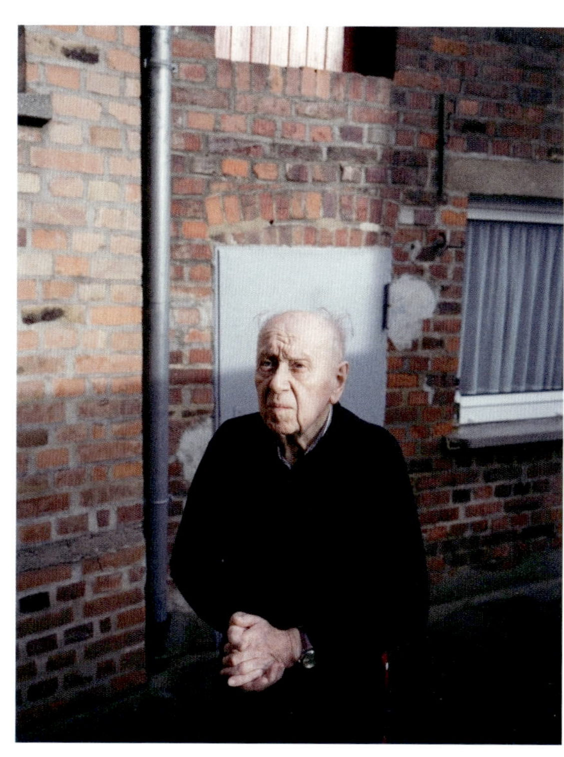

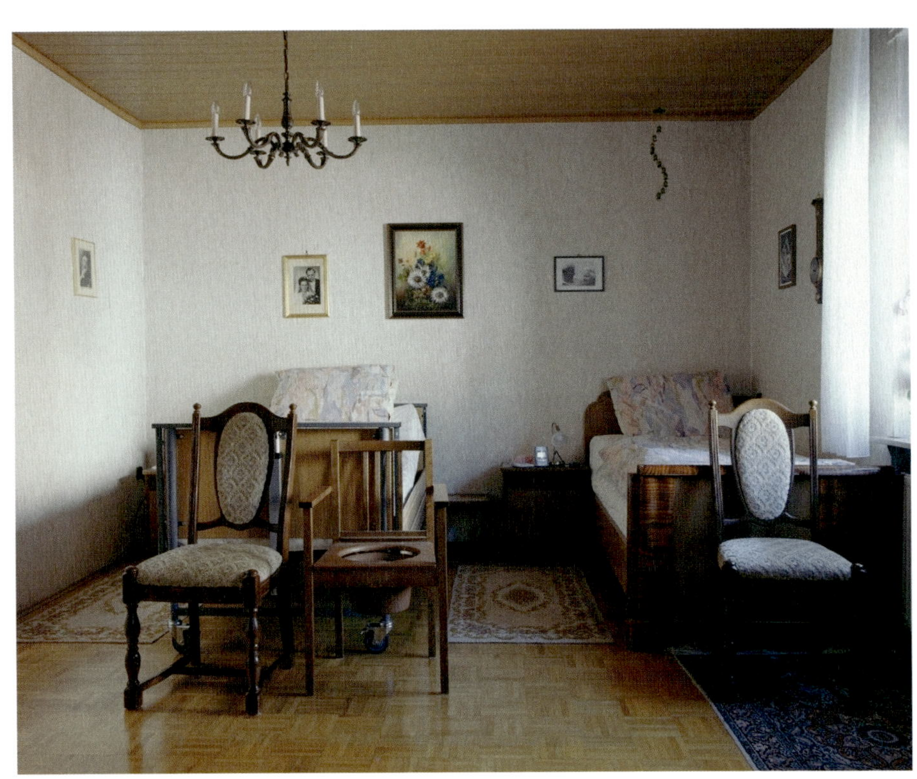

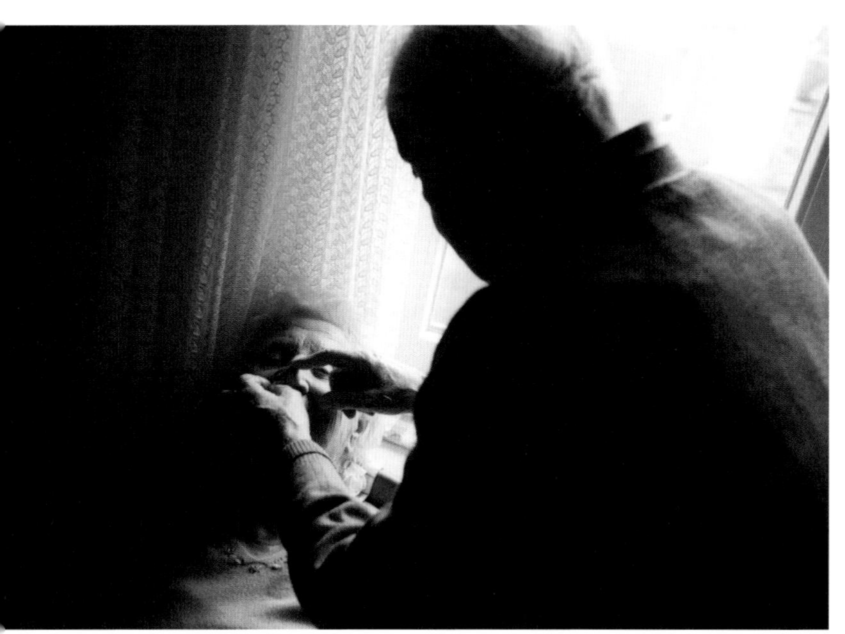

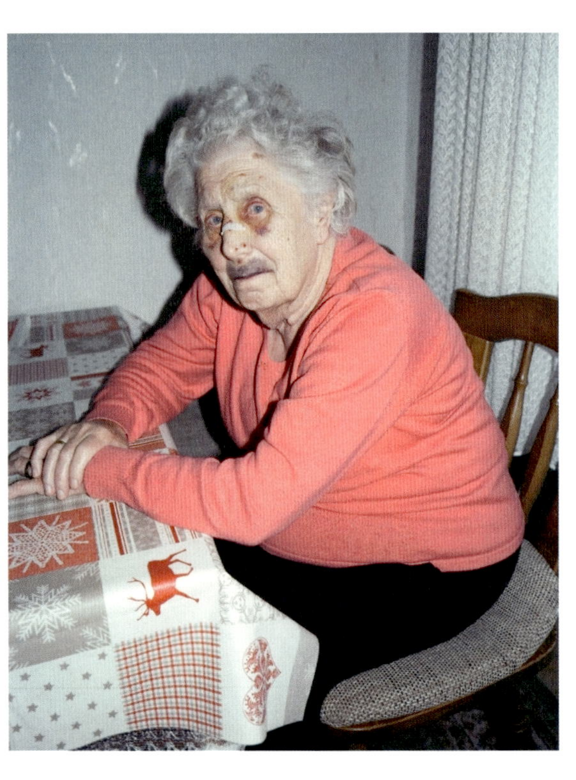

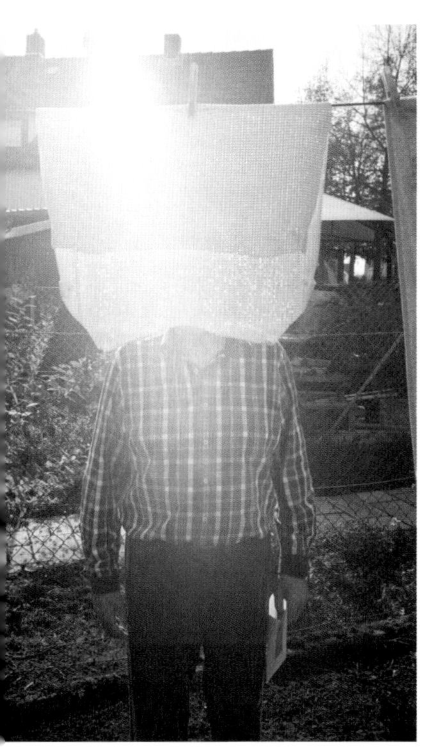

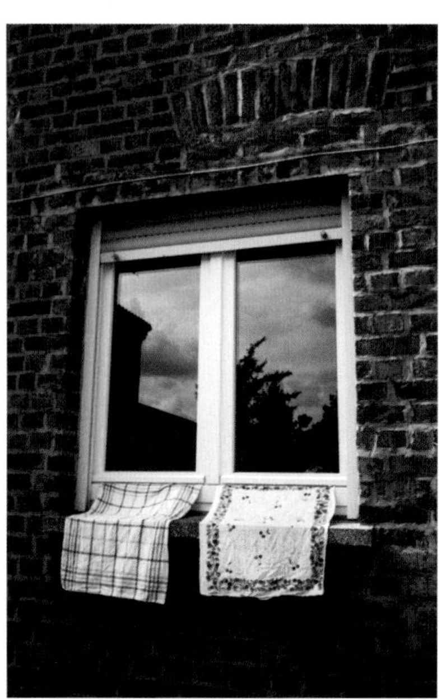

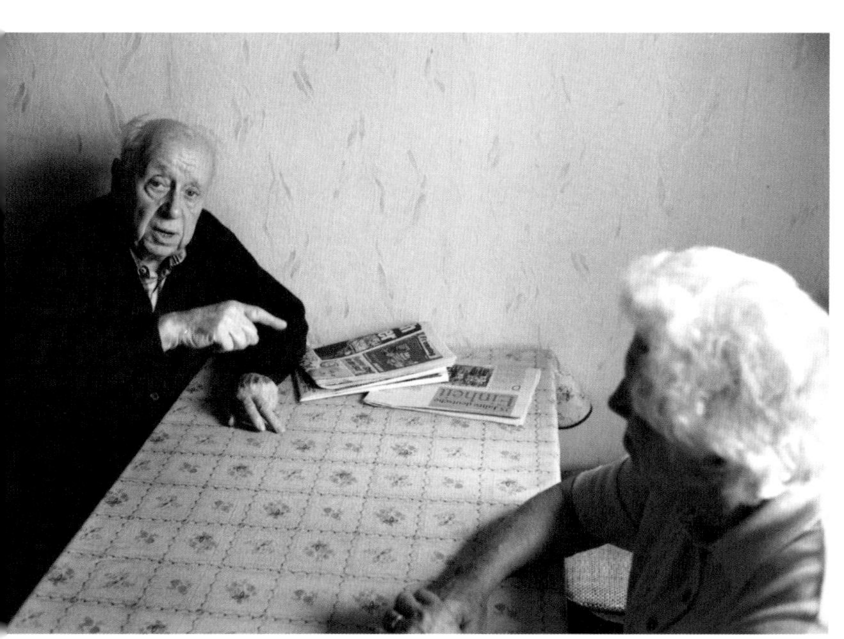

ALI ZARAAY

13

The Safe House

Ali offers us a small window into an orphanage, where lost and abandoned children find caregivers, get AIDS treatment and have the chance of education and life. He takes us to the remote village of Nakuru in Kenya, where Mama Jane opened a safe house with the support of the Loving Voices NGO for physically or emotionally scared children to find a happy, warm and loving place.

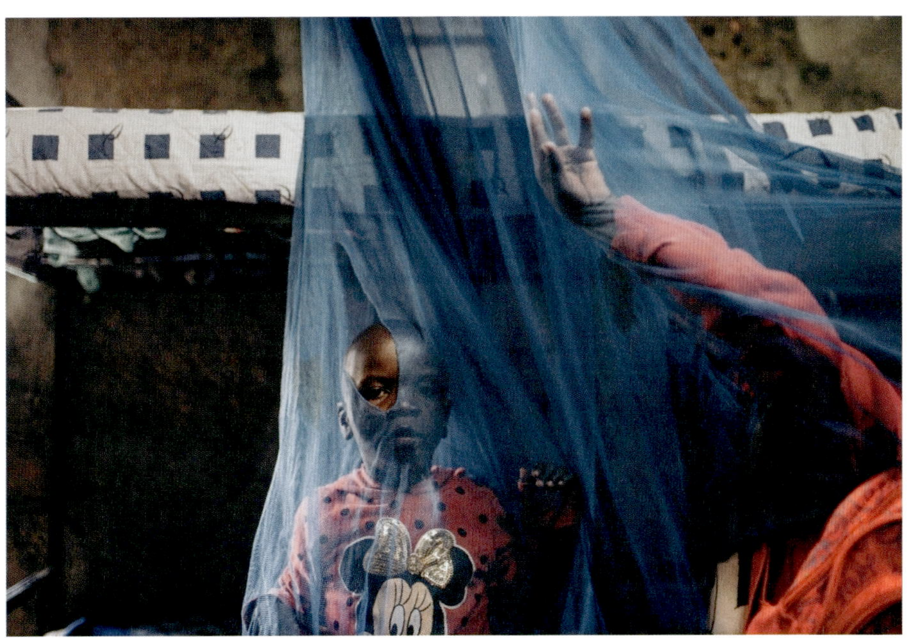

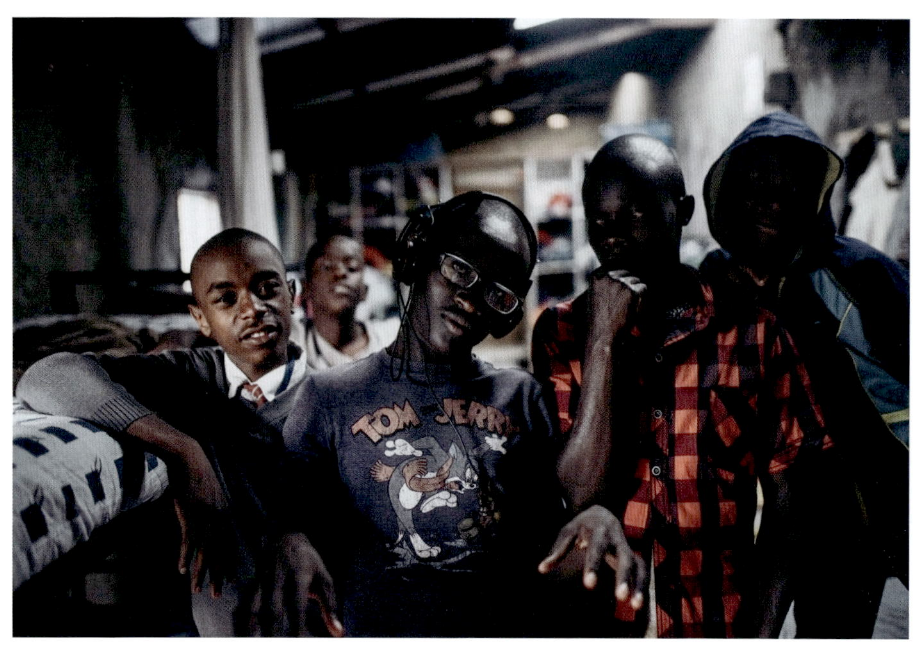
TOM

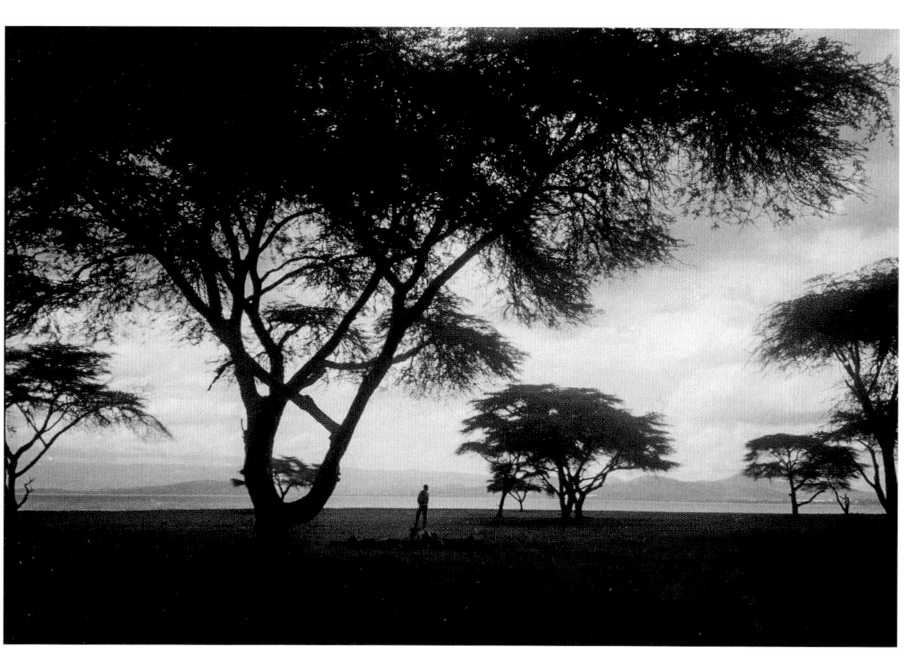

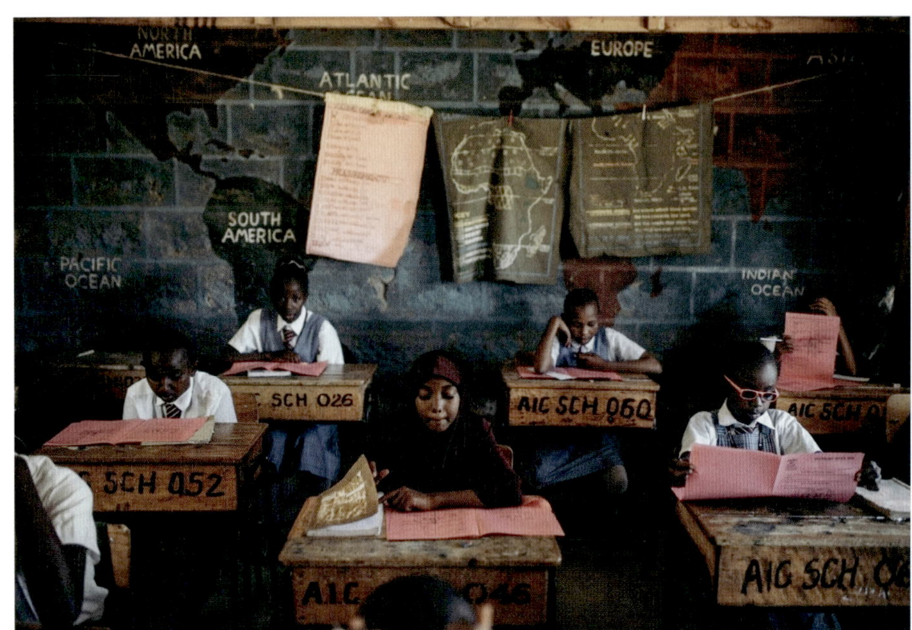
NORTH AMERICA
ATLANTIC
EUROPE
SOUTH AMERICA
PACIFIC OCEAN
INDIAN OCEAN
SCH 026
AIC SCH 060
SCH 052

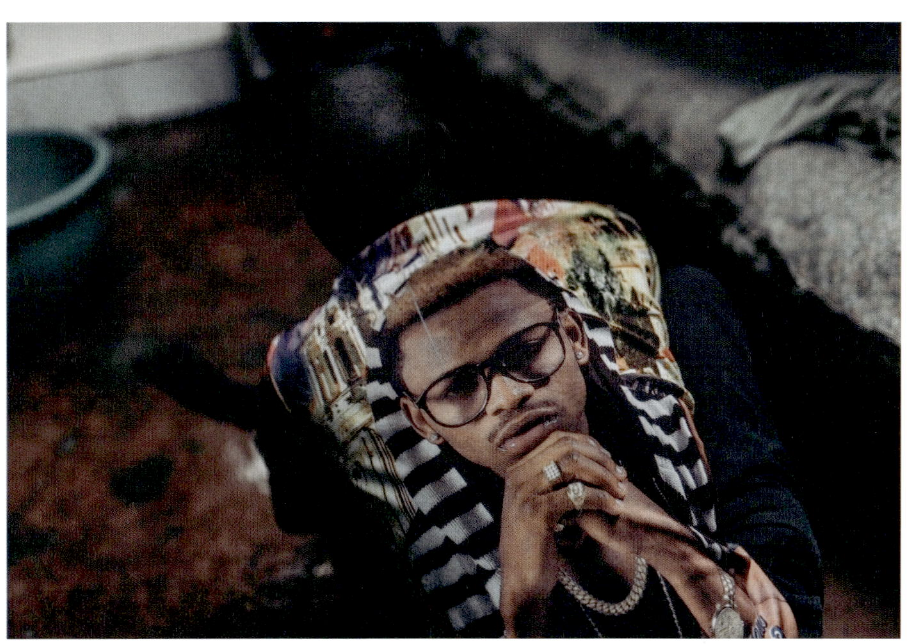

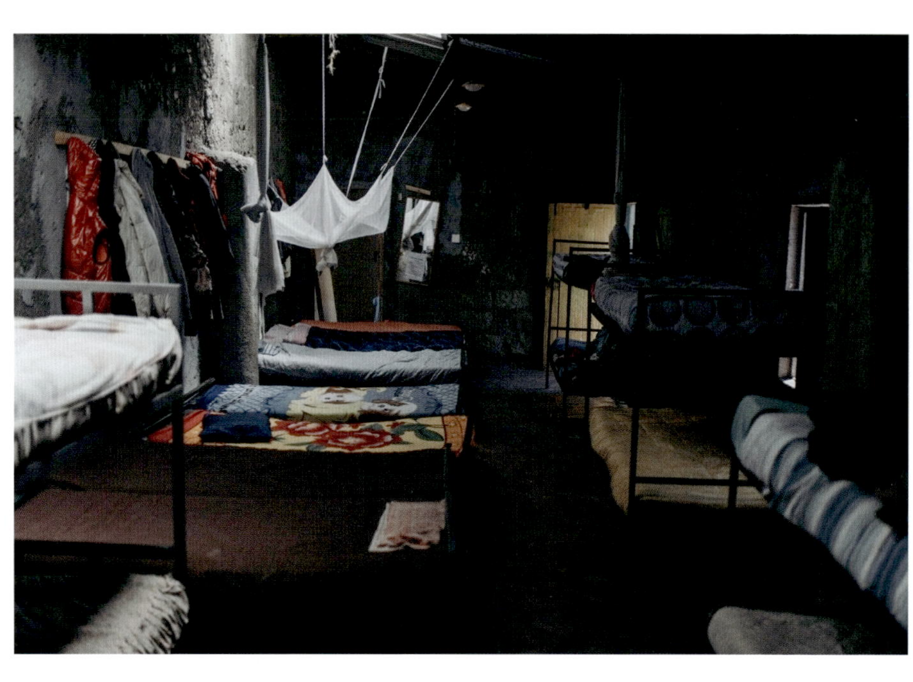

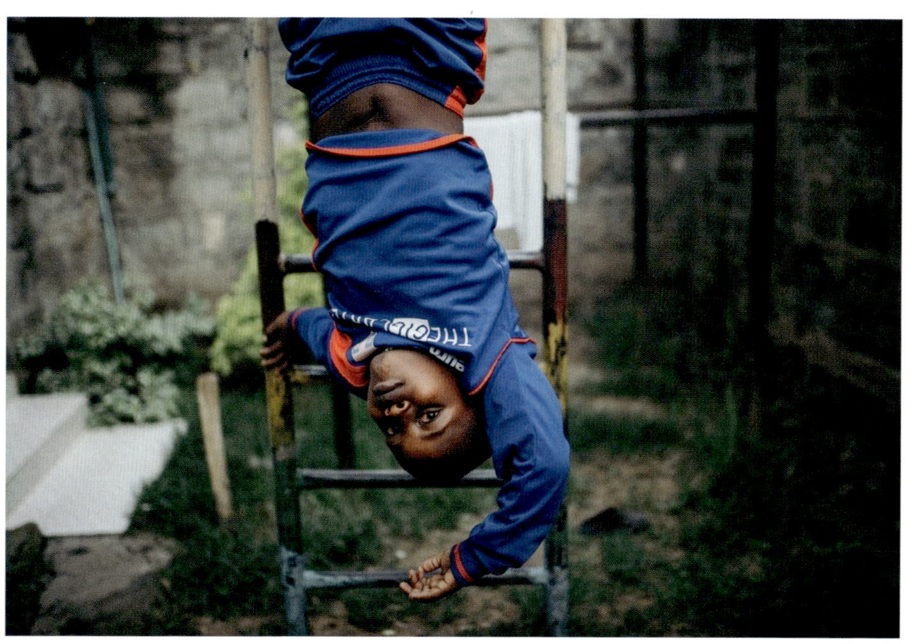

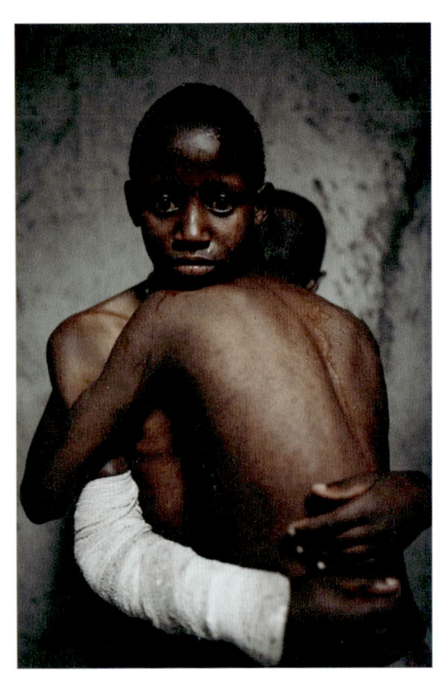

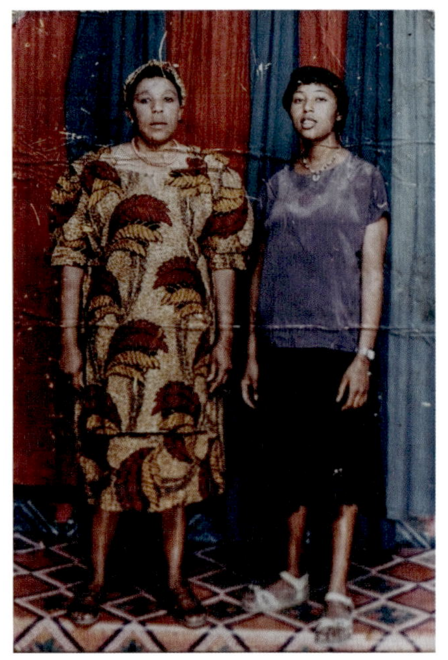

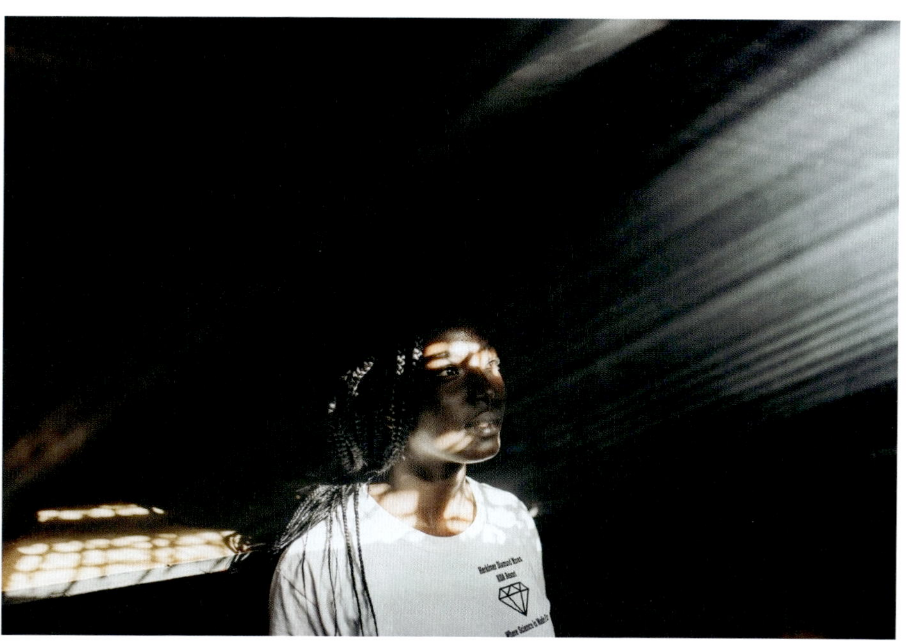
Herkimer Diamond Mines

SANTIAGO MESA

14

ETERNAL

Violence has many faces, but only one form: it is cyclical. Santiago's pictures show Medellìn, the second largest city in Columbia that has been bleeding a war for more than 30 years. A war for control of the territory. A war between drug trafficking gangs. A war that counts more than 600 homicides per year.

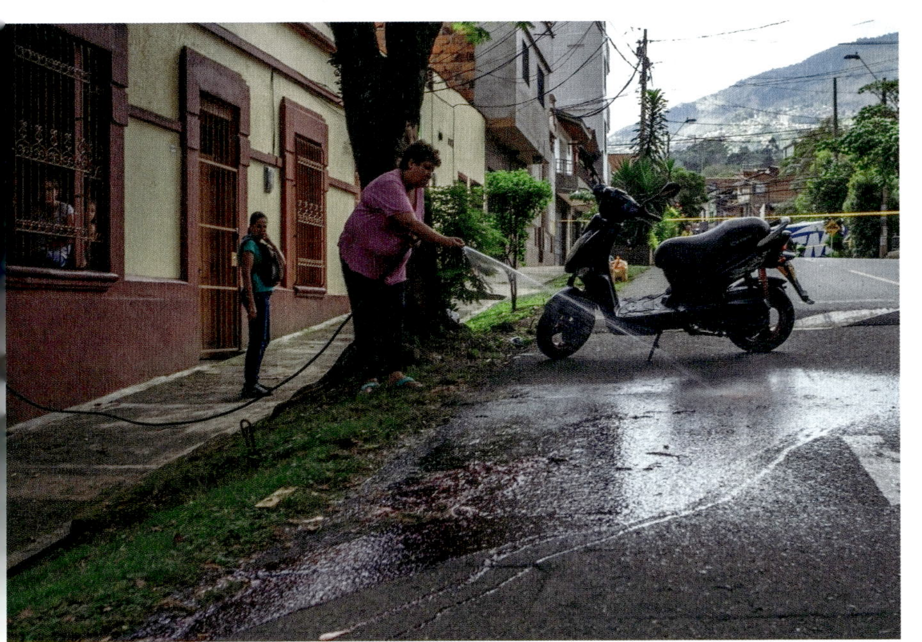

Spring

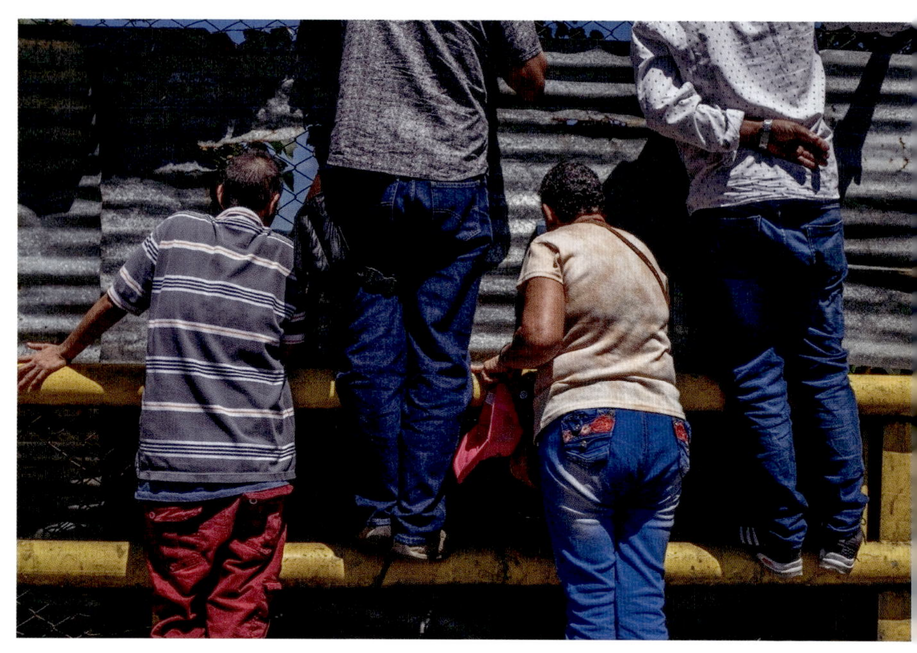

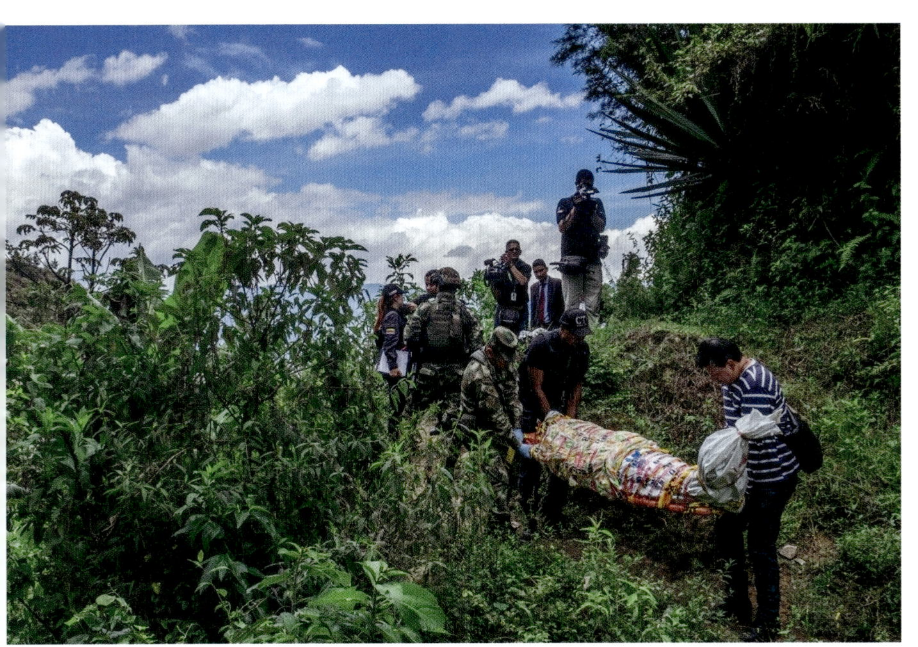

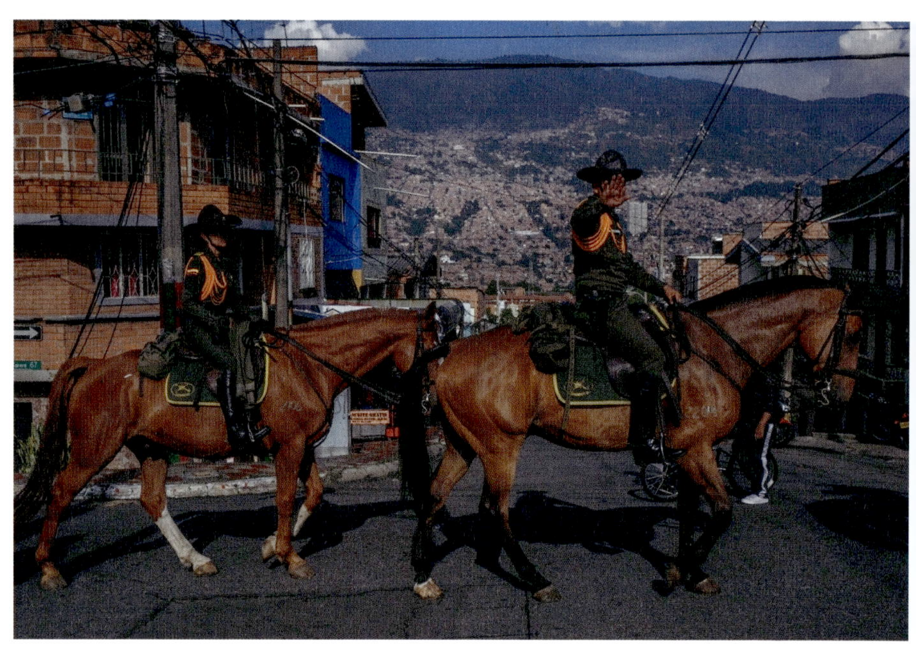

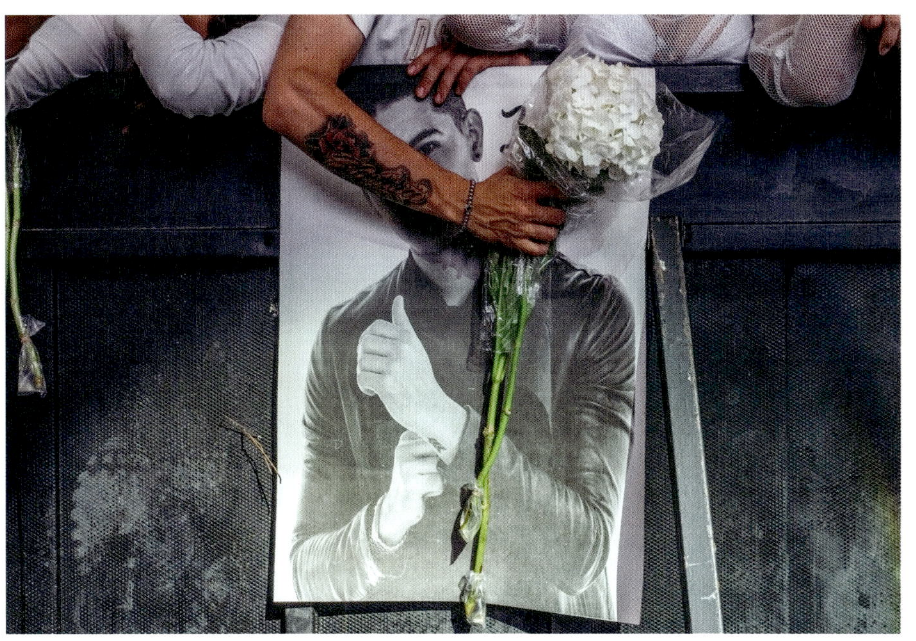

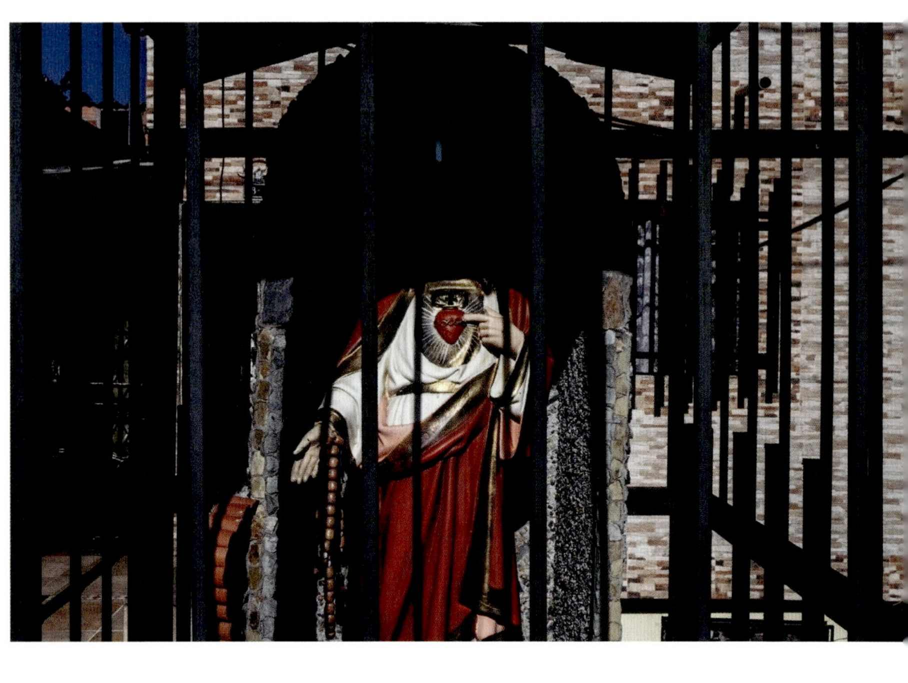

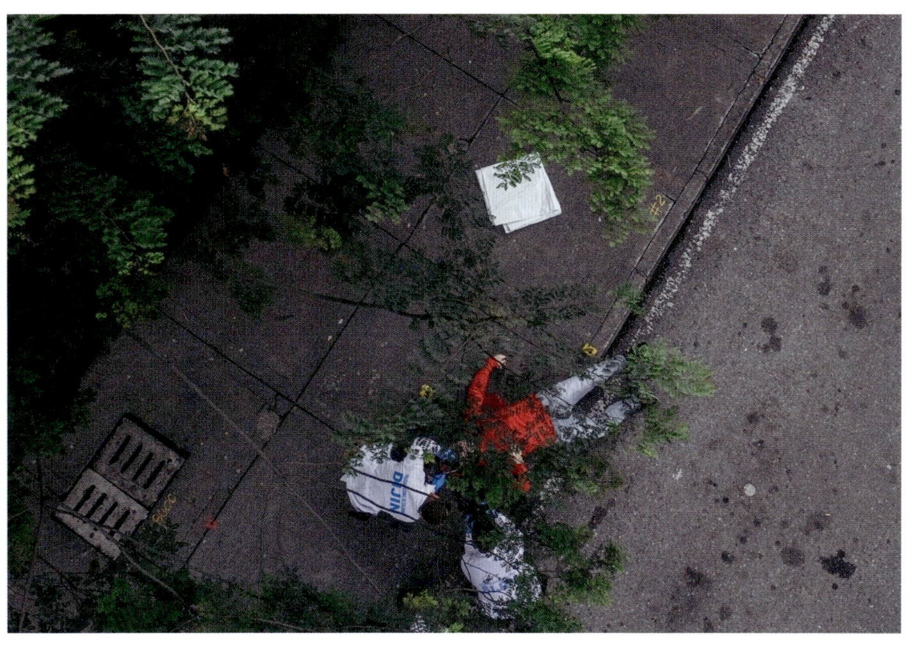

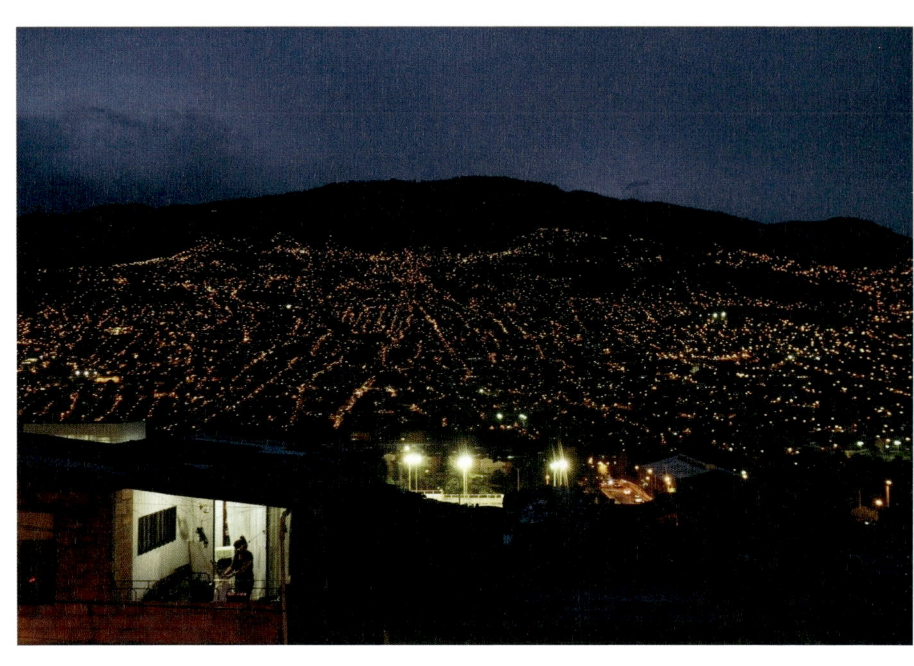

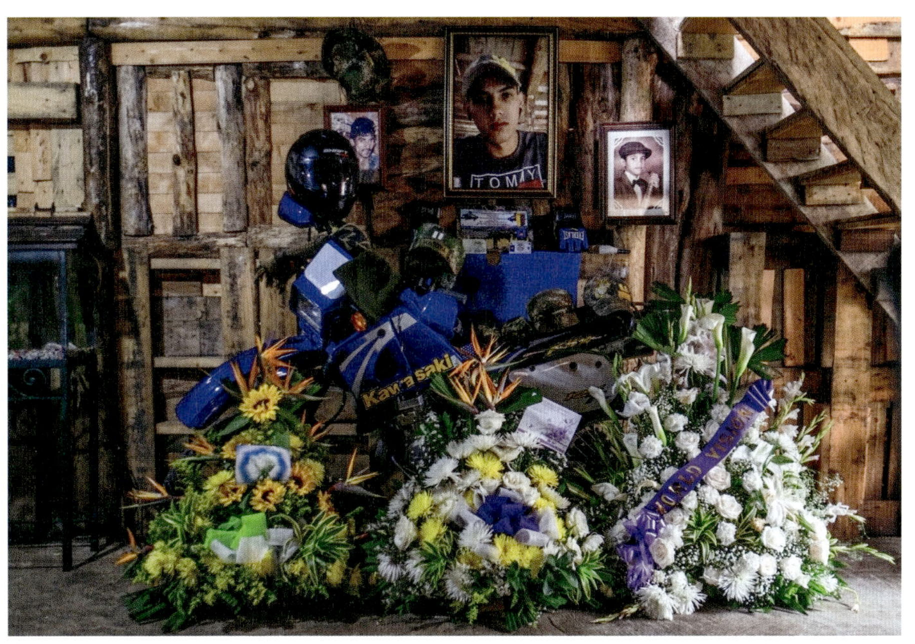
WORLD VISION

JOSH KERN

15

LOVE Me

The self-doubt, the ecstasy and the fulfillment of the creative act is central to Josh's work. He aims to capture the feeling of excitement an artist feels when a new idea is taking form or when there is just chaos in his head. The result is a series of notebook scans, where his life, captured on film, mixes with his thoughts, expressed in ink.

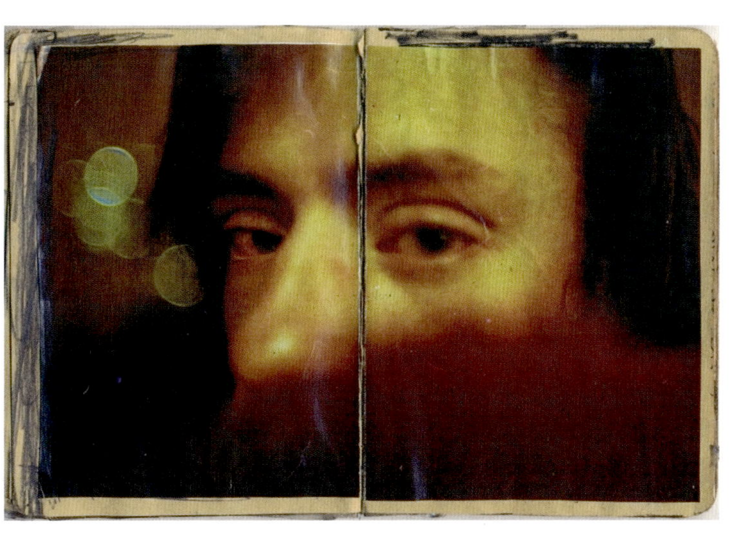

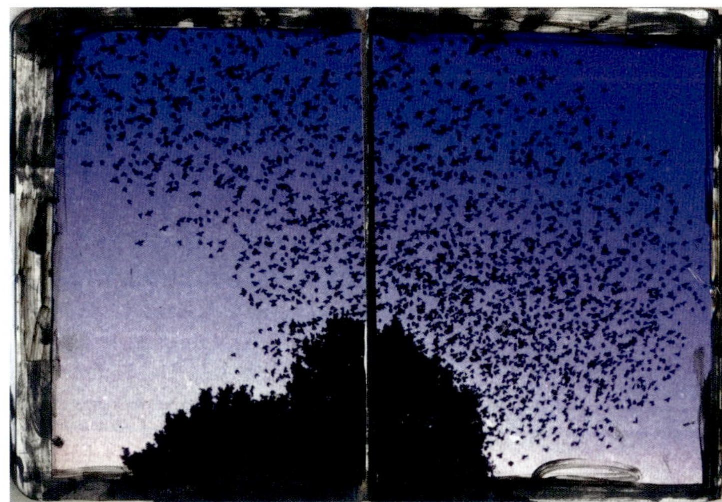

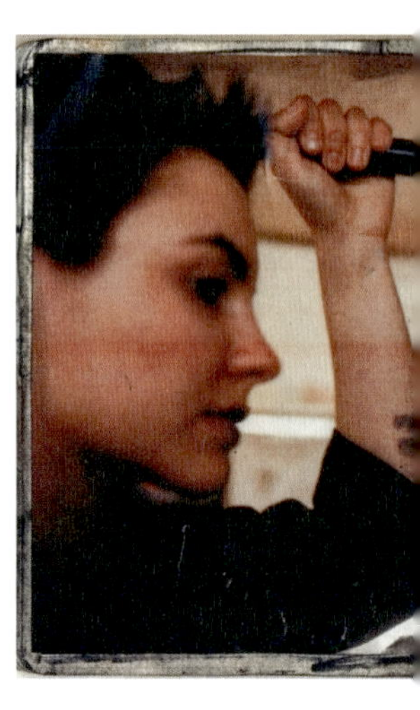

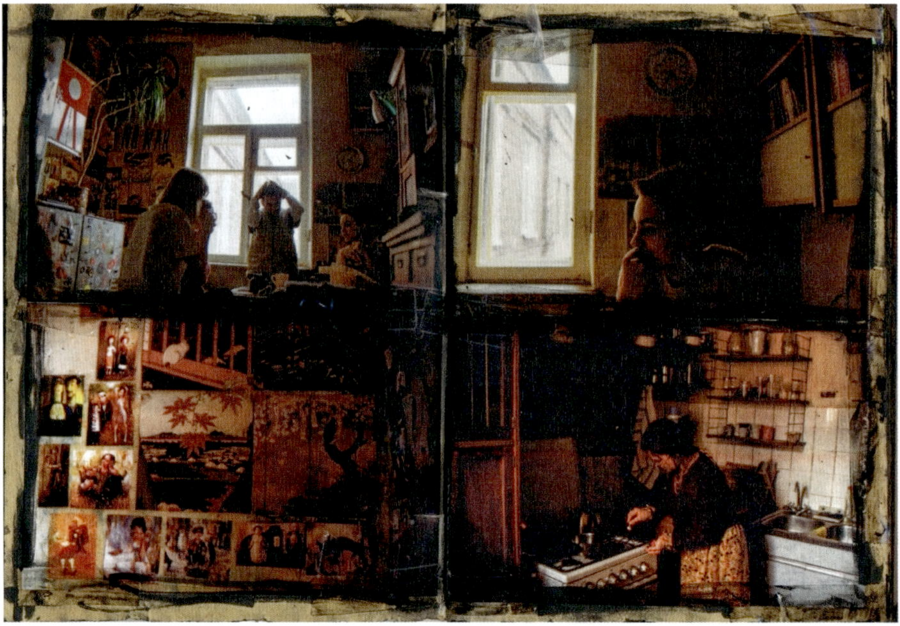

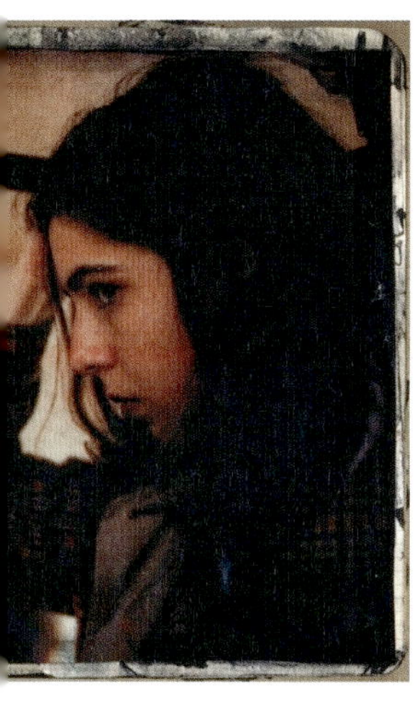

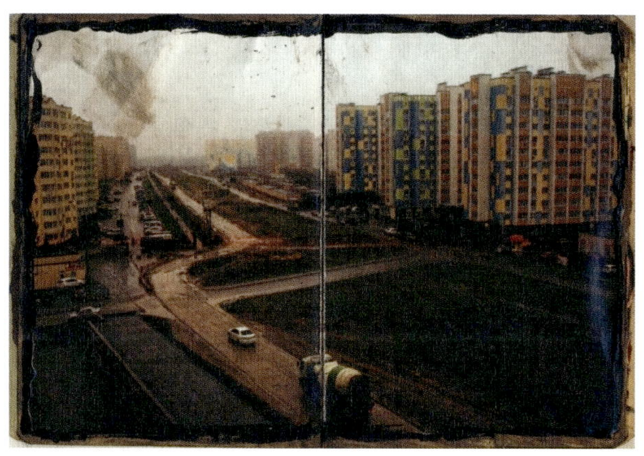

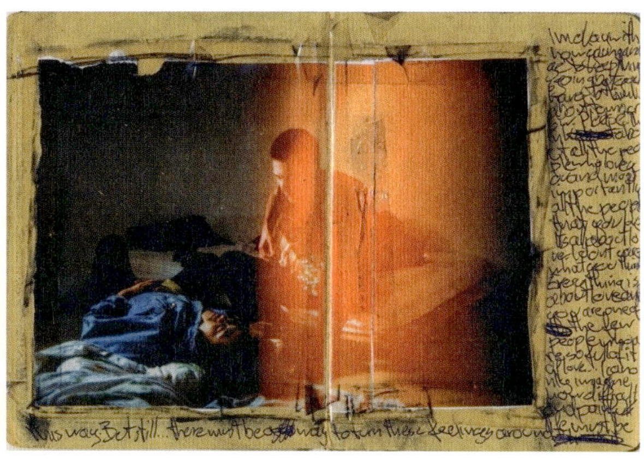
this way. But still... there must be a way to turn these feelings around

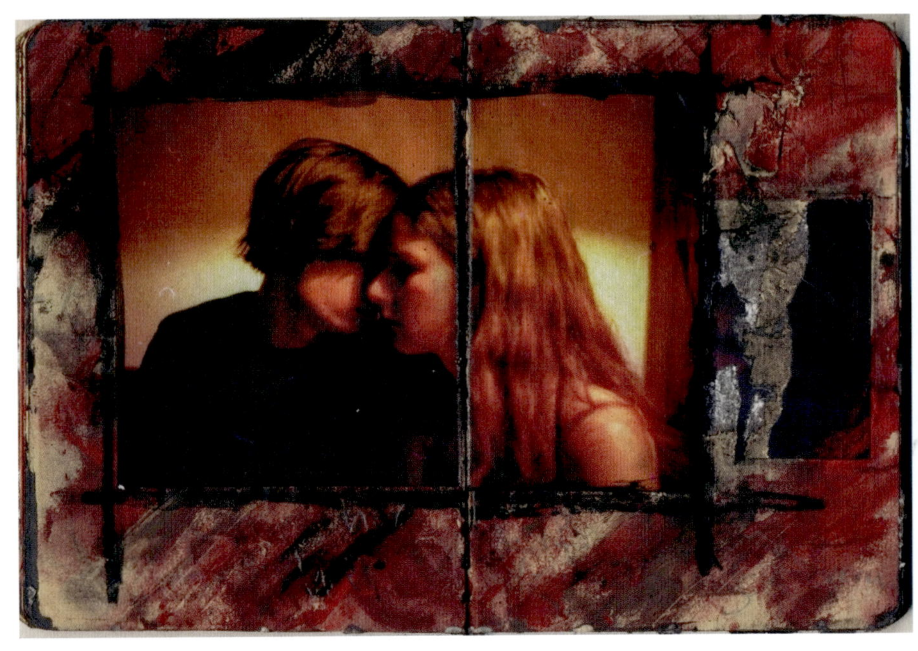

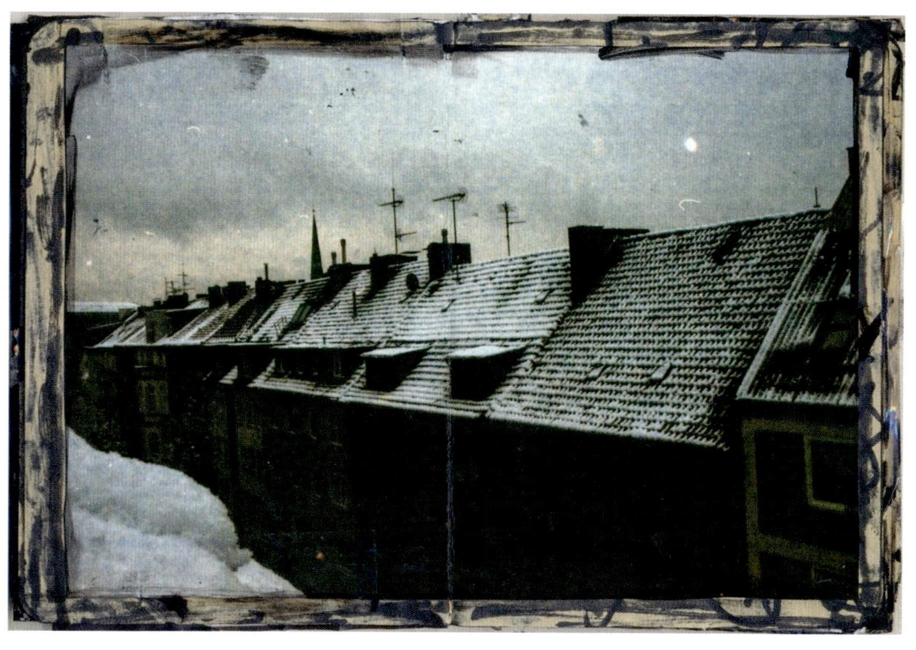

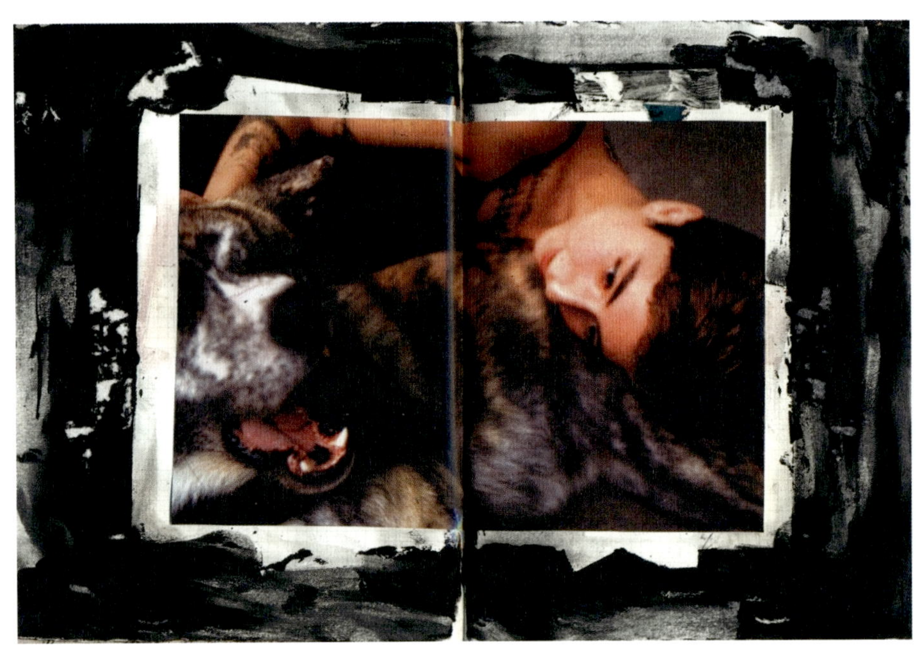

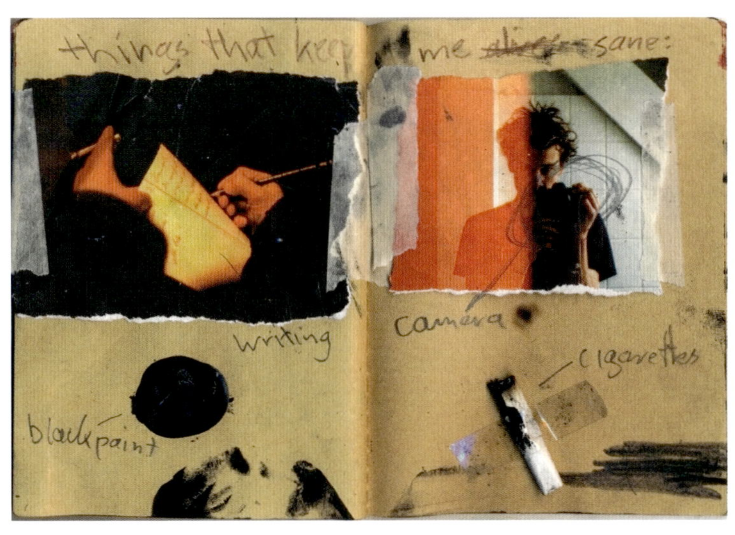
things that keep me sane:
writing
camera
cigarettes
blackpaint

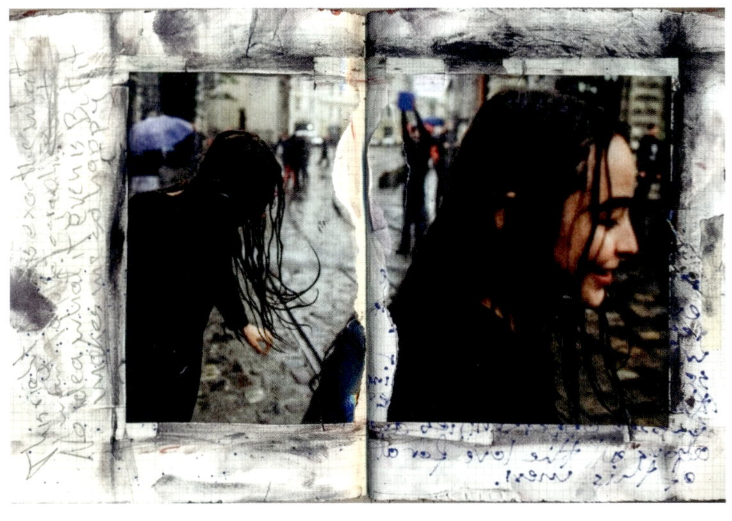

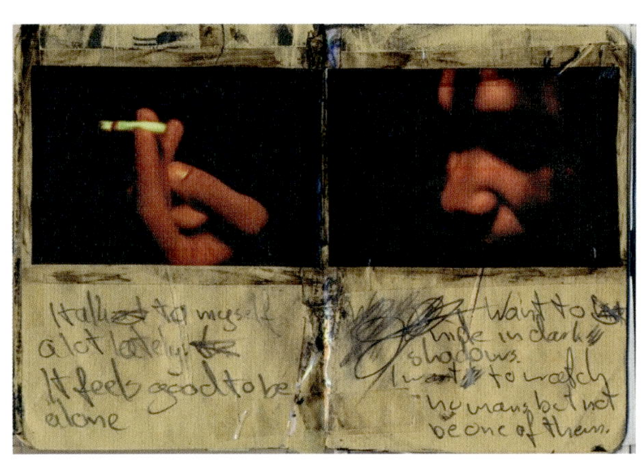
I talk to myself
a lot lately.
It feels good to be
alone
Want to
hide in dark
shadows.
I want to watch
the many but not
be one of them.

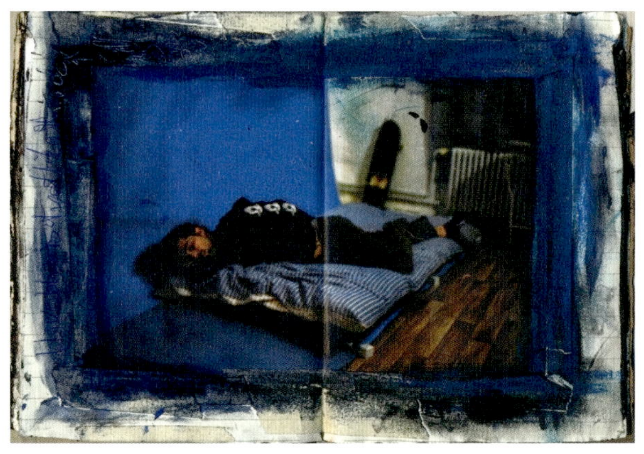

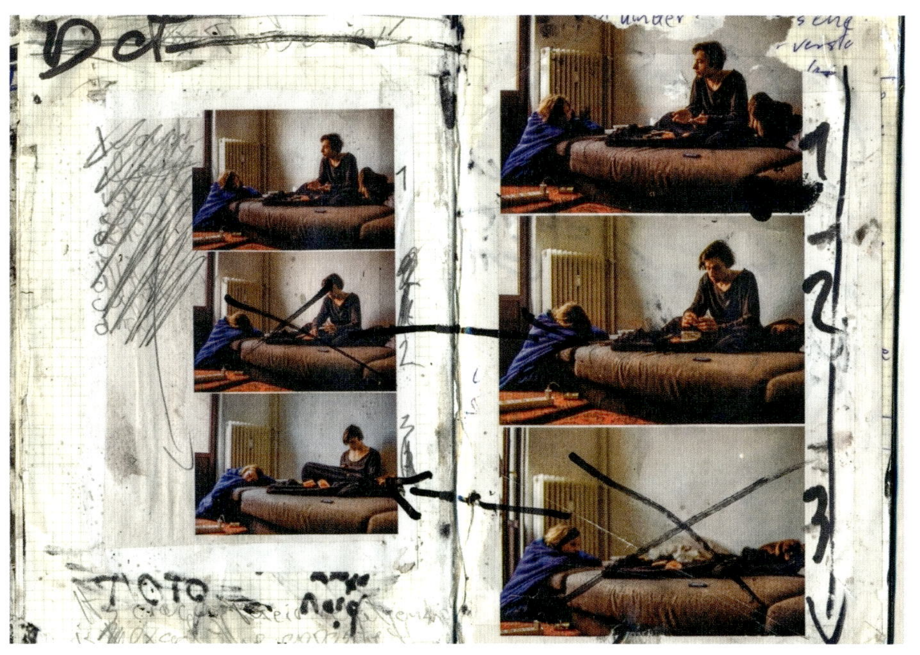

ESMEE VAN ZEEVENTER

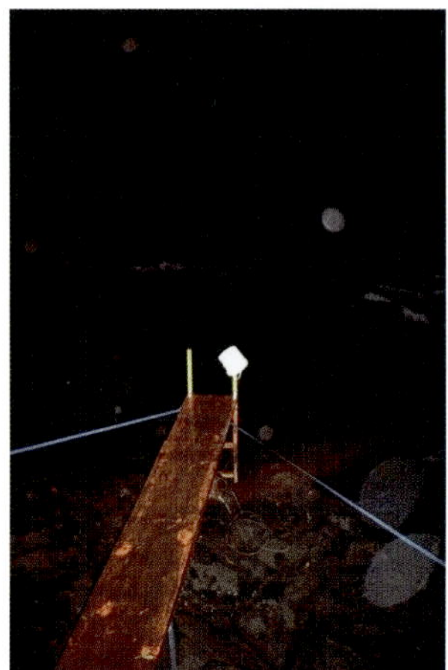

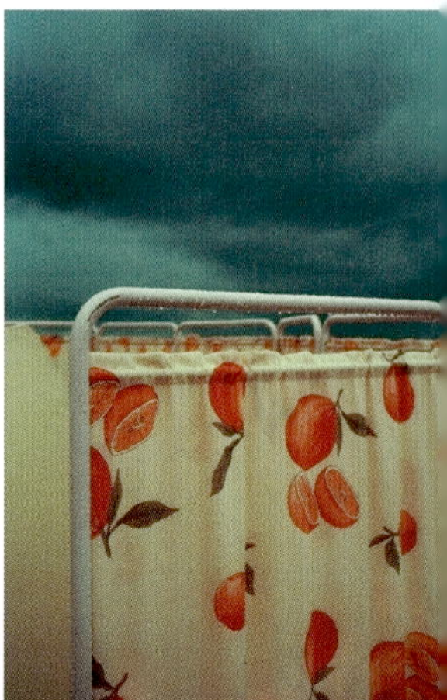

While moving around, Esmee often finds herself stimulated by random things that make her get lost in a scene that may have happened, or may be about to happen. Arbitrary, everyday encounters. The remarkable within the unremarkable.

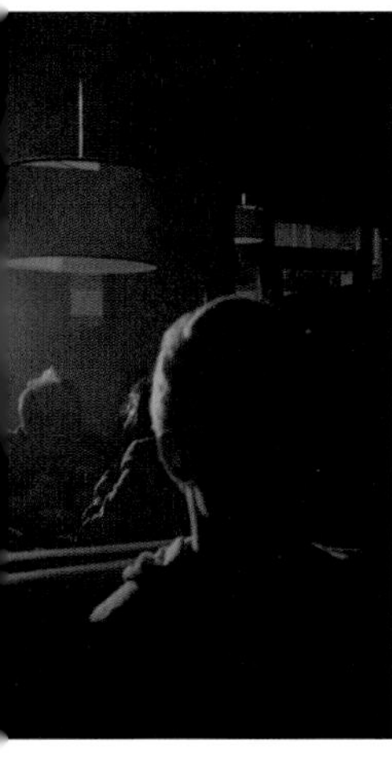

$treet POETRY

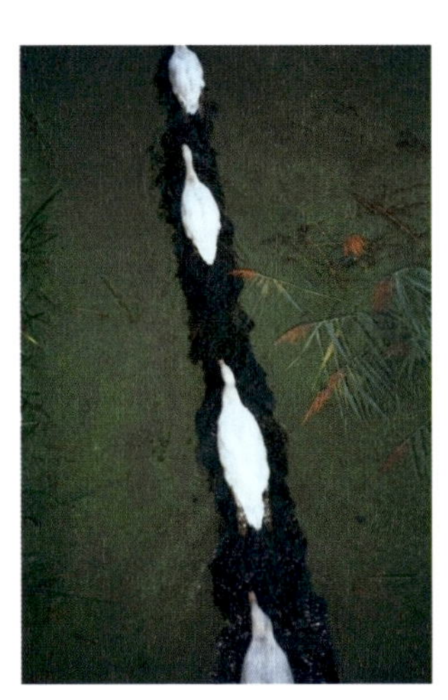

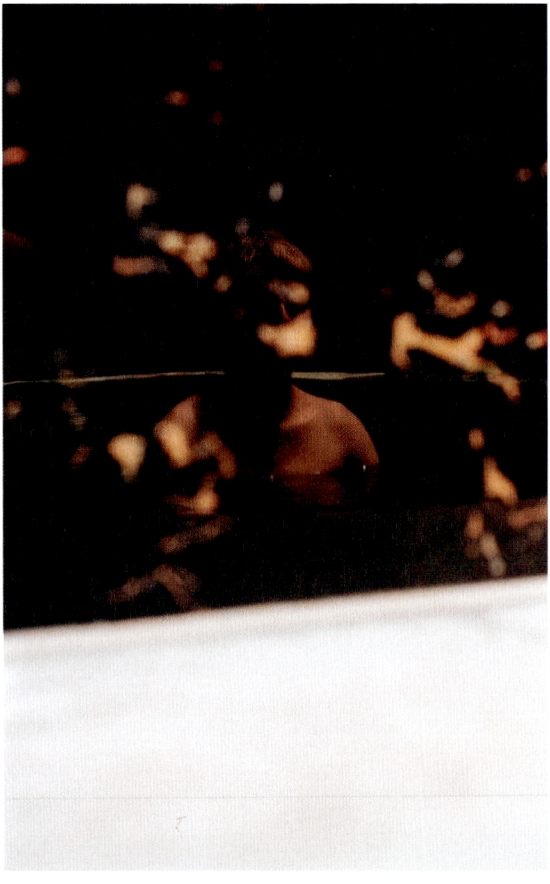

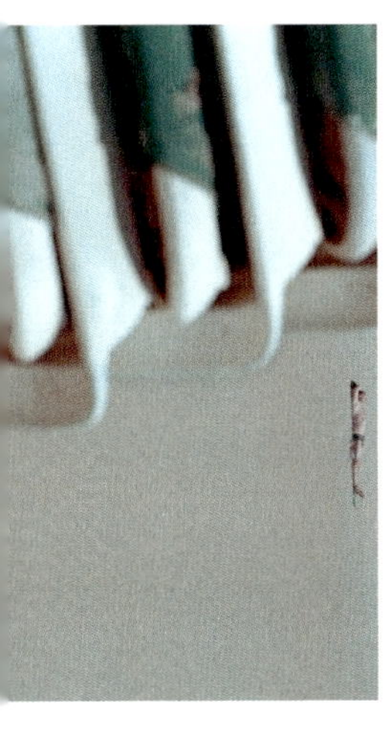
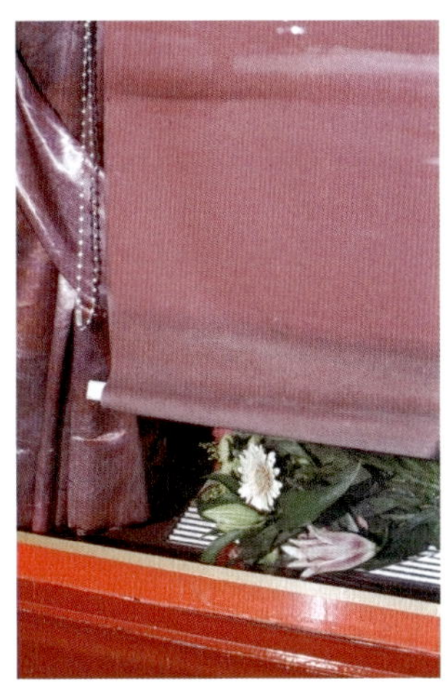
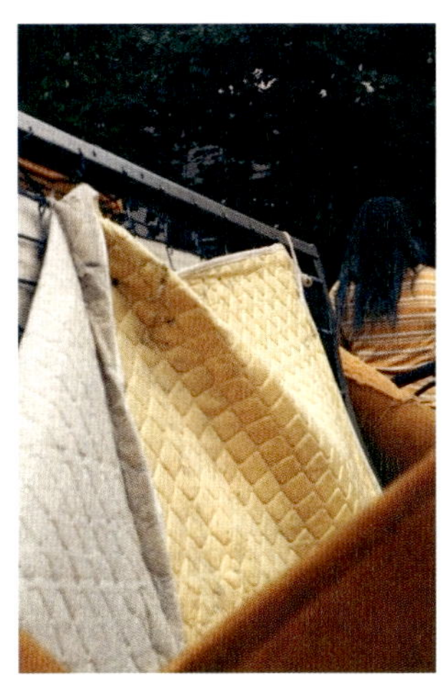

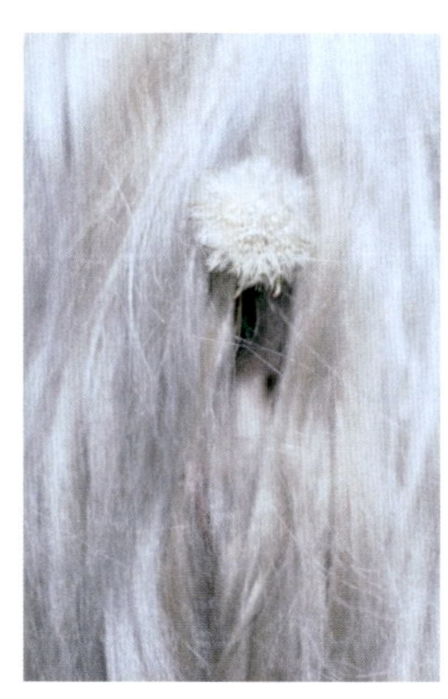
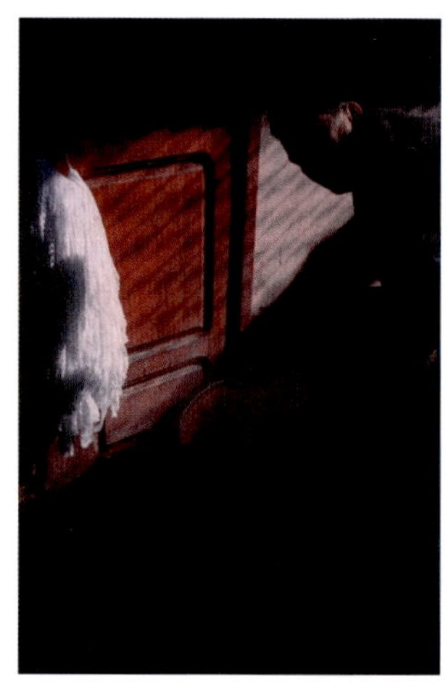

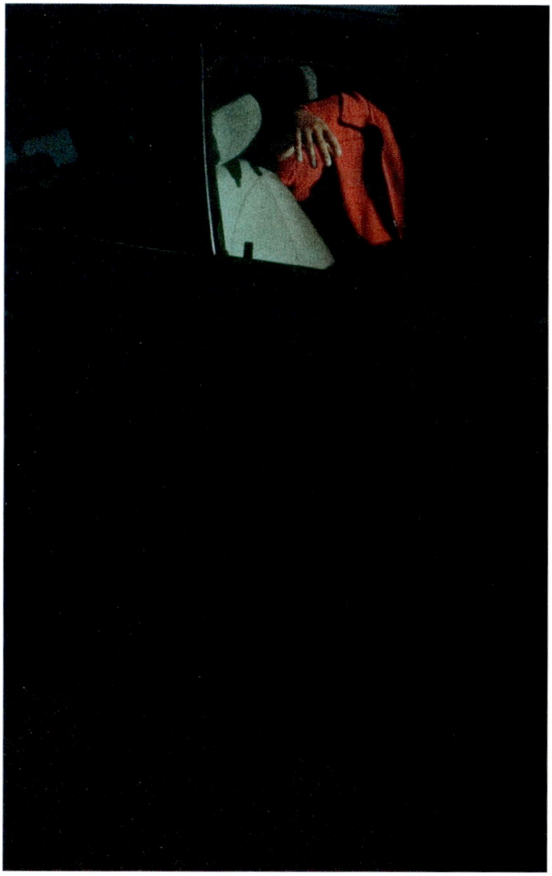

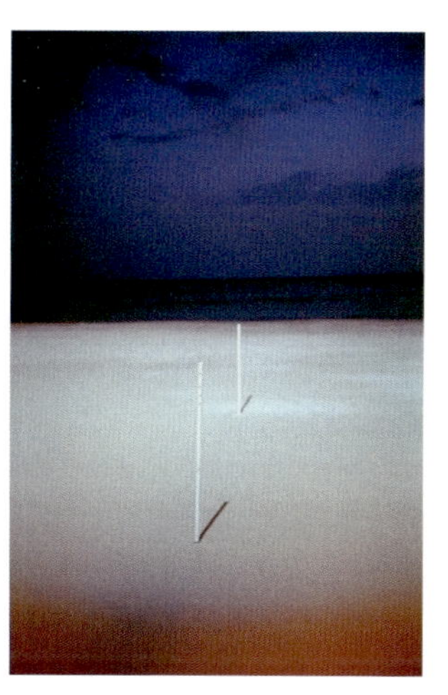

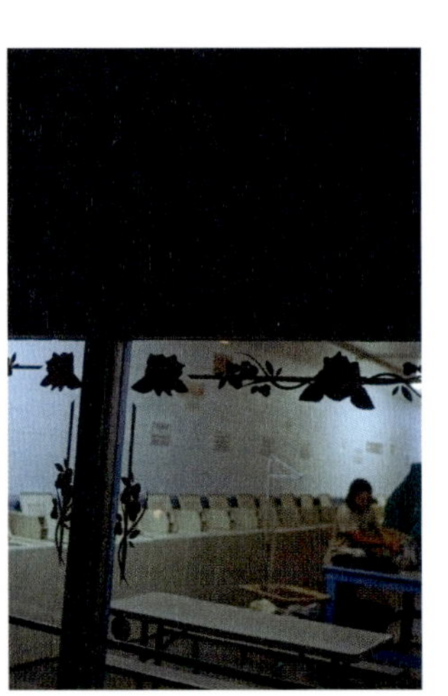

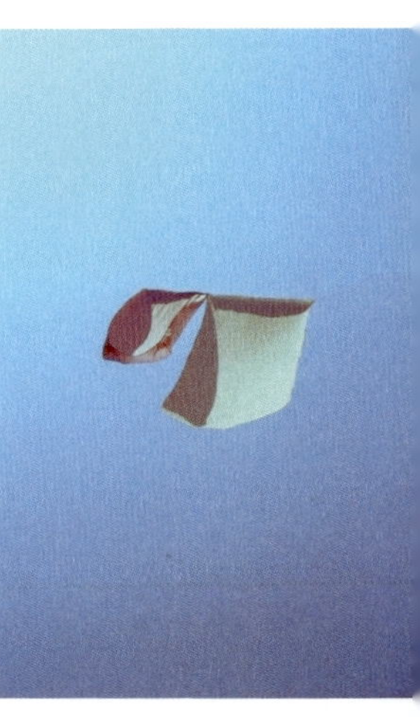

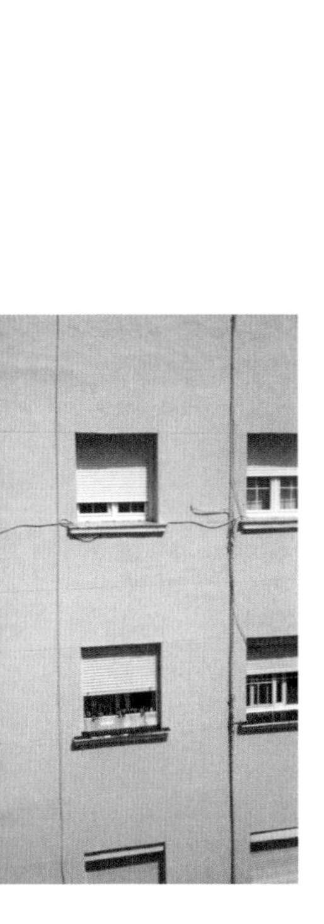

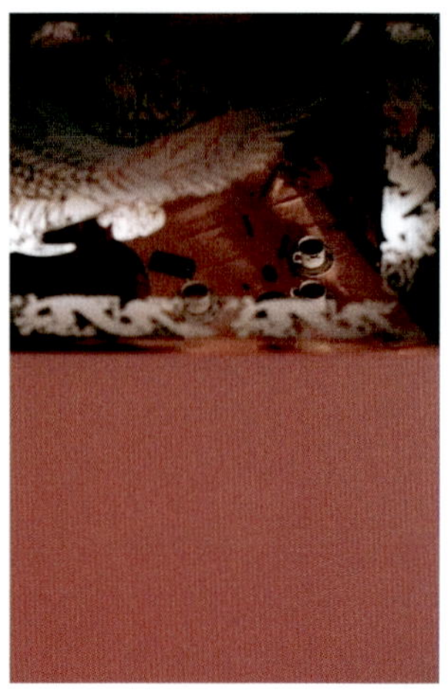

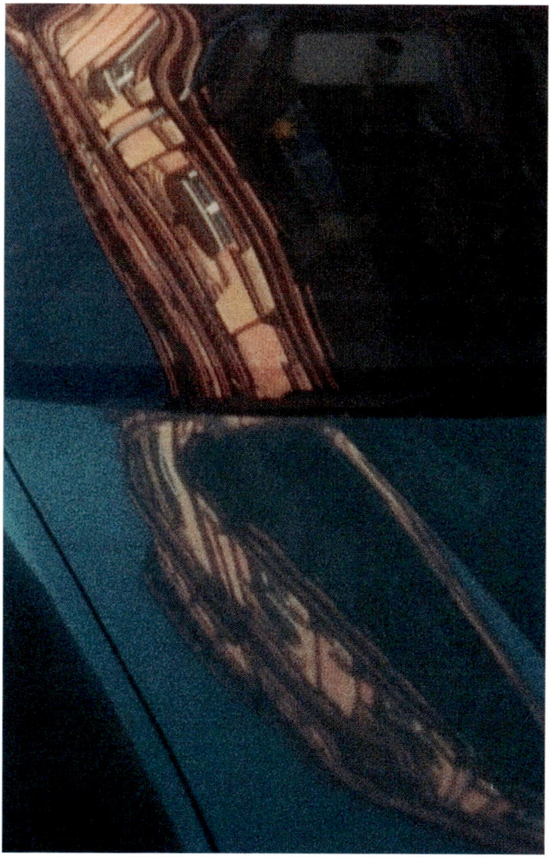

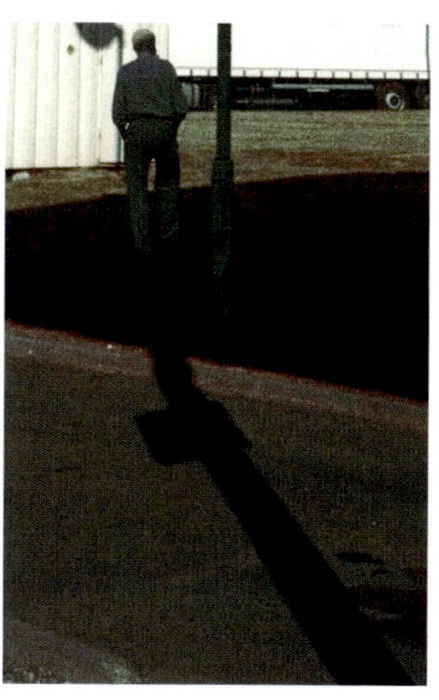

WHILE THE MOONLIGHT SHOWERS UPON MY DARK ROBE

Pressure to perform, career, comparatively early marriage. The life of young Chinese is shaped by conservative ideas of family and society. Andy finds many of them feeling overwhelmed and questioning these traditions. Instead of living according to their parents' wishes, they want to realize their own dreams. Young people in an old world, demanding self-realization and self-determination.

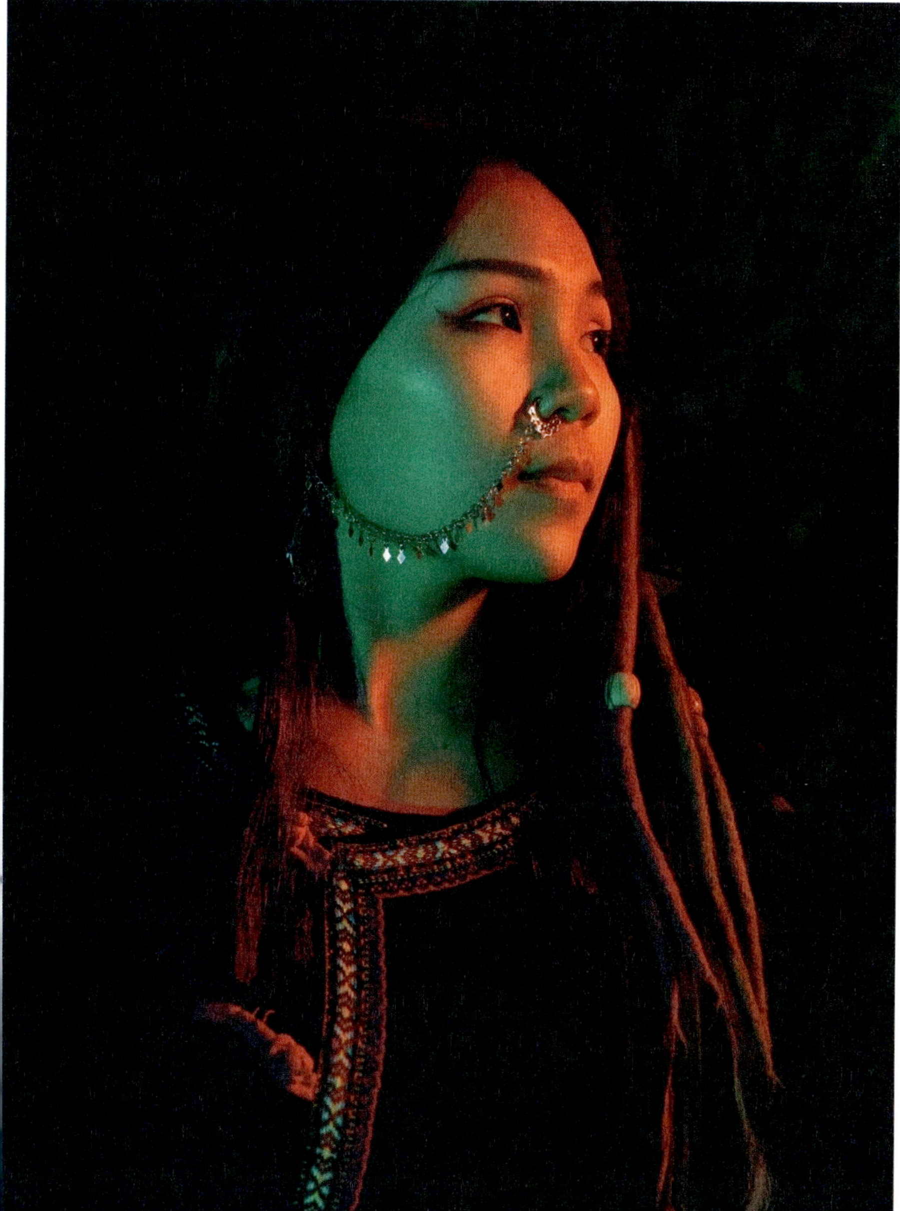

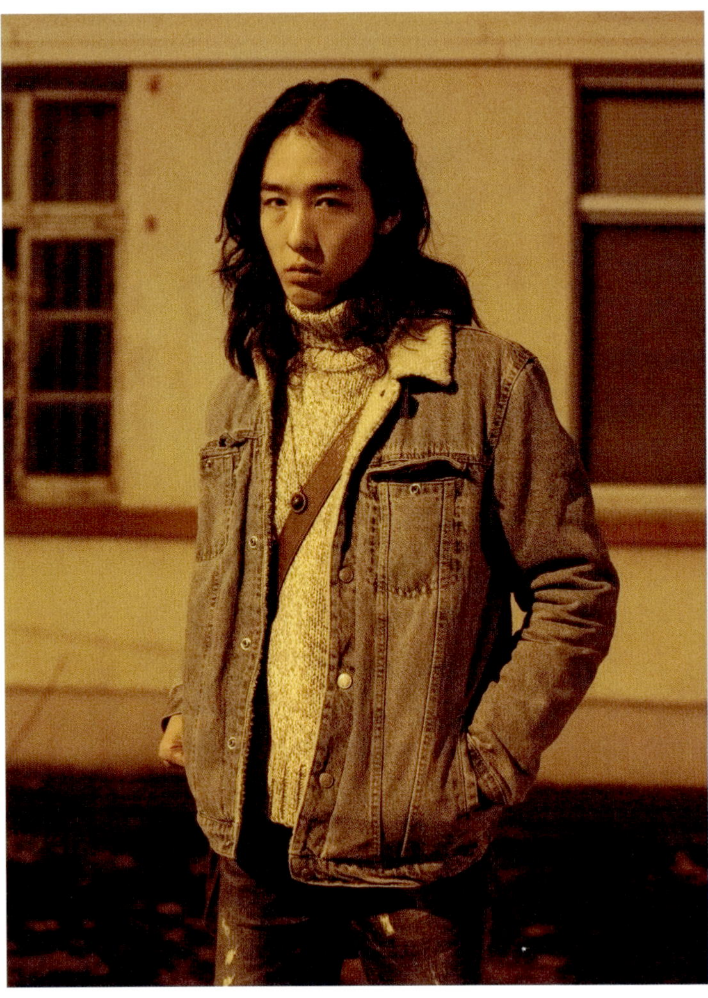

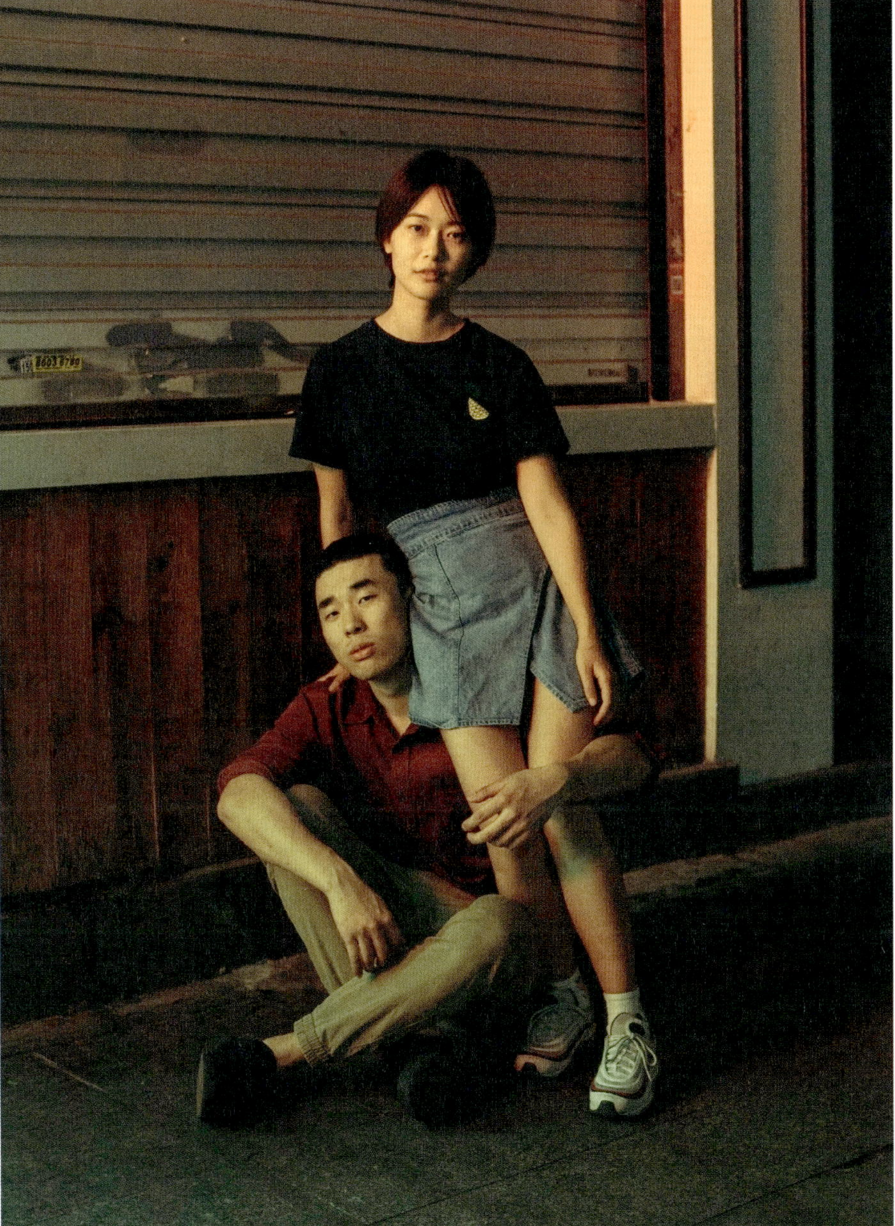

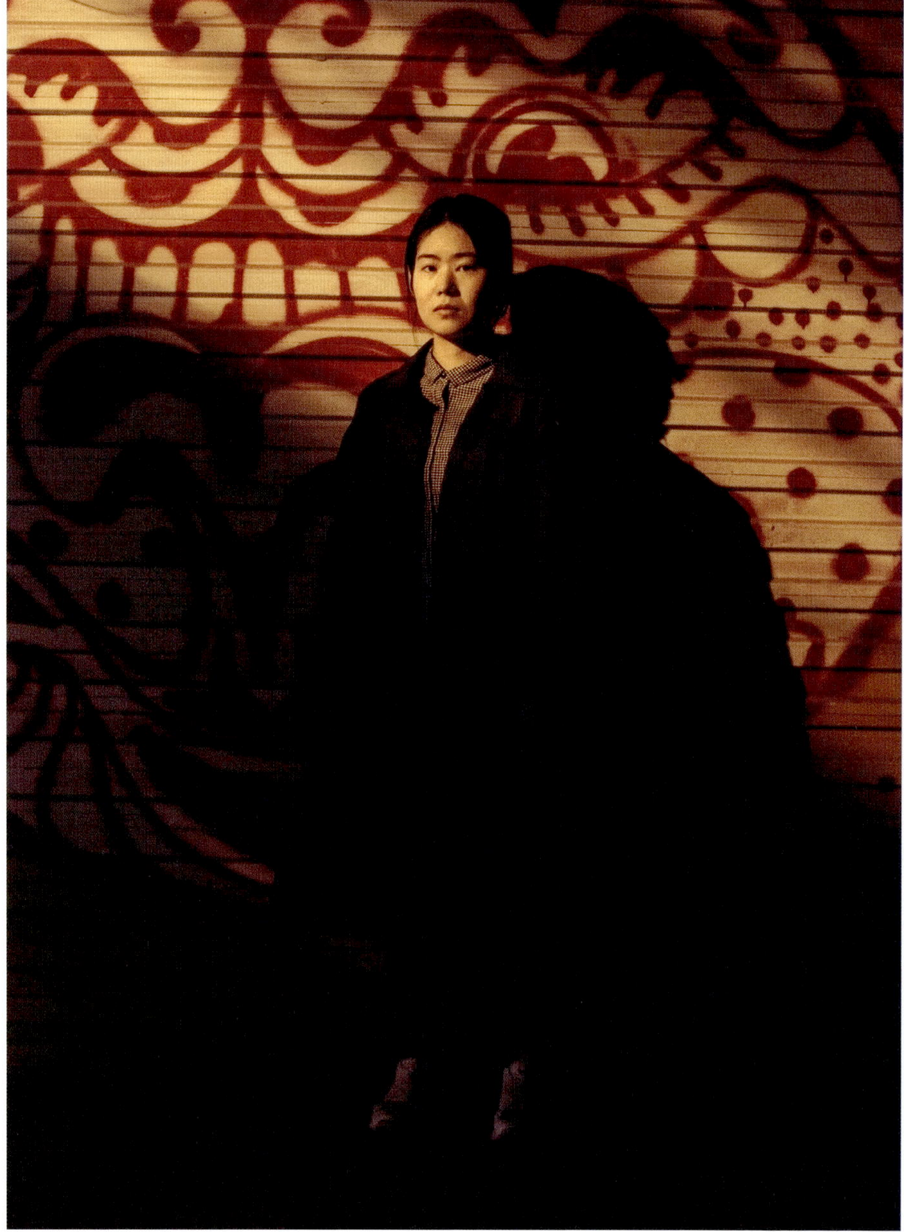

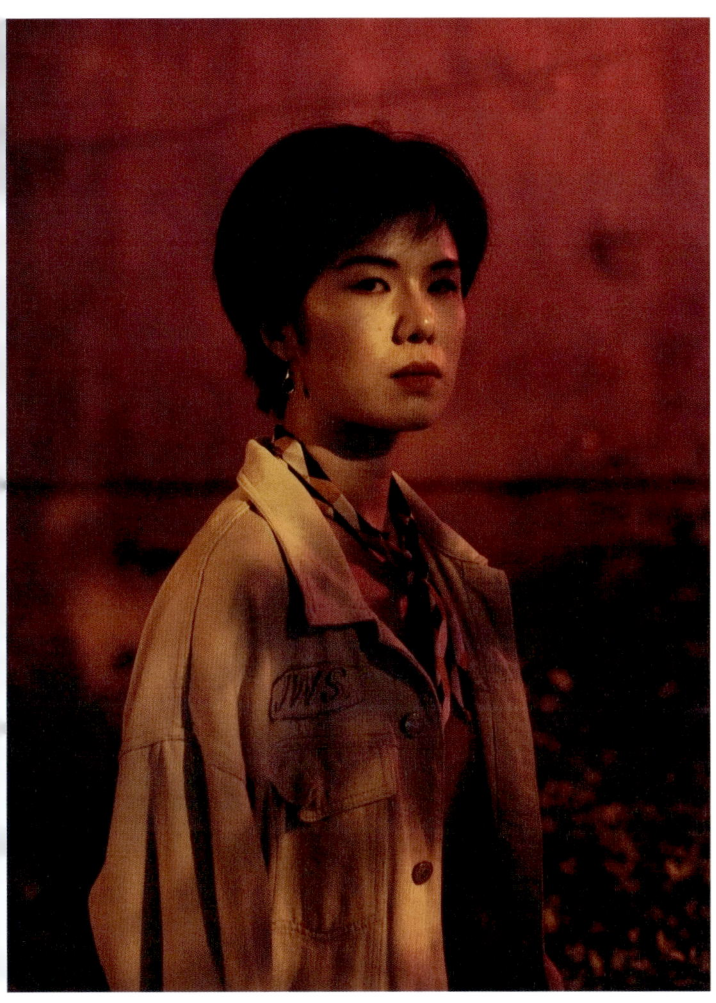

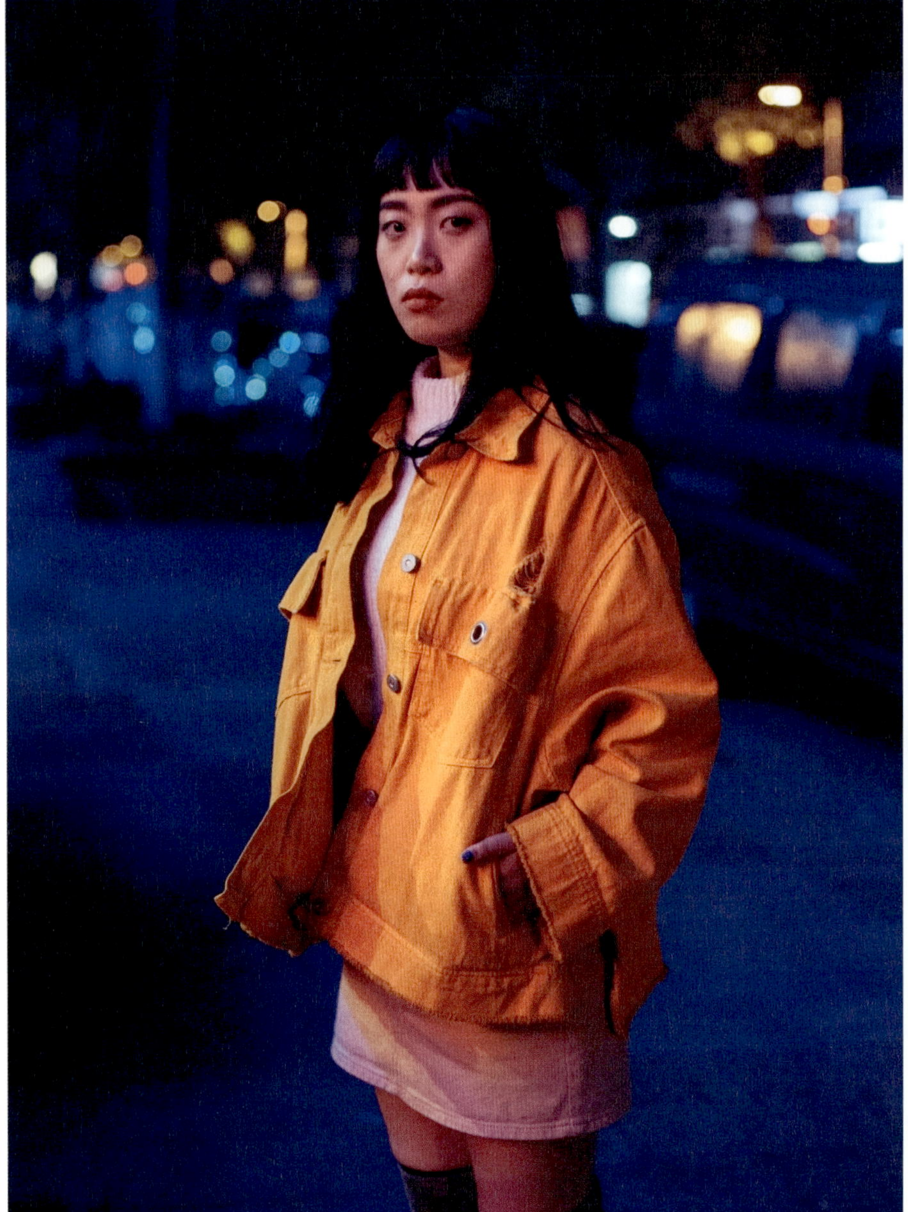

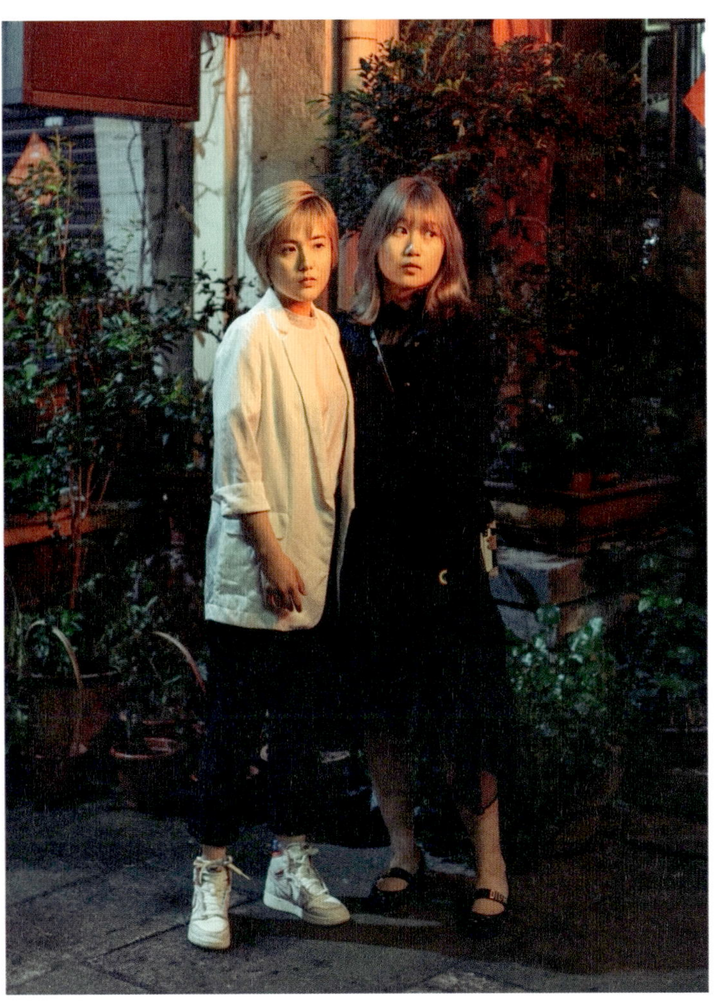

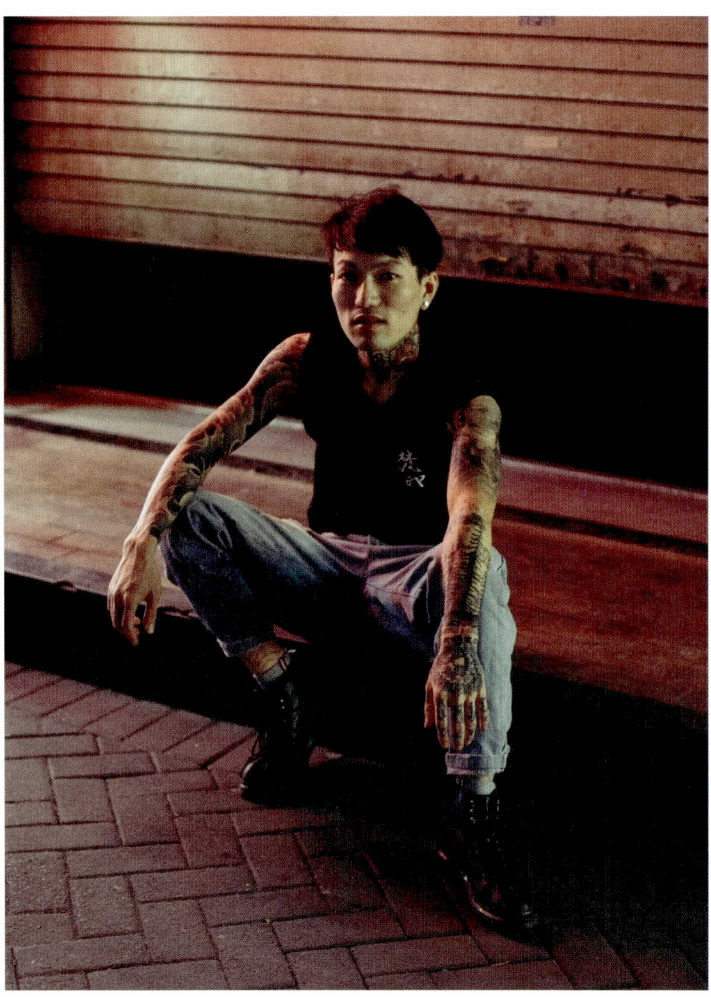

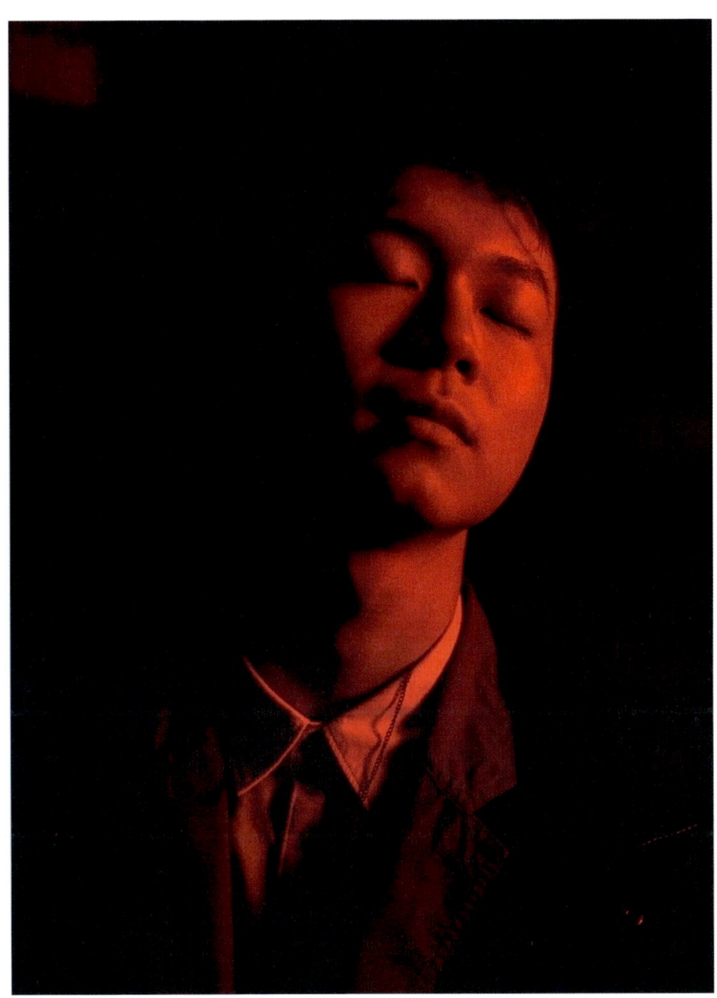

Radical

In contrast to classical pornography, which depicts old-fashioned role models and male dominance, the producers of queer and feminist pornography aim to break these stereotypes. They advocate diverse sexualities and want to show a positive and respectful perspective on sexuality towards all genders. Nick visited Berlin, the worldwide capital for the feminist & ethical porn scene.

LUST

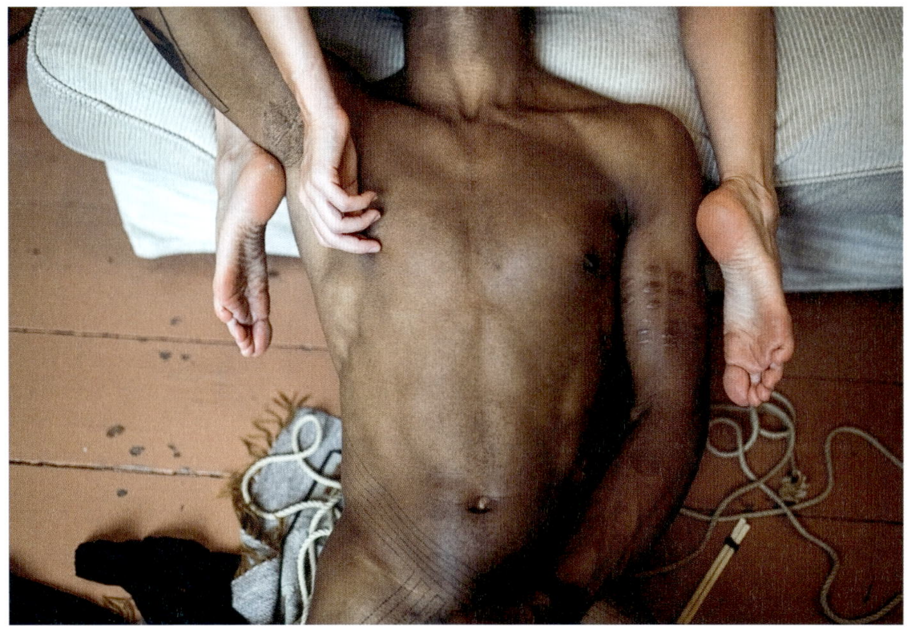

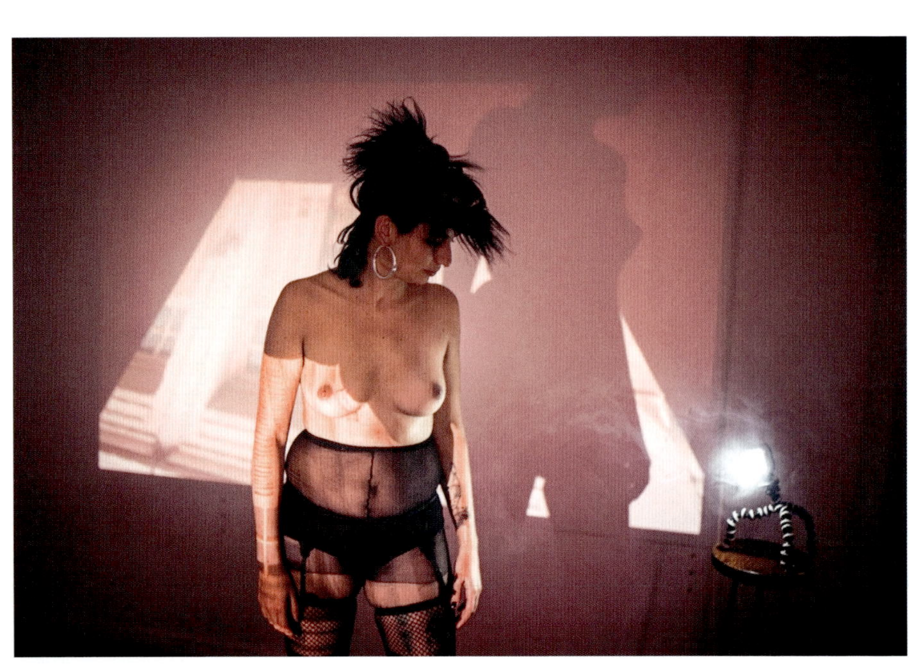

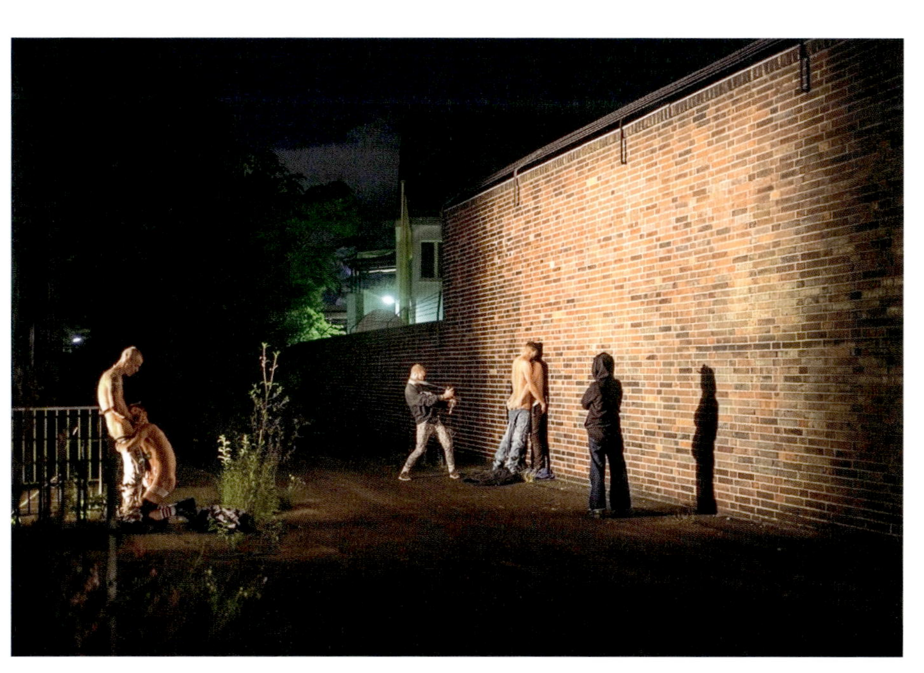

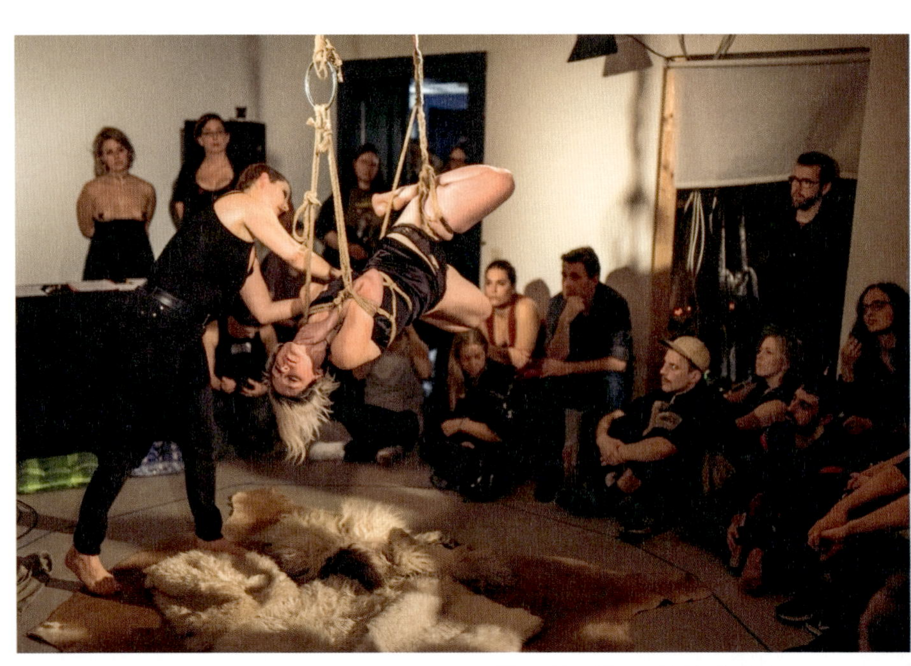

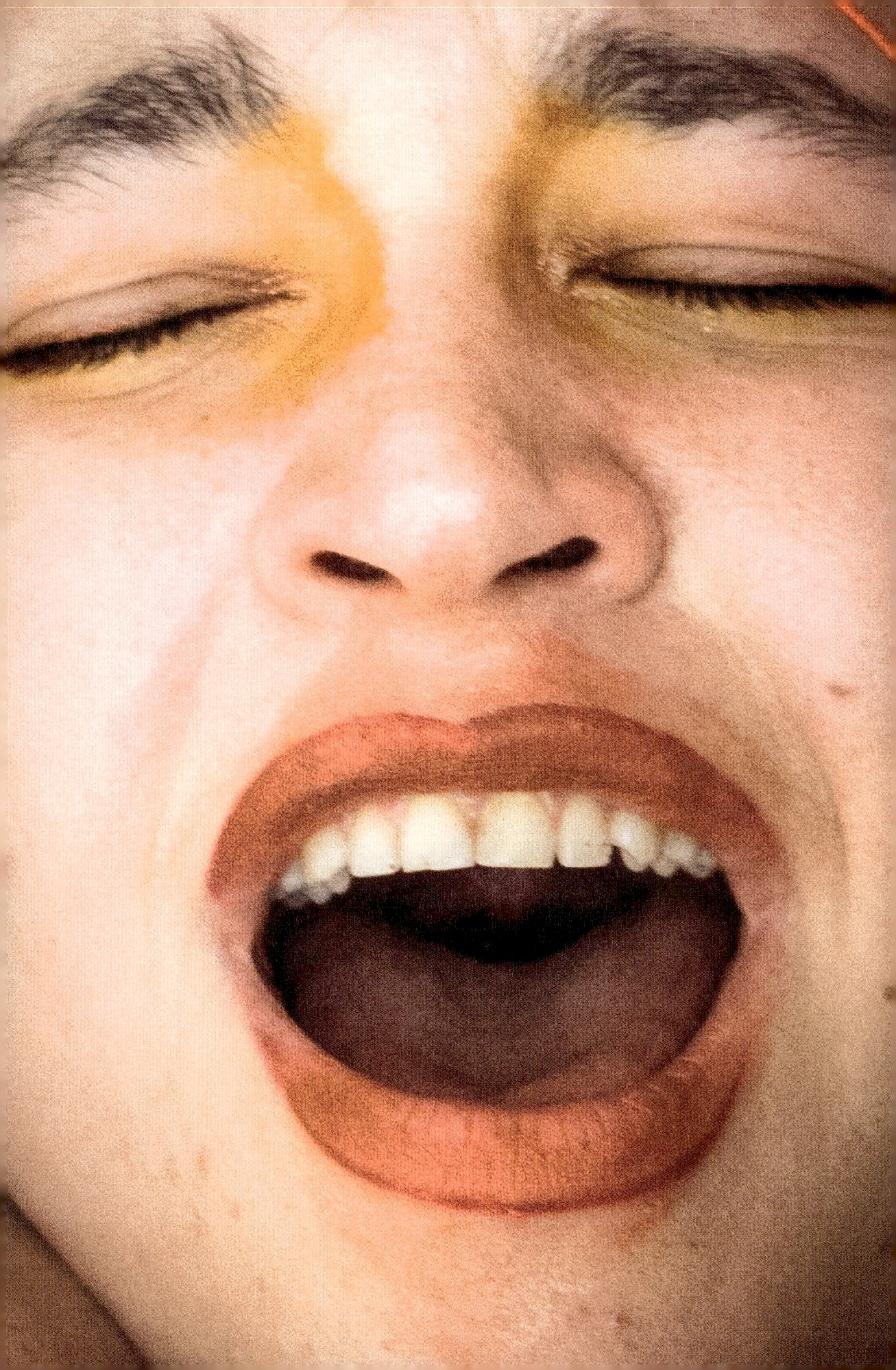

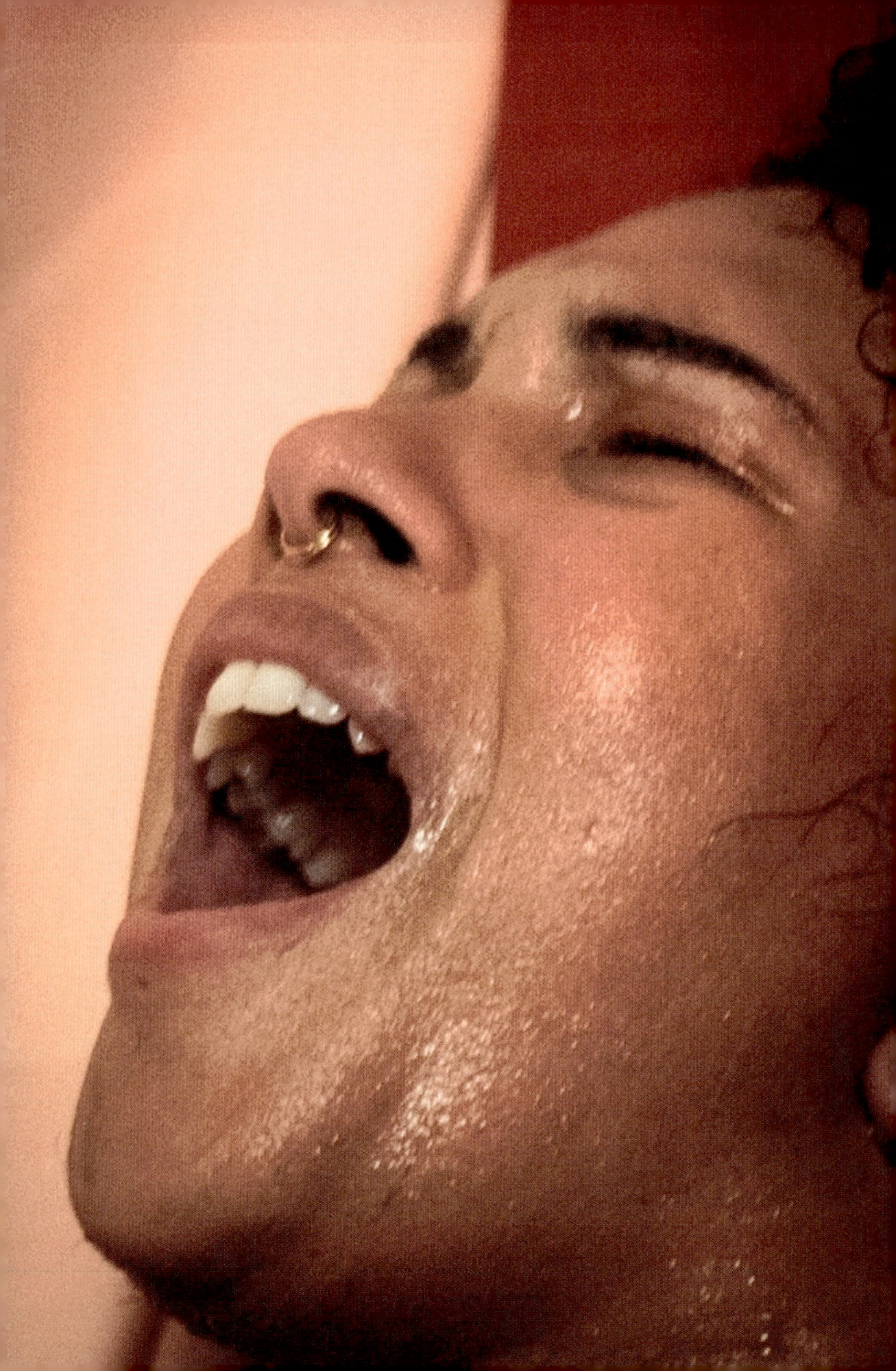

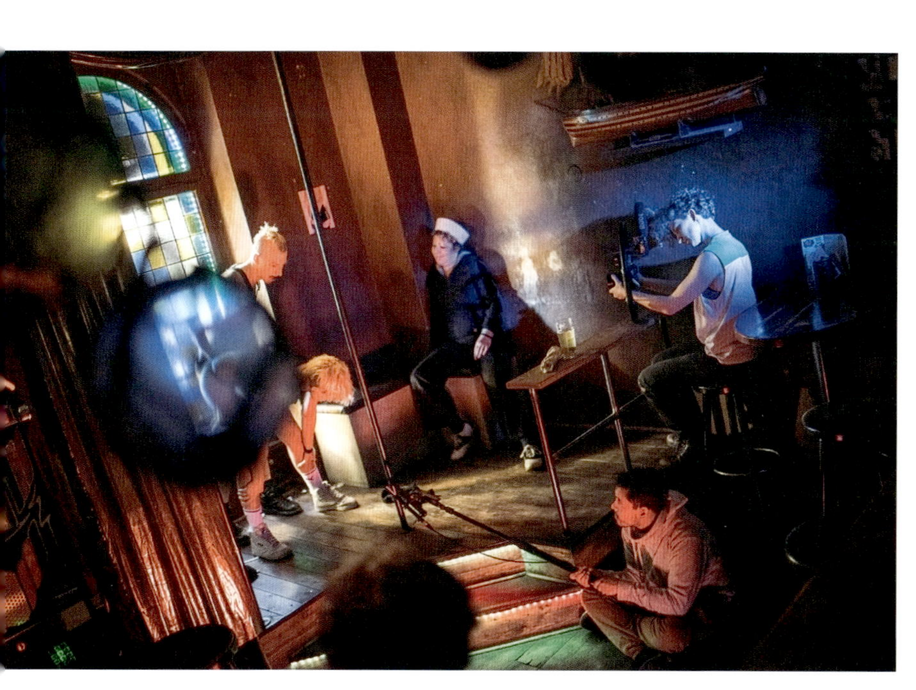

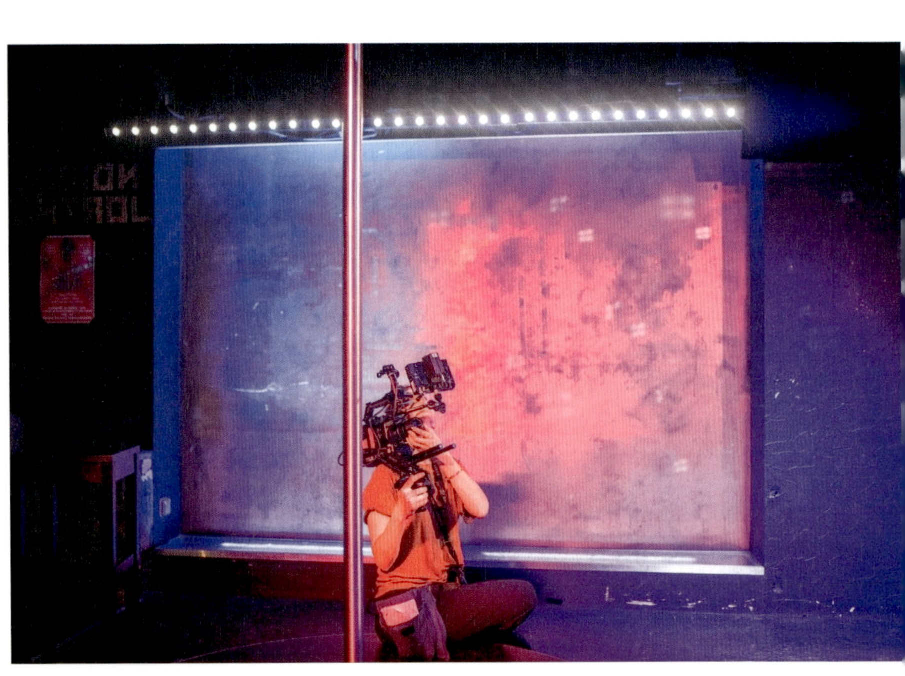

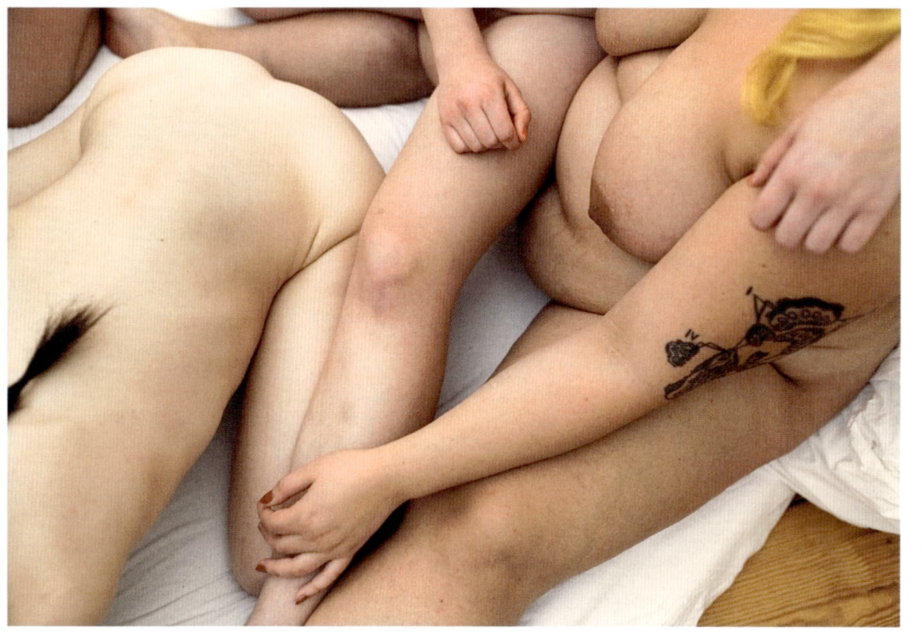

19

MALTE UCHTMANN

Even though Germany got known for its "welcome-culture", the country creates material and immaterial borders that make it more difficult for refugees to settle. Malte's work is a visual study of the architectural infrastructure for the accommodation of refugees in Germany, exploring the embedded social and political structures, asking: to what extent is architecture impairing integration in Germany?

Arriving

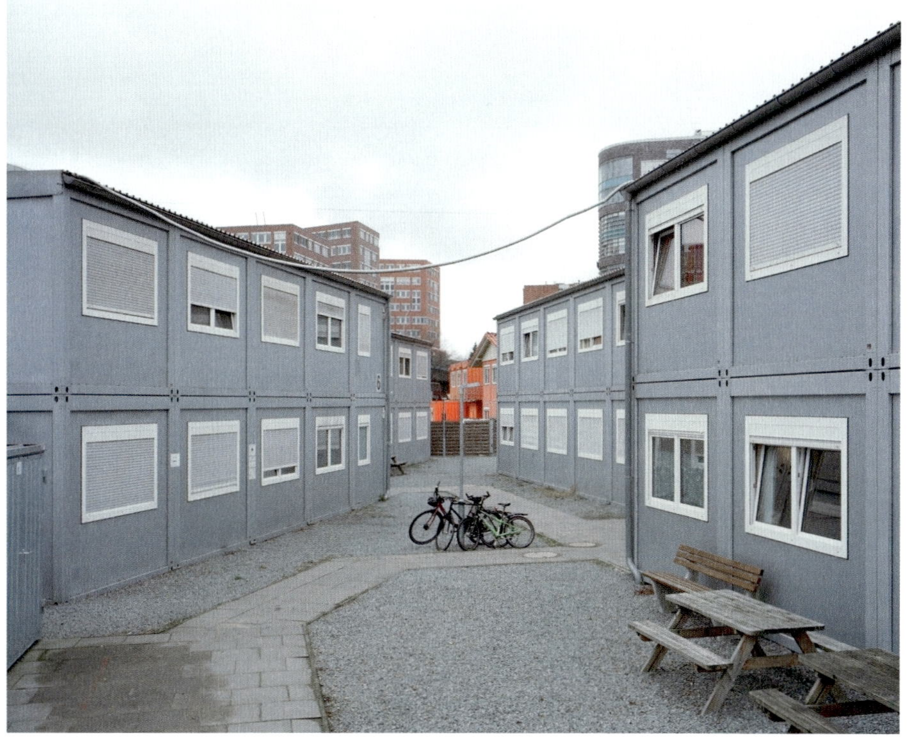

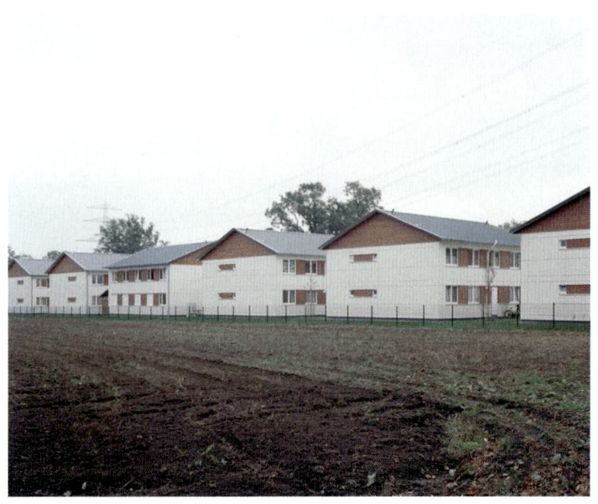

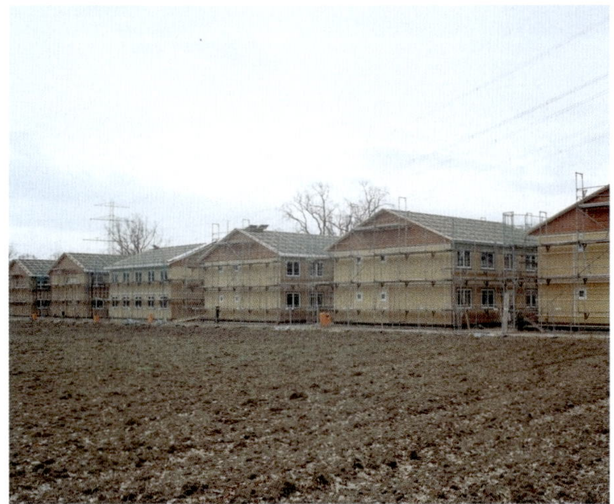

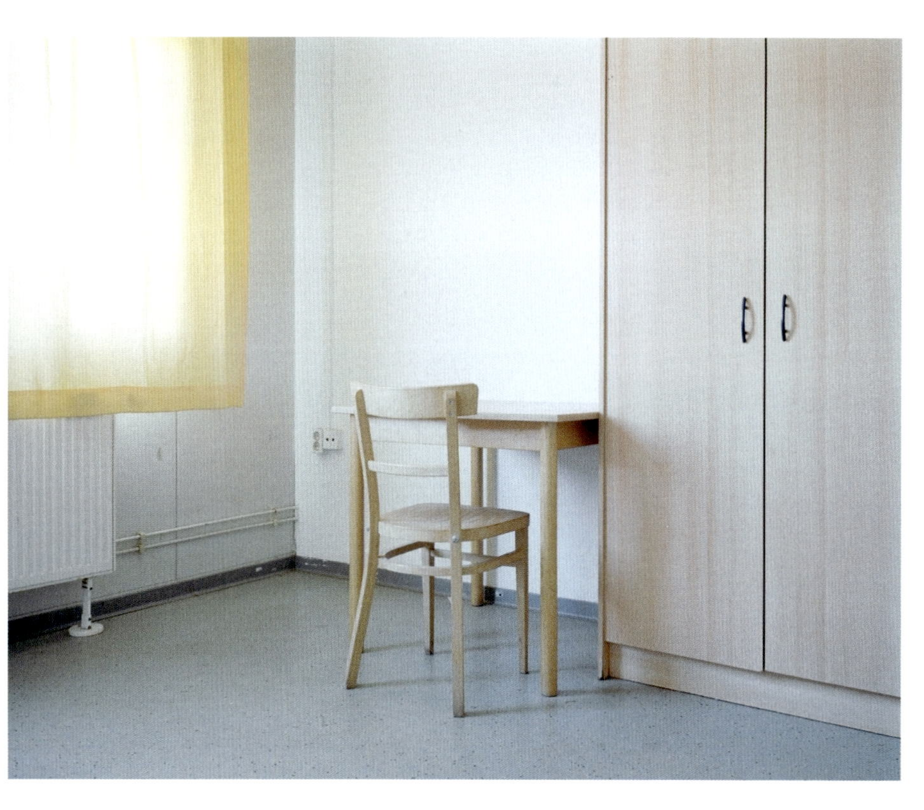

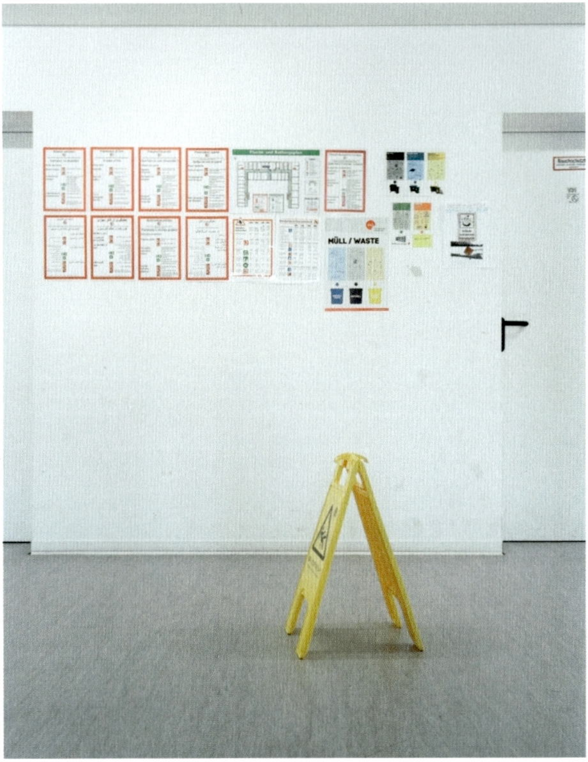

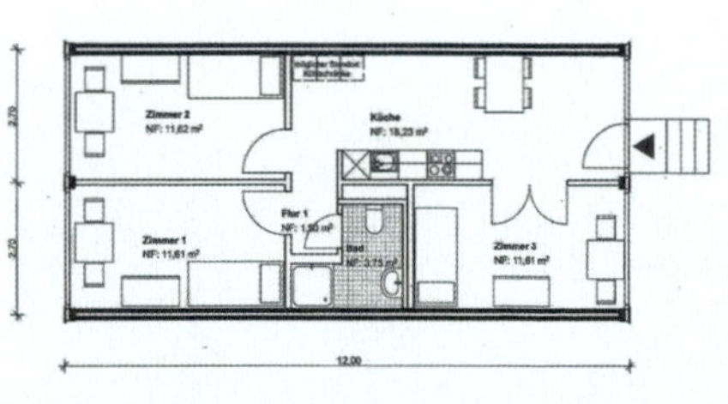
Zimmer 2
NF: 11,62 m²
Küche
NF: 18,23 m²
Flur 1
NF: 1,50 m²
Zimmer 1
NF: 11,61 m²
Bad
NF: 3,73 m²
Zimmer 3
NF: 11,61 m²
2,70
2,70
12,00

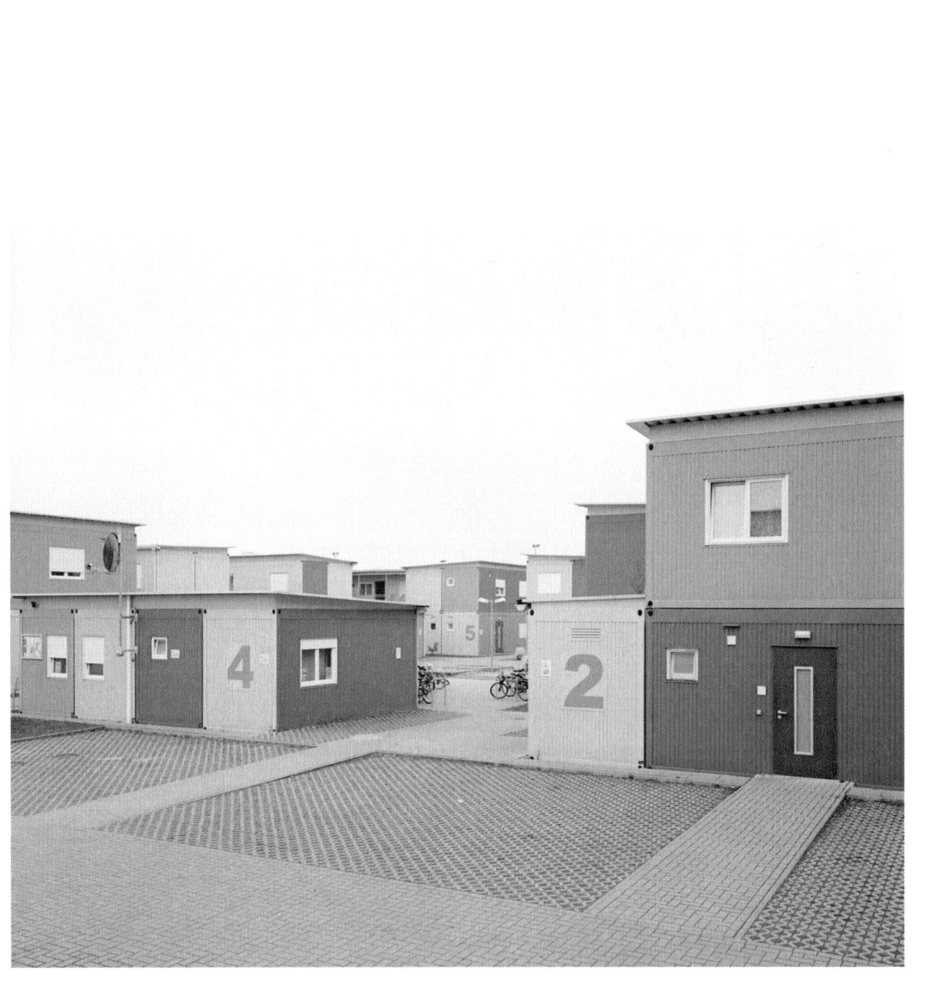
4
5
2

Anlage 1

Anforderungen an die Unterbringung in Gemeinschaftsunterkünften

1. Die Gemeinschaftsunterkunft muss den öffentlich-rechtlichen Vorschriften (insbes. des Bau-, Hygiene- und Brandschutzrechts) sowie den gewerbeaufsichtlichen Bestimmungen und sonstigen Verpflichtungen entsprechen. Die Unterkunft ist in einem Zustand zu halten, der den Anforderungen an eine menschenwürdige Unterbringung entspricht.

2. Für jede Person soll eine Wohnfläche von mindestens 7 Quadratmetern zur Verfügung stehen. Ausnahmen von mindestens 6 Quadratmetern Wohnfläche sind zulässig. Bei der Berechnung der Wohnfläche bleiben sonstige Flächen wie Flure, Toiletten, Küchen, Wasch-, Dusch- und Trockenräume sowie Gemeinschafts- und Verwaltungsräume unberücksichtigt. Die maximale Zimmerbelegung soll 4 Personen nicht übersteigen.

Zur Grundausstattung gehören:

2.1 Pro Person

a) ein Bett mit Matratze, ein Kopfkissen und eine Einziehdecke,

b) ein abschließbarer Kleiderschrank; bei Familienunterbringung zwei entsprechend große Schränke,

c) eine Lichtquelle (Lampe),

d) Handtücher und Bettwäsche.

2.2 Pro Zimmer

a) ein Tisch sowie Stühle entsprechend der Anzahl der Bewohner,

b) ein Abfalleimer,

c) Gardinen und Verdunklungsmöglichkeiten,

d) Möglichkeiten zur Aufbewahrung von Lebensmitteln, soweit diese nicht in einer Gemeinschaftsküche (Nr. 4 Buchstabe c) vorhanden sind.

3. Soweit keine Wohneinheiten mit eigener Nasszelle zur Verfügung stehen, sind gemeinschaftlich genutzte Sanitärräume für Männer und Frauen getrennt einzurichten. Die Sanitärräume müssen abschließbar sein. Folgende Mindestausstattung ist zu gewährleisten:

a) ein Waschbecken für maximal 8 Personen,

b) ein Duschplatz für 10 – 12 Personen,

c) ein Toilettenplatz für 8 weibliche Bewohner,

d) ein Toilettenplatz und ein Urinalbecken für 15 männliche Bewohner,

e) Zubehör für Wasch- und Toilettenräume.

Bei Duschanlagen ist zwischen den einzelnen Duschplätzen ein Sichtschutz anzubringen.

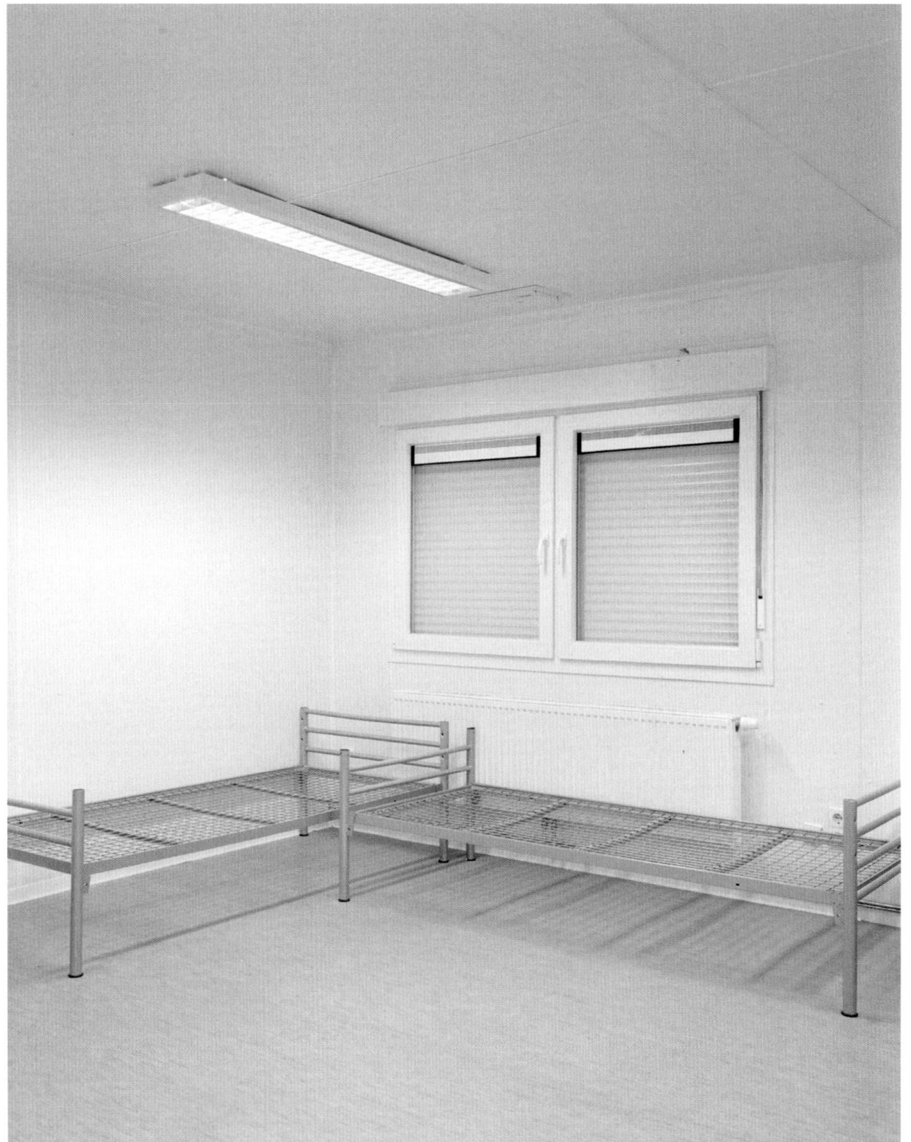

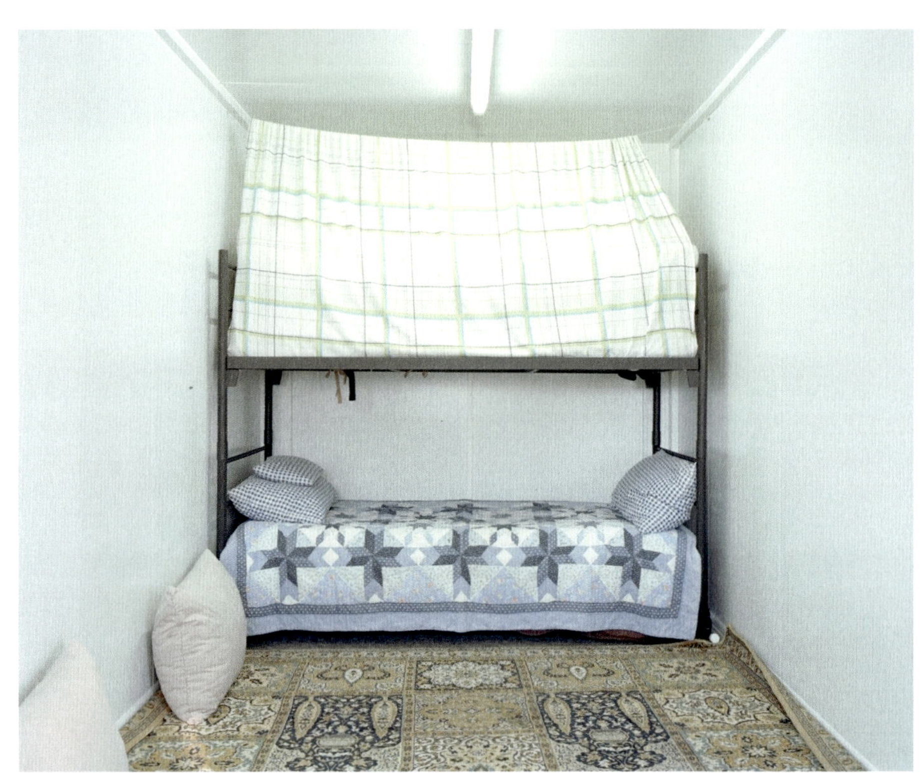

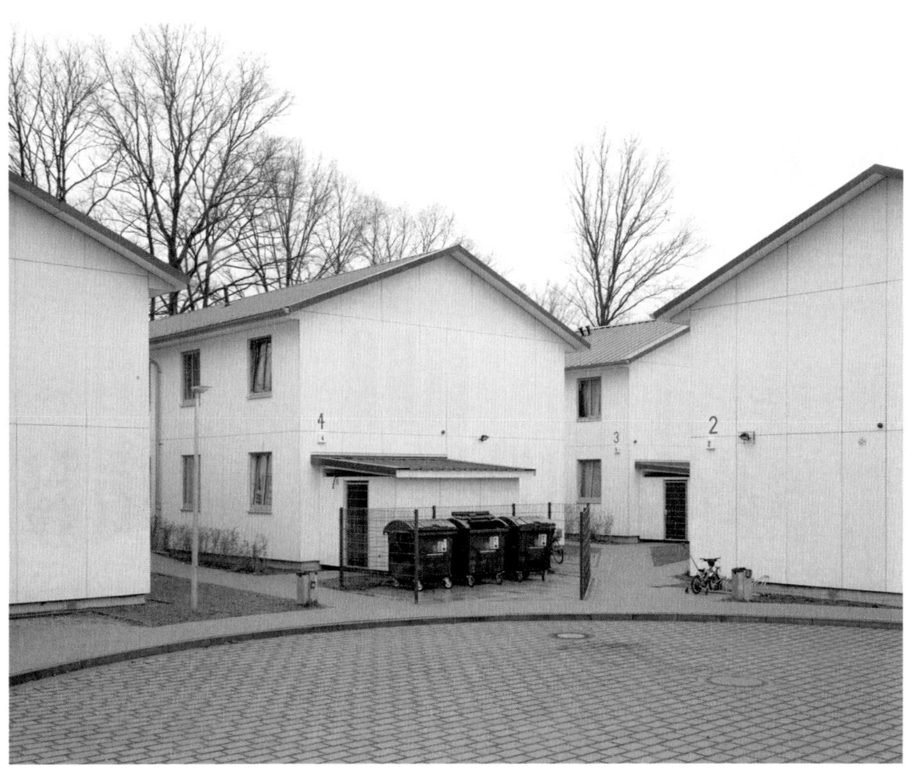
4
3
2

FRANZISKA KAUFHOLD

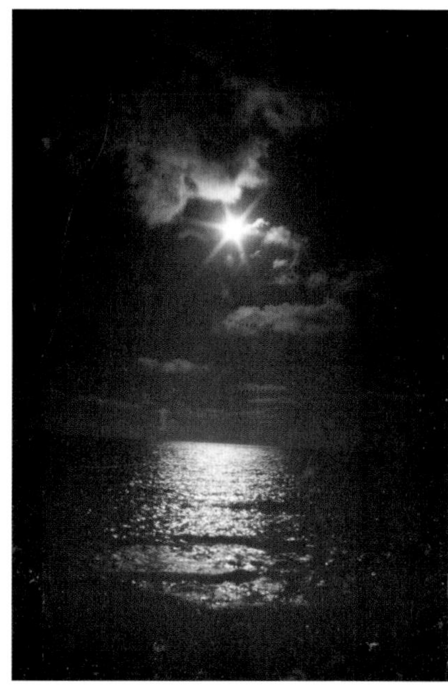

DÄMMER

20

Long silent remote winters are always followed by ecstatically exhausting, overfilled high seasons here. Franziska's pictures are a story about island adolescence, about affection, rapture, apathy and life in a bubble. It is a story about doing everything and not getting caught, or sleeping for days and having nobody even notice. About wandering and finding the way home, just to get lost once again. More than anything, this is about growing, annual reunions and the ambivalent relationship between us and the island we call home.

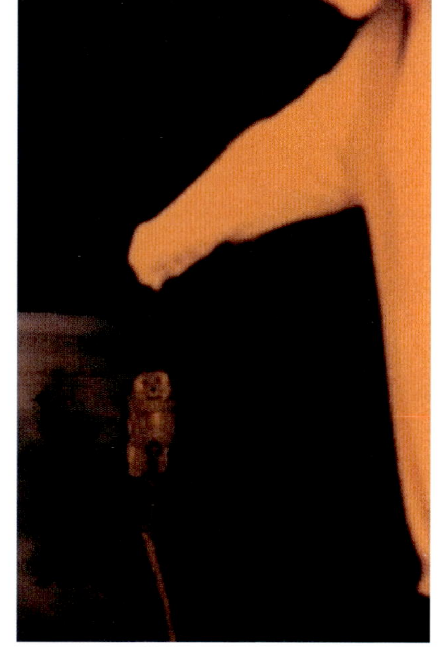
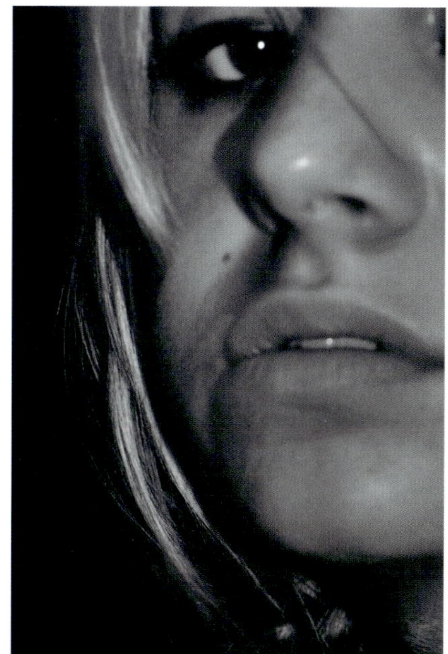

$ C H L A F

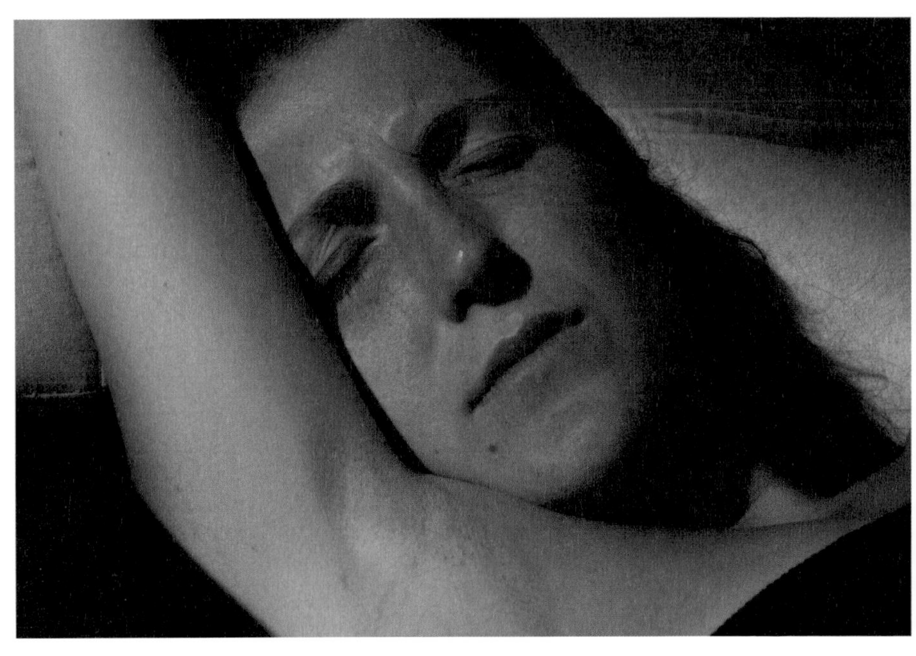

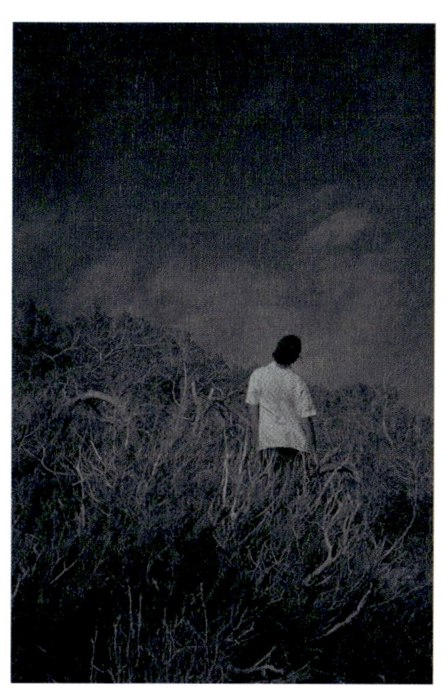

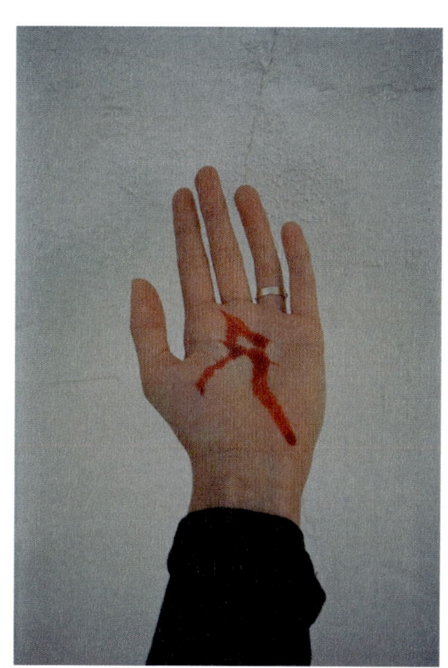

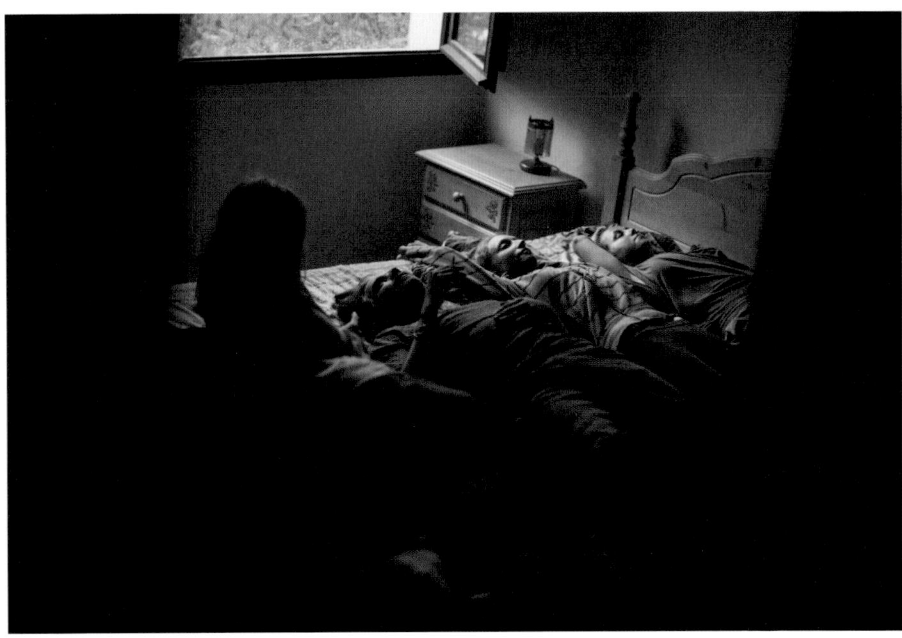

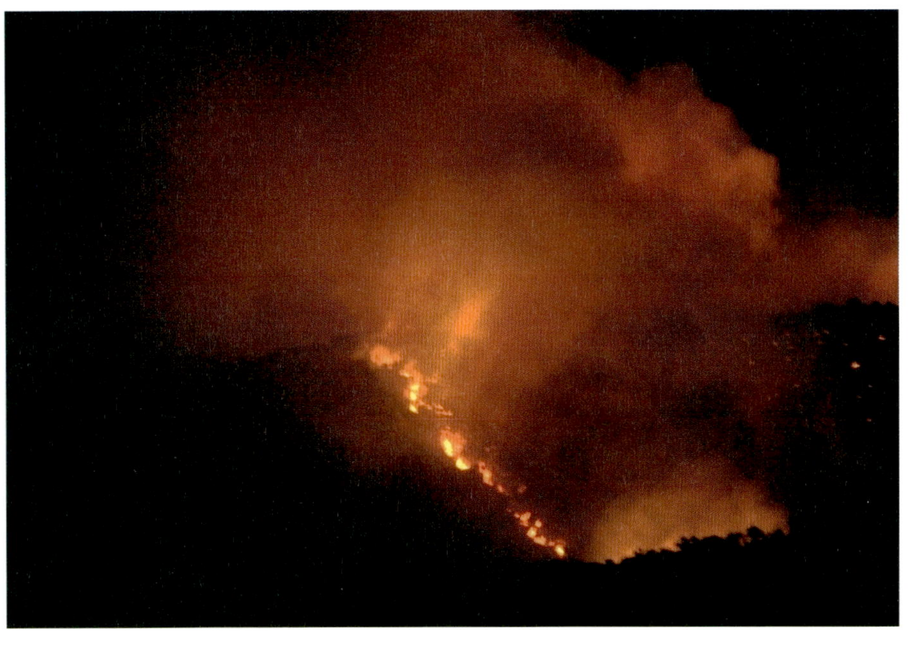

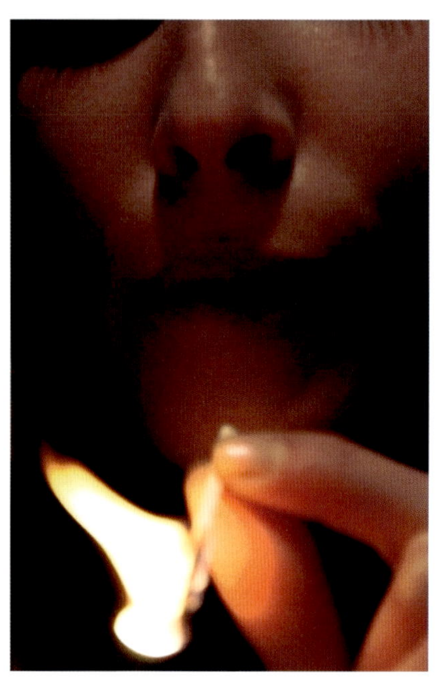

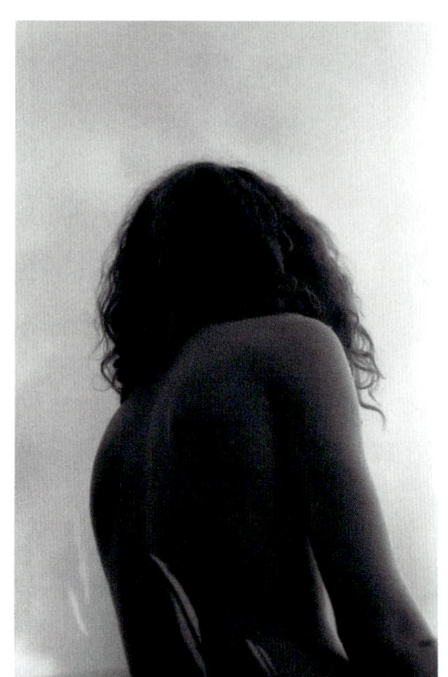

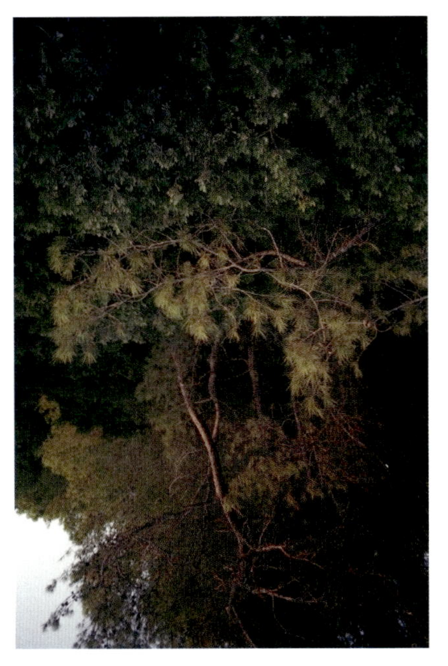

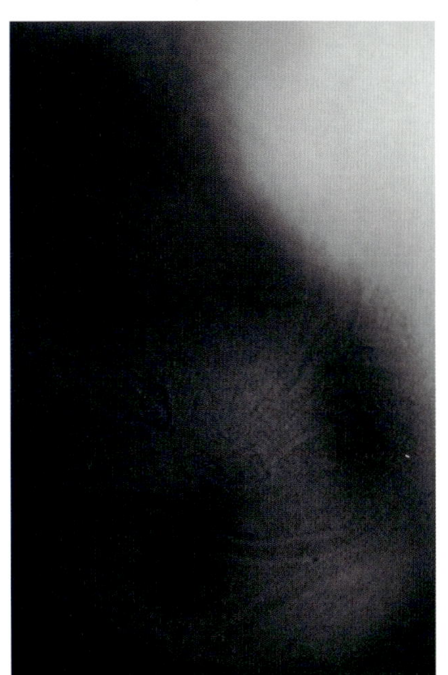

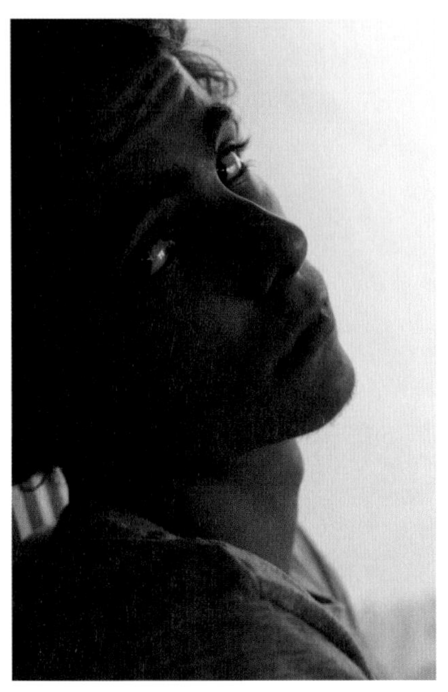

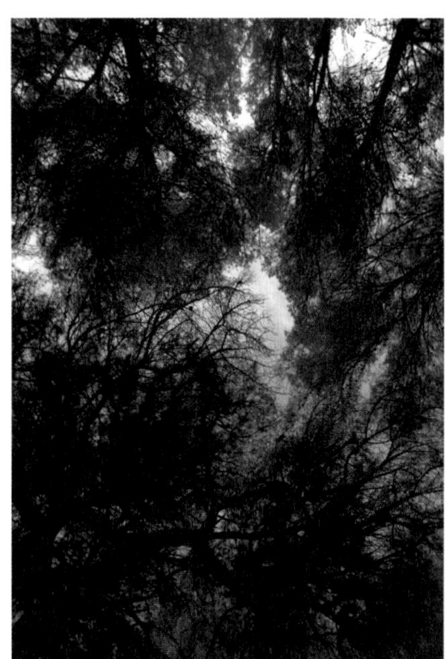

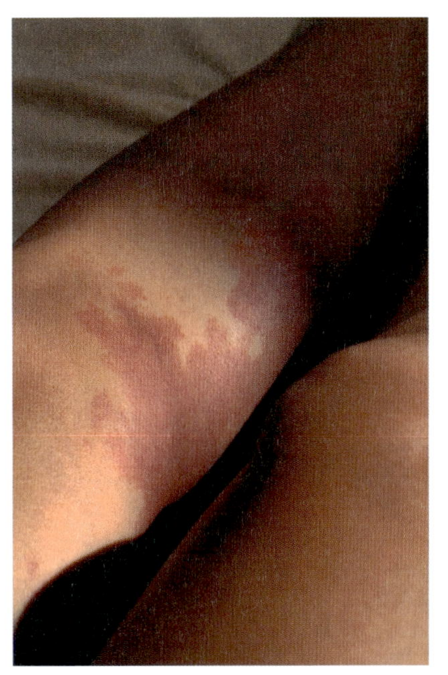

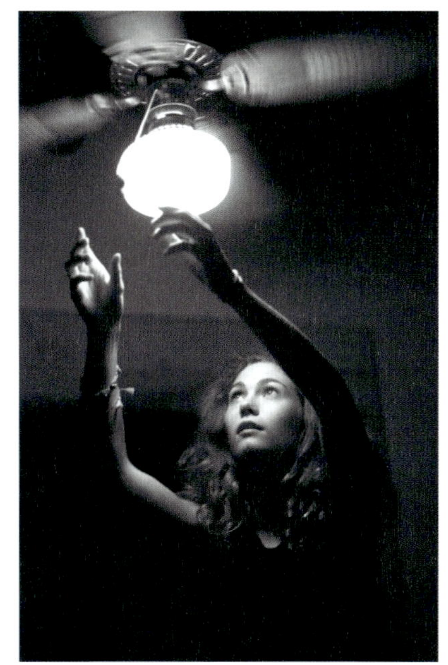

JASPER BASTIAN

21

A Road NOT Taken

The border between Belarus and Lithuania, two countries previously part of the Soviet Union, used to be rather fluid allowing residents to share and love the same territory. However, in 2004, the European external border became a reality. Jasper takes us to physically divided villages, to families torn apart and aims to show bonds between individuals and communities that suddenly severed.

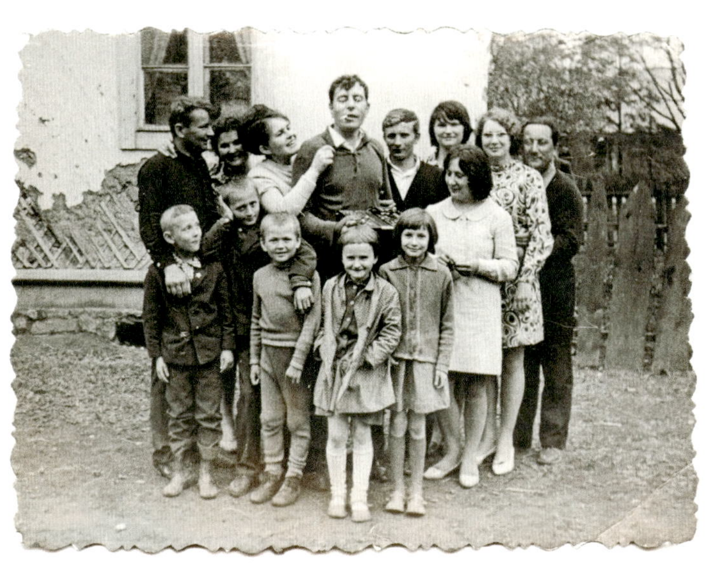

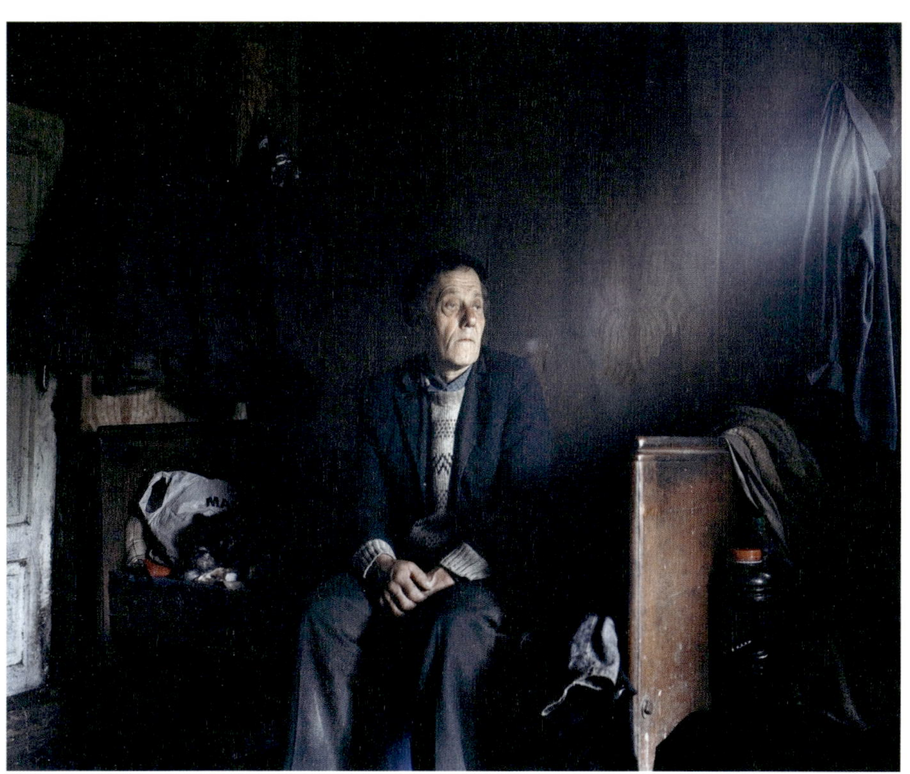

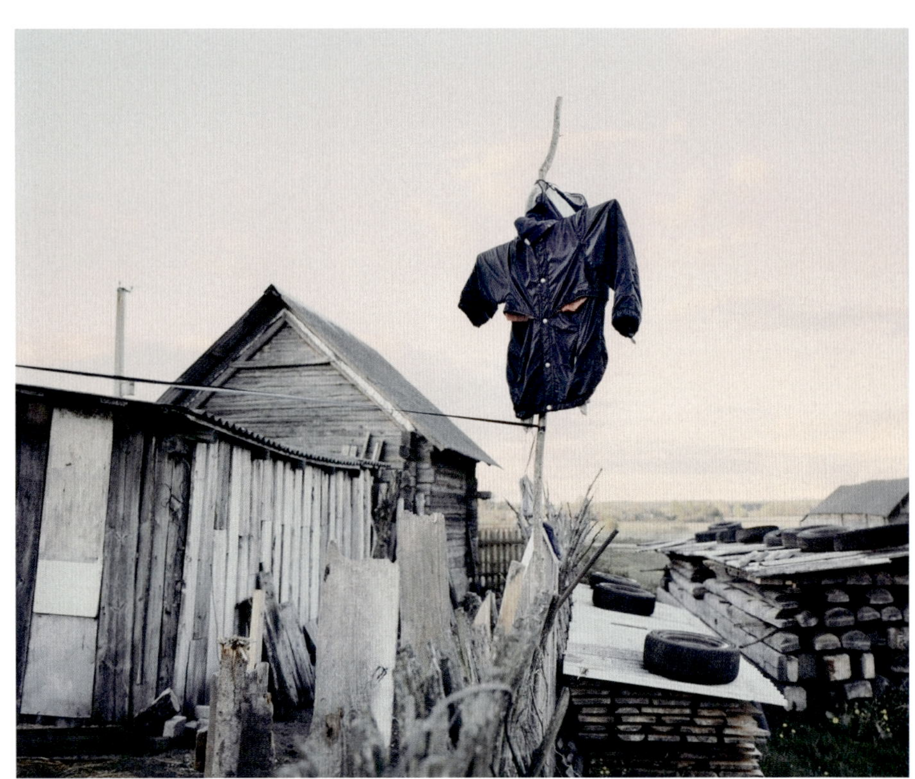

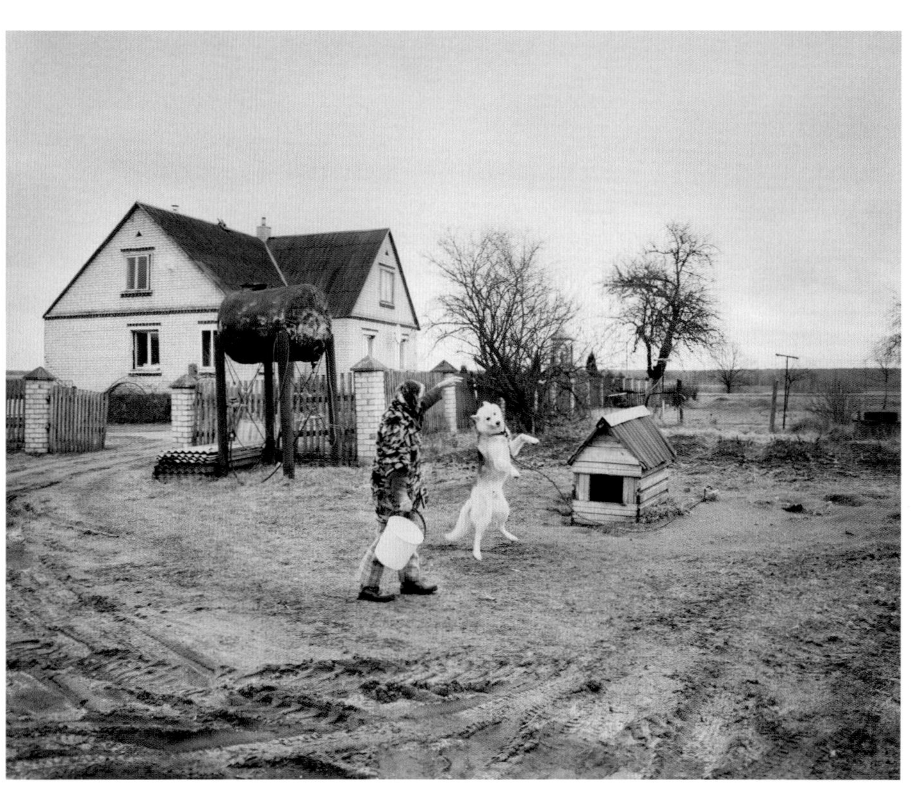

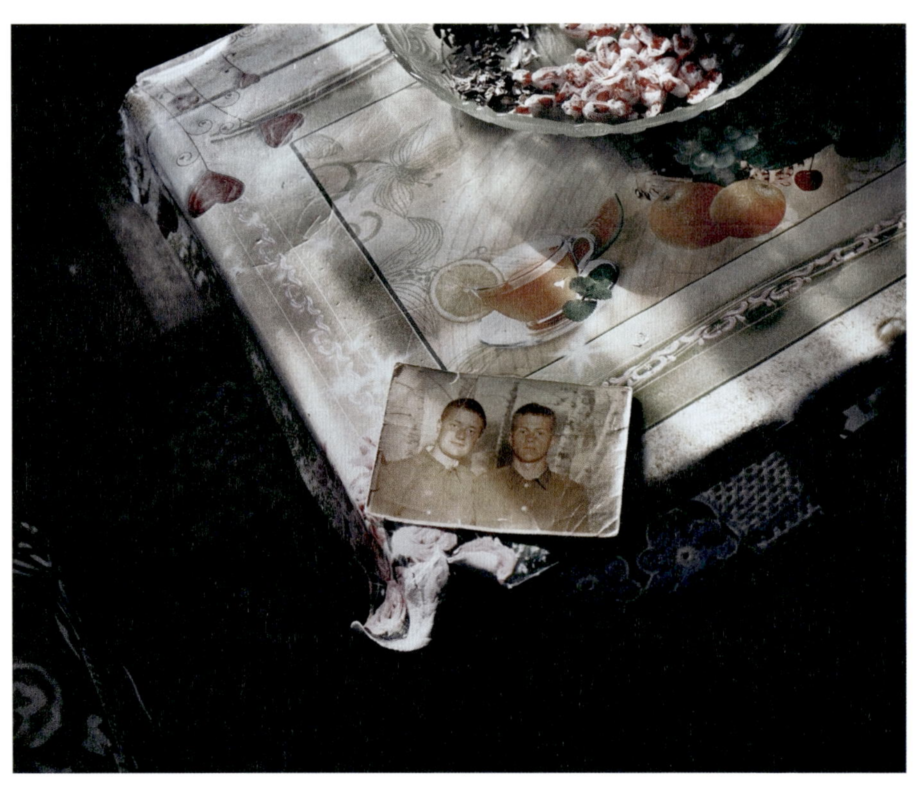

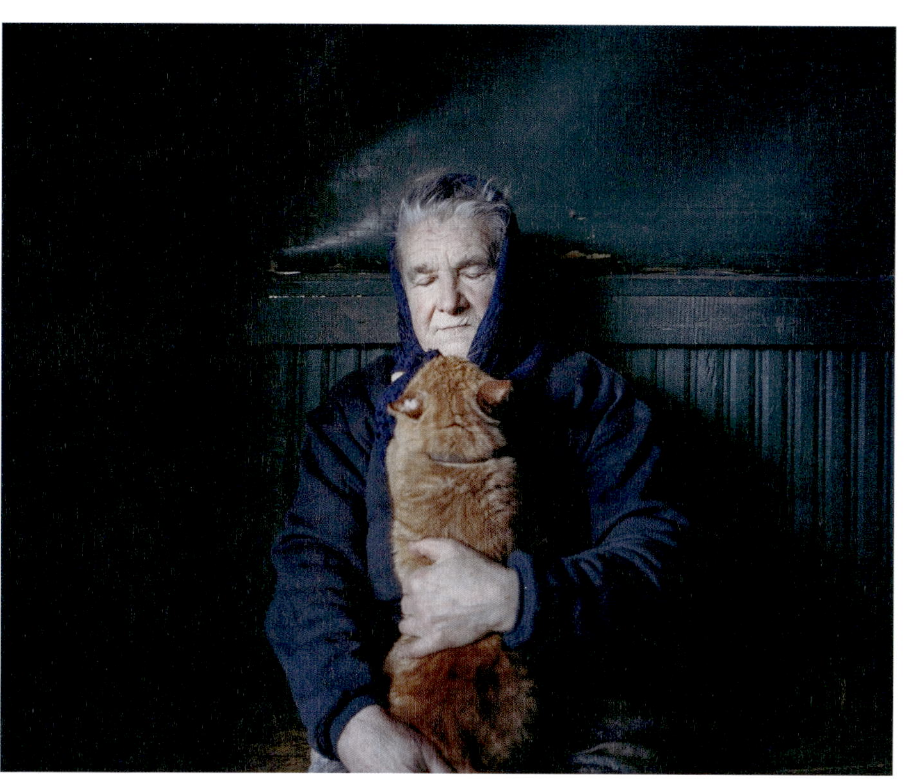

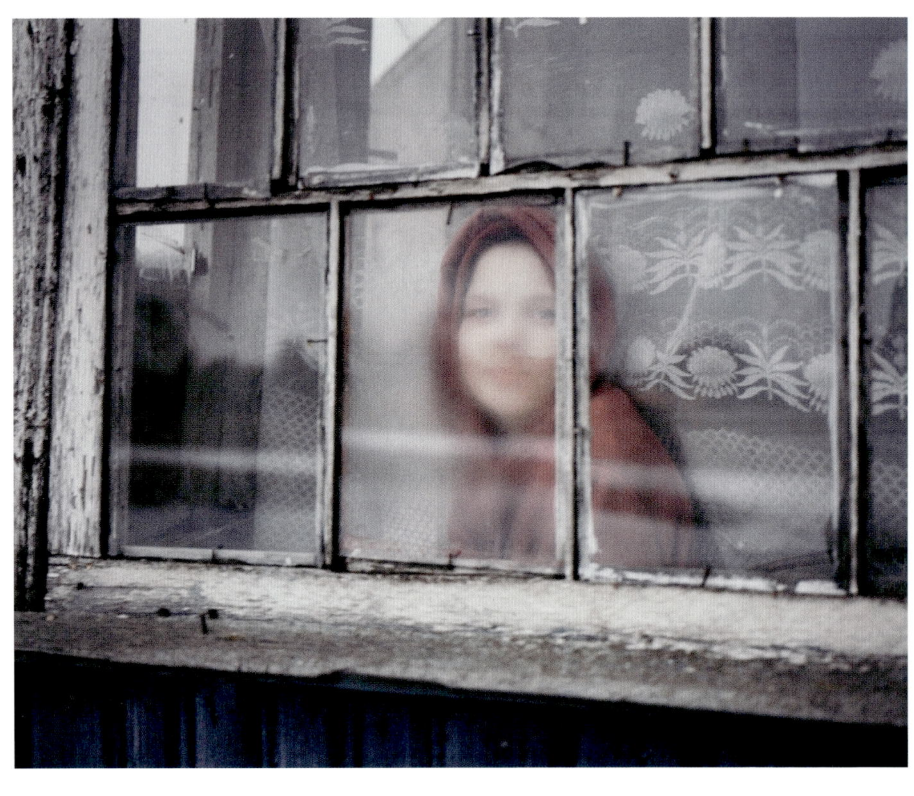

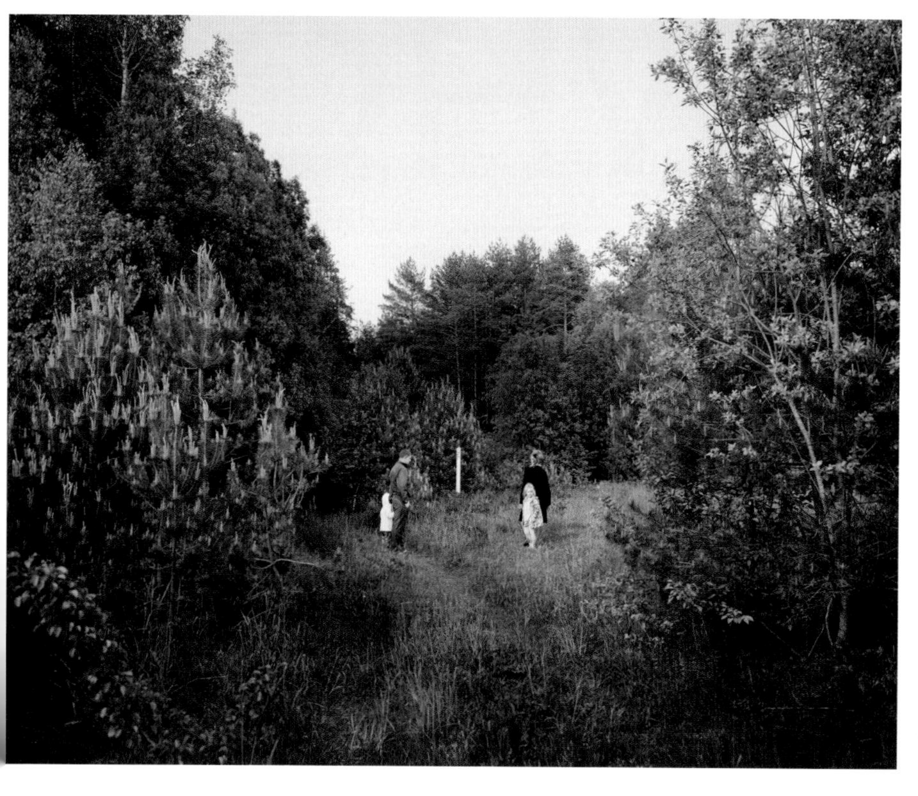

JAN BORRECK

22

WHO

YOU?

Dwelling over what could have been has never led to change. Jan was diagnosed with Alopecia Areata (round patches of hair loss) at age 6. Much of his time growing up focused on how the external world perceived him. In his adolescence, he was discharged from military service for not having hair, promoting the question of what he could have become if he had hair. To reflect on that, his series of self-portraits show men that could have been him.

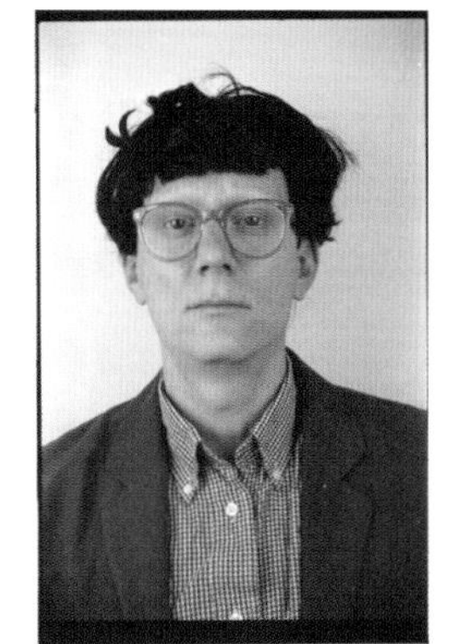

AM

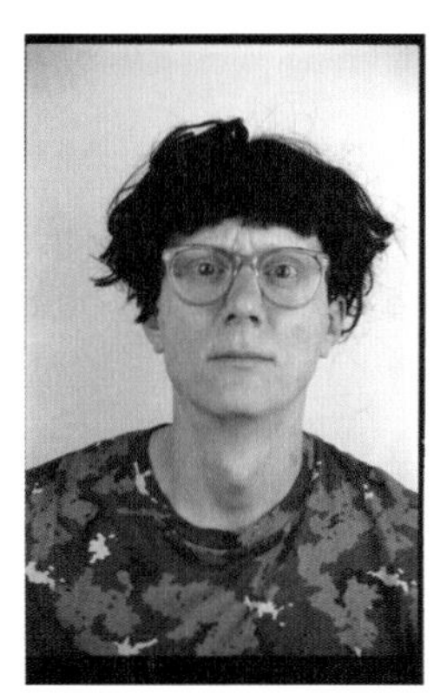

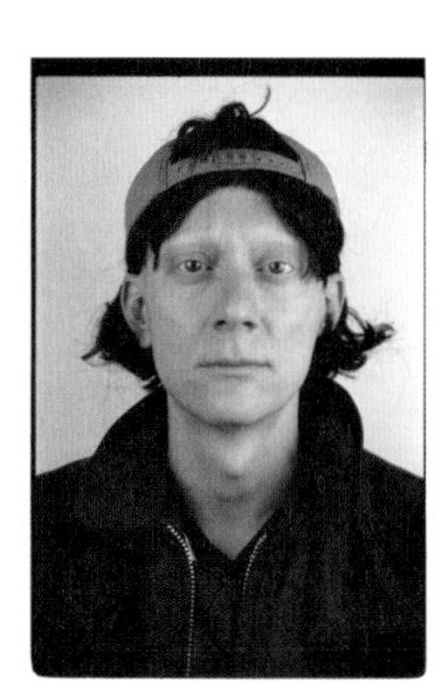

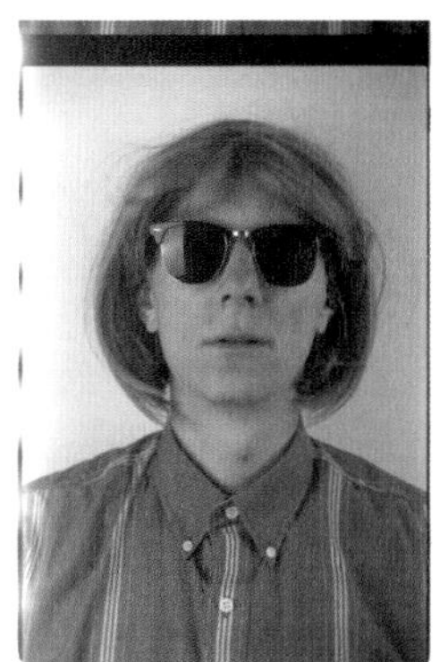

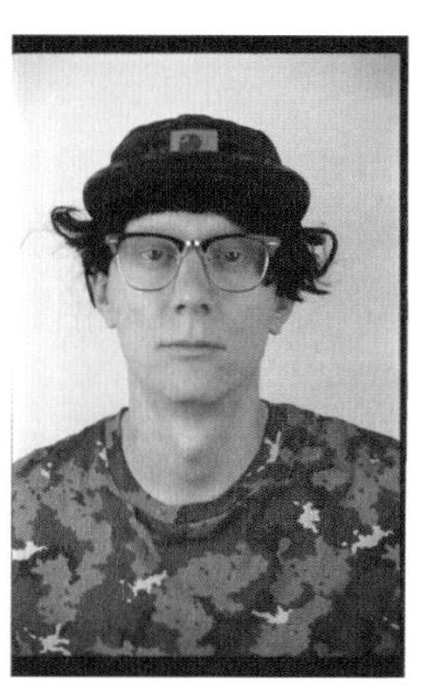

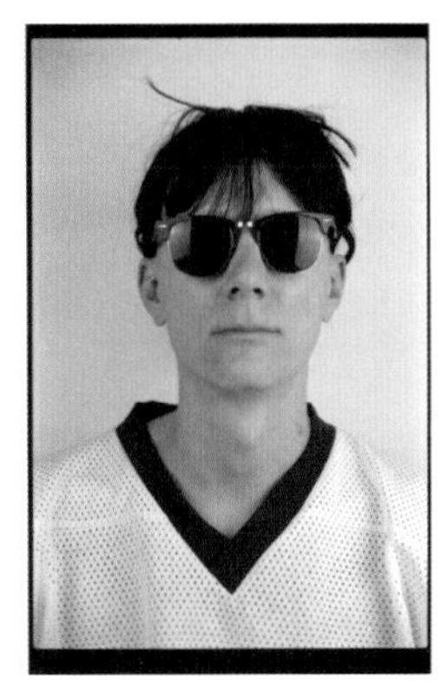
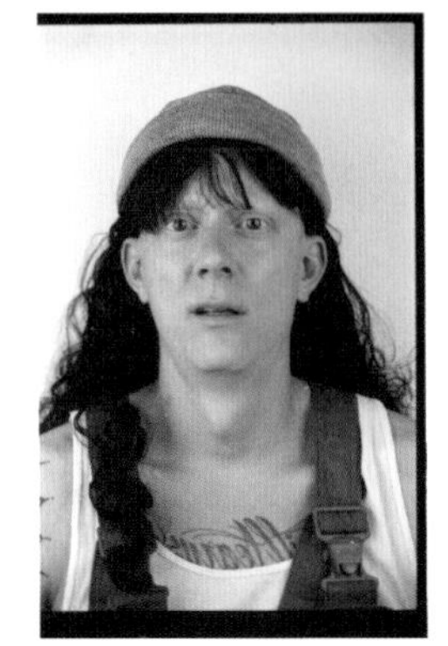
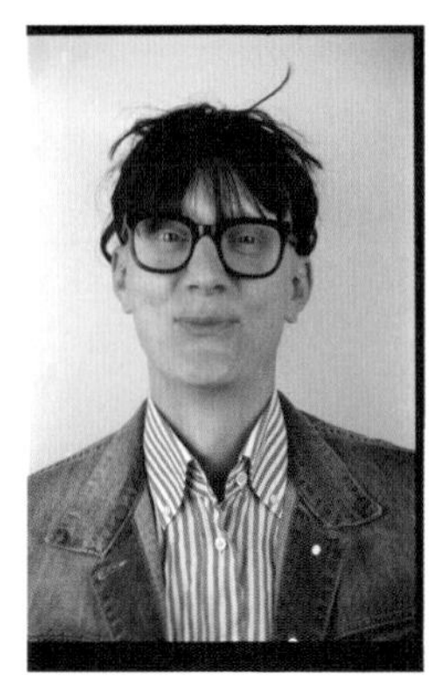
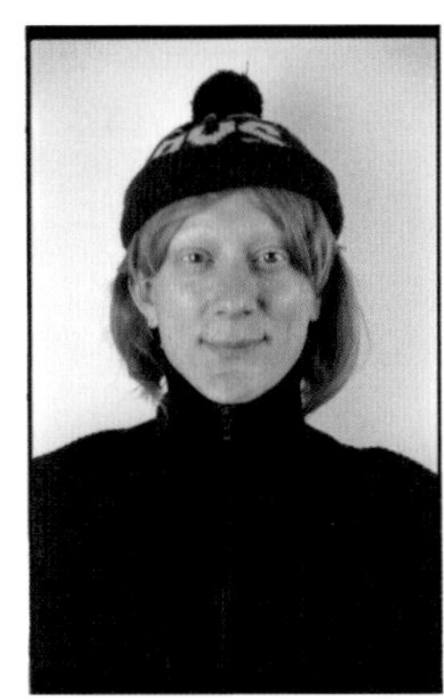
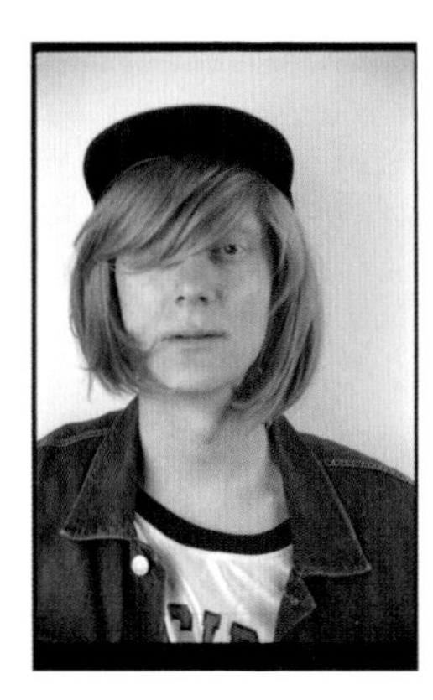

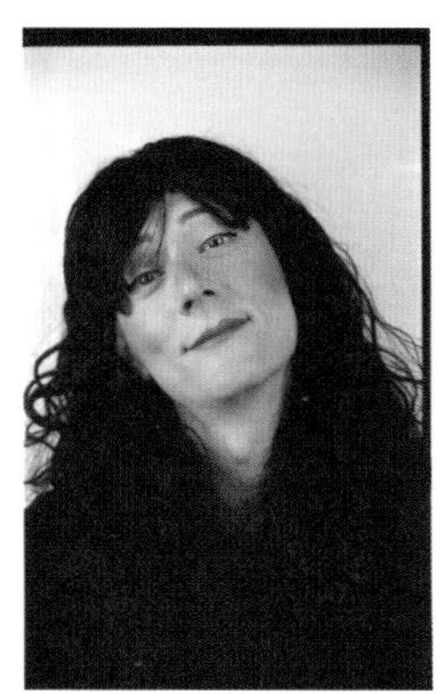

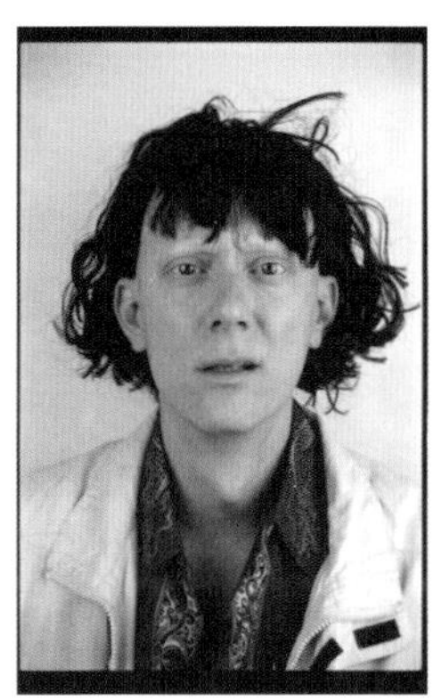

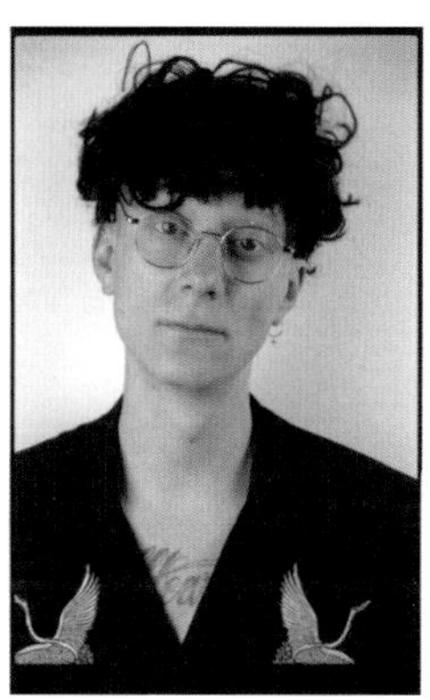

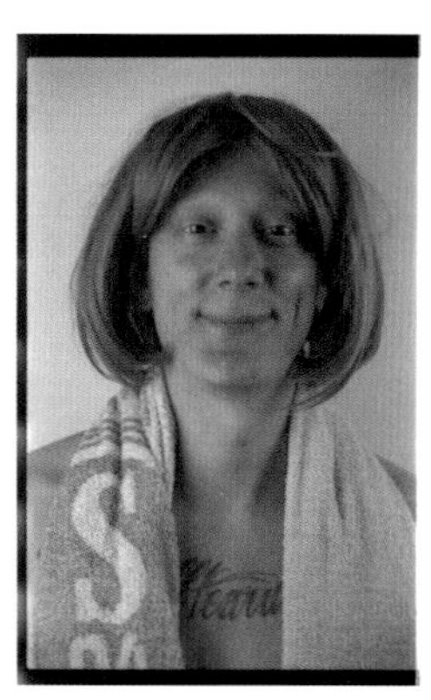

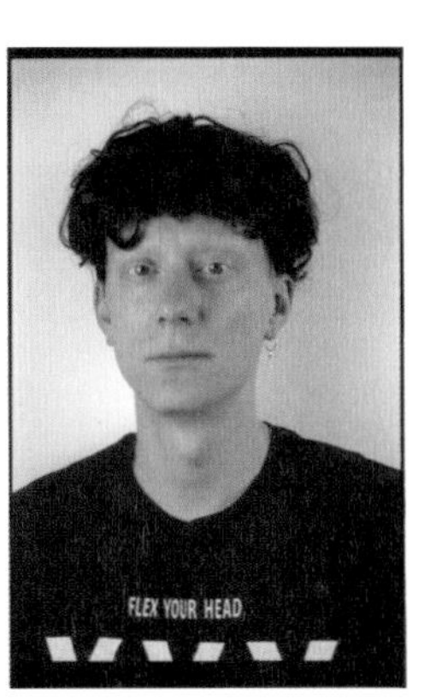
FLEX YOUR HEAD

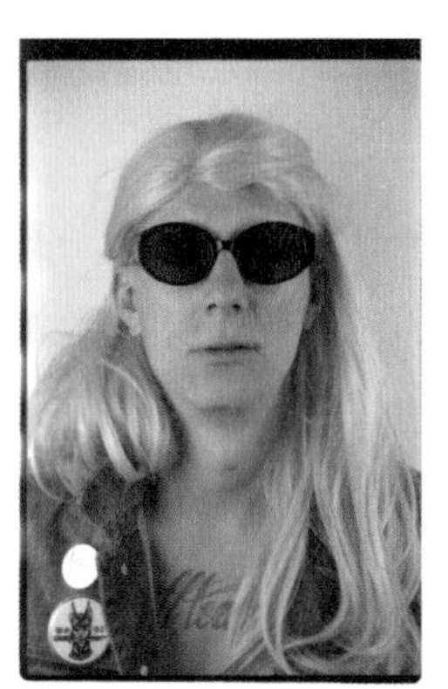

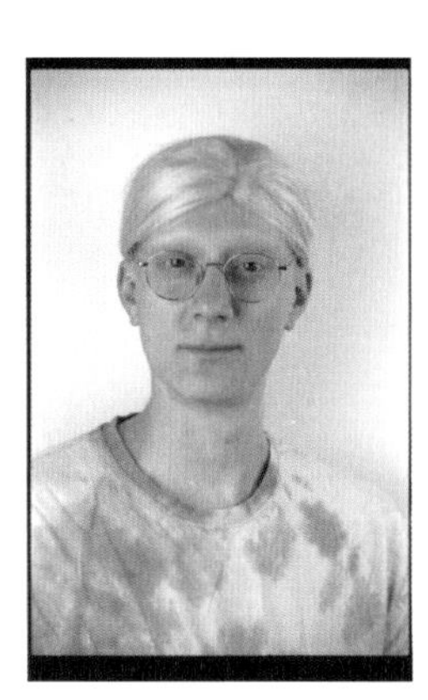

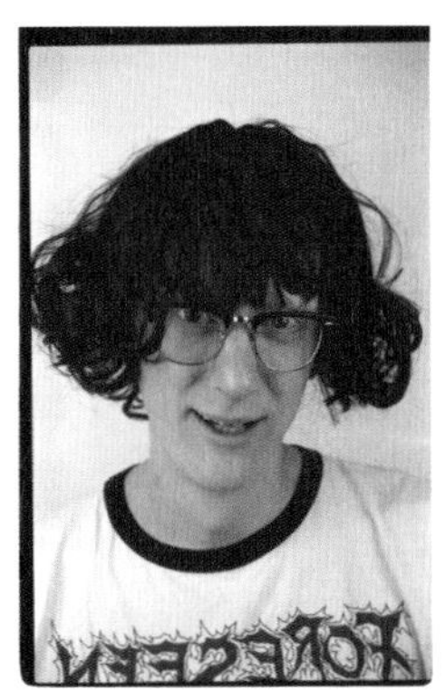

KATJA ABFALG

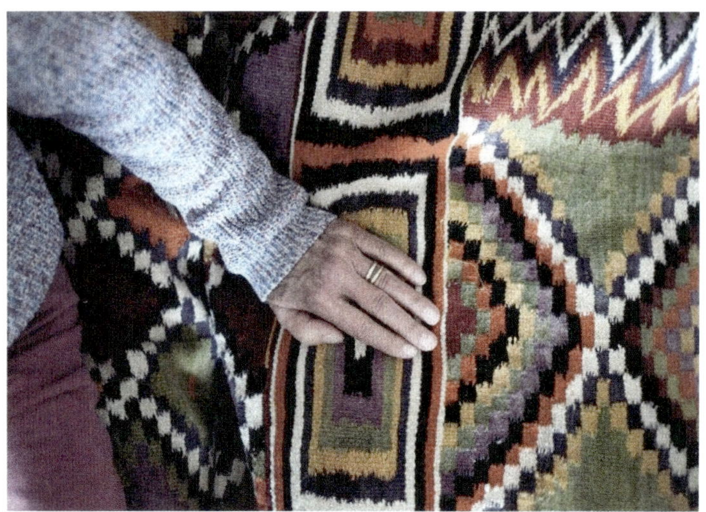

23

Diary

AT

Katja's grandmother suffers from dementia and was unable to move into a nursing home due to the pandemic. Luckily, she got to stay home. Katja was able to stay with her during these strange times creating a diary that deals with farewell, memory and family by mixing photographs, archive material and handwritten text.

I'm spending my time
during the Corona crisis
with my grandmother.
I came to her place
before Corona escalated
and now it seems like
I'm going to stay with
her until the situation
calms down.

Grandma's

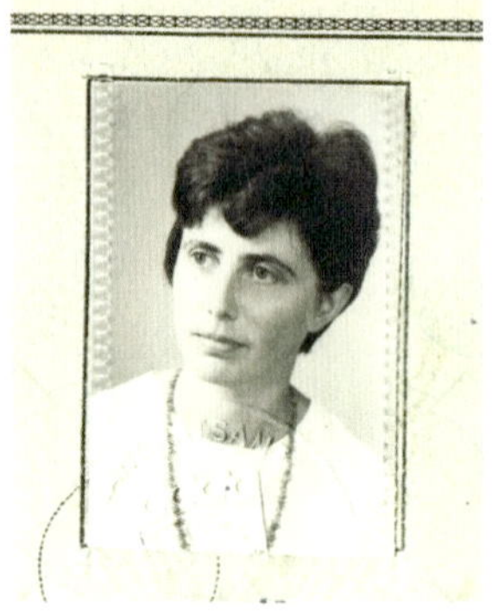

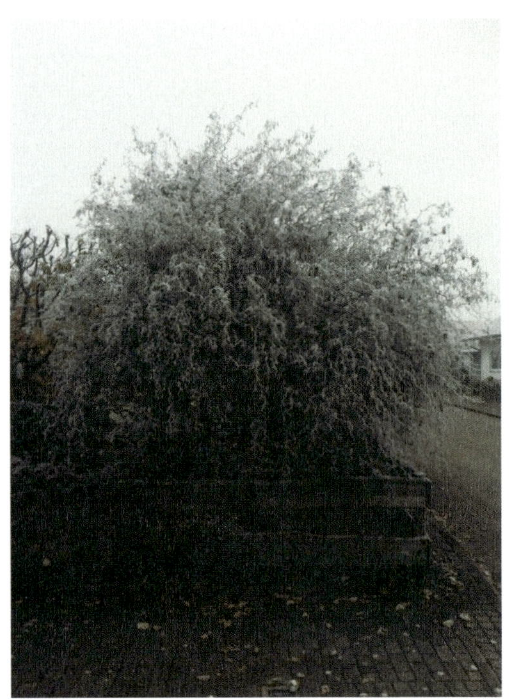

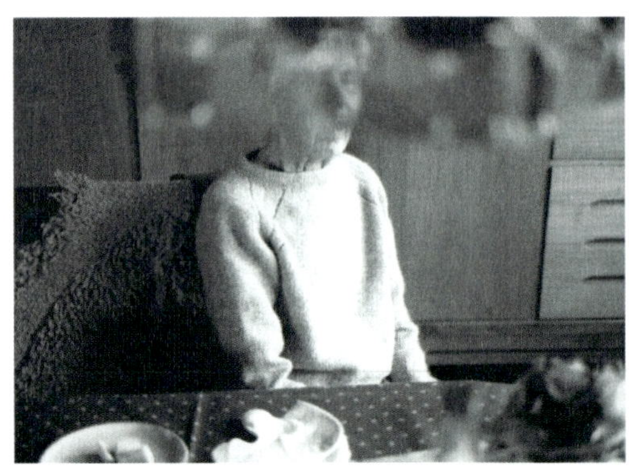

01.04.2020

Grandma in 1967, a year after my Dad was born.

25.03.2020

I talked to some family members today. They have decided not to visit Grandma for the time being in order not to bring the virus with them. Understandable and correct. But I wonder at what point they have to take the risk. I probably won't be able to stay here forever. Let's see, maybe I can. I wouldn't mind. And my calender has never been so empty, so maybe it will all work out just fine.

My grandma's dementia is progressing rapidly. I don't think she knows who I am anymore.

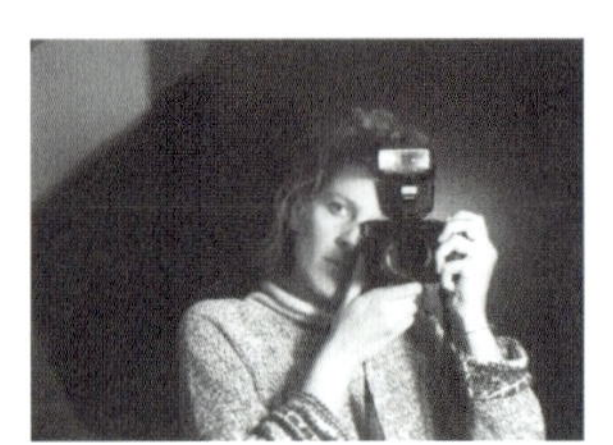

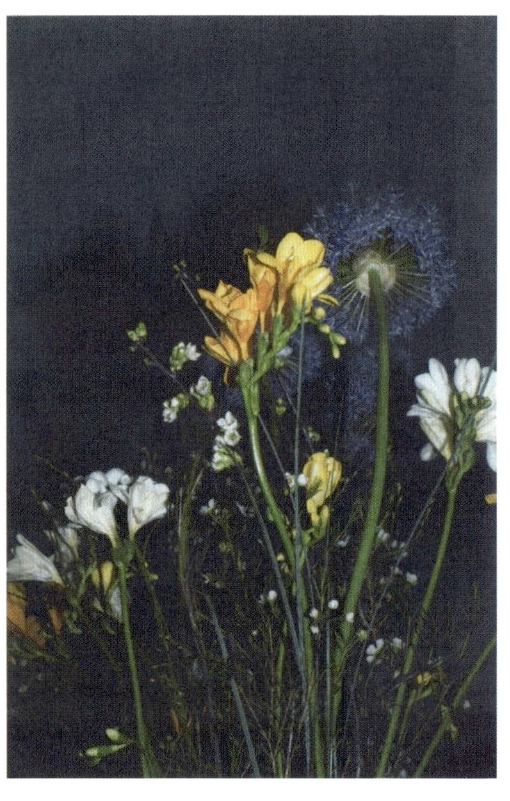

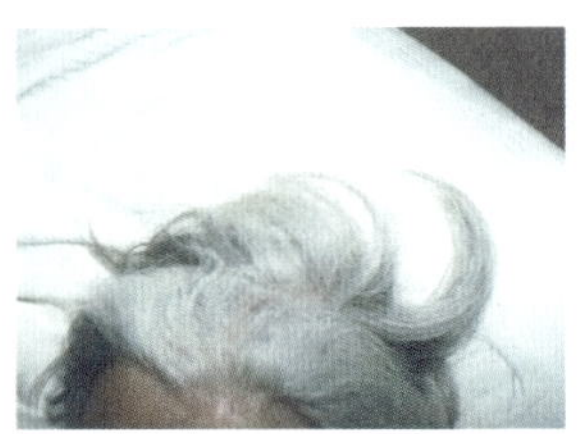

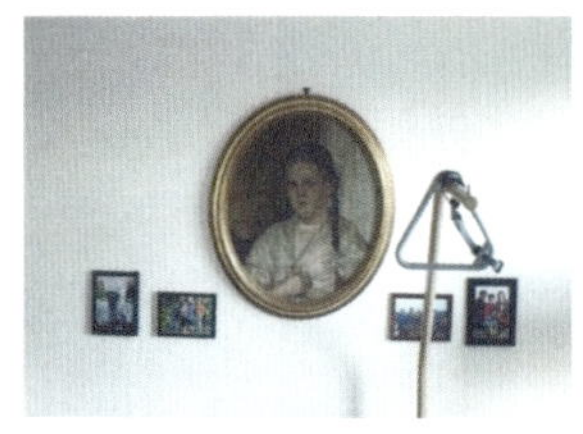

10.04.2020

One of my aunts and my two cousins left today. Tomorrow the next family members come to visit. Felt uninspired to take photographs today, the only one I took was a self portrait wearing my grandma's sweater.

19.04.2020

Grandma no longer has a feeling for day and night. She woke up at 3:45 am. and spoke for an hour. I'm awake and listening and can't go back to sleep. Her words are not clear but she seems to be talking to herself happily.

09.04.2020

Grandma is not leaving her bed anymore. It's nice that her new bed is in the living room, the place where we spend most of our day anyways.

Grandma said to my Dad: „You are a funny comb."
It's fascinating to wonder what she was actually thinking about and whether she forgot the word or the meaning. Forgetting is a strange thing.

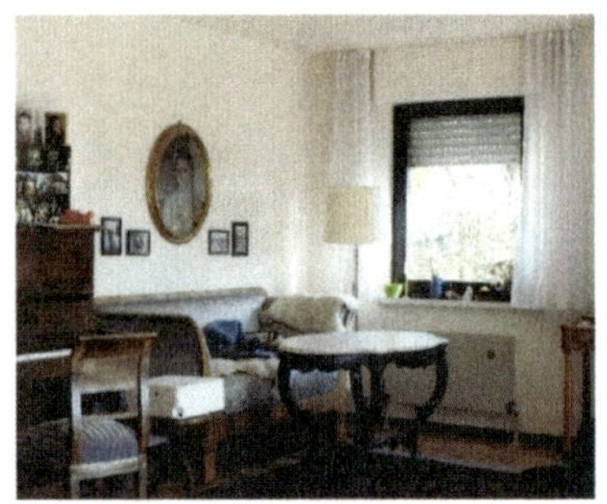
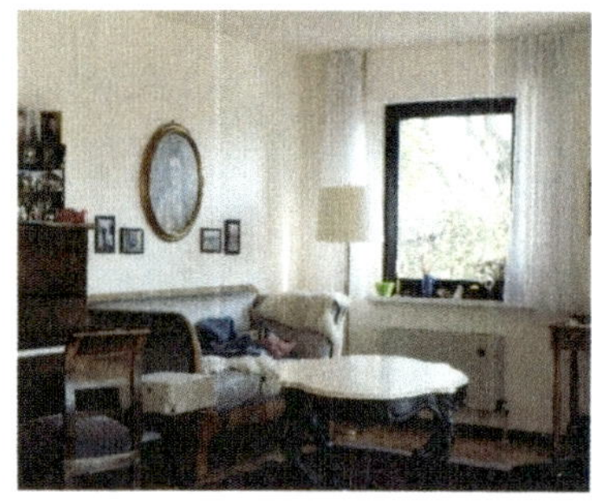
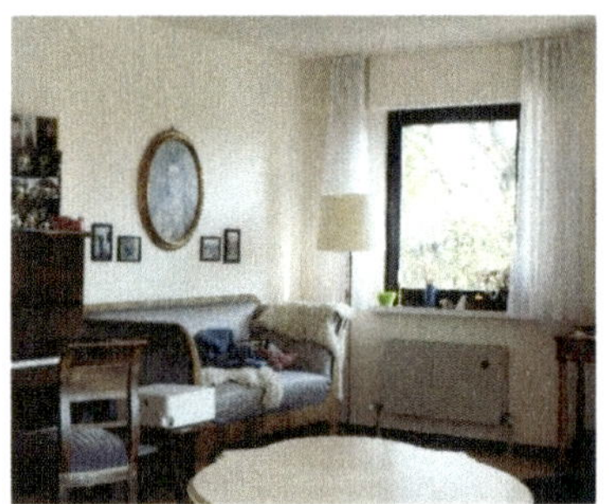
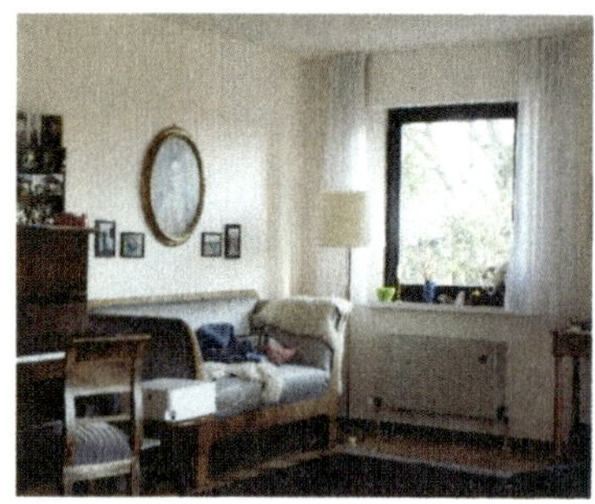
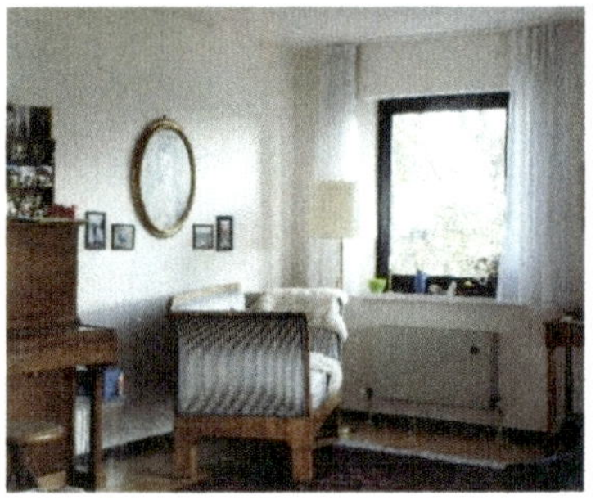
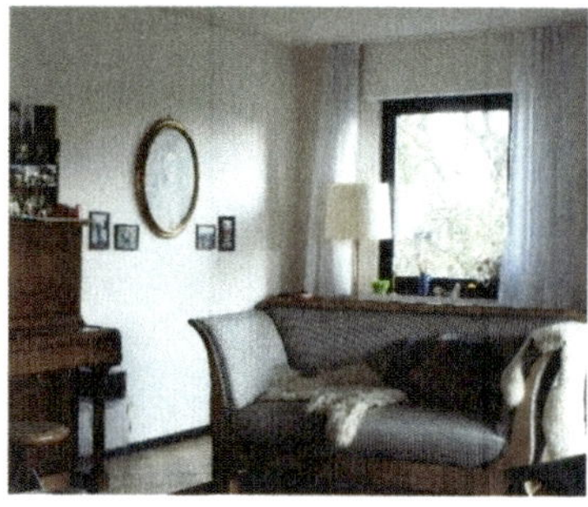
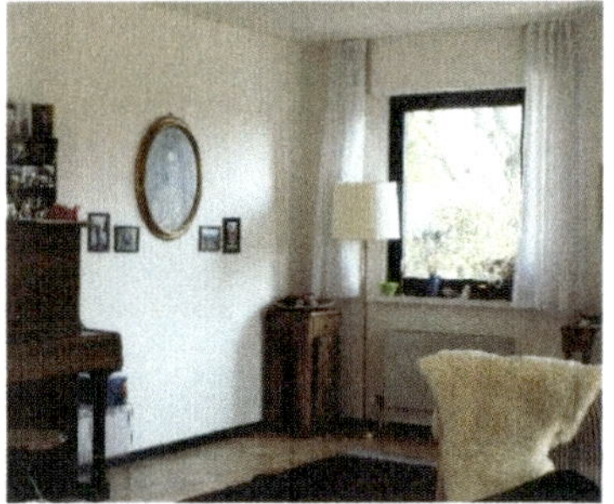
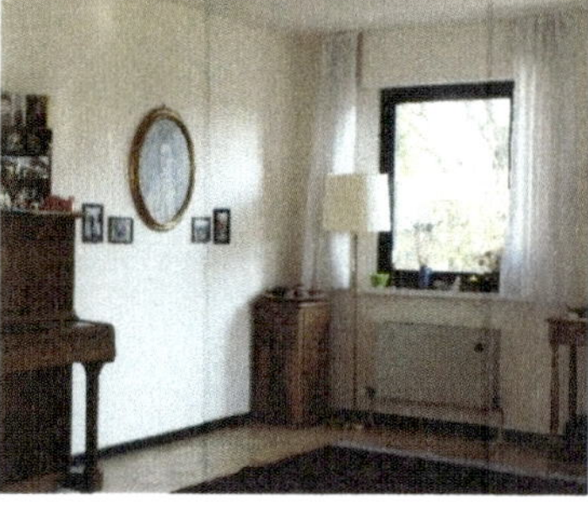

There were a few changes
today. The living room will
soon be Grandma's. On
Monday we will get a
nursing care bed.
And Grandmas kids, my
Dad and uncle and aunts,
are all coming soon. We
are ready to take the risk.

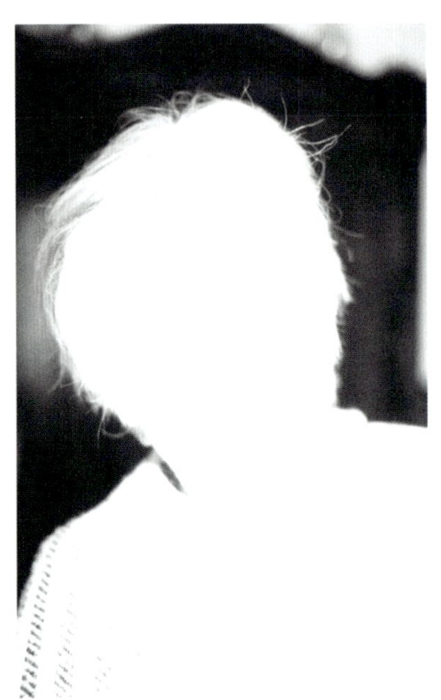

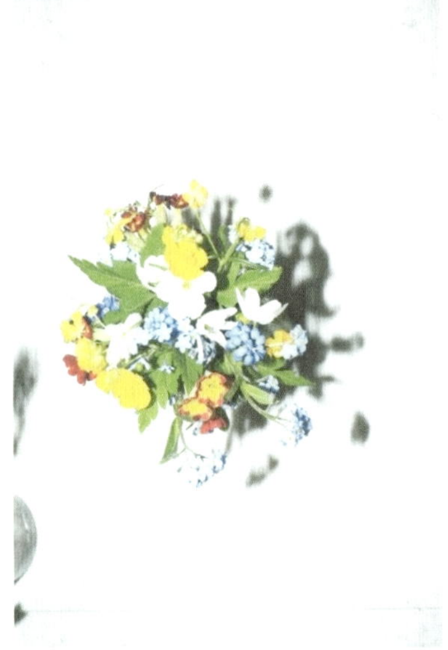

Yesterday, Grandma
said to me: „hi ghost",
after I said „hi Grandma".
Most of the time she
thinks I'm her sister.
Today I wasn't noticed
by her. Let's see who I
am in her reality tomorrow.

24.04.2020

At the beginning I thought I'd
stay with Grandma until the
situation with Corona calmed
down. It is now clear that I will
stay with her until she dies.

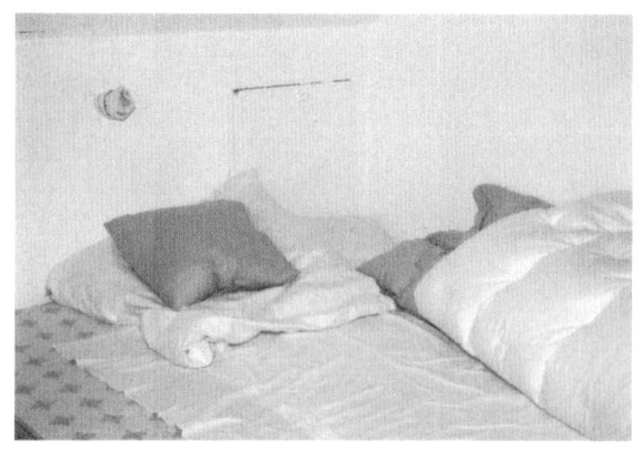

A calm day today.

FLORIAN DÜRKOPP

A field,

I meet you there

24

Florian spent four days and nights alone in the wilderness, without food and shelter — a time that is the core of a vision quest, a western adoption of a rite of passage. The seminar is packed with rituals, singing, dancing and sharing of innermost thoughts with the group in a spiritual atmosphere. While the young participants are seeking answers to the big questions of life, an esoteric philosophy is promoted.

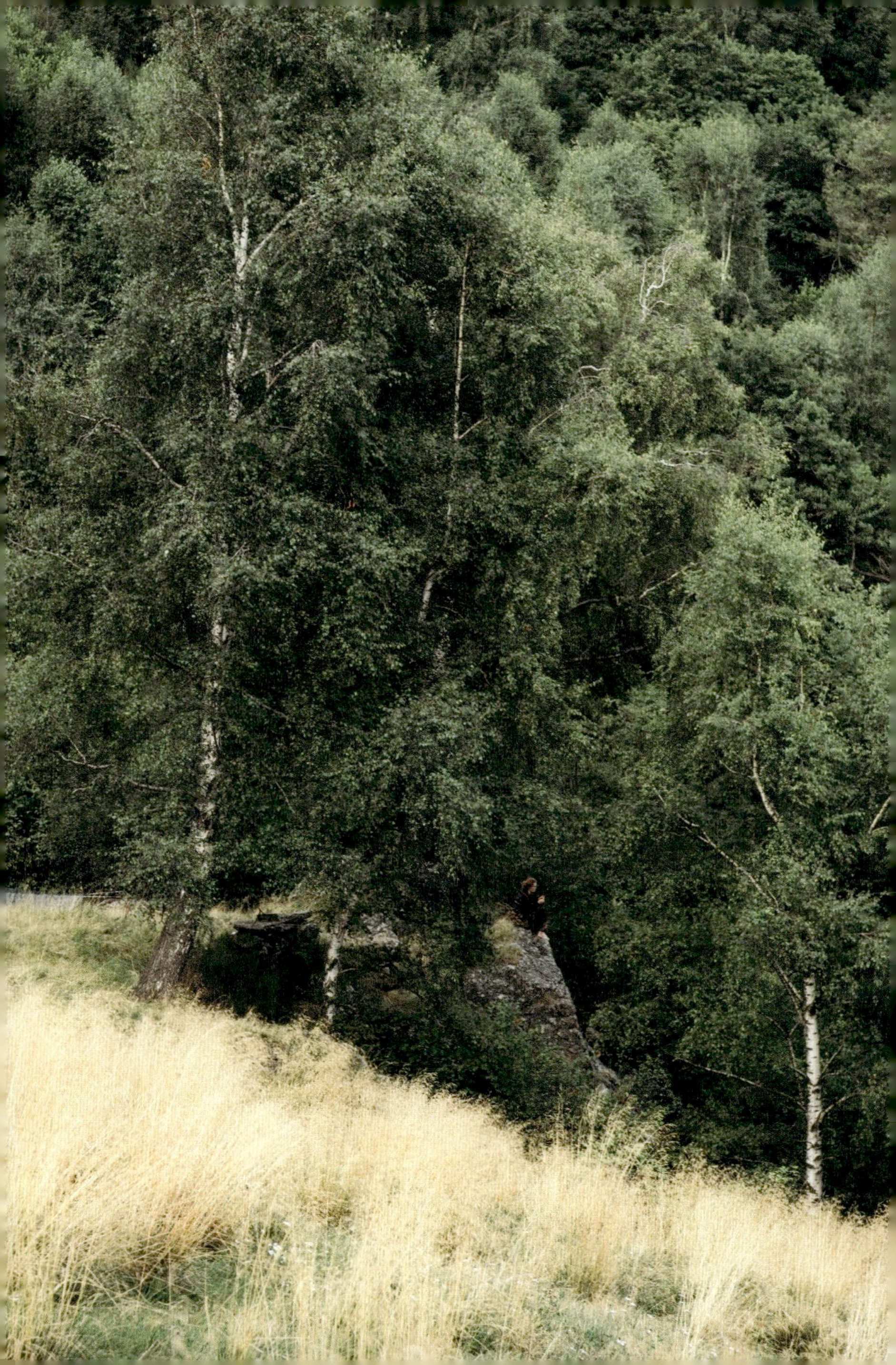

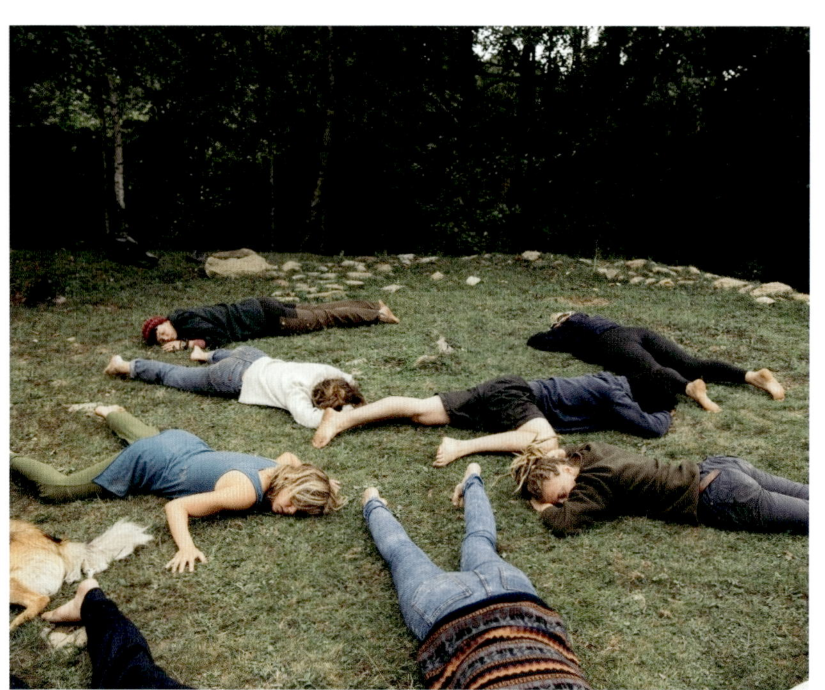

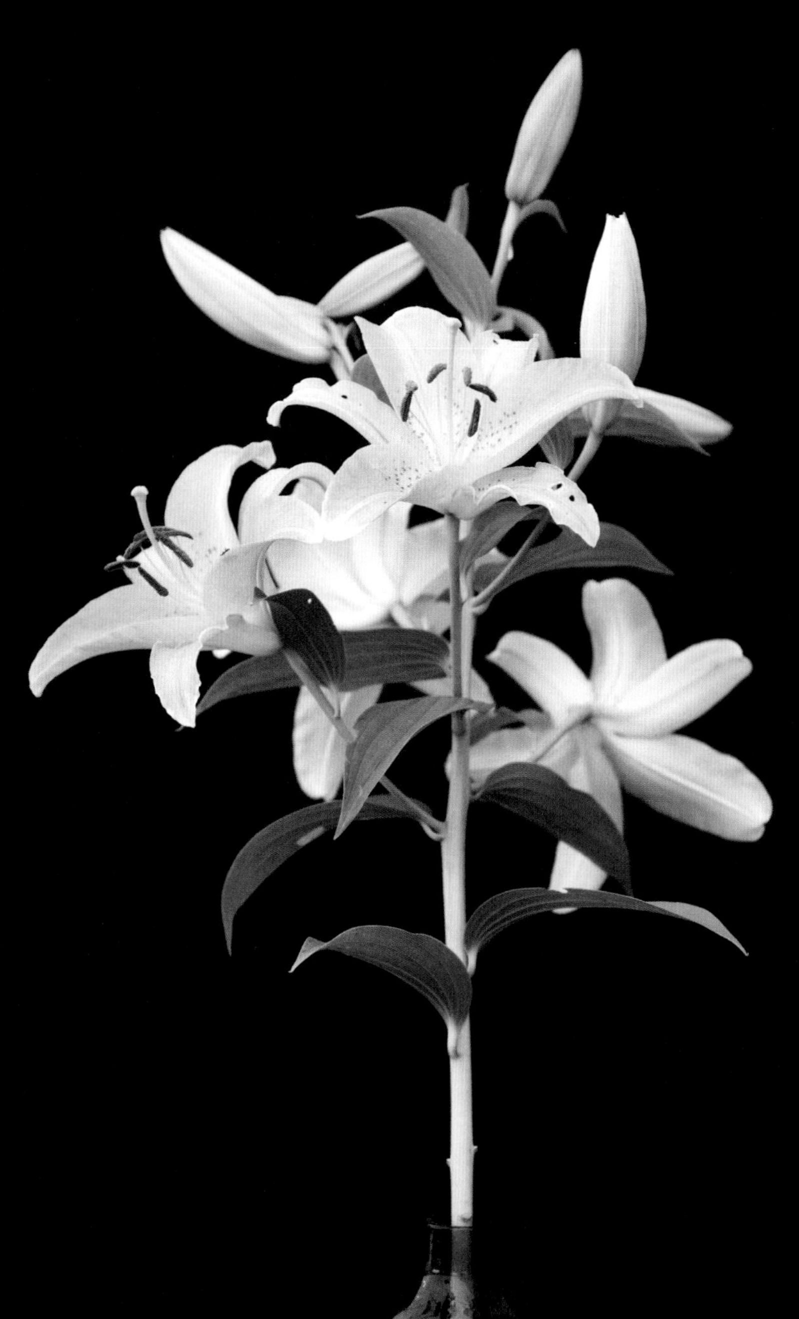

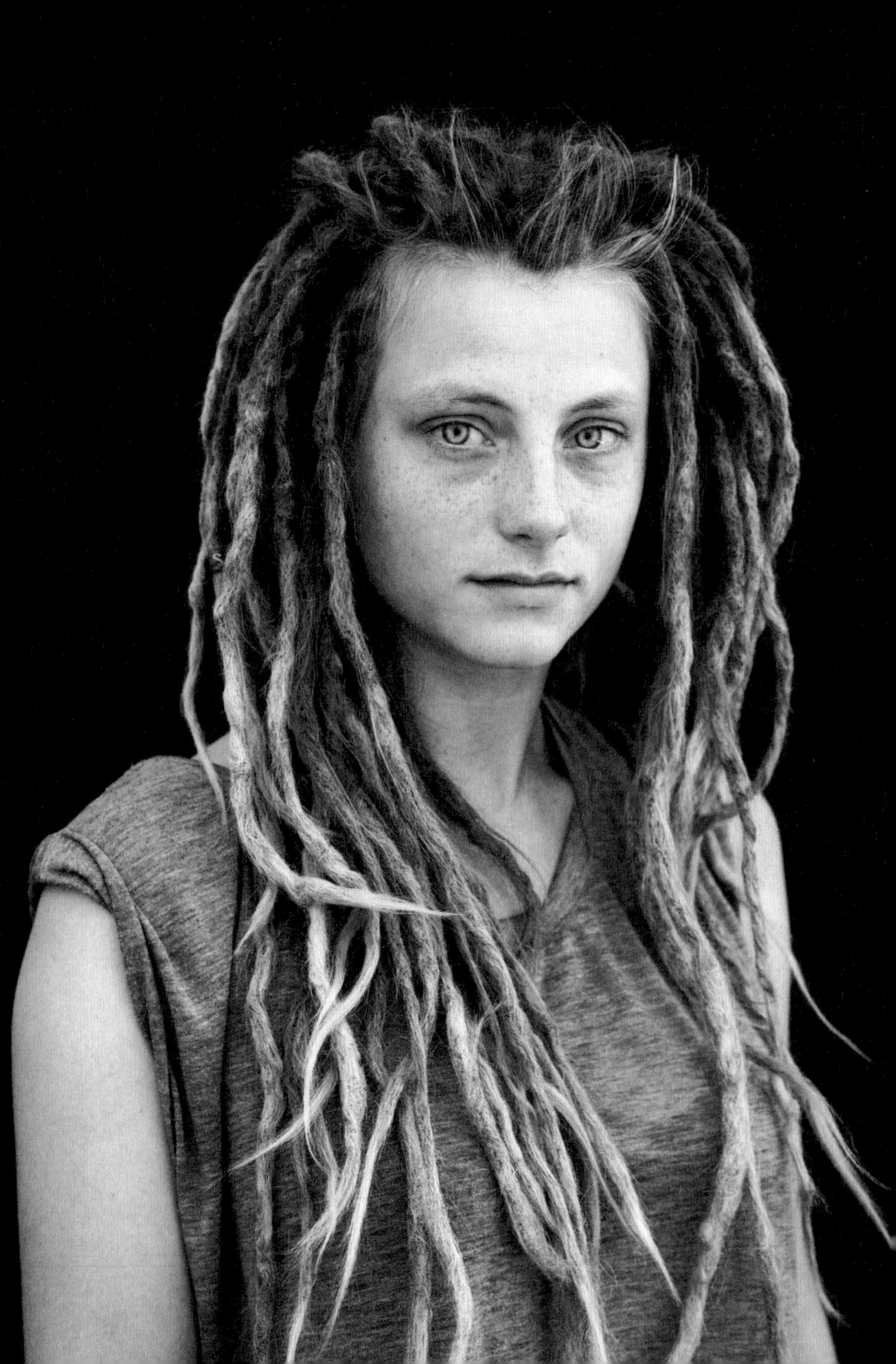

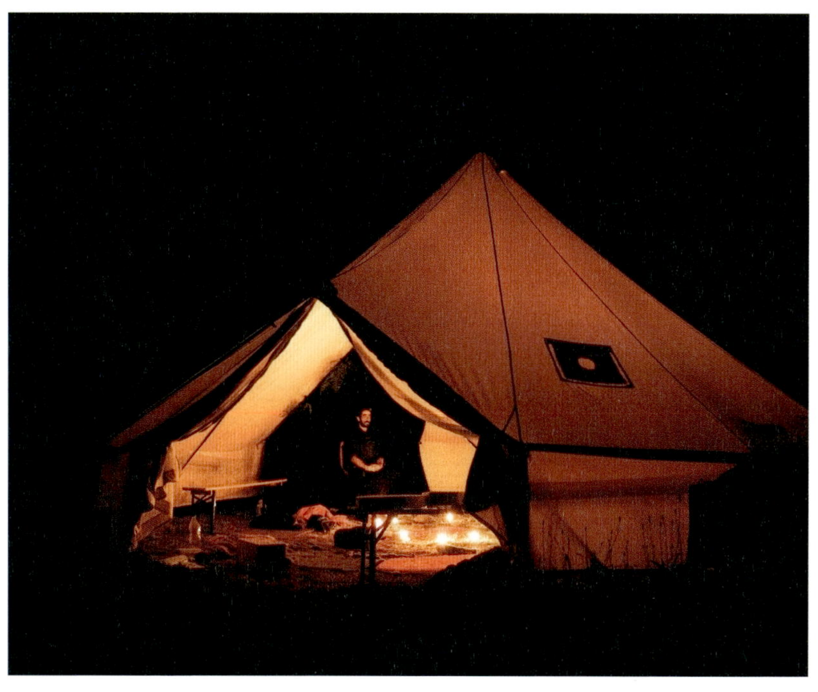

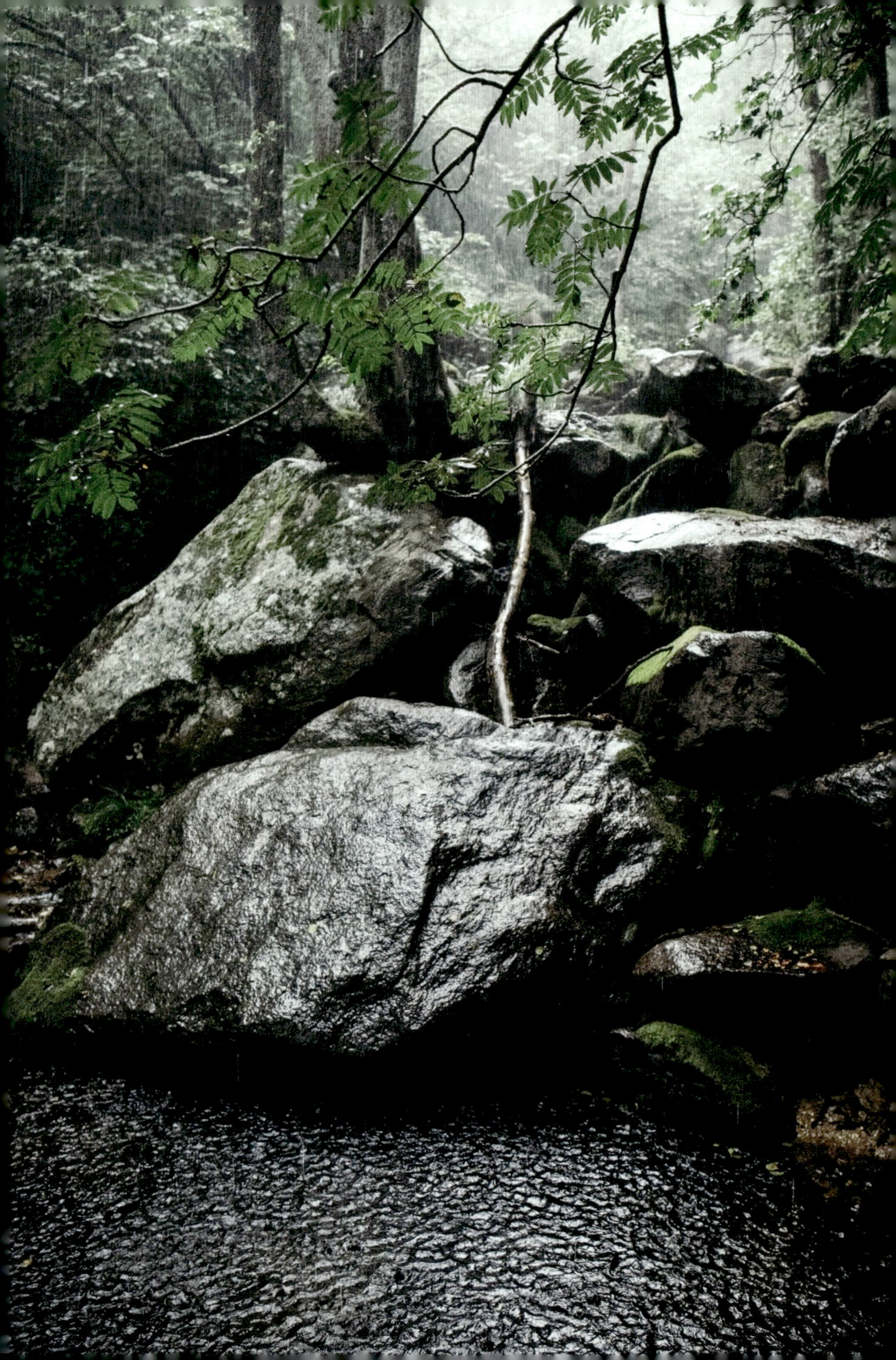

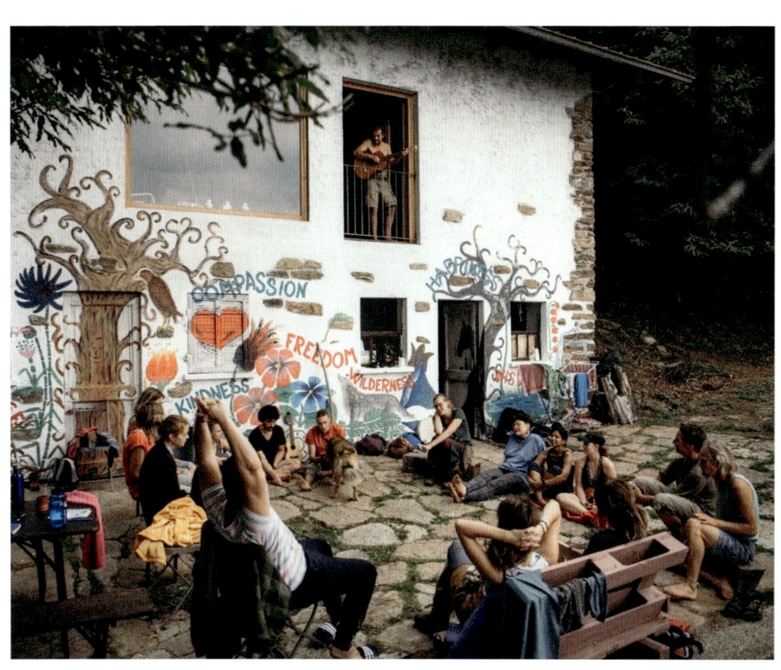
COMPASSION
FREEDOM
KINDNESS
WILDERNESS

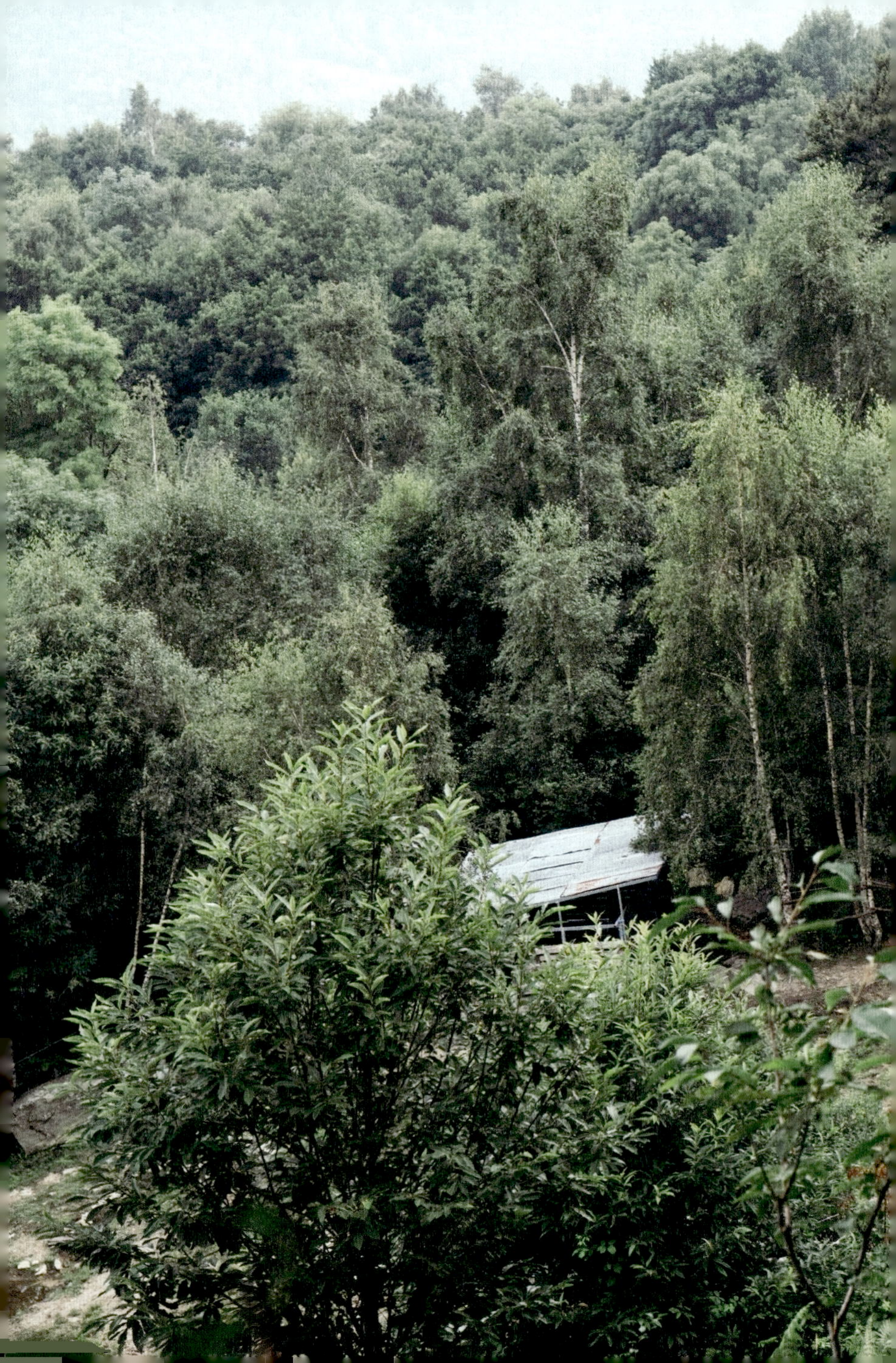

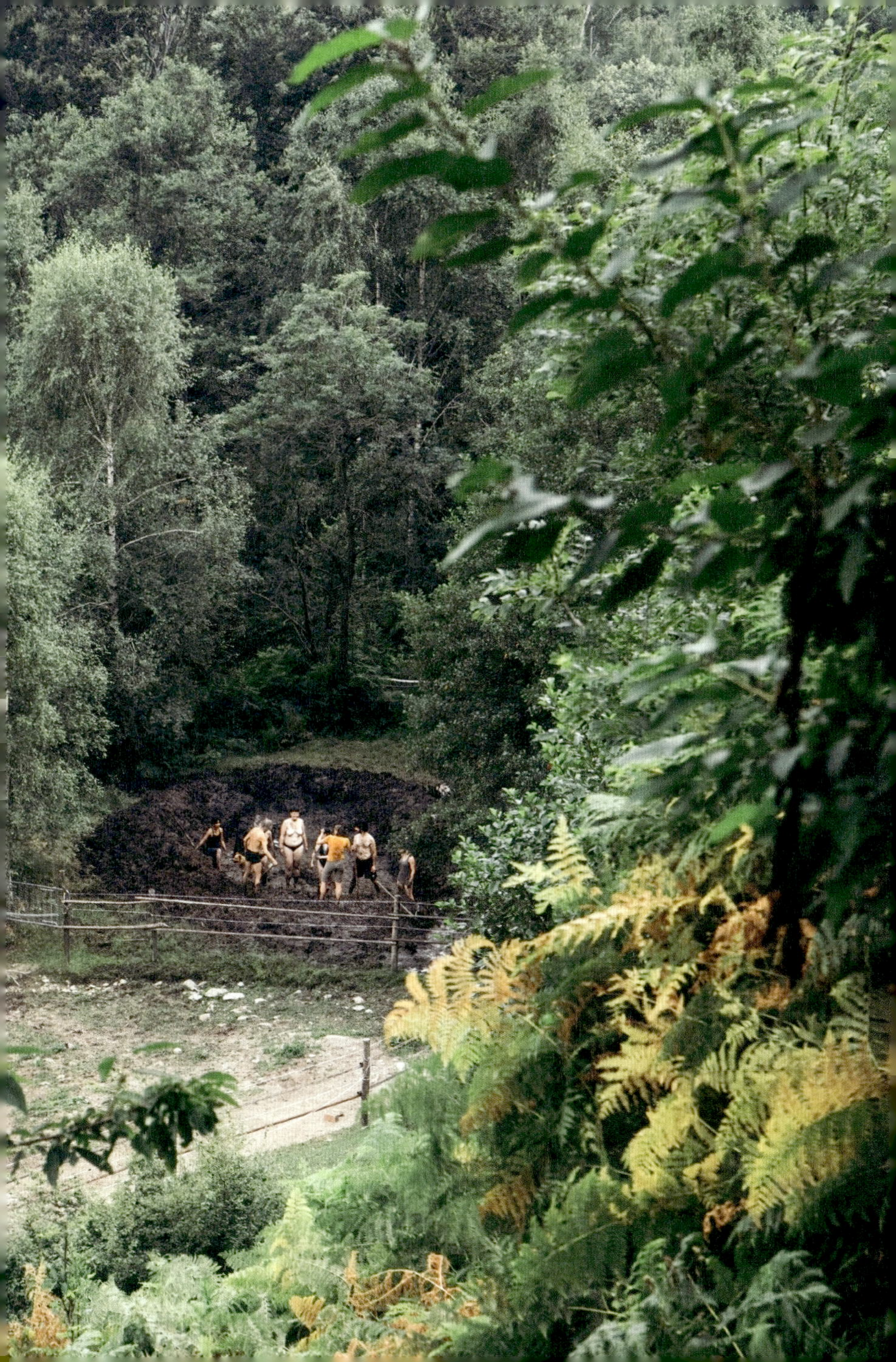

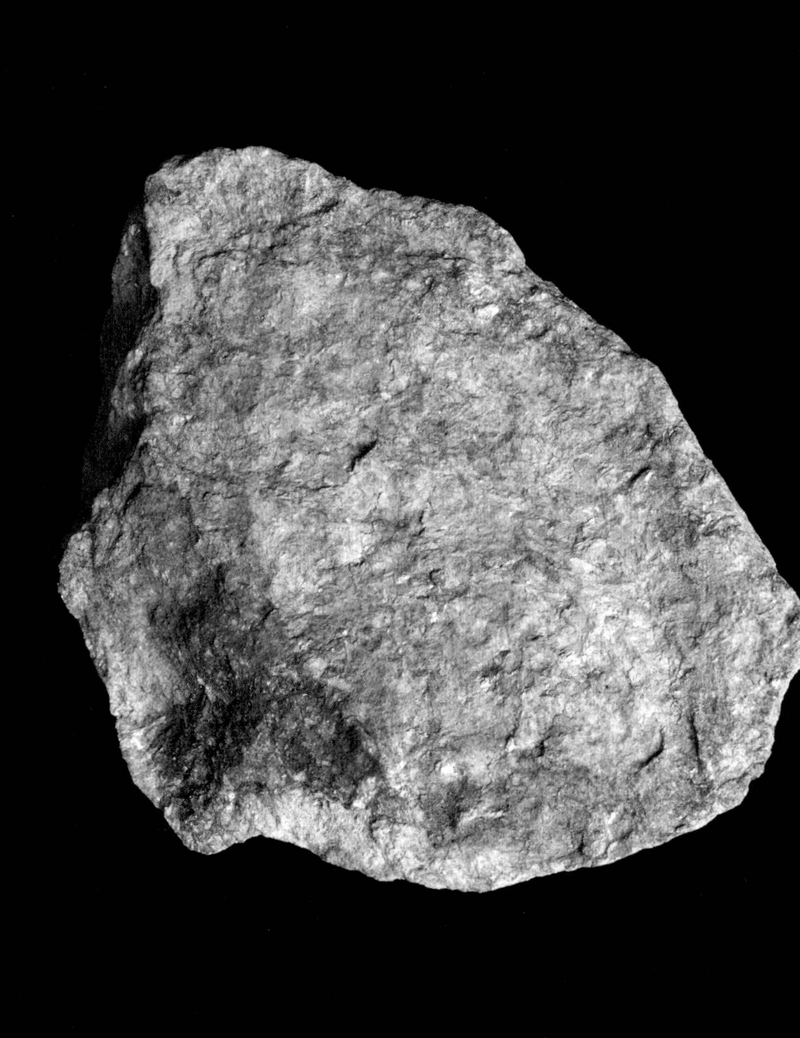

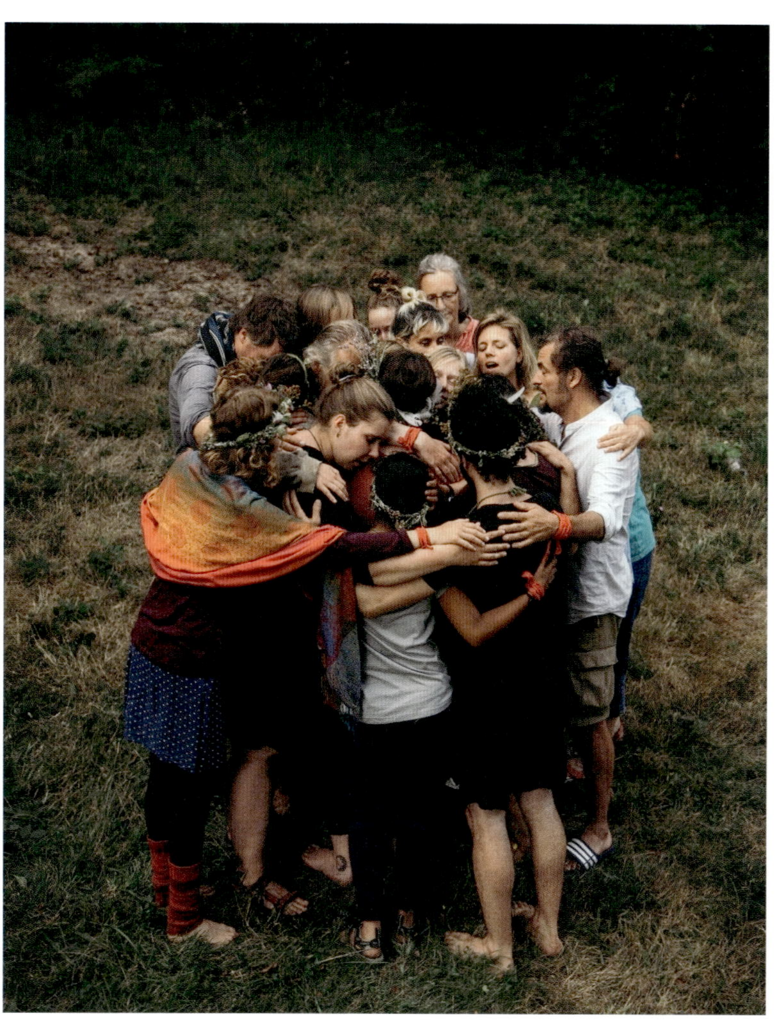

I HAD PLEASURE A GLIMPSE

In the summer of 2019, Chrystyna was diagnosed with Borderline Personality Disorder, Depression, and Anxiety. Since then, she documented her daily life, coping with her mental illness and using photography as a form of self-expression and therapy.

THE
TO CATCH
OF BEAUTY

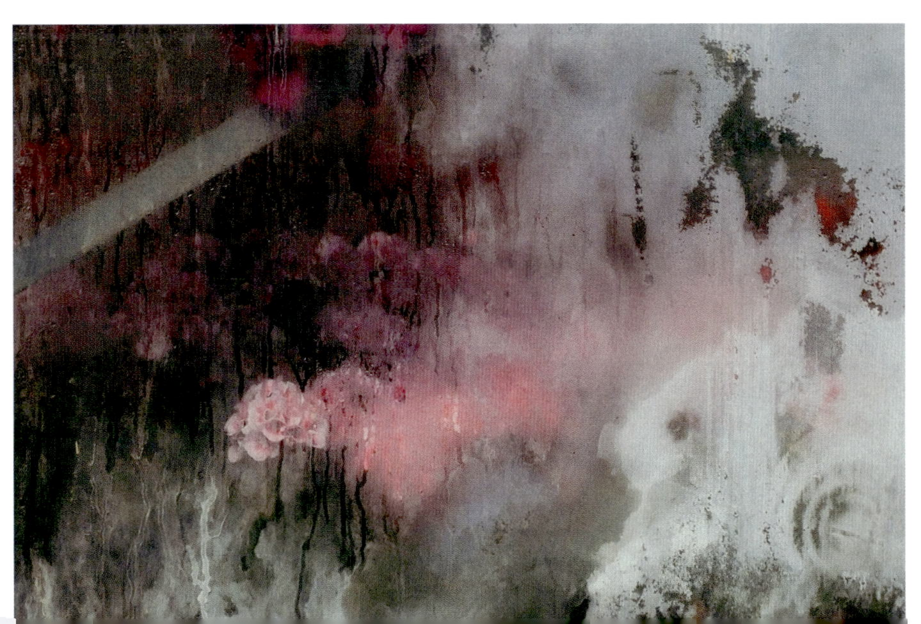

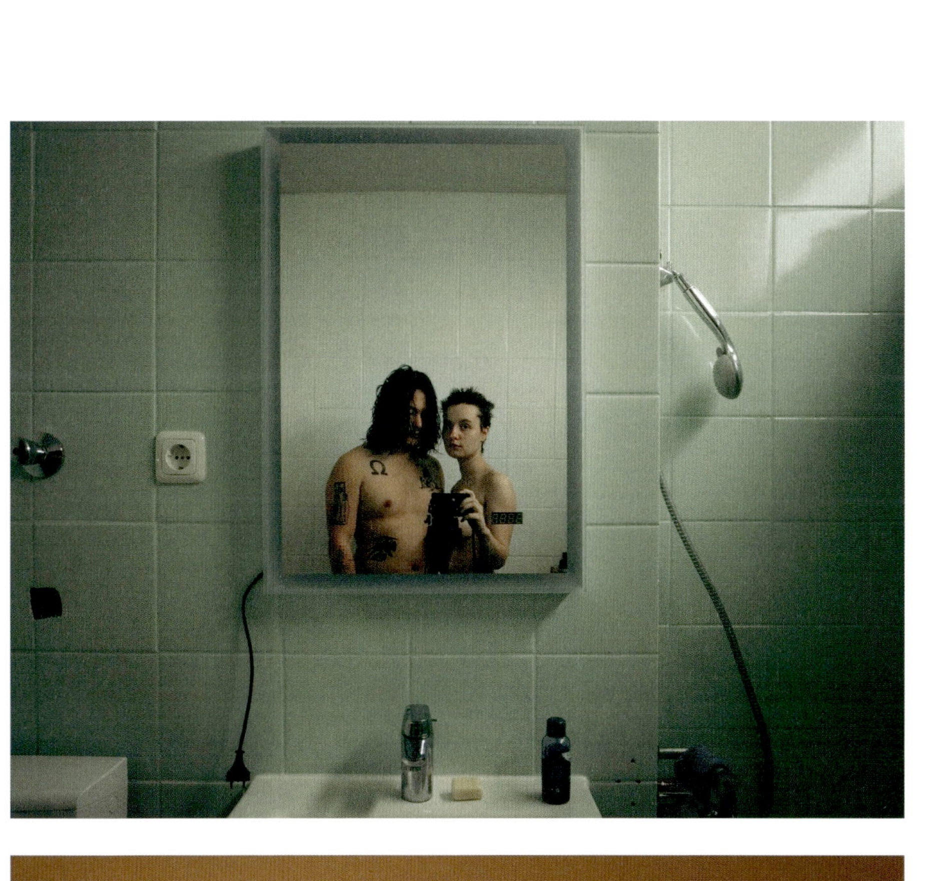

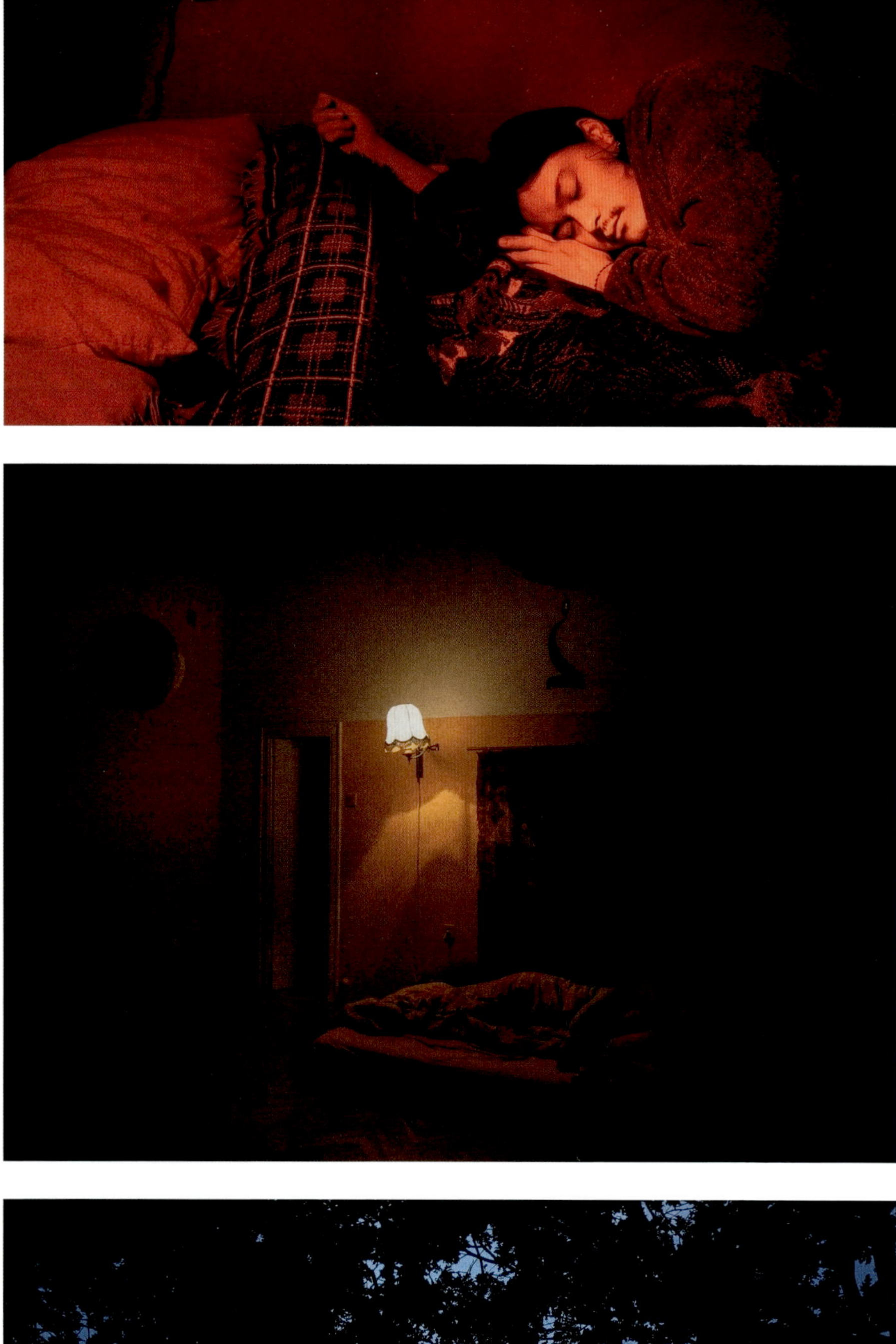

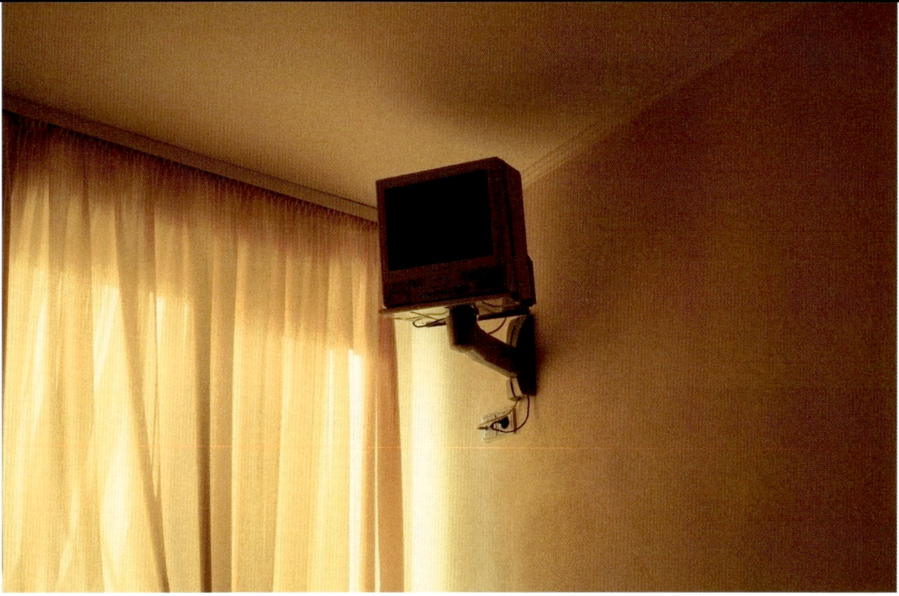

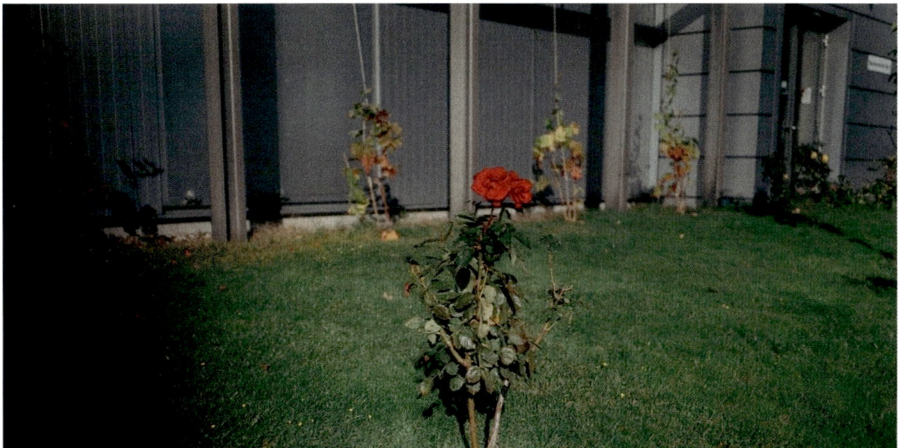

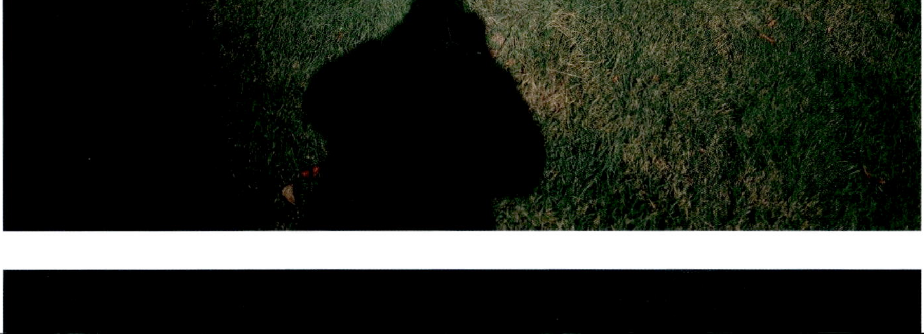

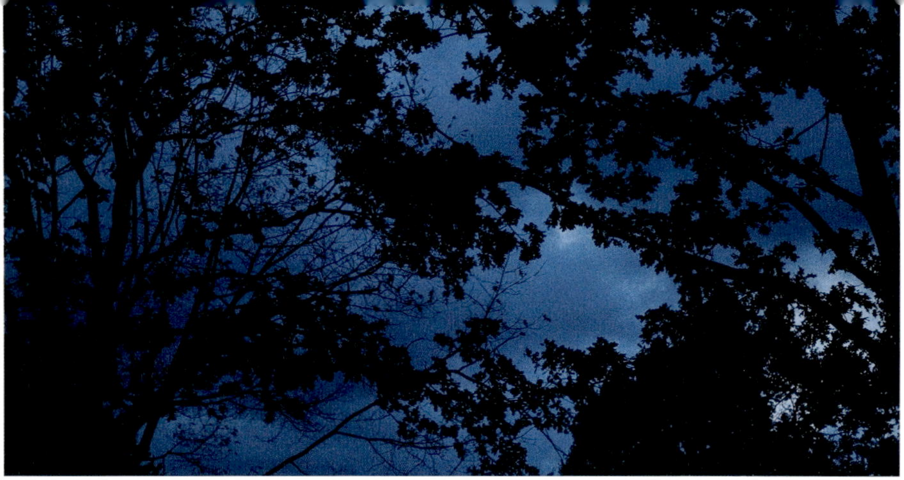

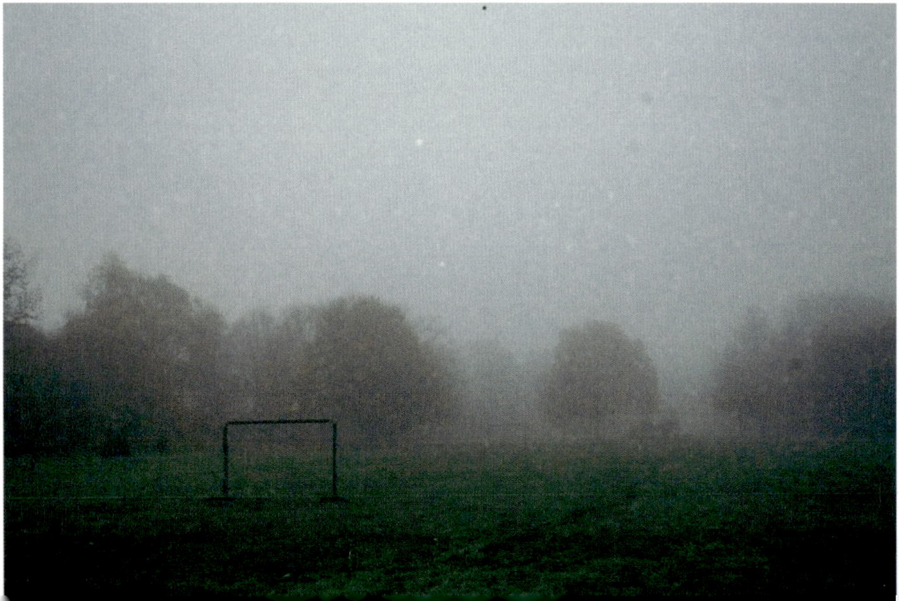

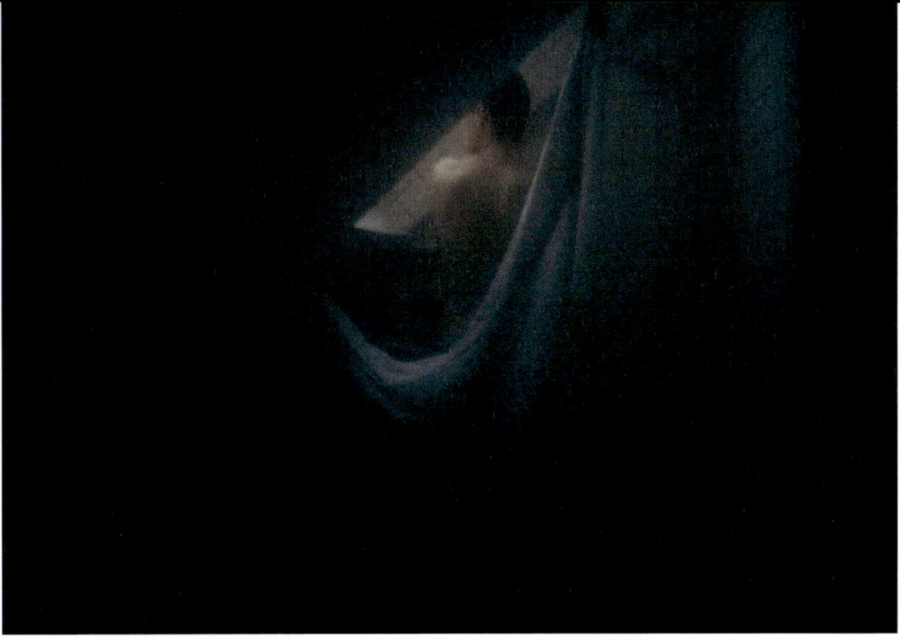

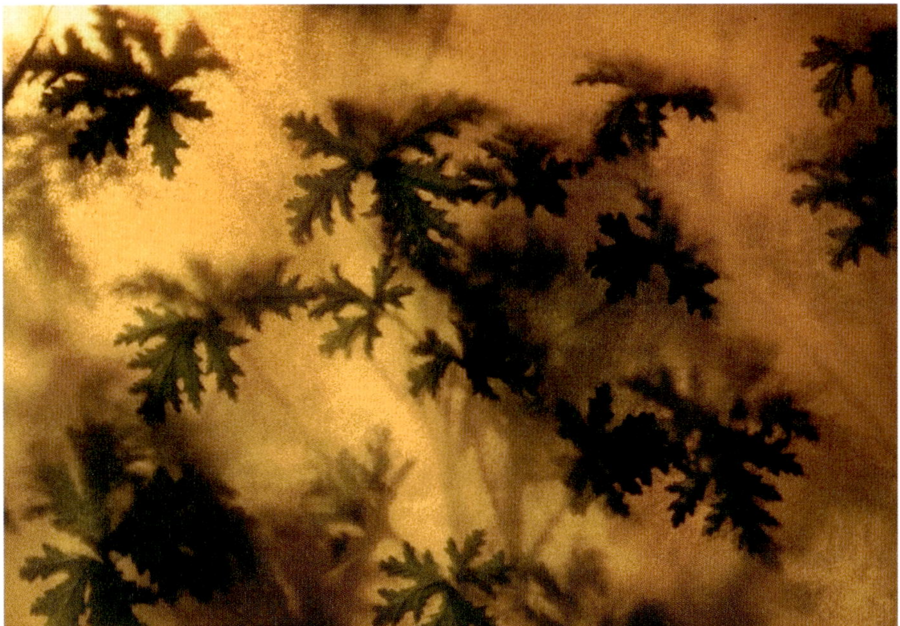

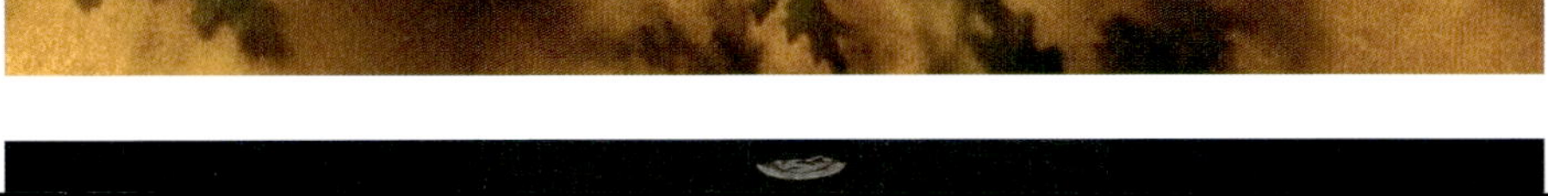

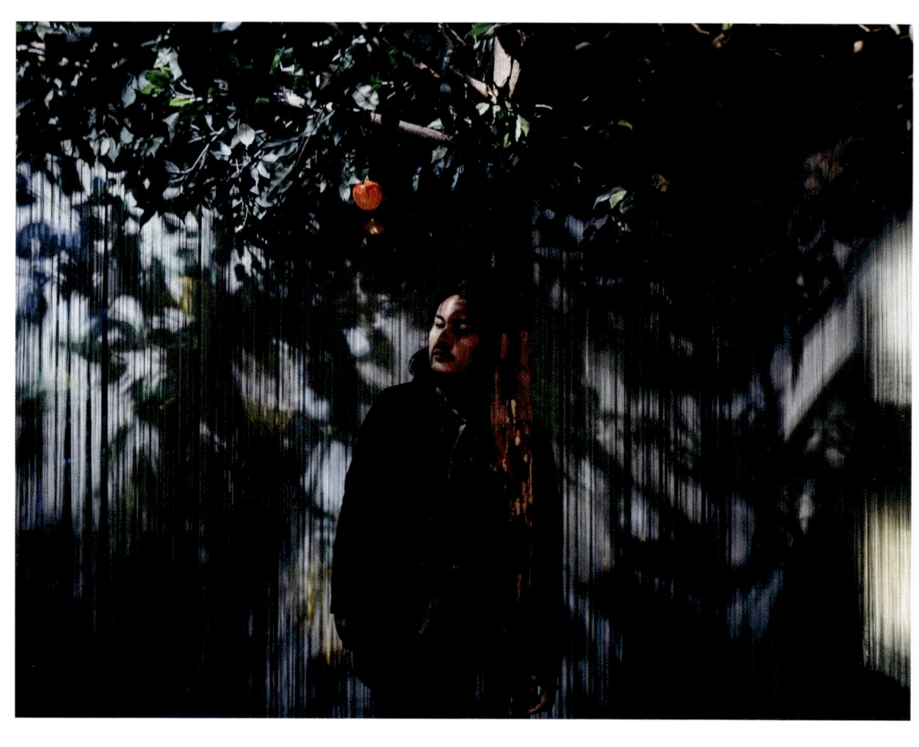

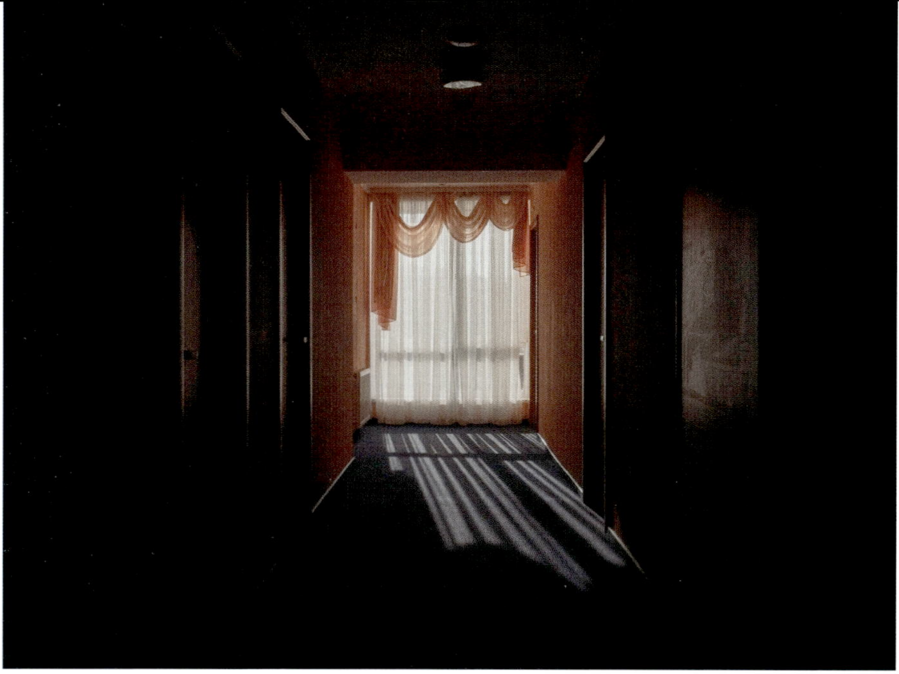

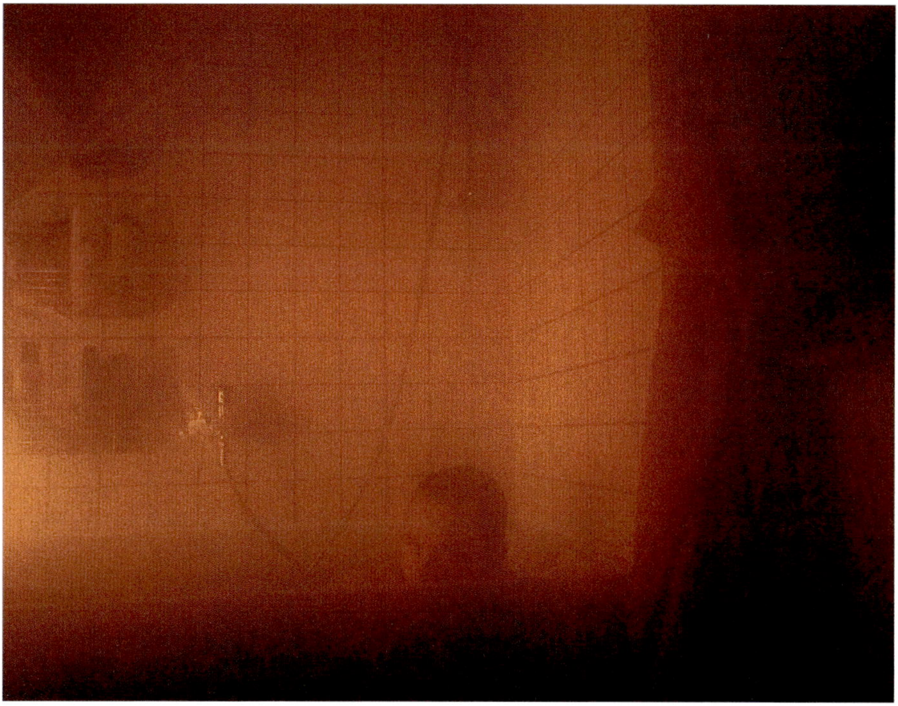

INGMAR B. NOLTING

Maß und

Ingmar's work is a journey through a Germany that is almost shut down. He took photographs on the frontlines and in the backyards of the Corona crisis, aiming to create a coherent, more comprehensive document of the situation. His photo-essay examines the state of German society—a nation that is often associated with bureaucracy, control and order—during an exceptional time of crisis.

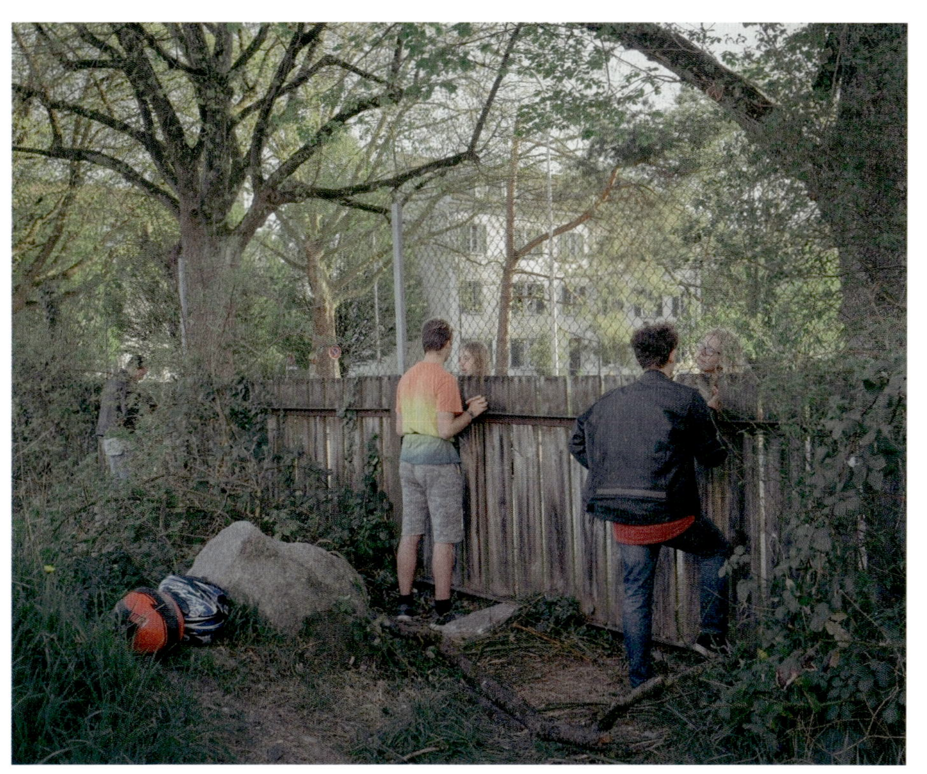

Mitte

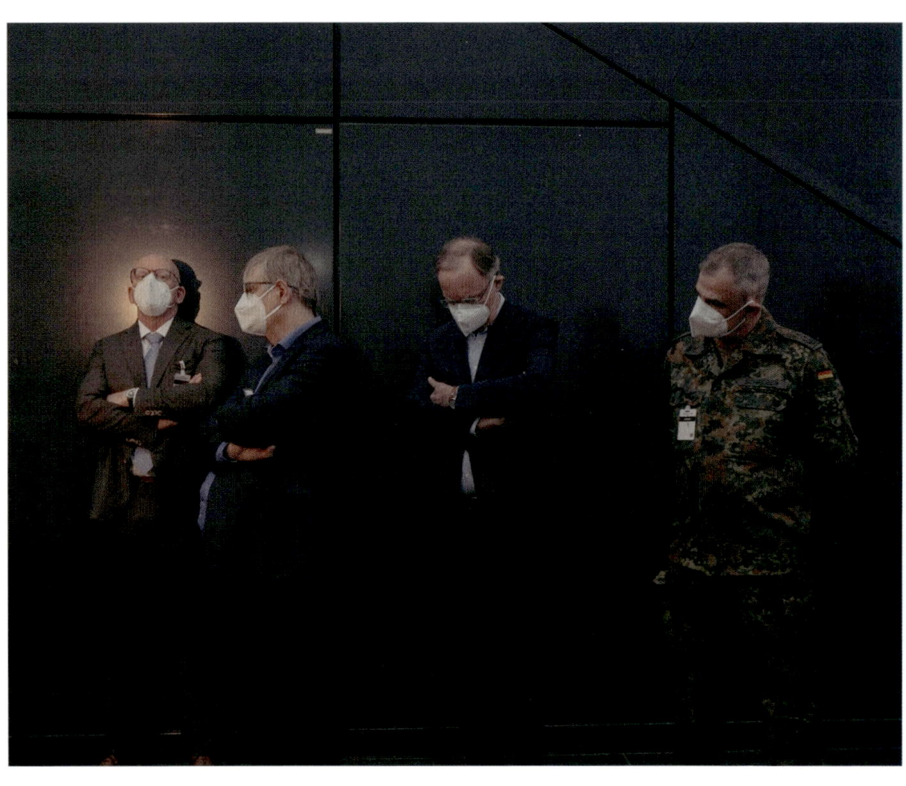

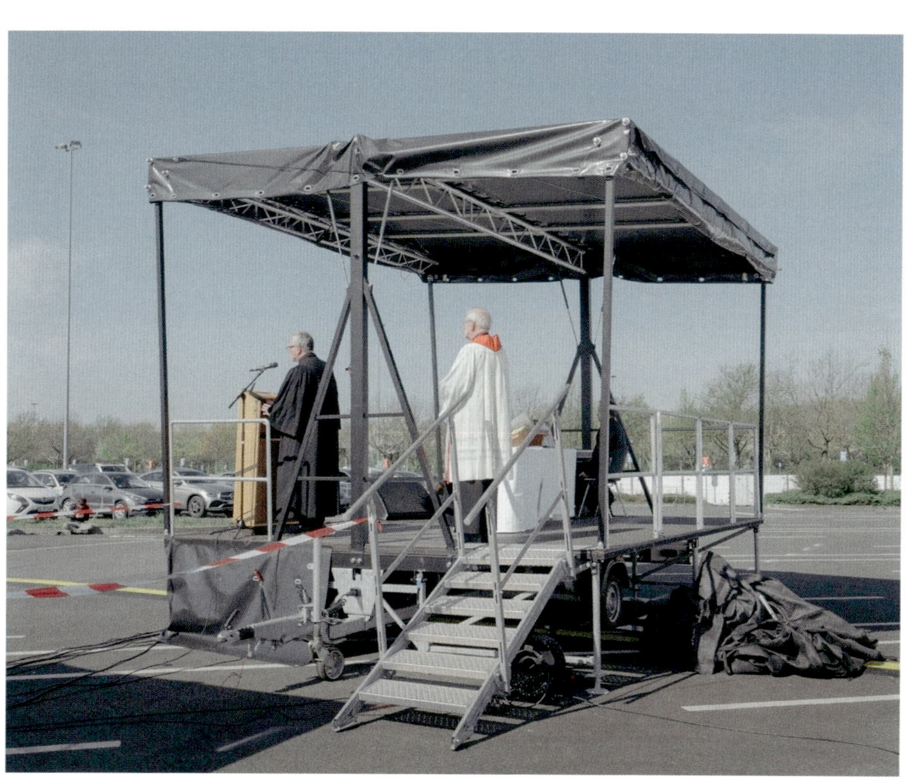

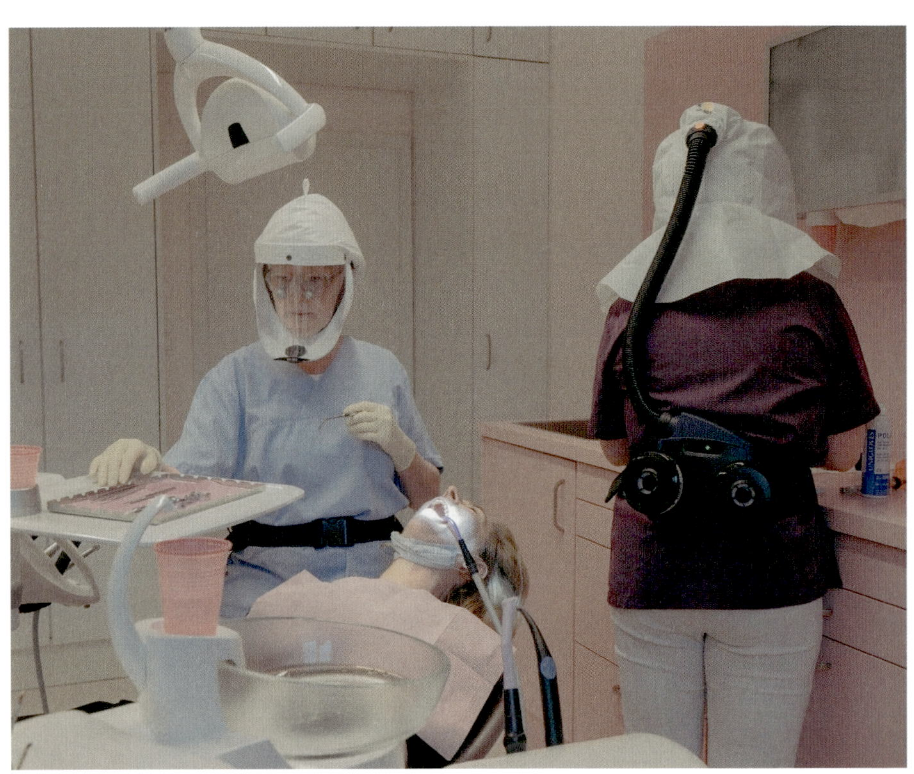

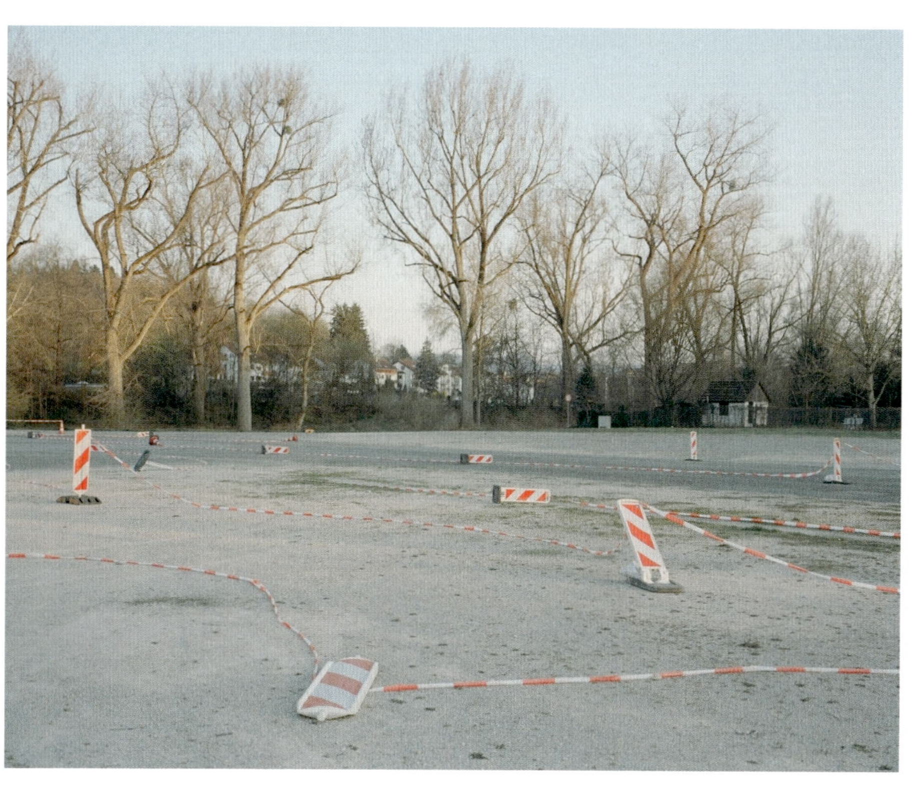

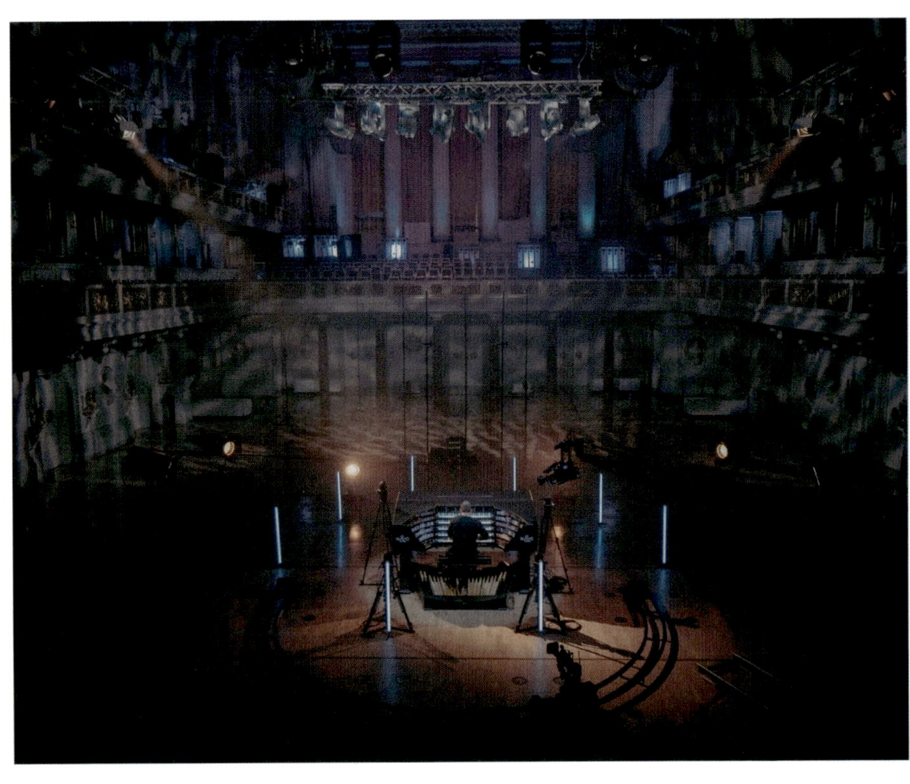

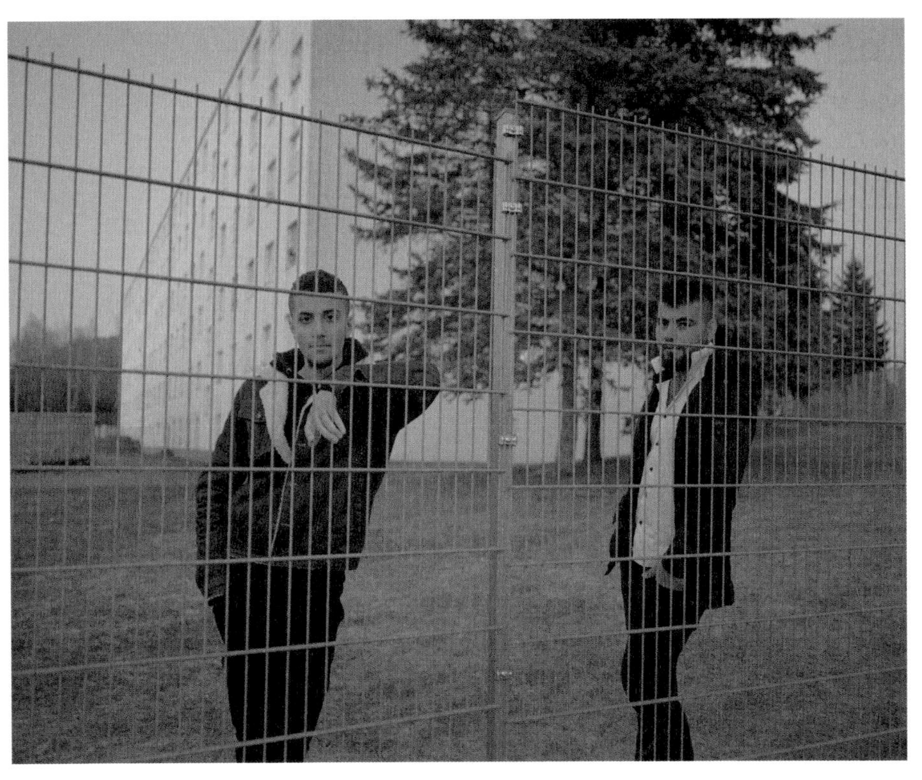

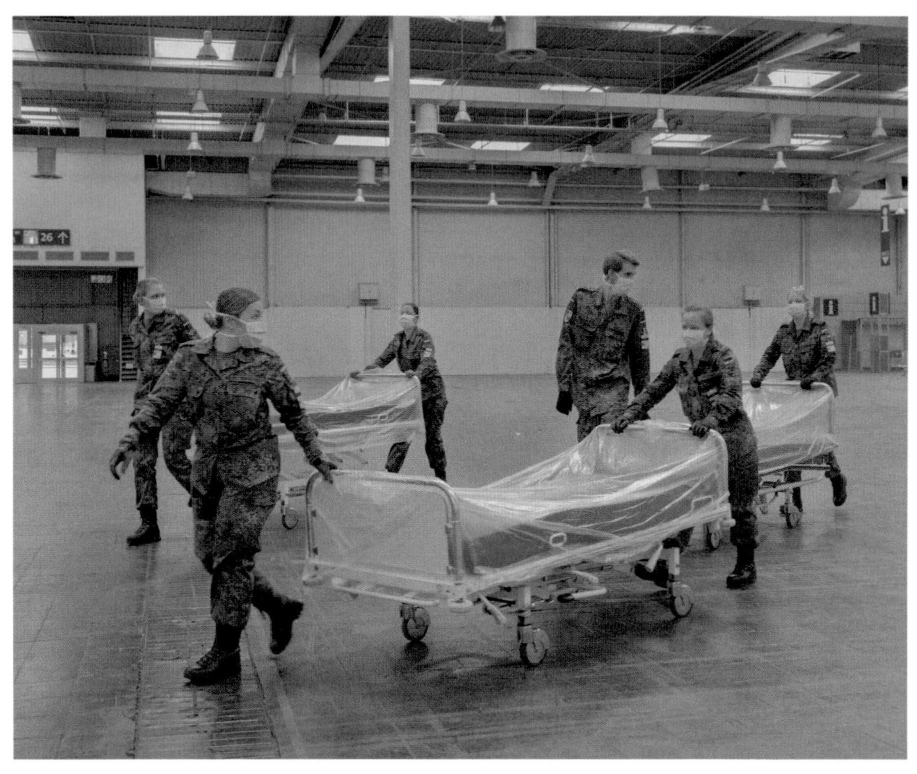
26 ↑

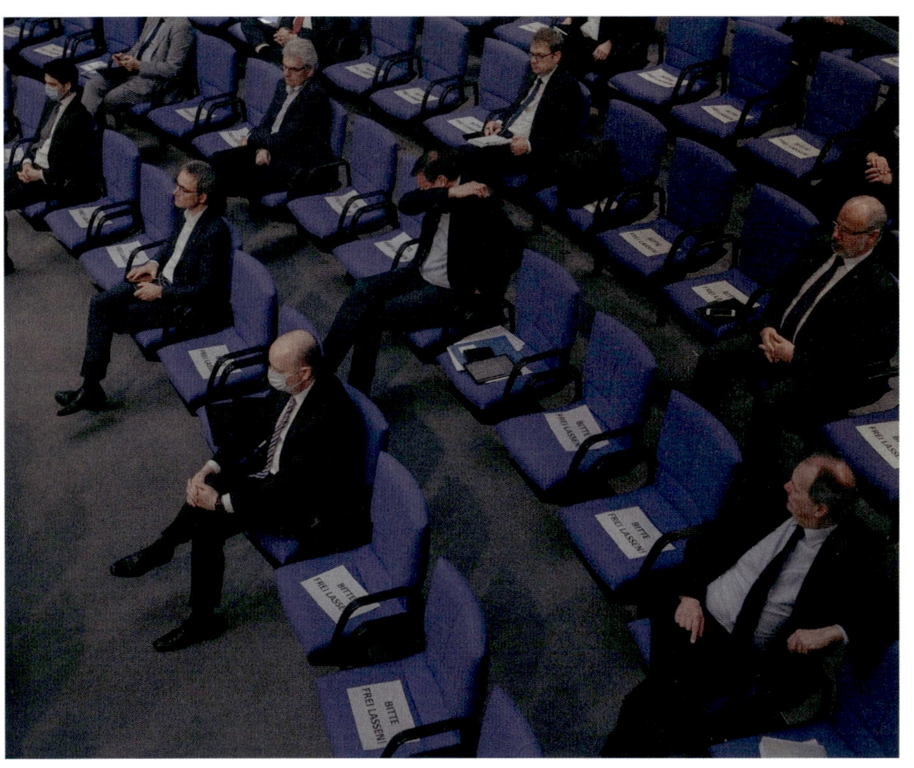
BITTE
FREI LASSEN!
BITTE
FREI LASSEN!
BITTE
FREI LASSEN!

KSENIA KULESHOVA

27

ABKHAZIA

Abkhazia, once one of the most beloved touristic regions of the Russian Empire and later of the Soviet Union, now is a lost place on the world map. Officially still a part of Georgia, separated after the civil war of 1992, it's a state recognized only by Russia and just a couple of other countries. Ksenia visits a land forgotten by the global media circus and international politics. Without any real industry, infrastructure or educational power, it survives on occasional nostalgic tourism from ex-USSR citizens, foreign Abkhaz diaspora and scarce Russian alimony.

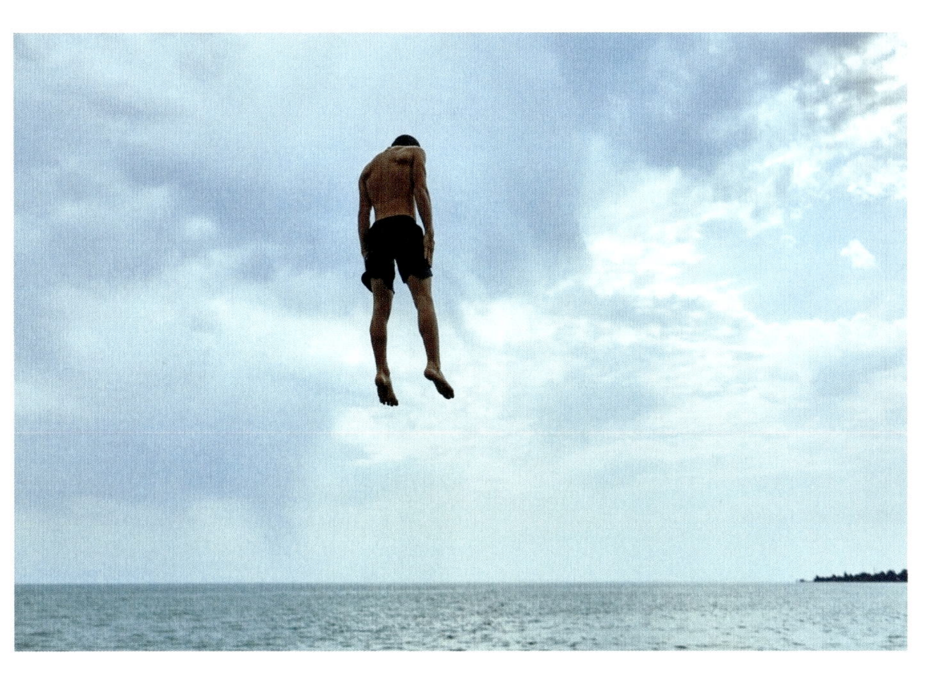

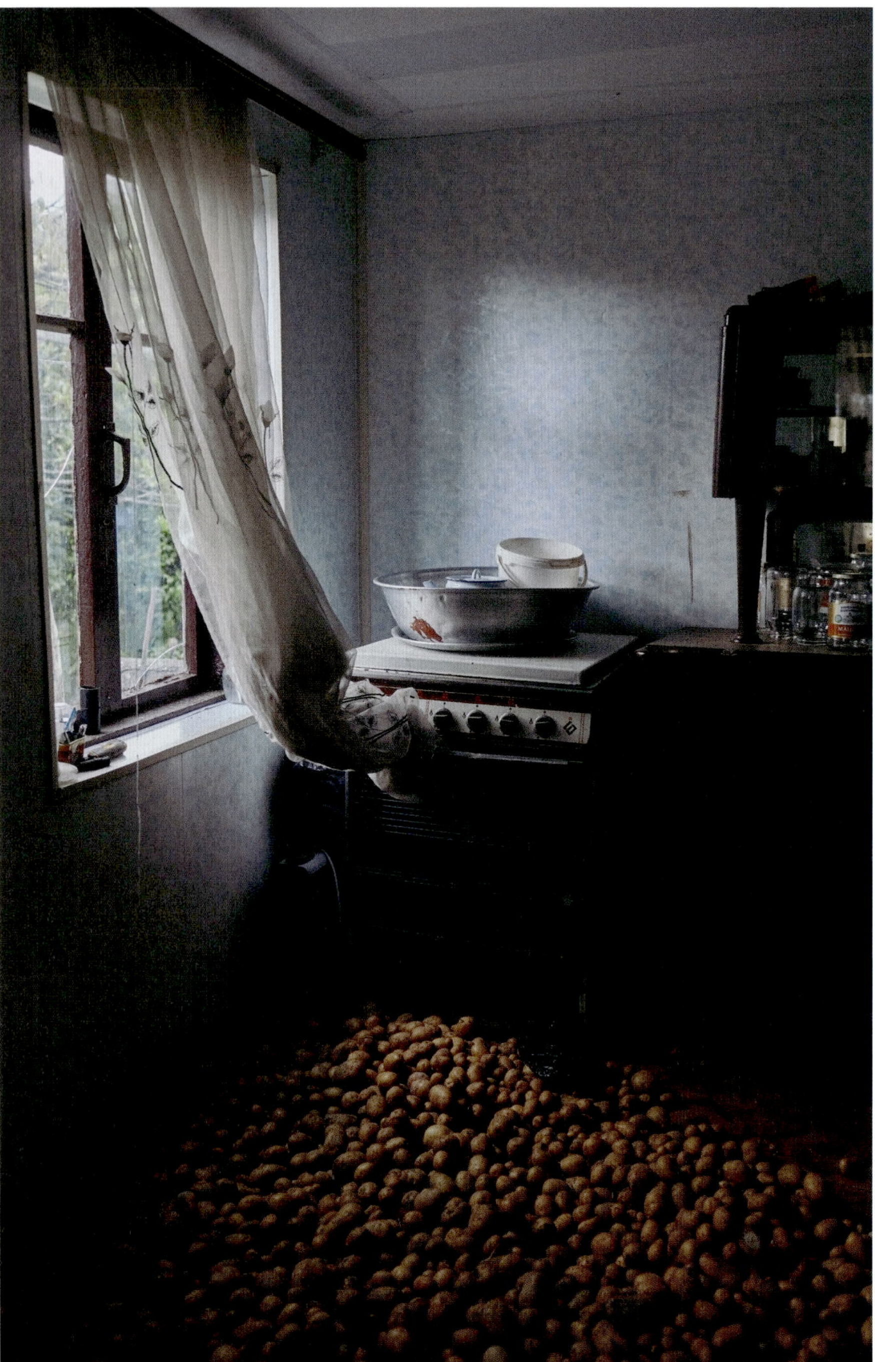

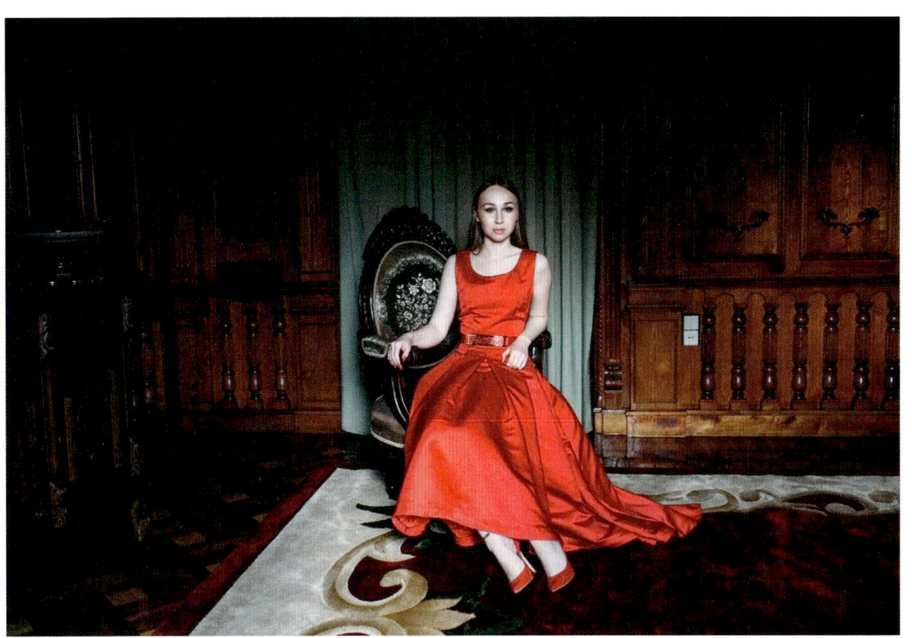

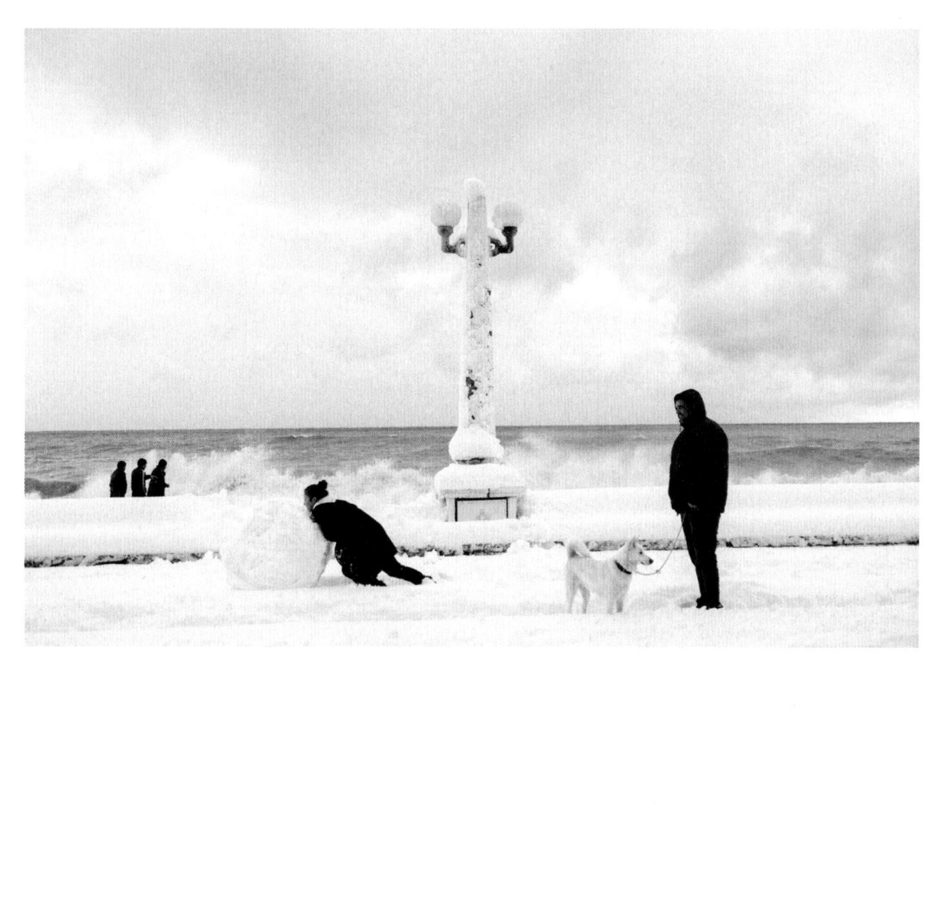

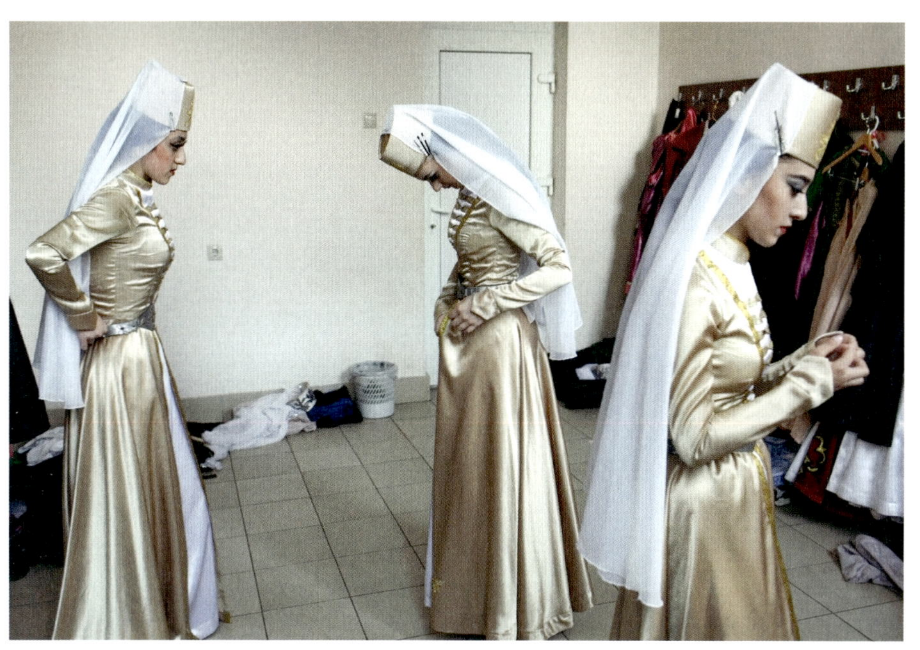

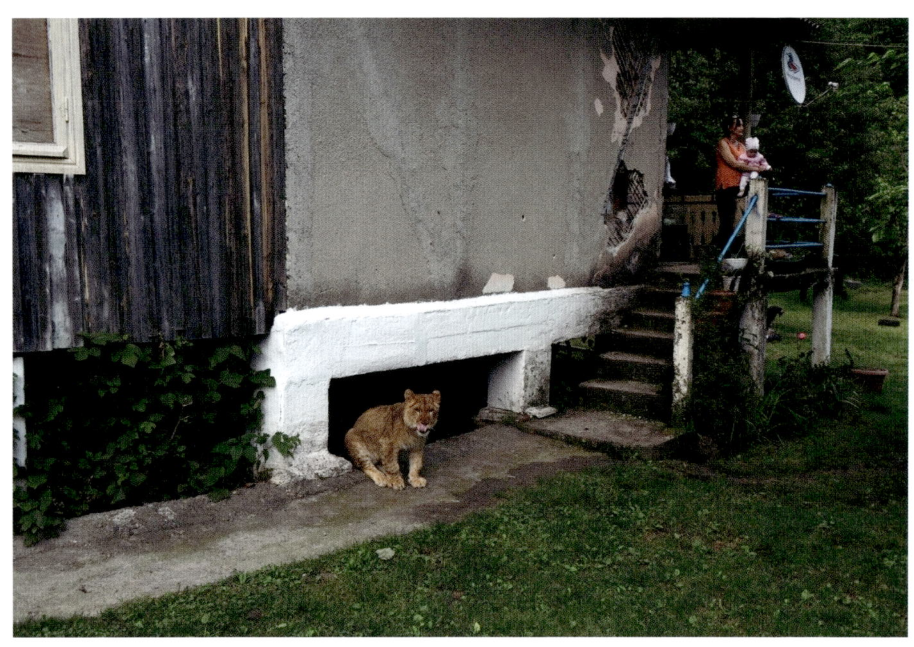

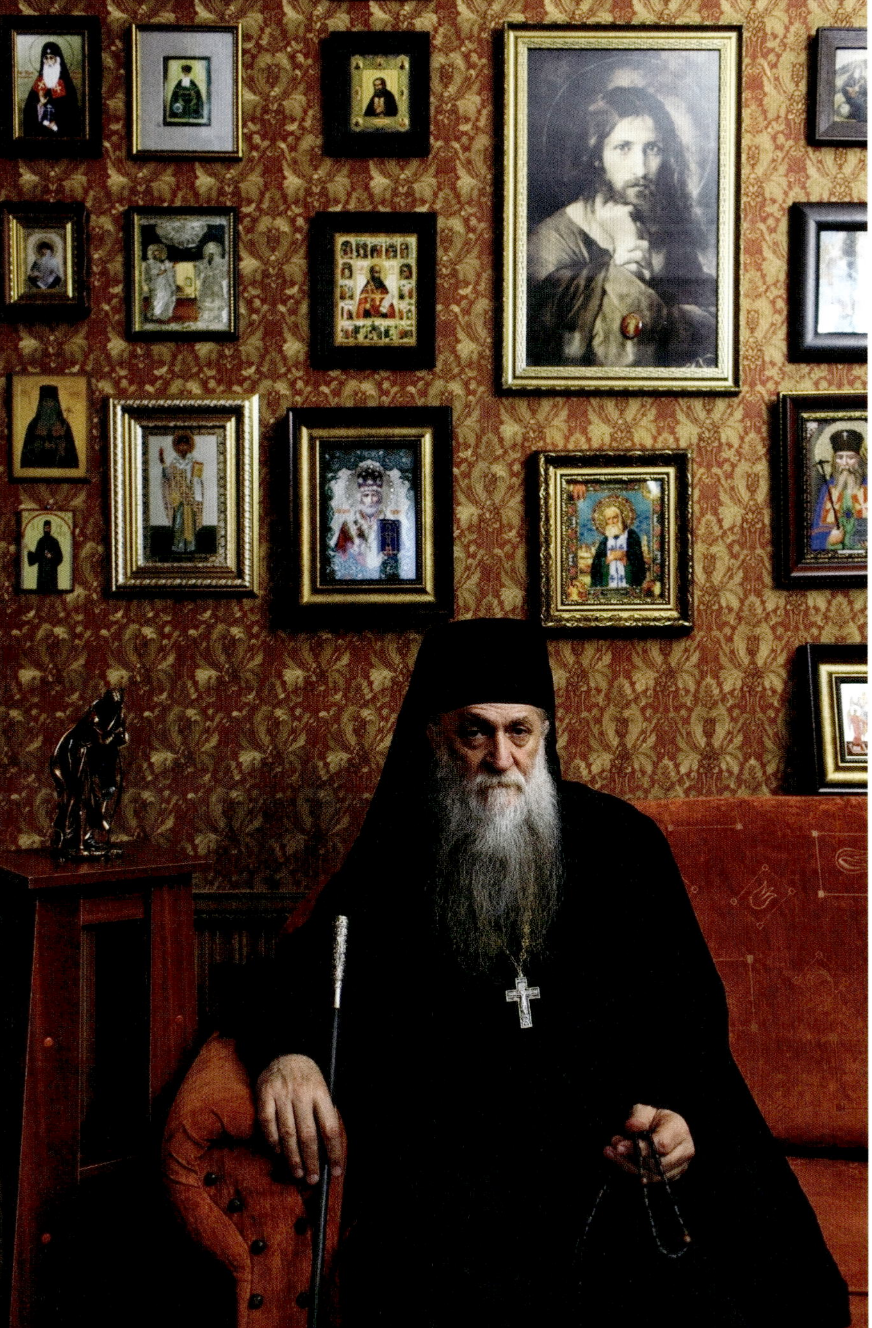

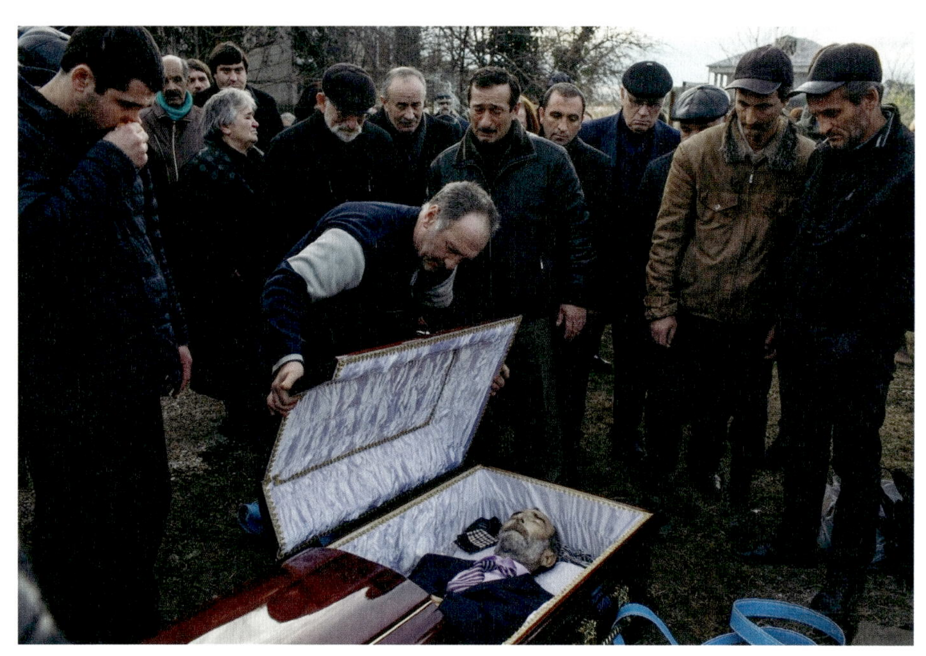

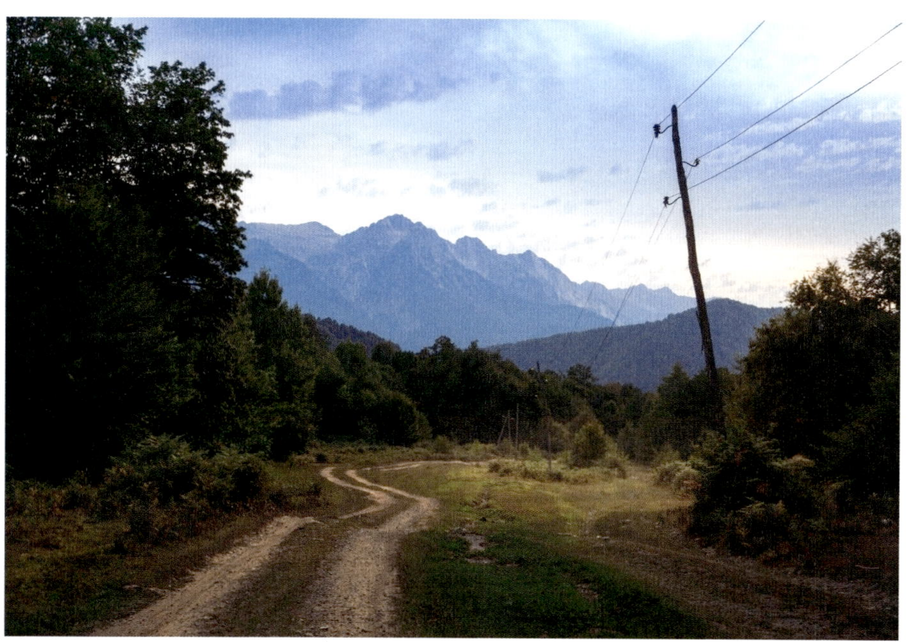

LEA FRANKE

28

Wir sind 15

The first love affects our whole life. We will never forget it. It can last long, end up short or sometimes even last a whole life. It's a unique fulfillment of a strong desire we never felt before. To examine this feeling, Lea accompanied Ronia and Lars during their first love and everything which goes along with it.

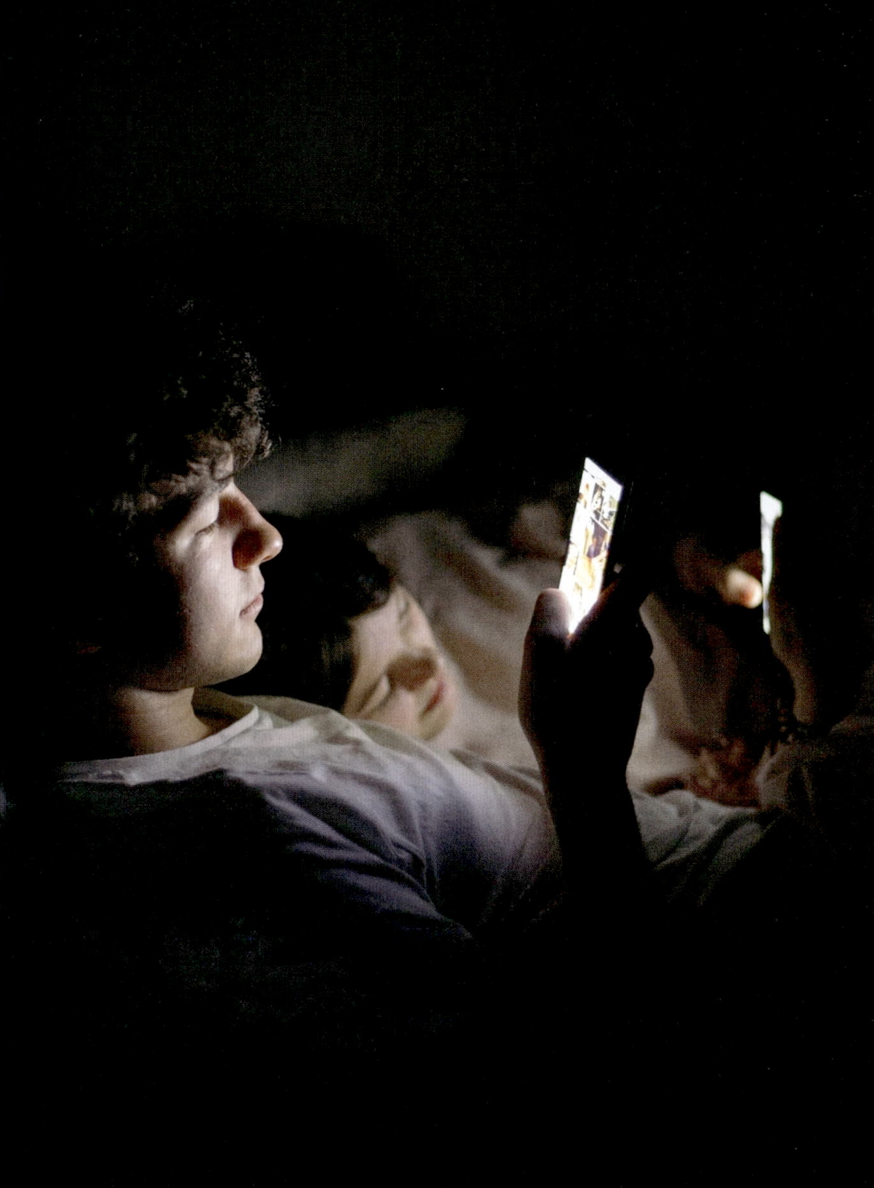

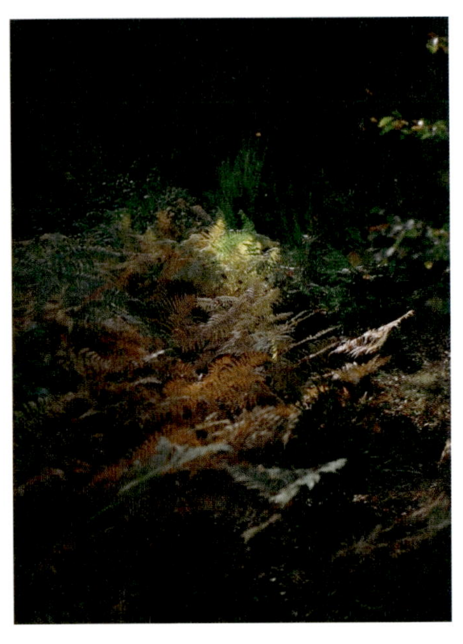

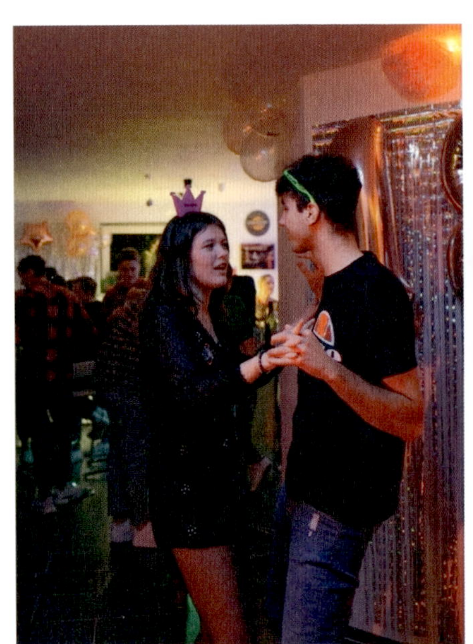

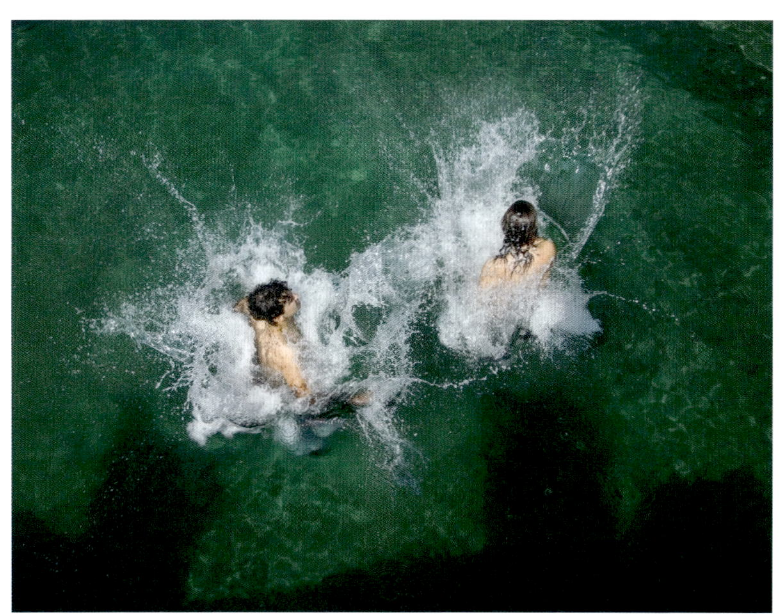

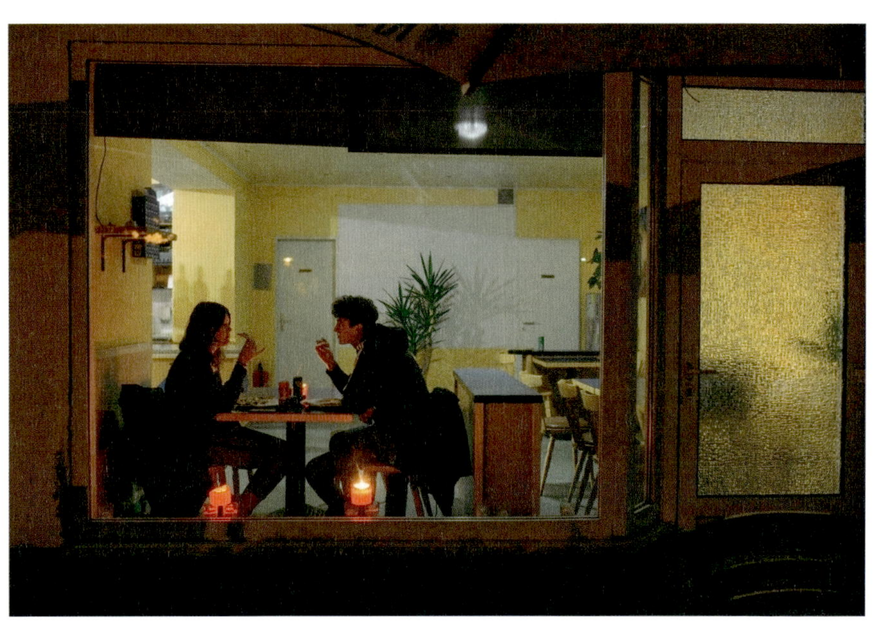

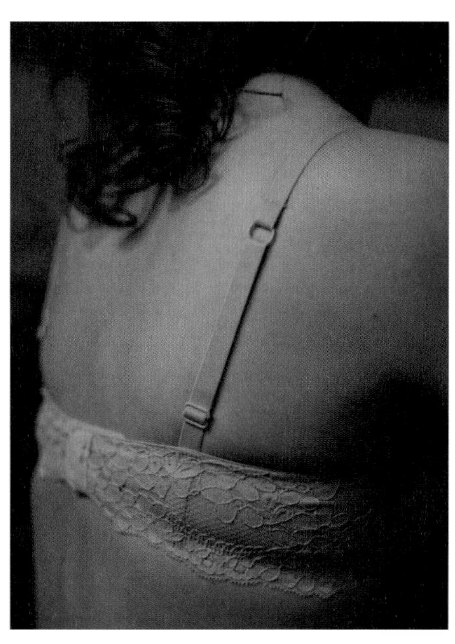

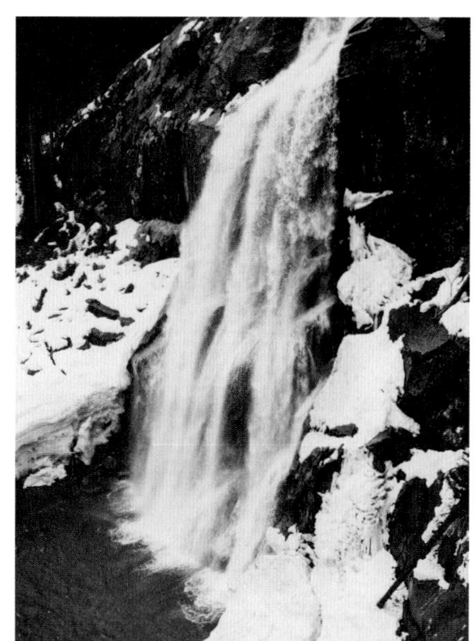

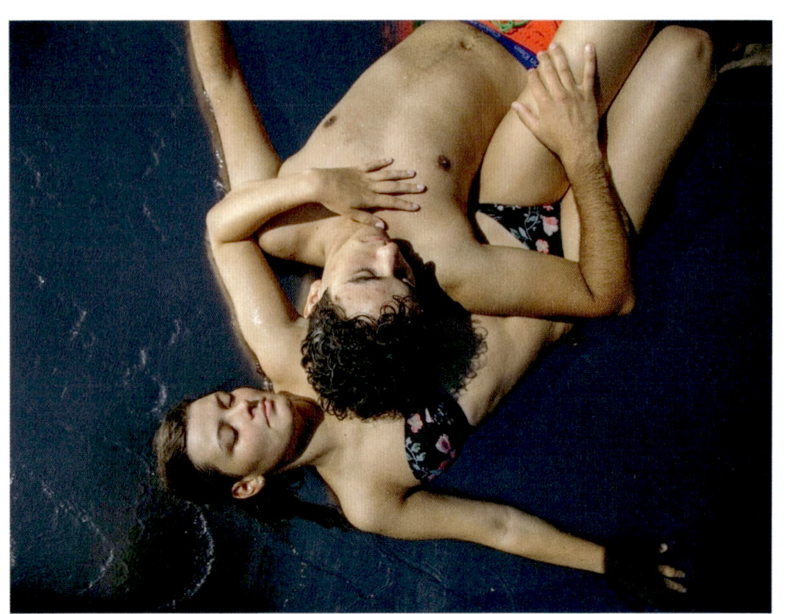

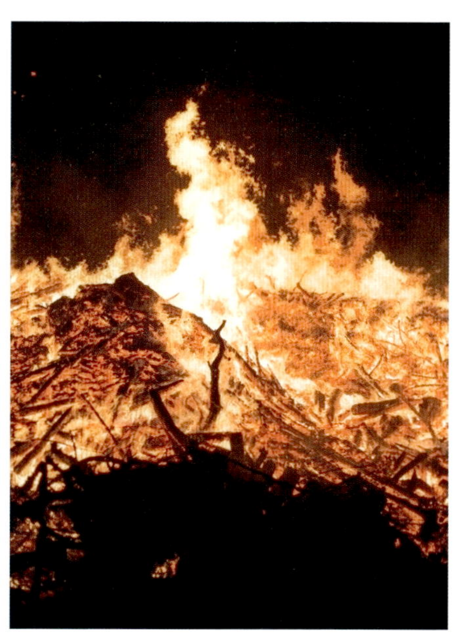

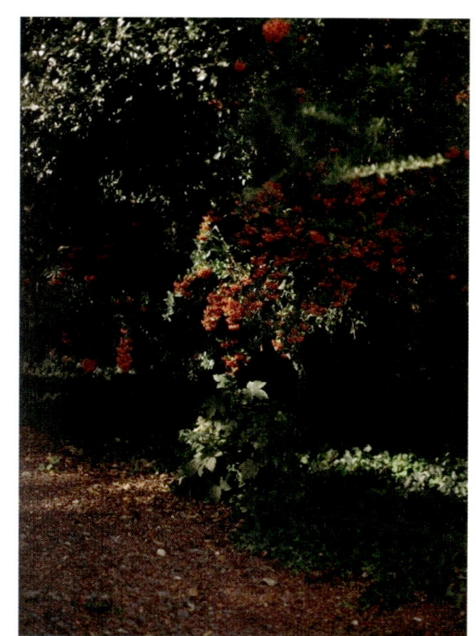

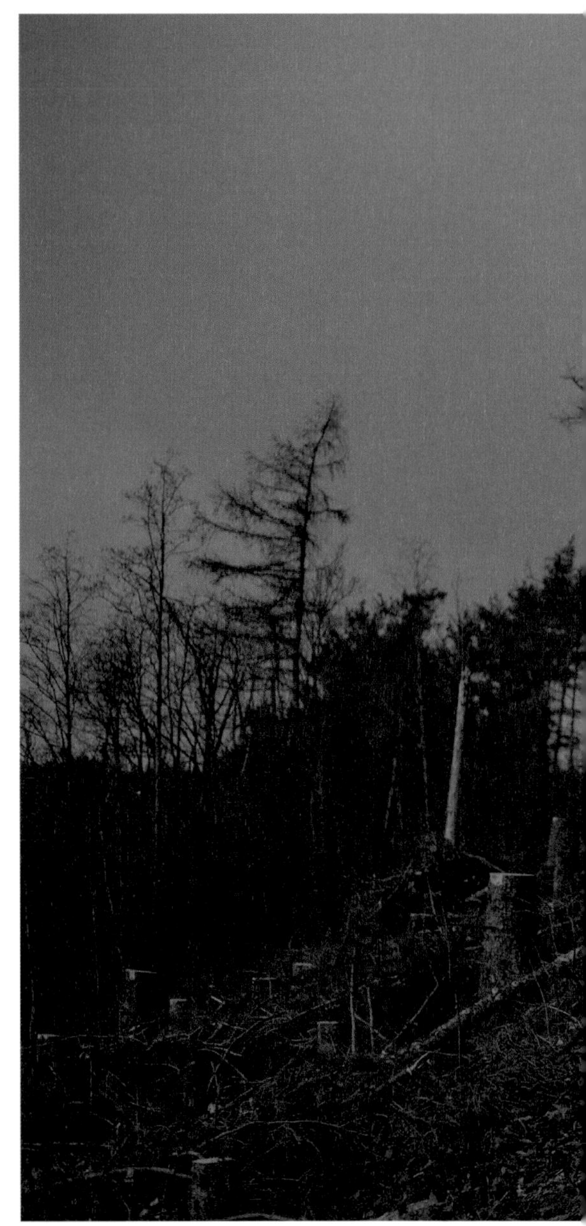

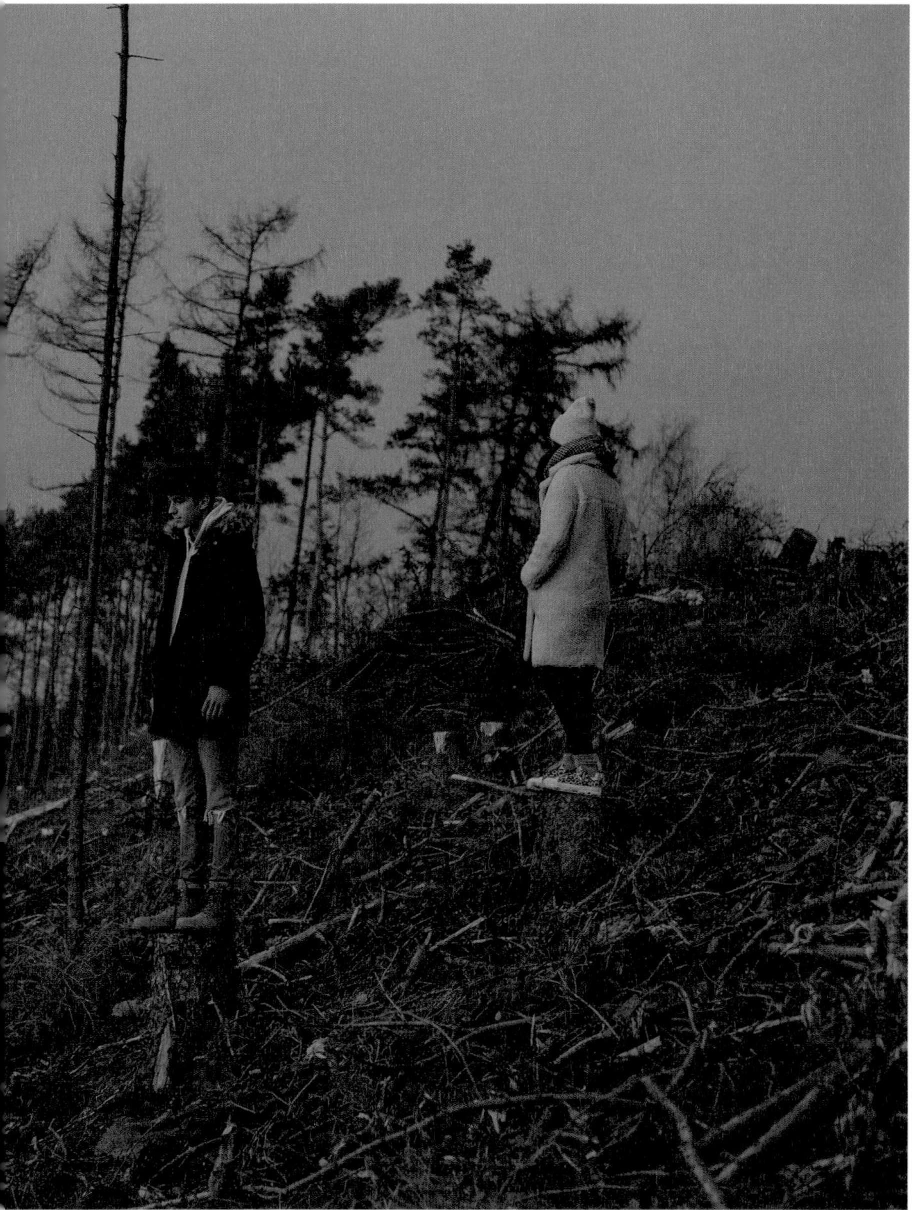

CHIARA WETTMANN

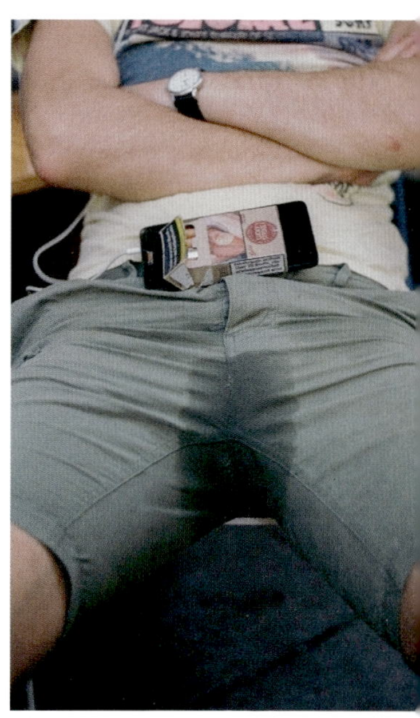

29

AIN'T

We meet many people in our lives and have thousands of conversations about different—but often the same—topics. This flood of exchange intensifies even more in an urban way of living, through which we often stumble blindly. And yet we also find closeness and harmony. Chiara guesses that this fleetingness is perhaps exactly what we sometimes lack in times of Corona-due isolation.

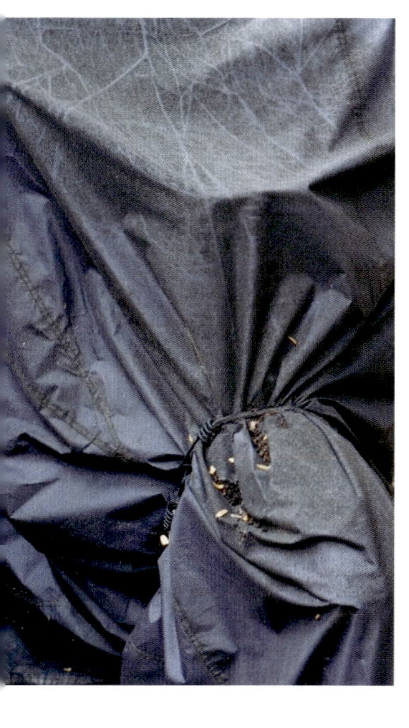

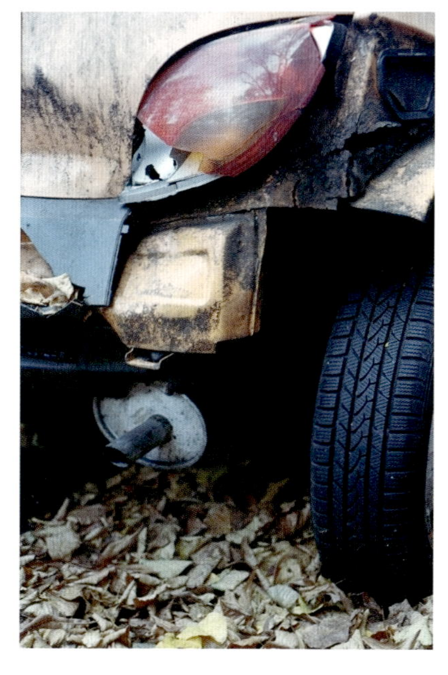

NO

Conversations

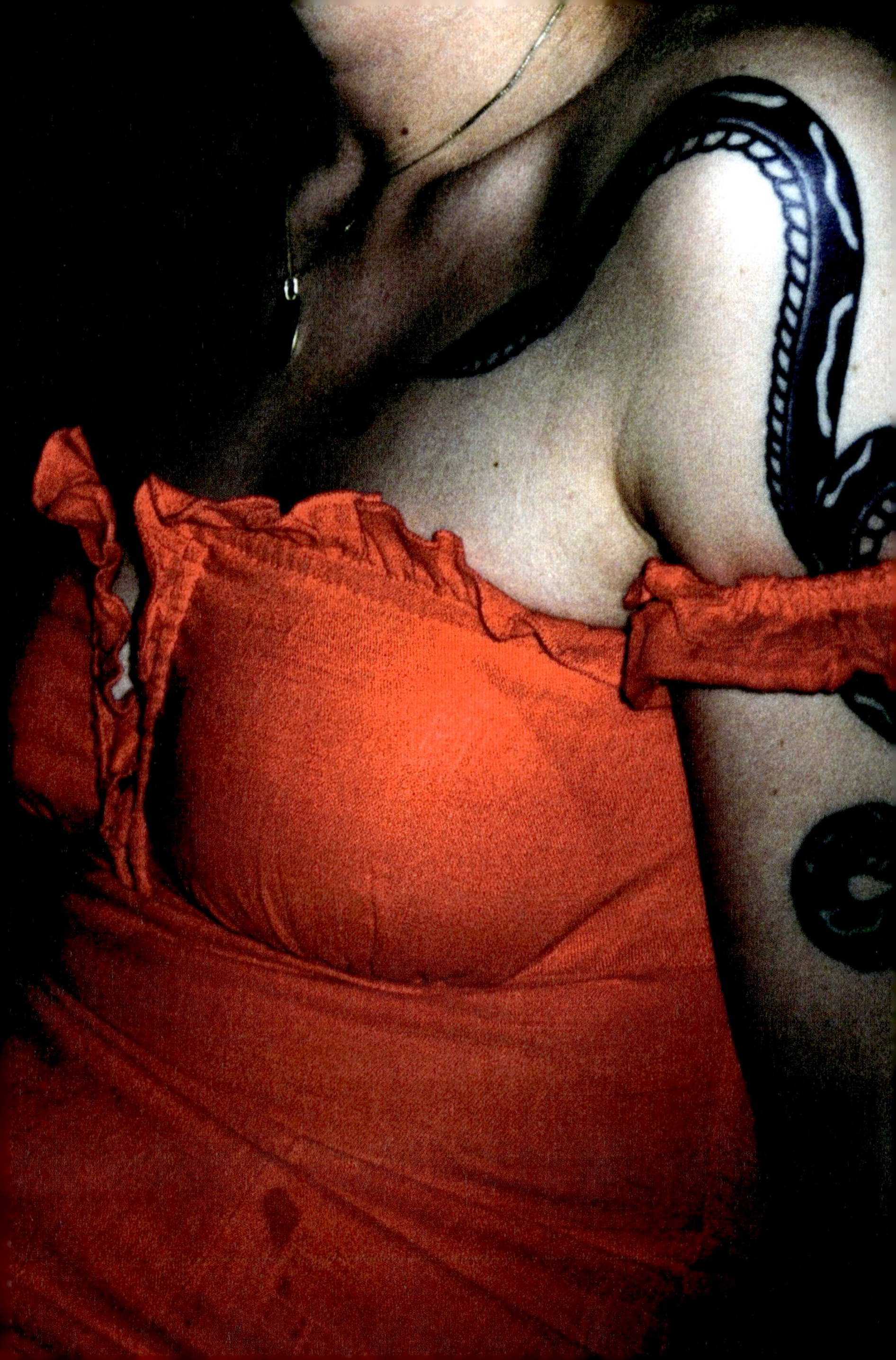

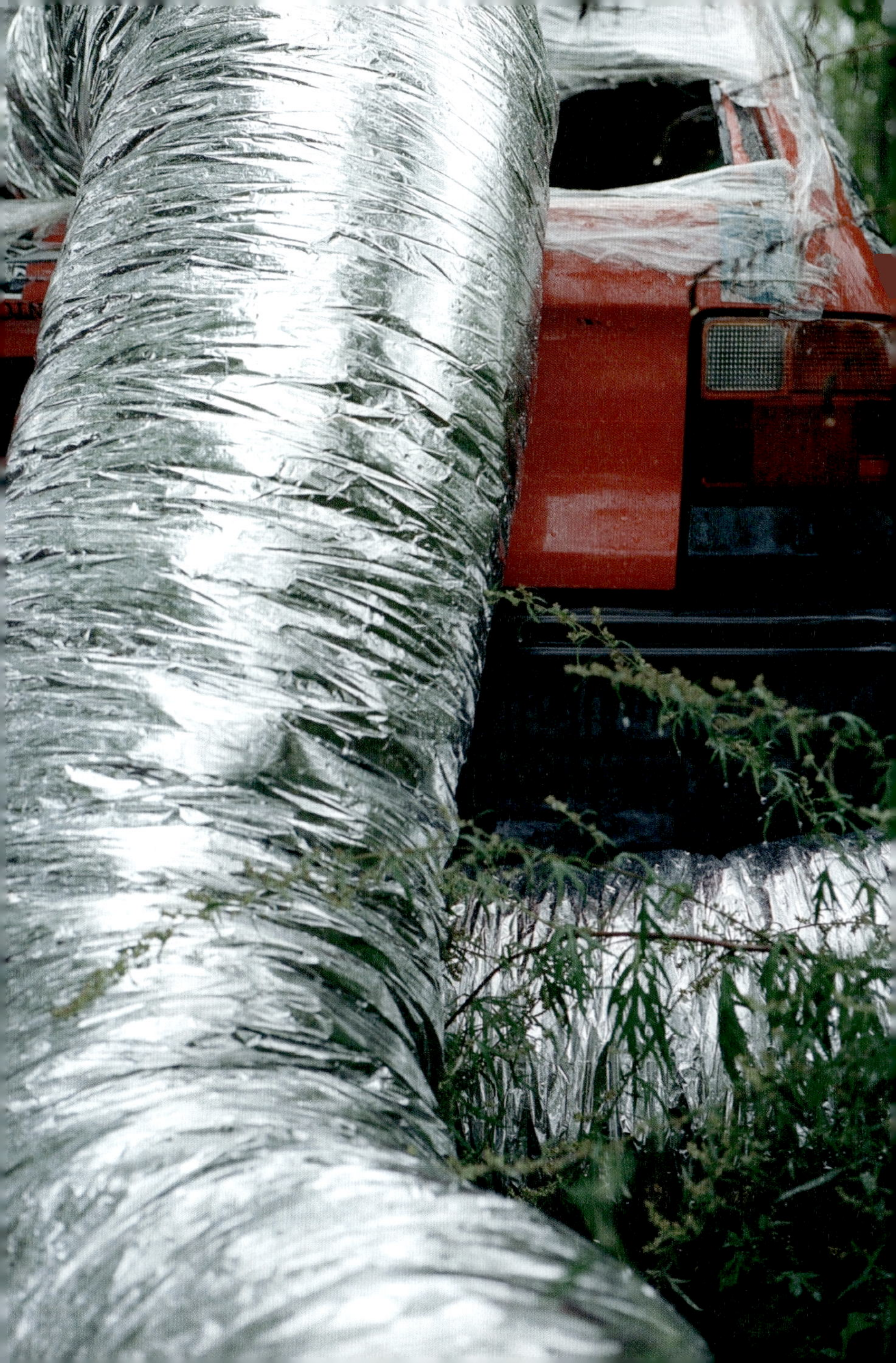

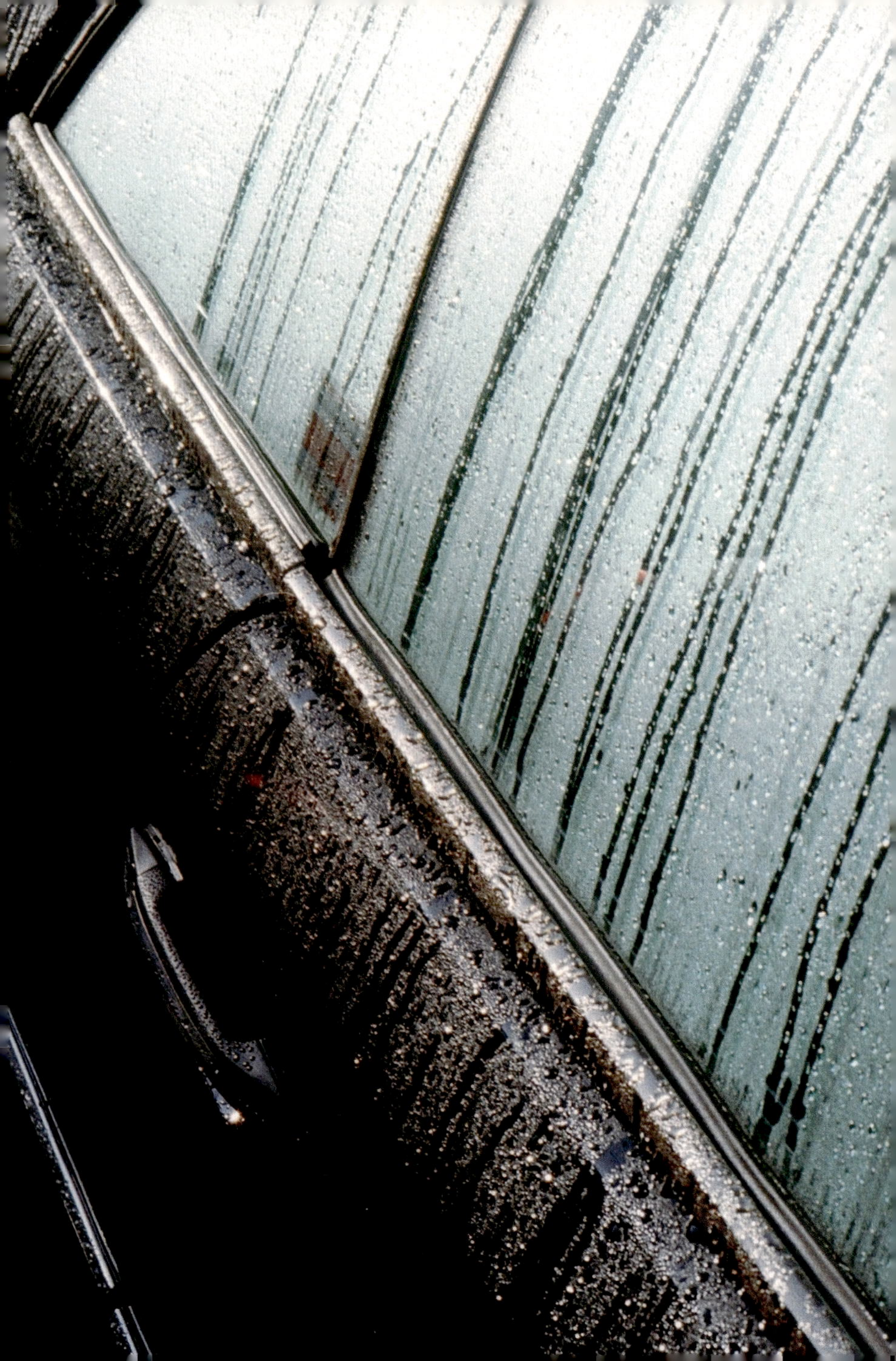

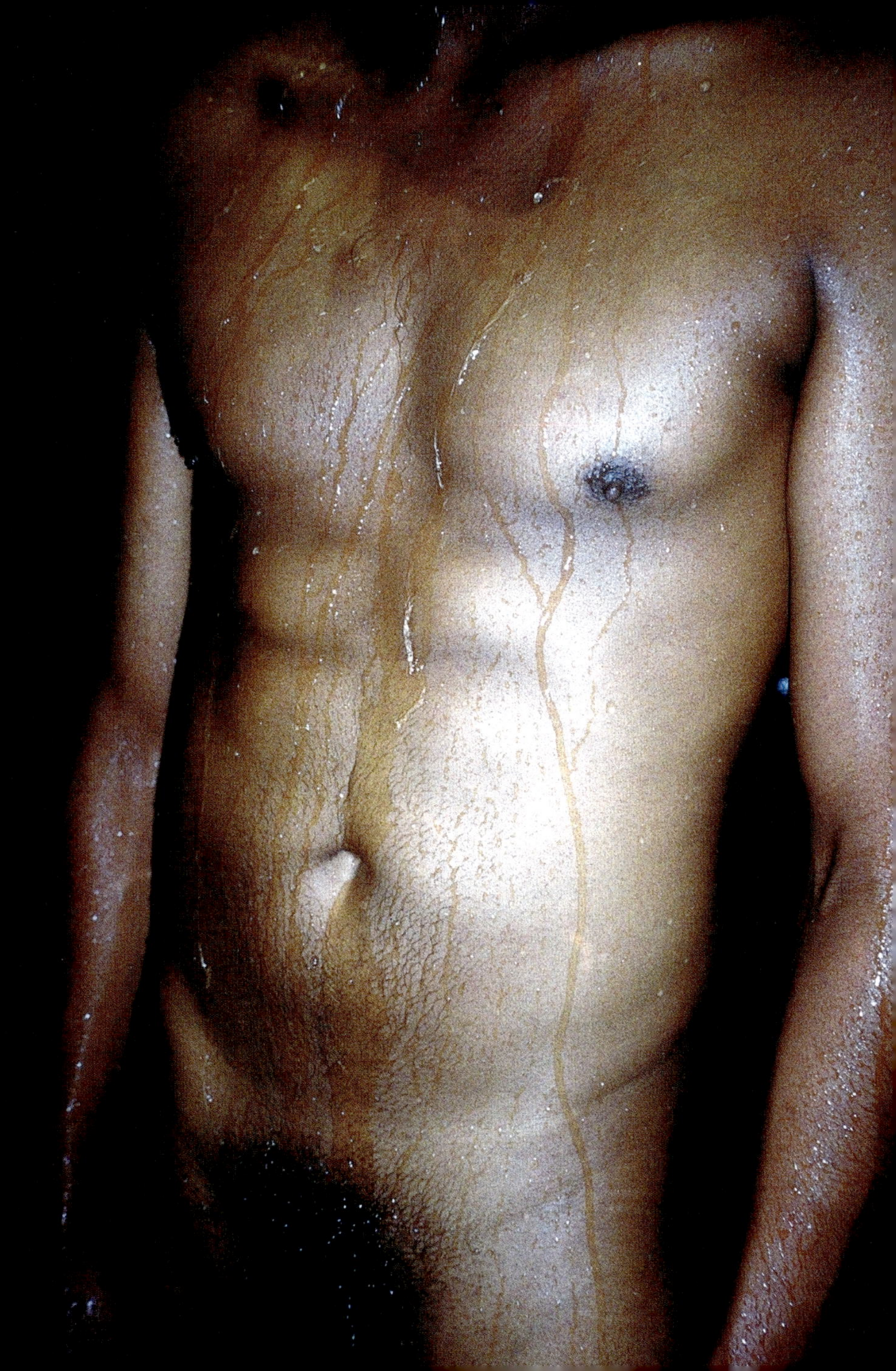

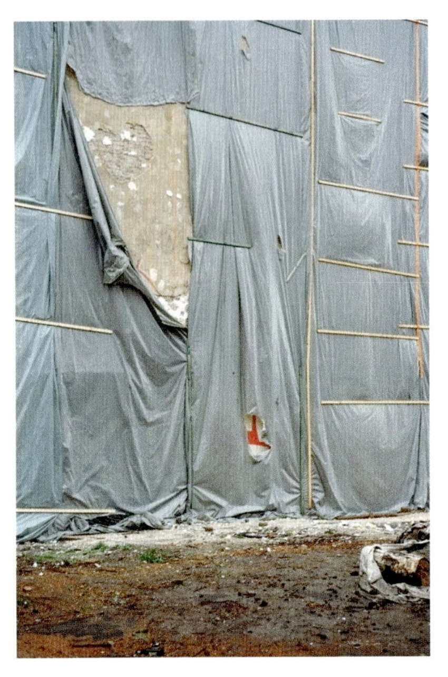

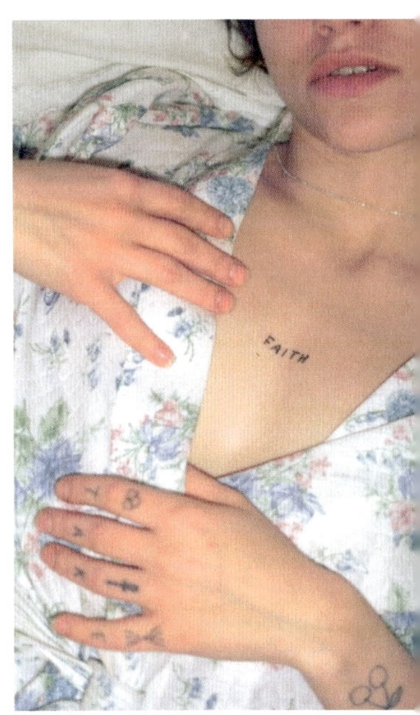
FAITH

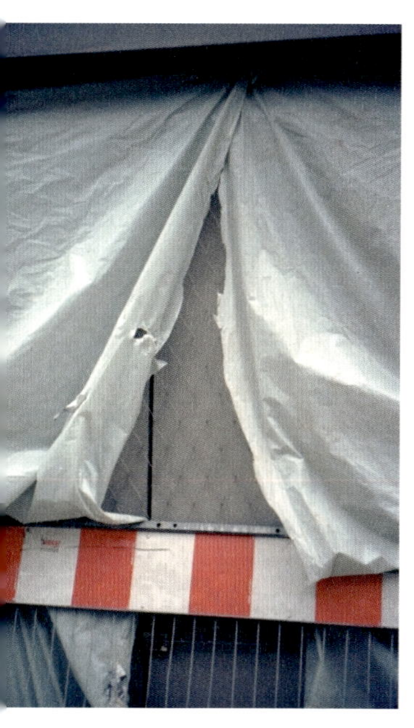

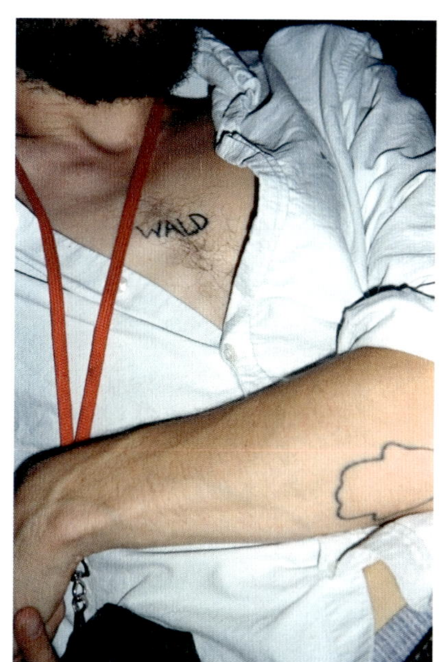
WALD

TAMARA ECKHARDT

The Children of CARROWBROWNE

30

As Ireland's largest minority group, Travellers are ostracized from Irish society for their nomadic way of life and pushed to the periphery of urban spaces. On the outskirts of Galway, situated right next to the city dump, is the Carrowbrowne Halting Site, home to eight Traveller families and their children. Tamara's project aims to offer a glimpse into the daily life of young Traveller children.

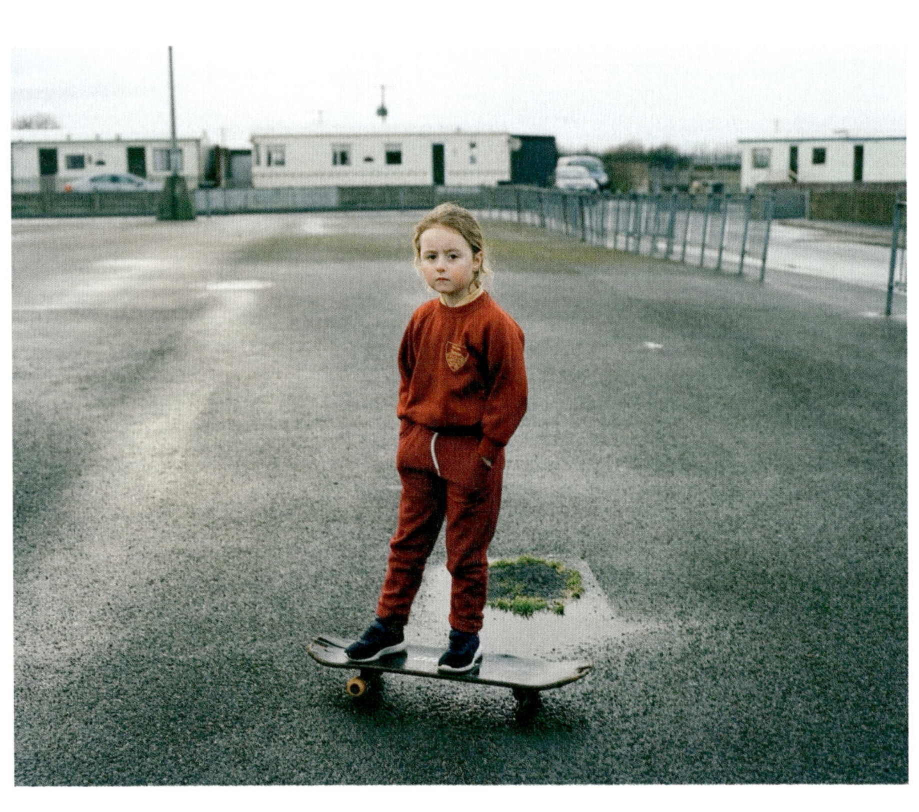

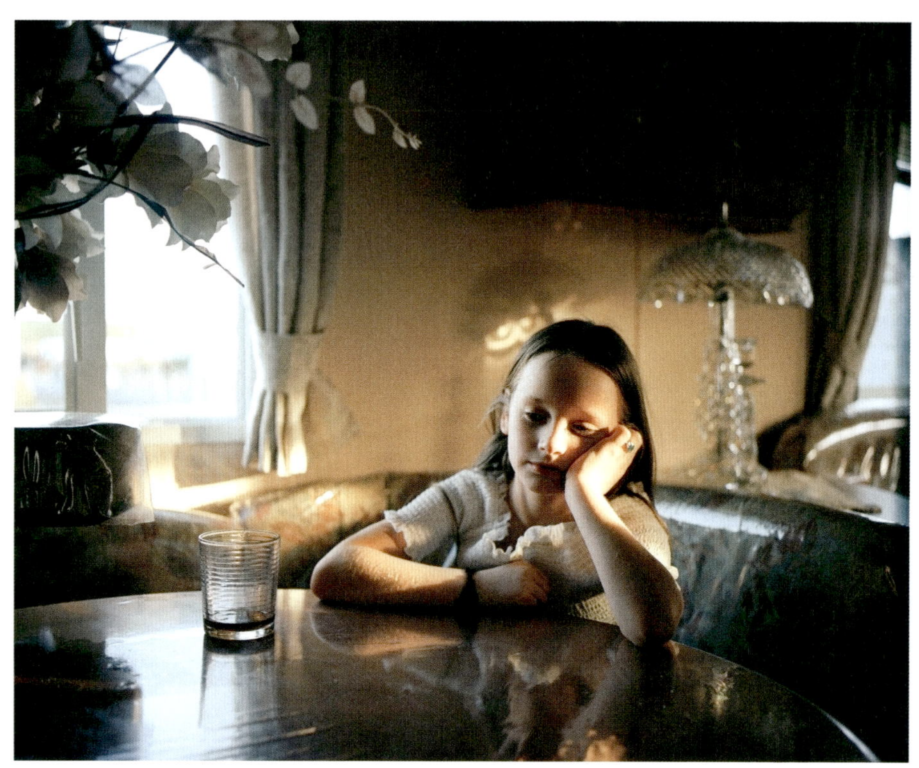

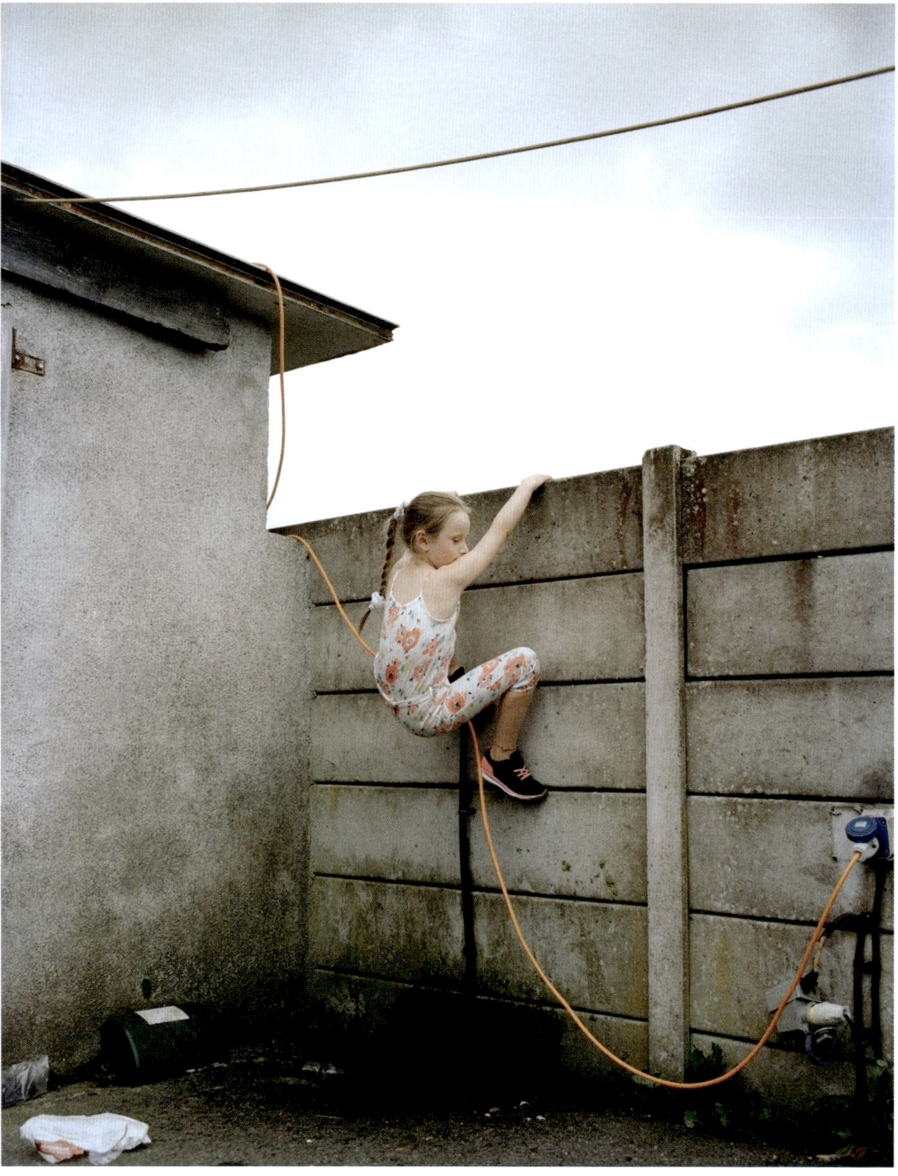

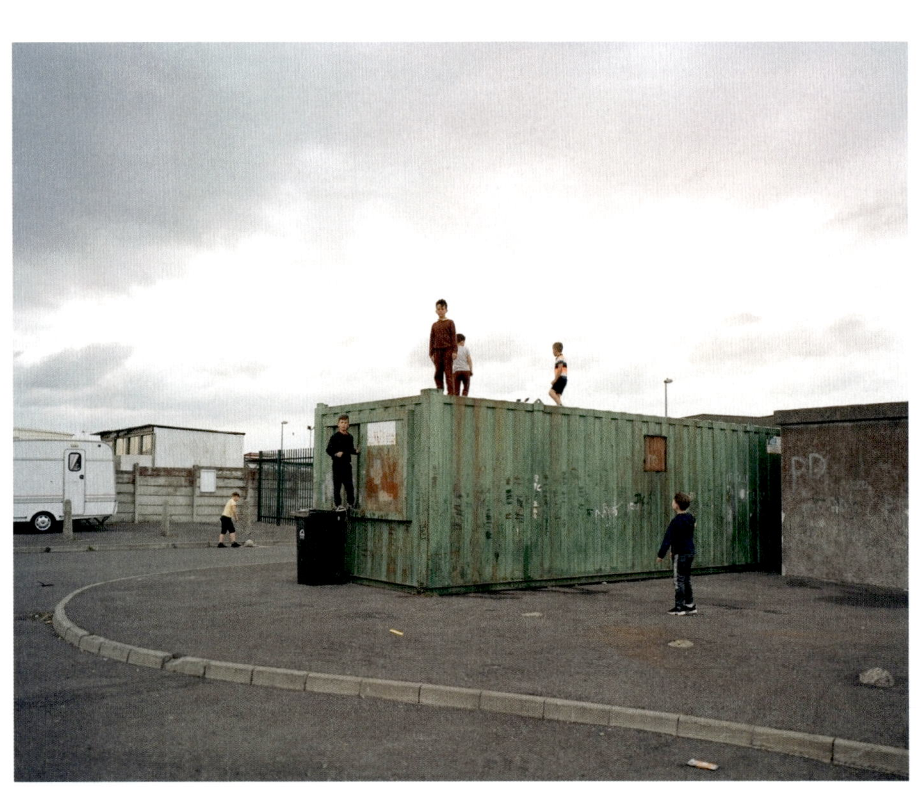
PD

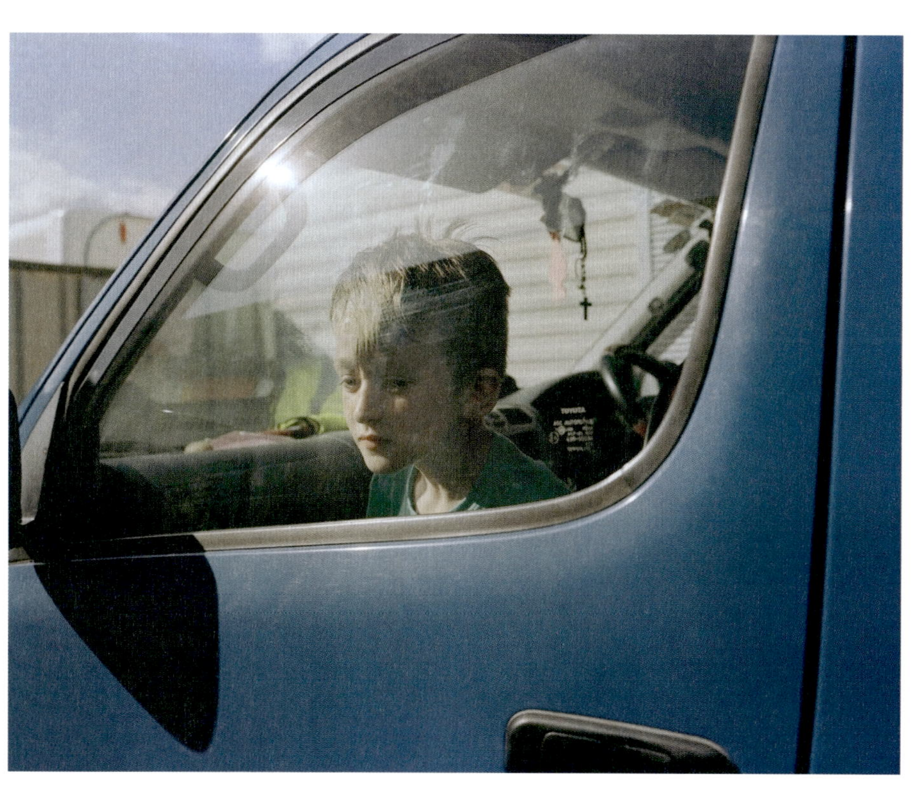

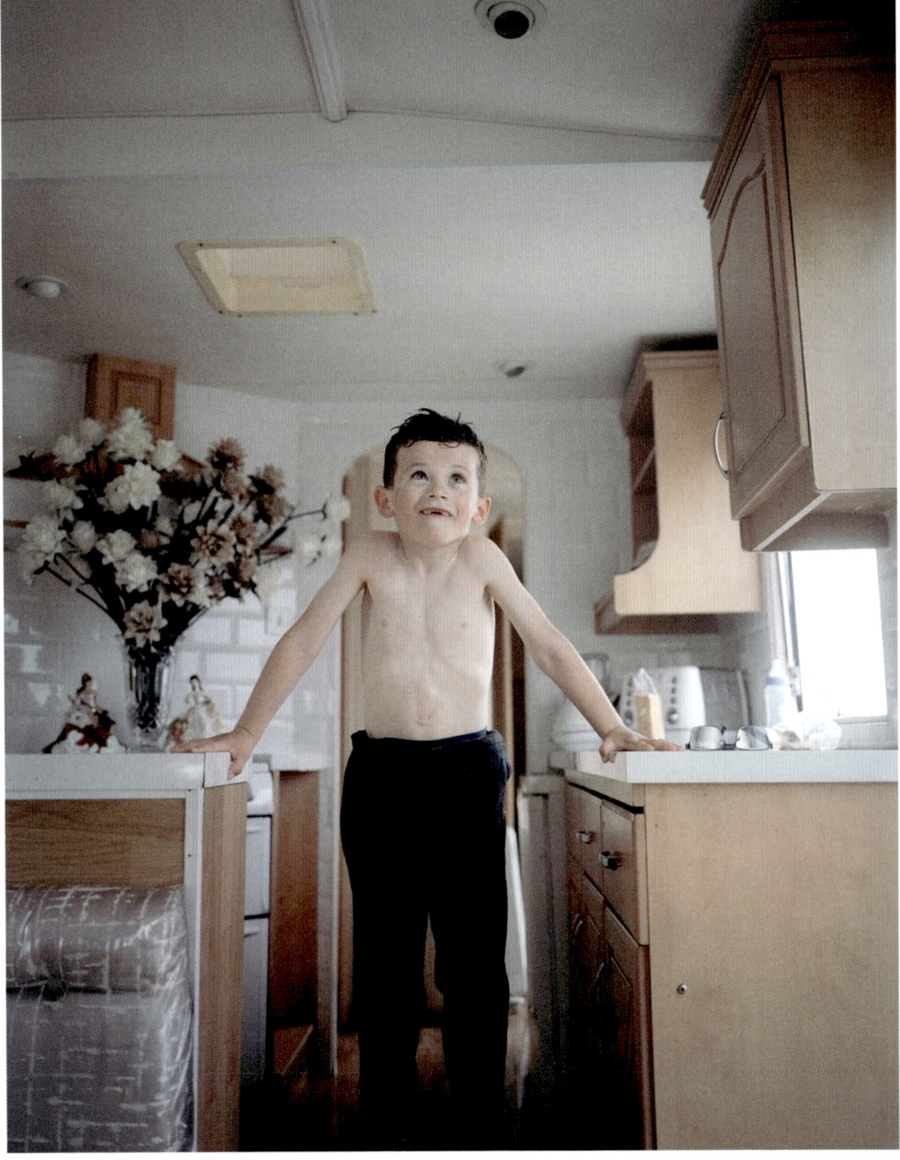

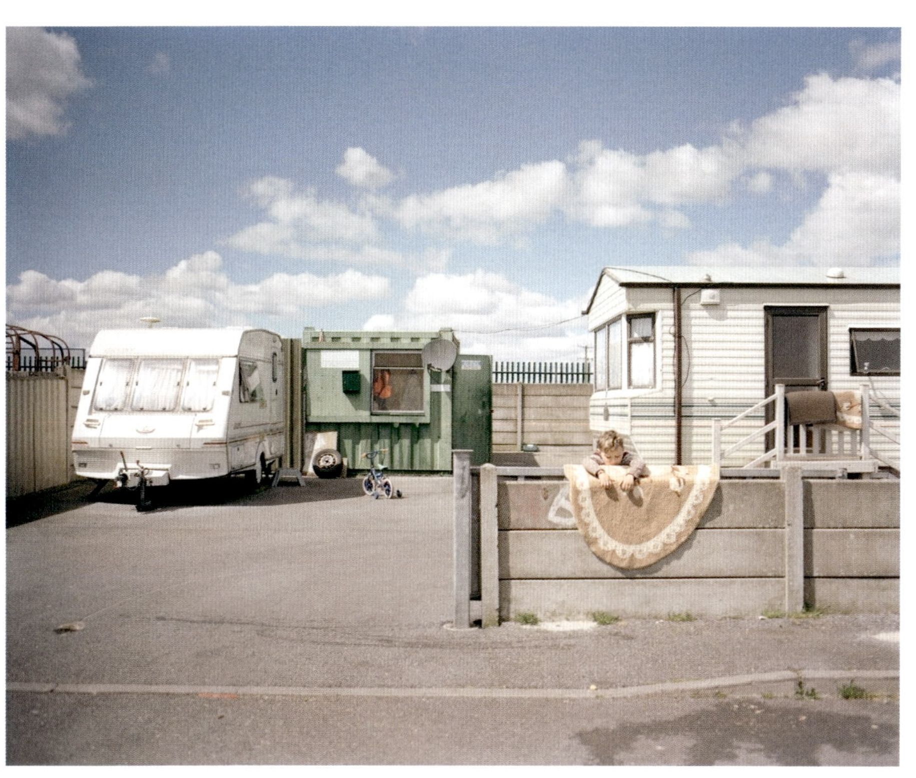

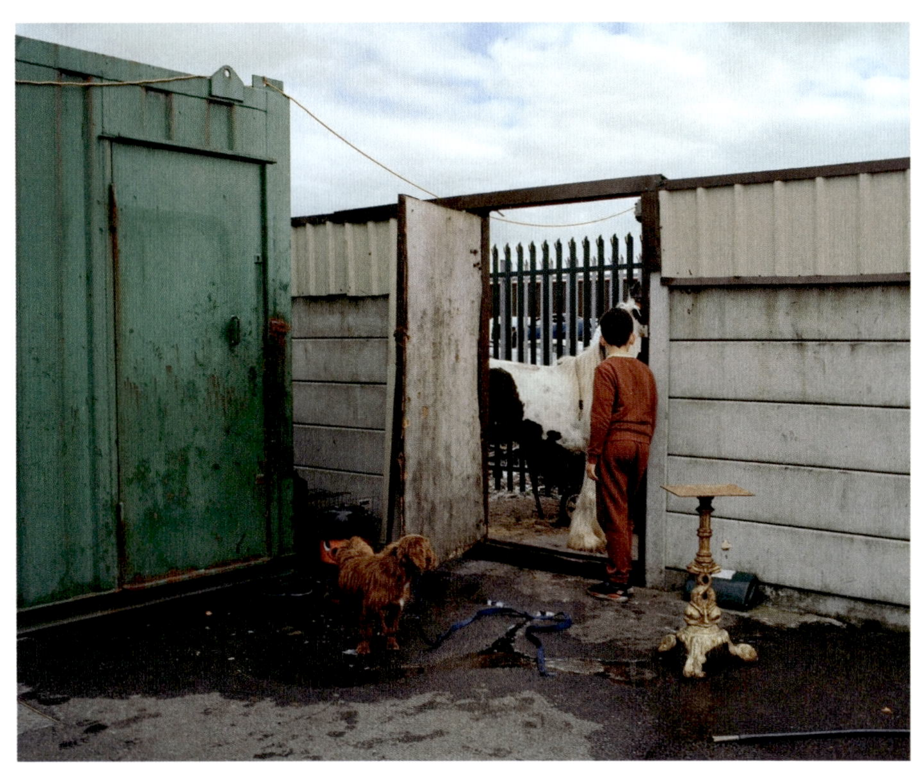

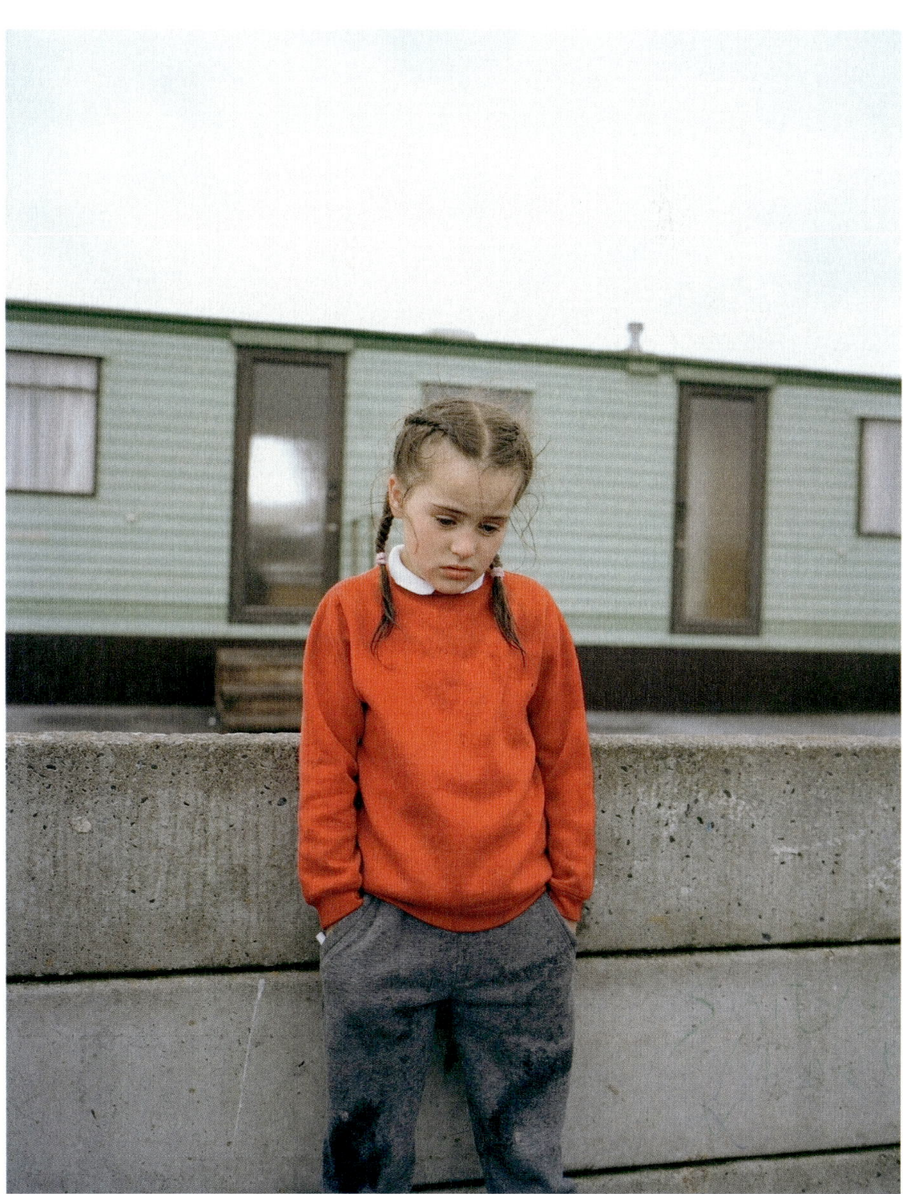

31 JAN A. STAIGER & DANIEL NIEDERMEIER

simili modo

What happens if we don't act with foresight? We make mistakes. How do we enable ourselves to get access to a world that has so far only been pure imagination? We create playable worlds of make-believe. Jan and Daniel document isolated systems that meet their designated function of imitating given regularities and consequently set the course of transformation that we as society will notice in the long run.

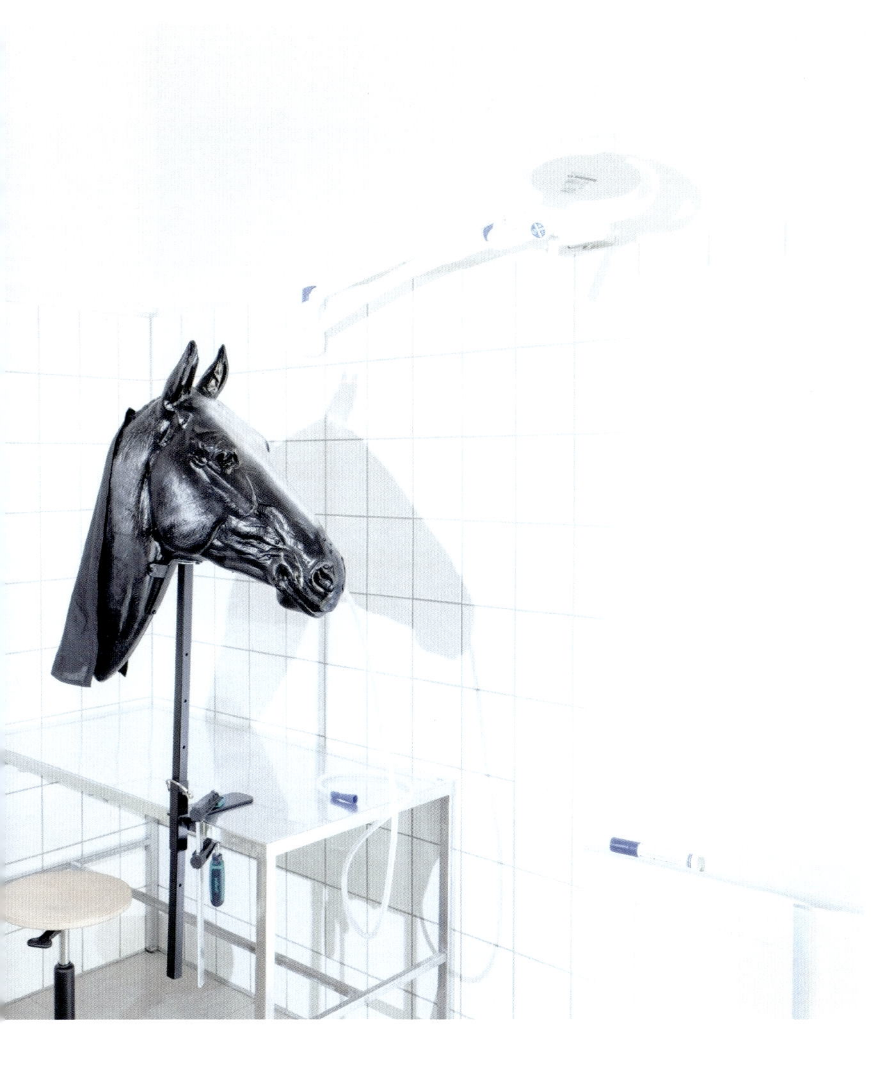

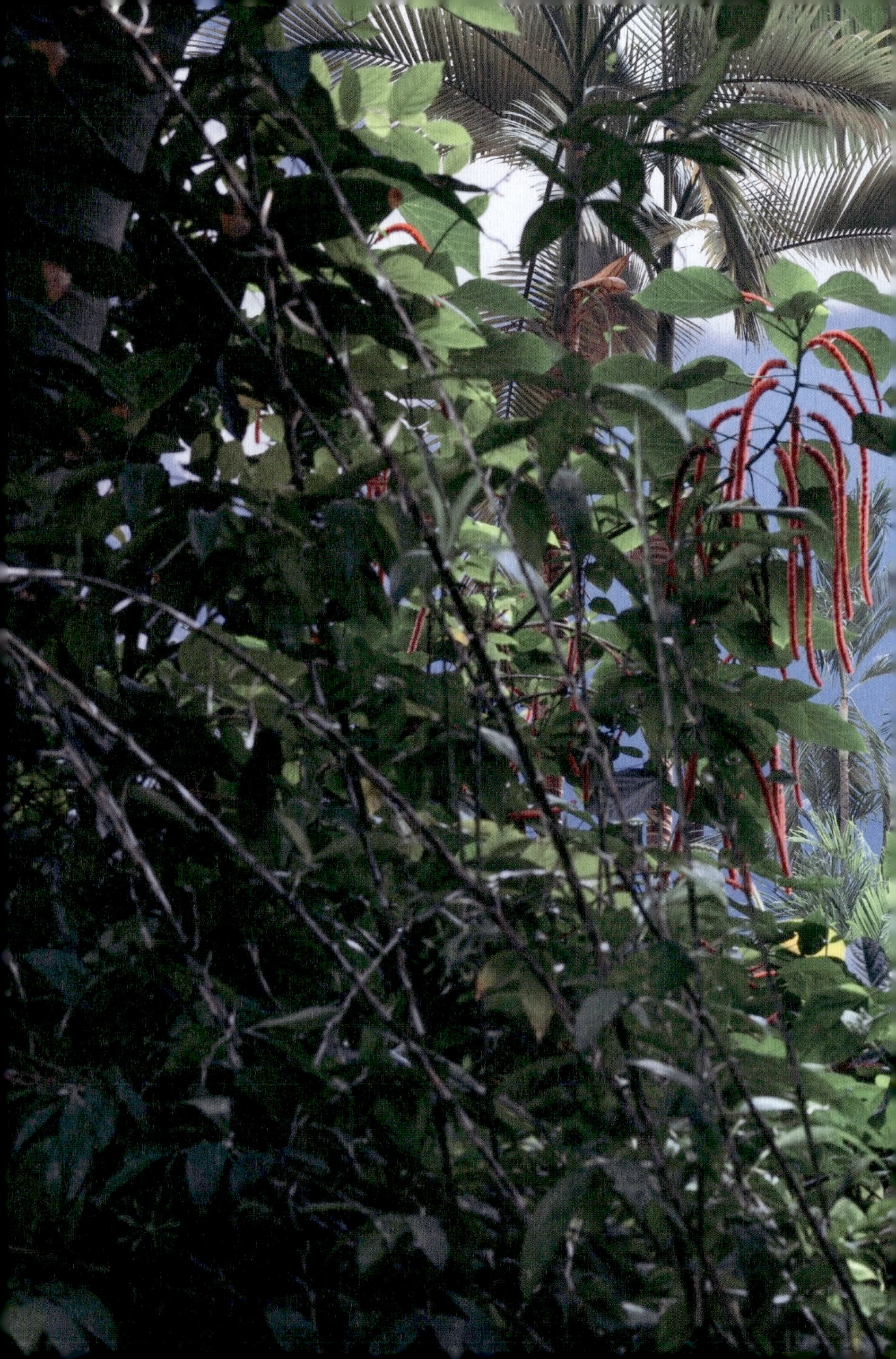

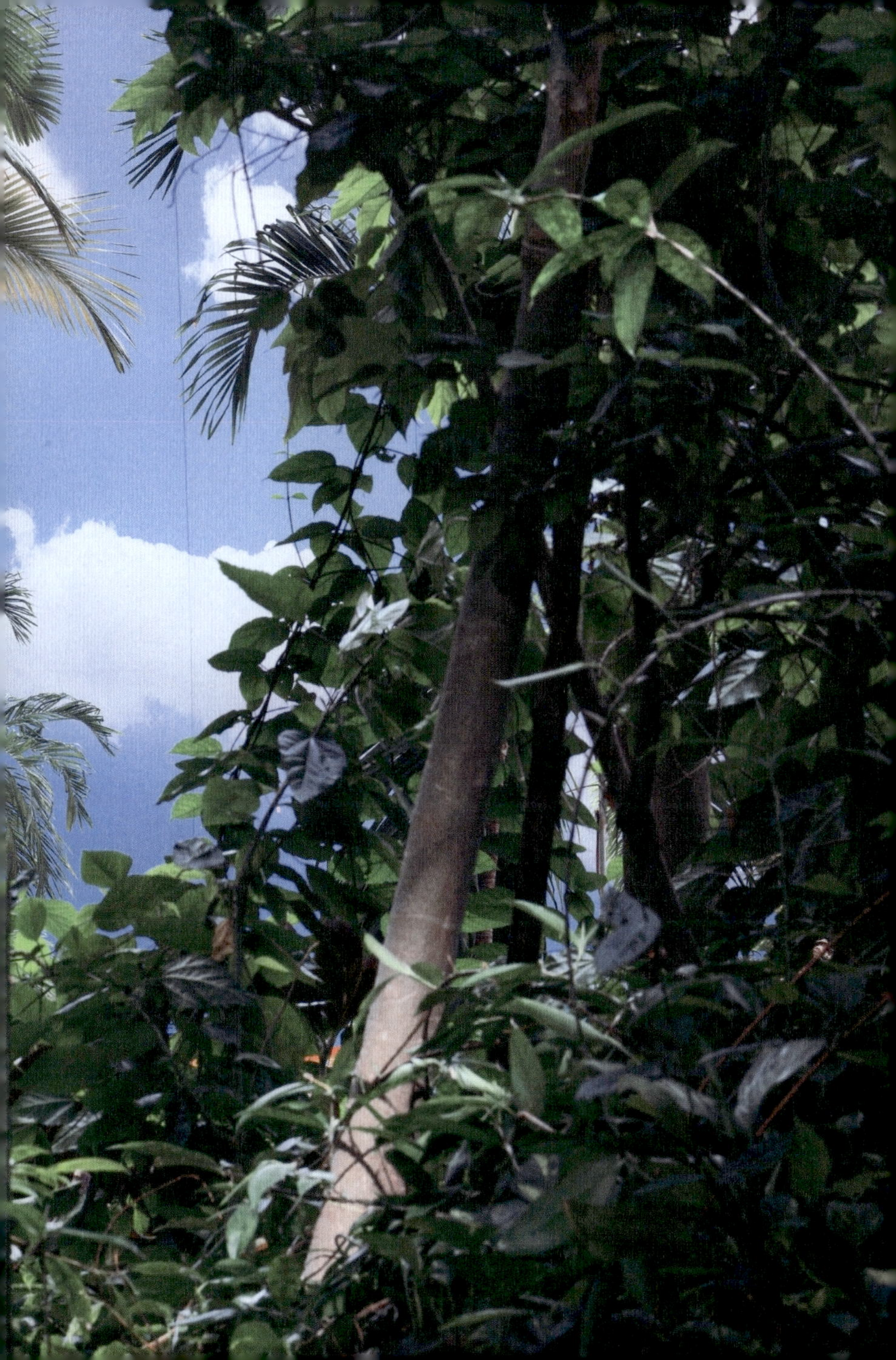

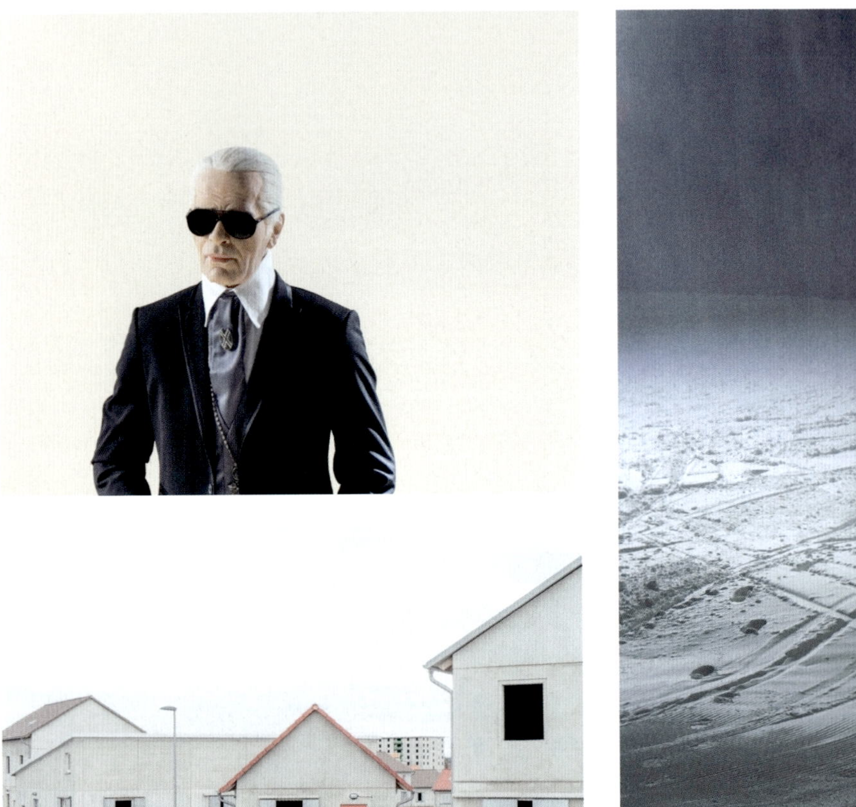

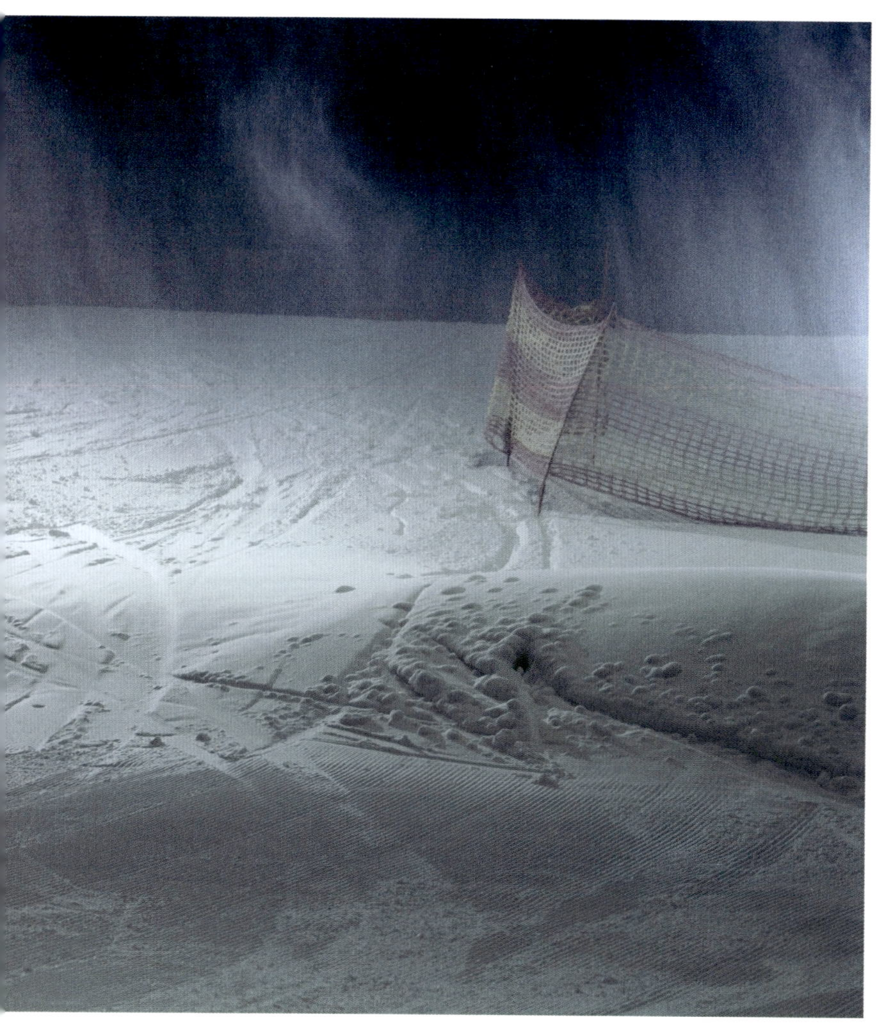

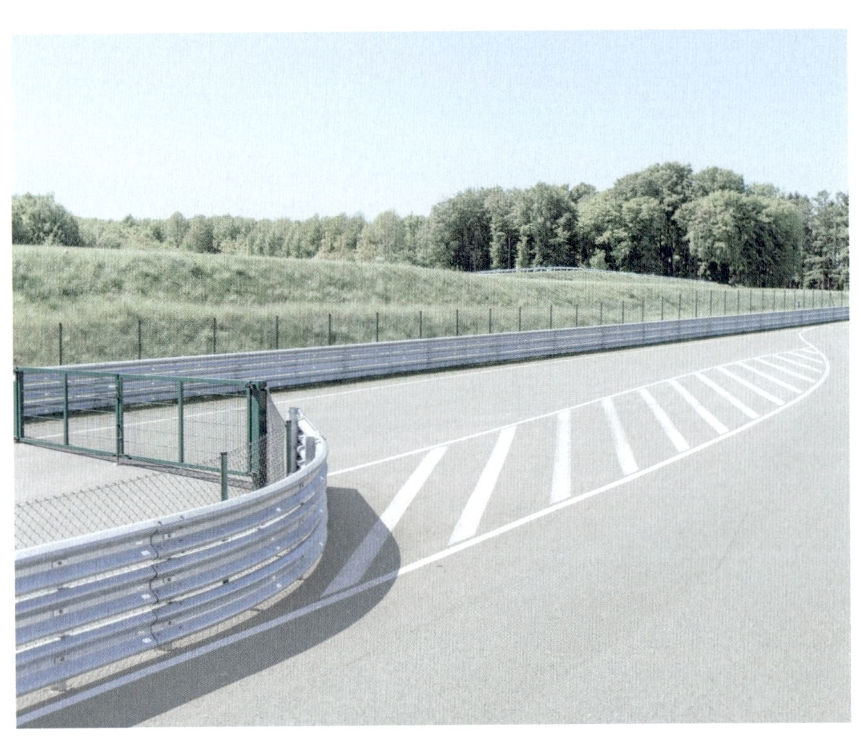

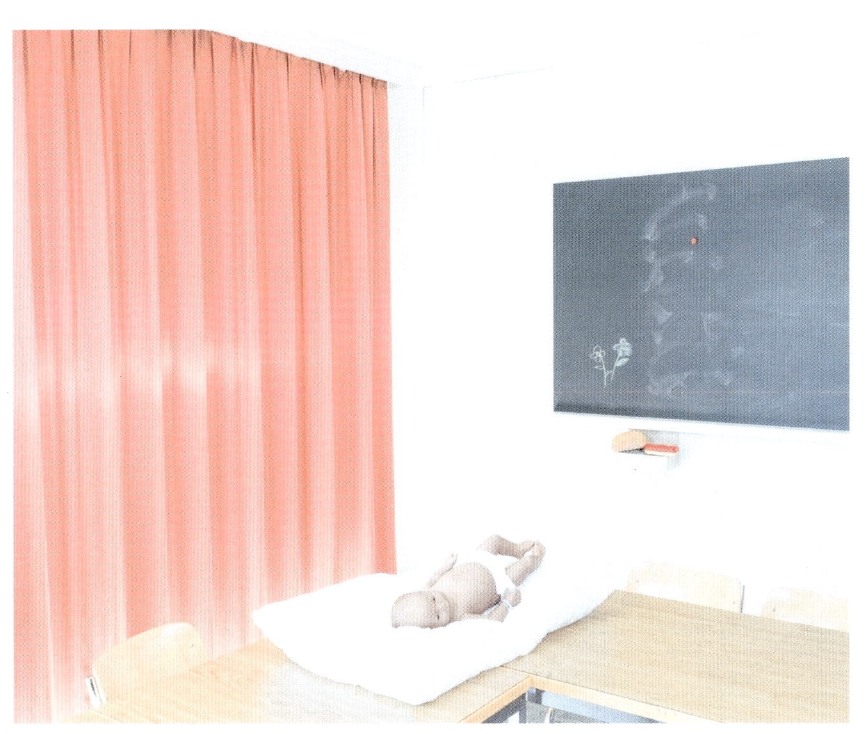

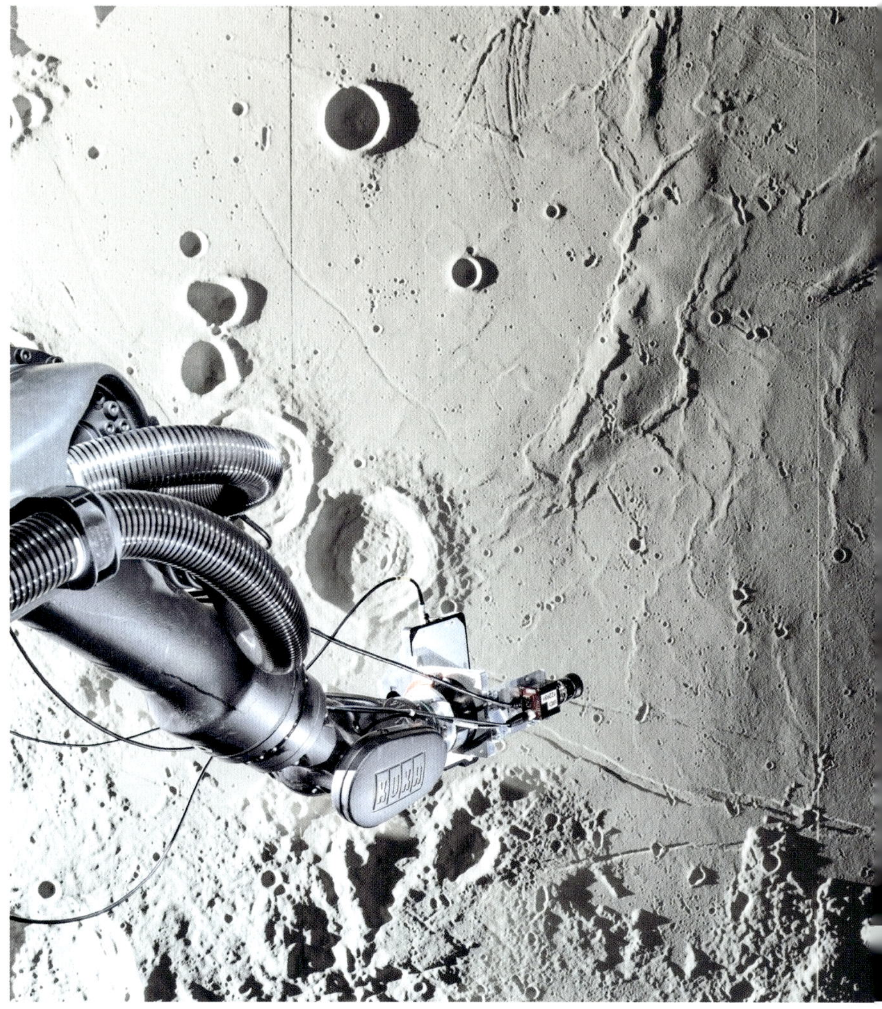
KUKA

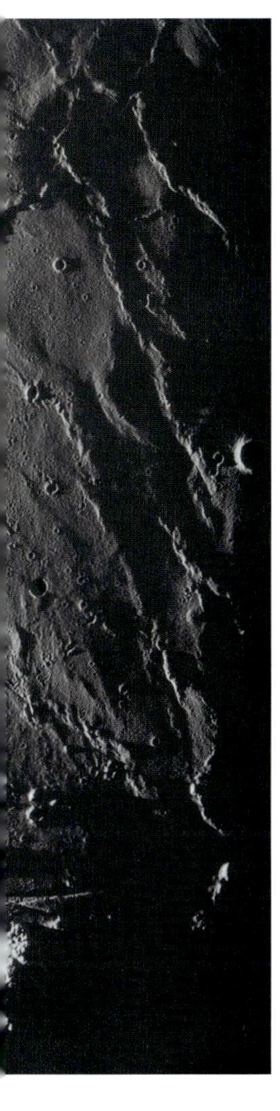

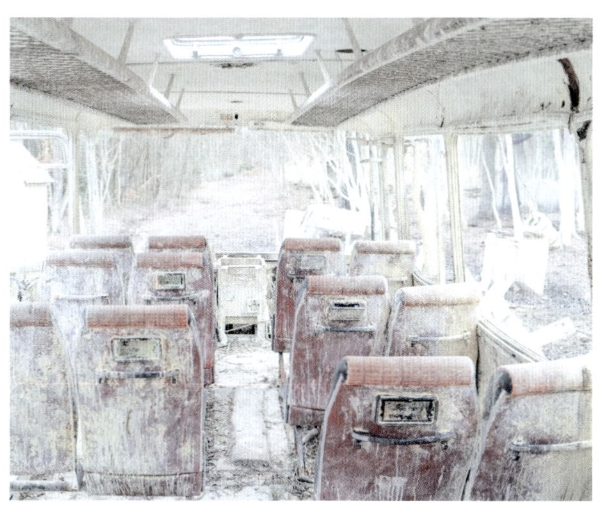

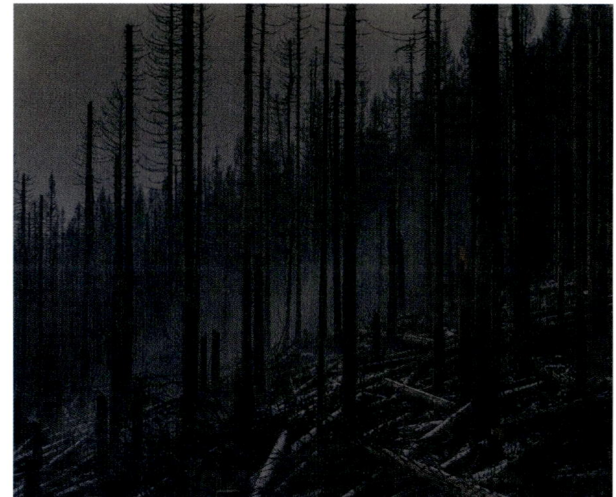

LUCREZIA ZANARDI

32

Present Traces of a Past Existence: A Photographic Research

Following the means of ethnographic researchers, Lucrezia's project reshapes the story of the Dutch intellectual, Etty Hillesum (Middelburg January 15, 1914-Auschwitz November 30, 1914—her journey, the places and atmospheres about which she writes, by combining archive research and photographic intervention. When presented as an exhibition, sound and words are superimposed on the images in an attempt to give the archived past a new structure.

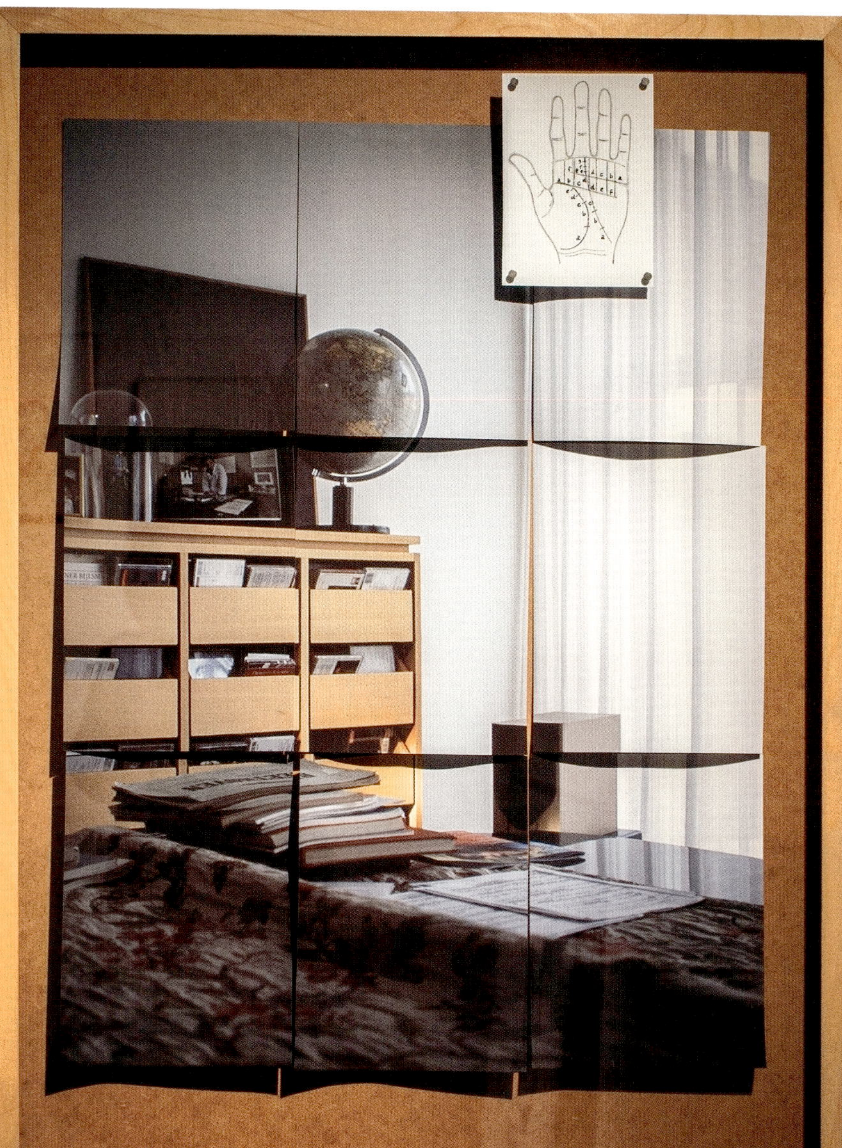

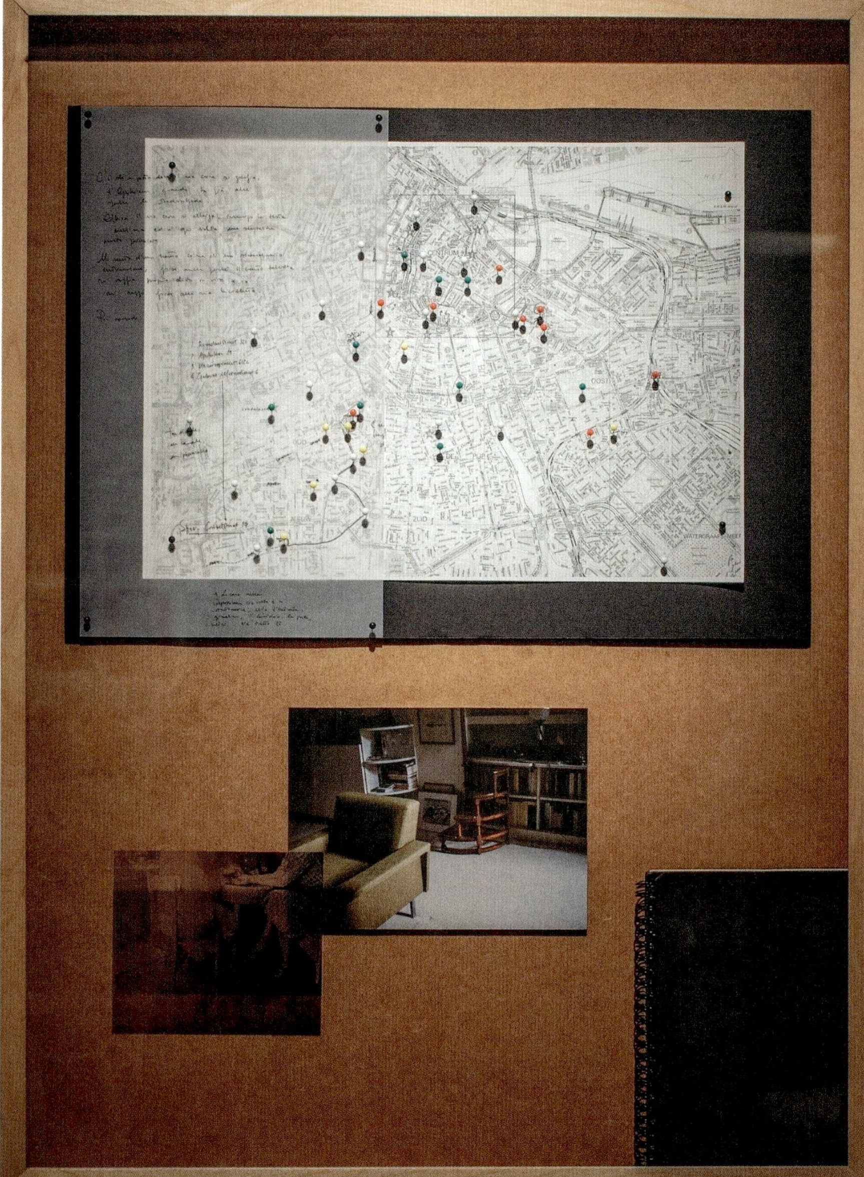

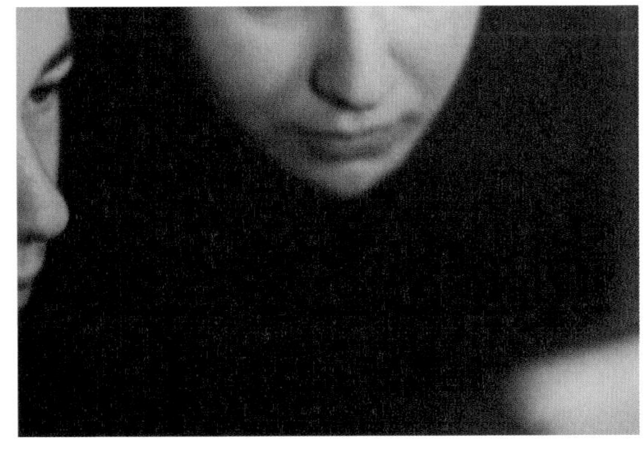

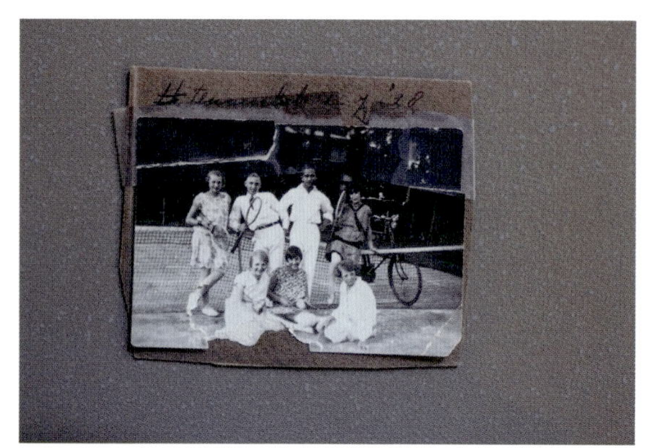

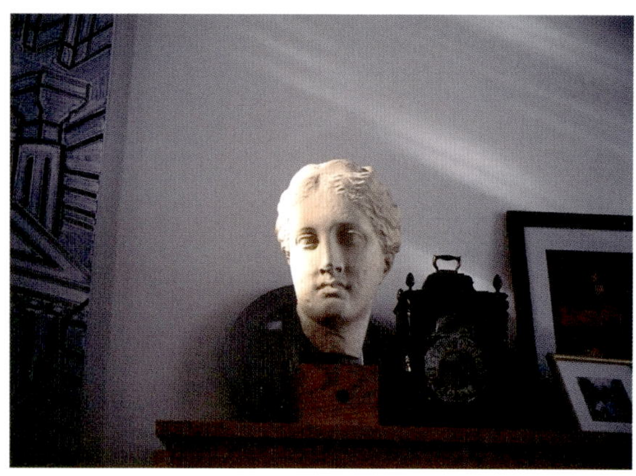

Ja, Ja, Ja, „ de
liegt in den Man
dein!" und tan
woher kommen
trockneten ent

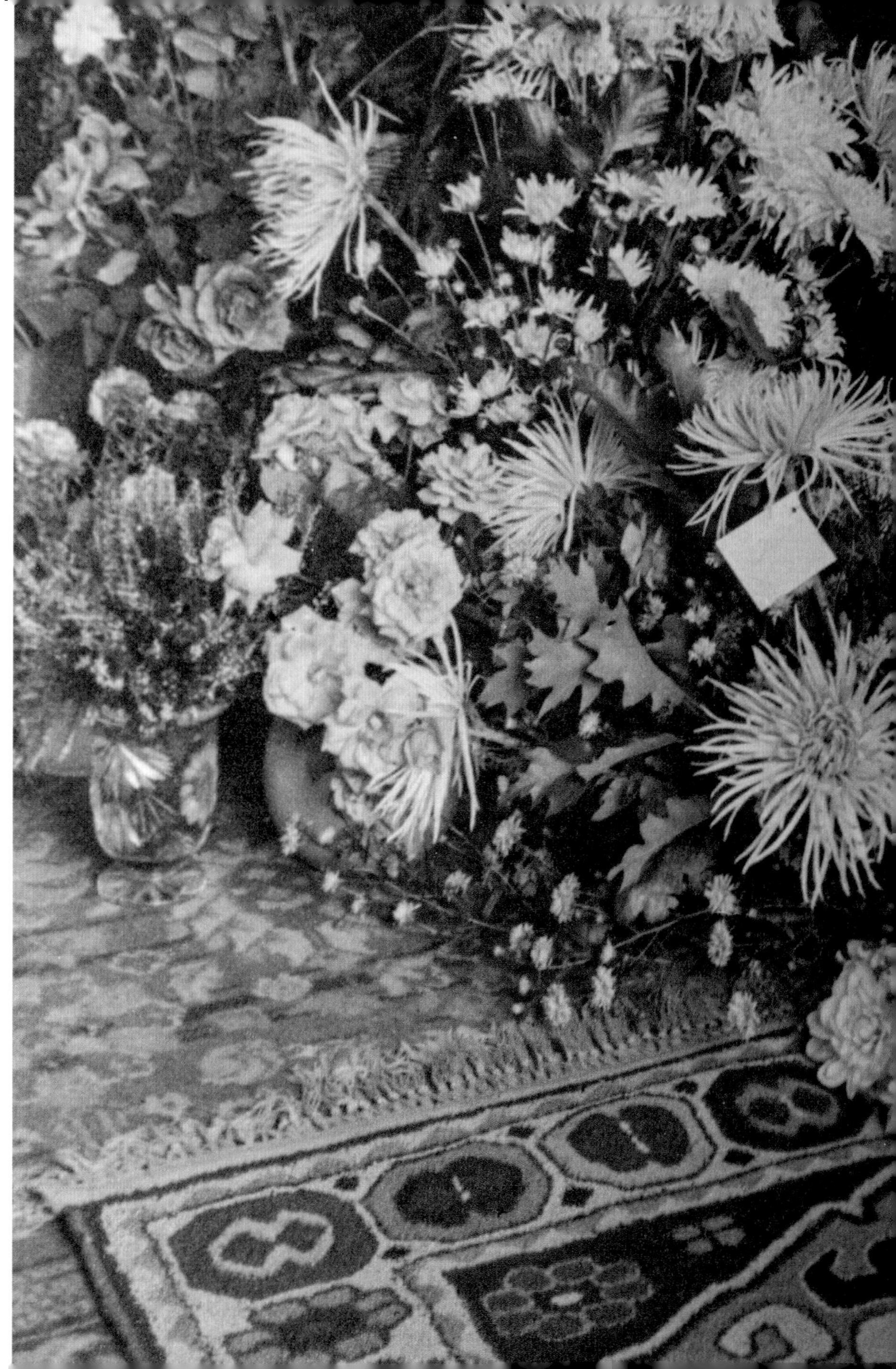

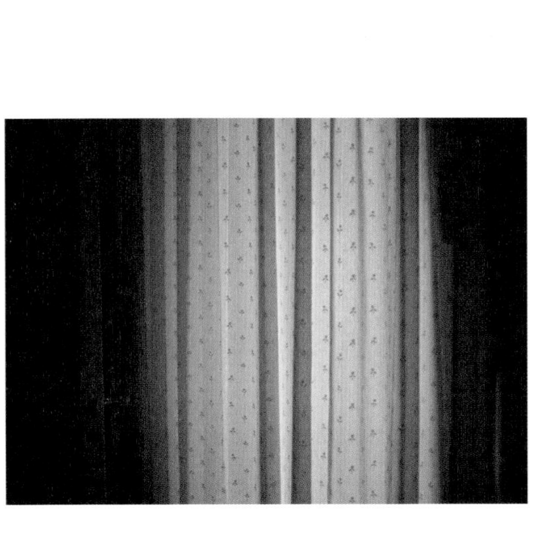

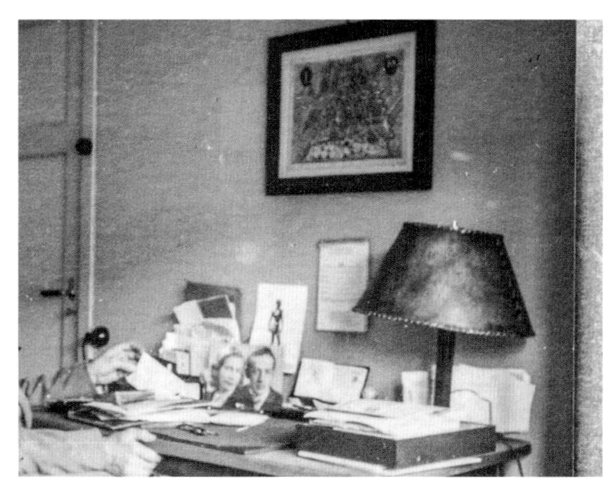

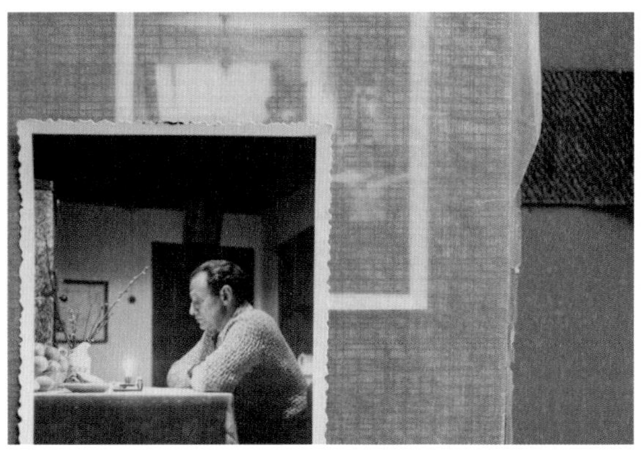

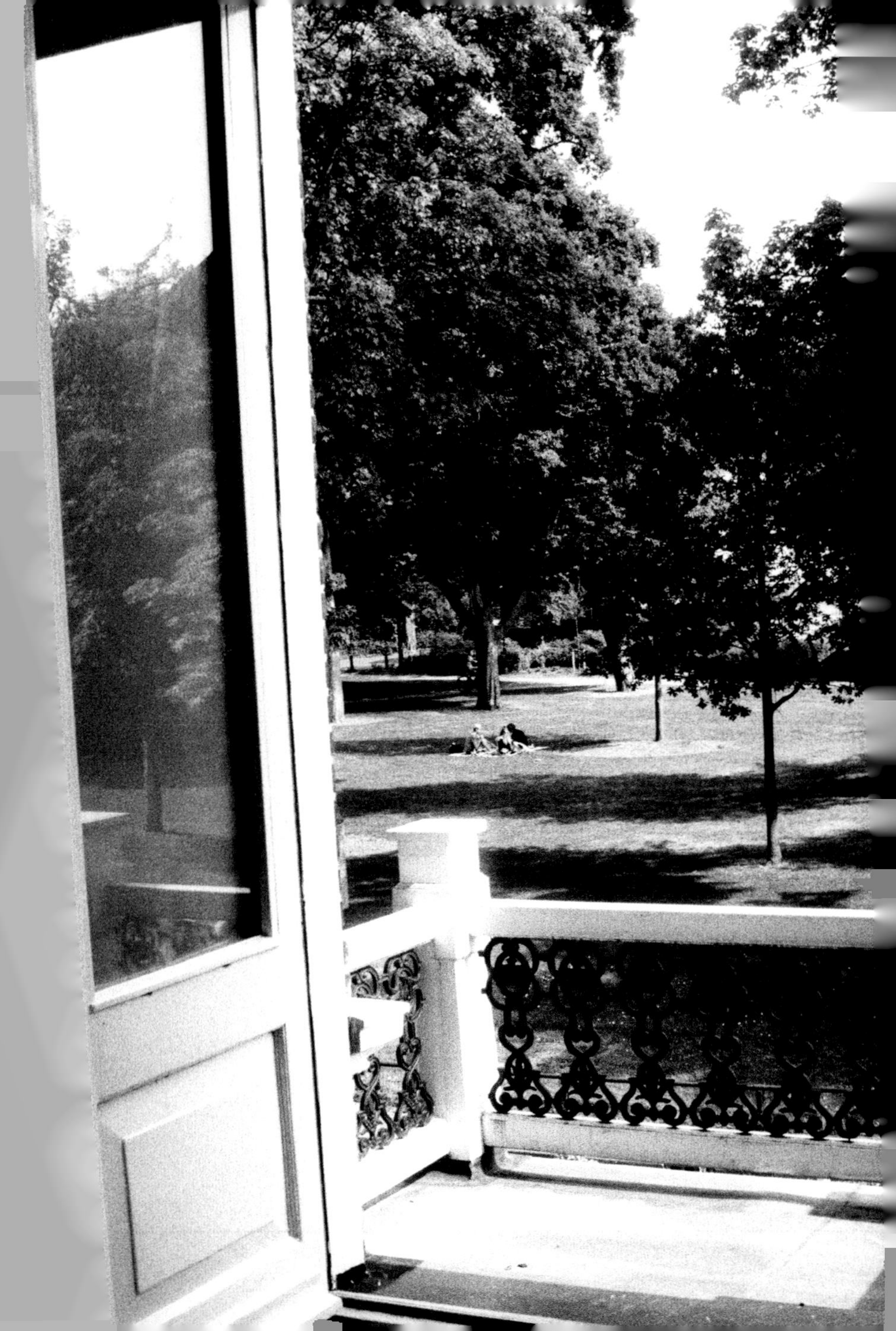

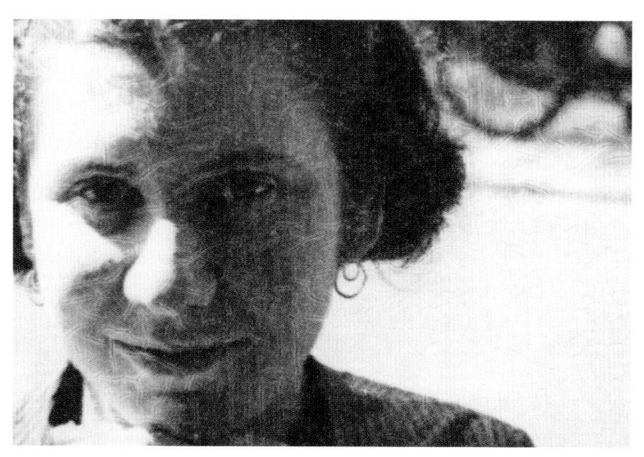

Stark philosophische Hand.

Musikalisch im Sinne des mu
könnte farbig dichten.

Sensibel, nervös.

~~Die Hand hat eine starke, e~~
~~... noch nich~~
zuzugeben, da das Rationale
Opposition zu dem Rationale
nicht statt gefundene Ausei

SHIRIN ABEDi

MAY I HAVE THi$ DANCE?

33

Shirin's pictures show Nona (18), Mojdeh (21), Reyhaneh (22), Elham (24) and Yasamin (22), who belong to the same ballet group in Tehran. They are part of the Iranian post-war generation, which stands up for self-determination, freedom and equality. Whereas, during the revolution the abolition of ballet symbolized independence from the West. Today, dance stands for the longing of a generation for Western freedom.

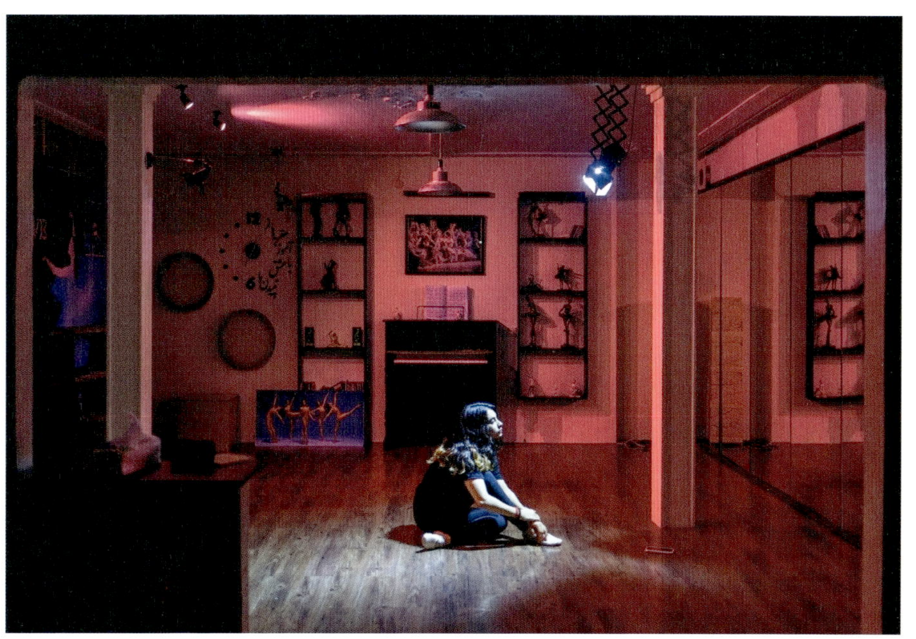

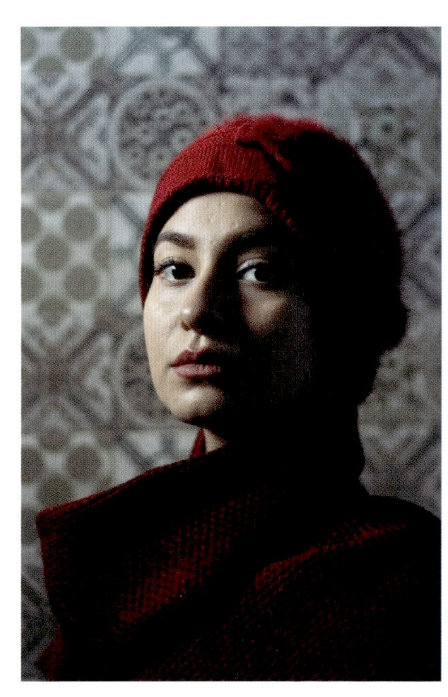

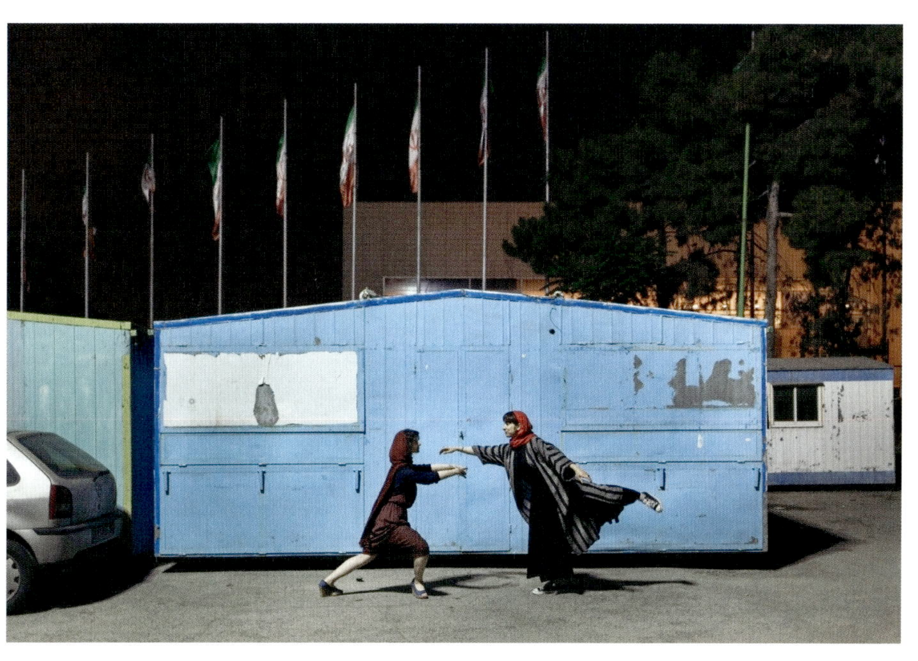

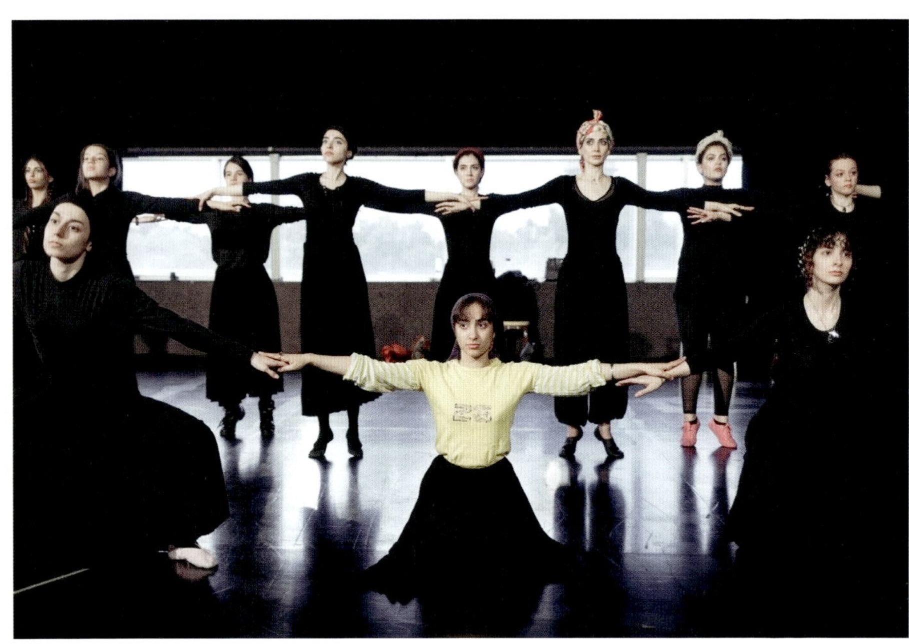

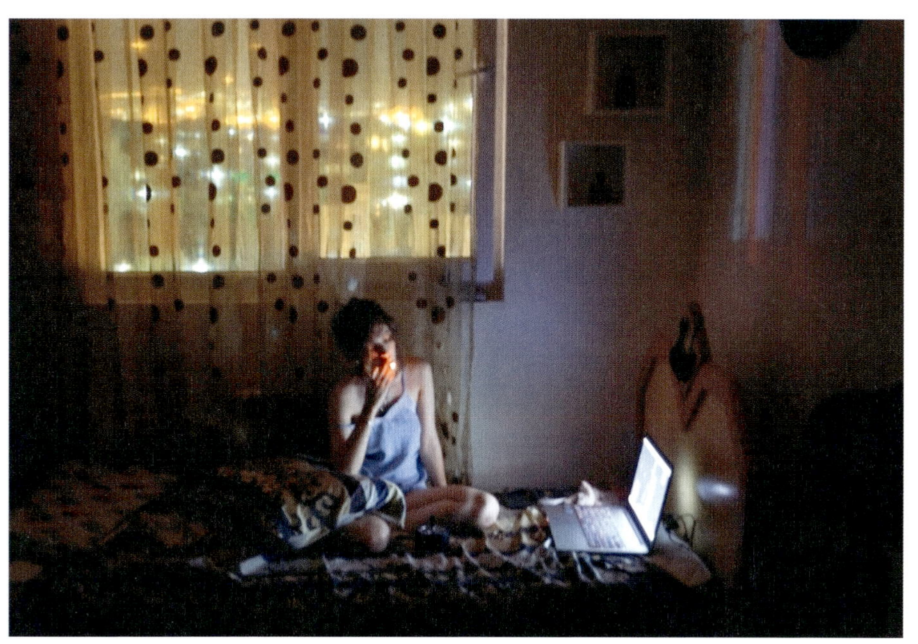

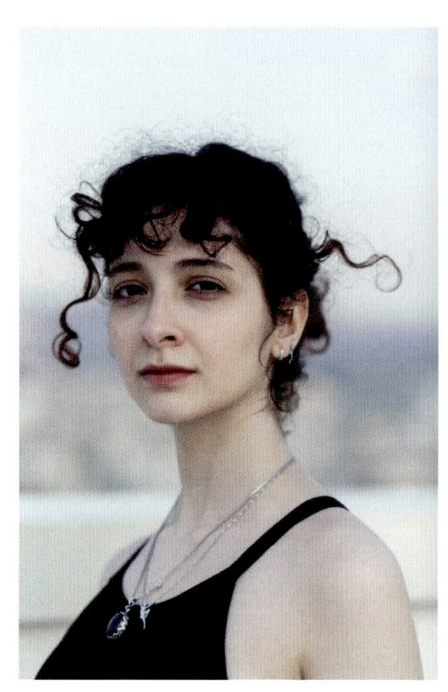

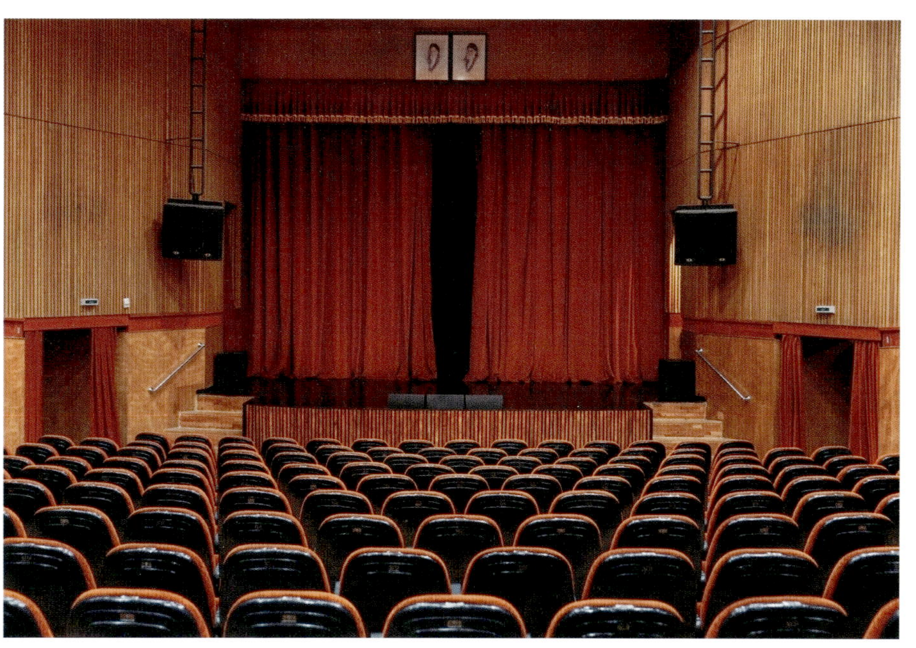

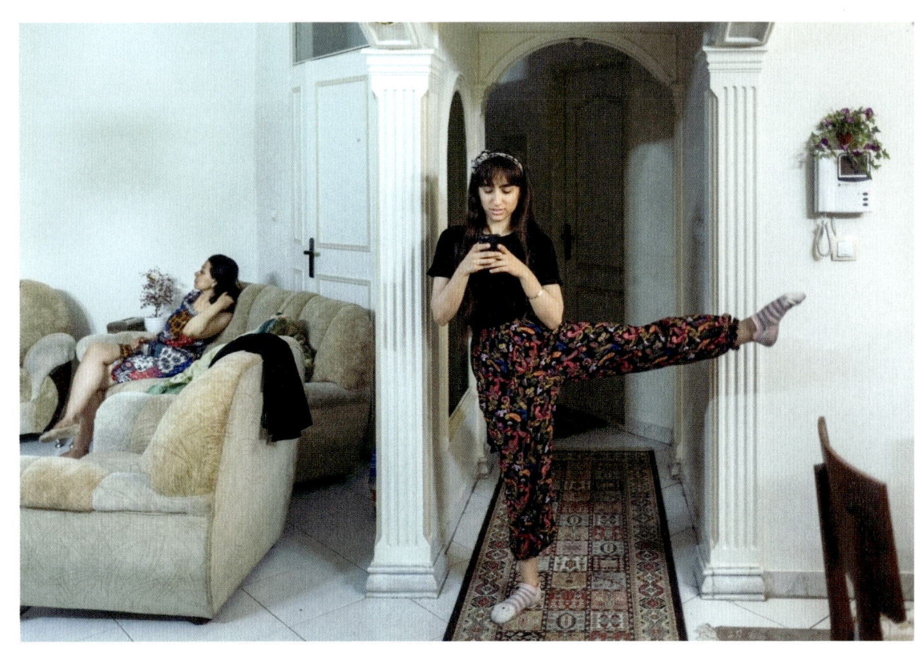

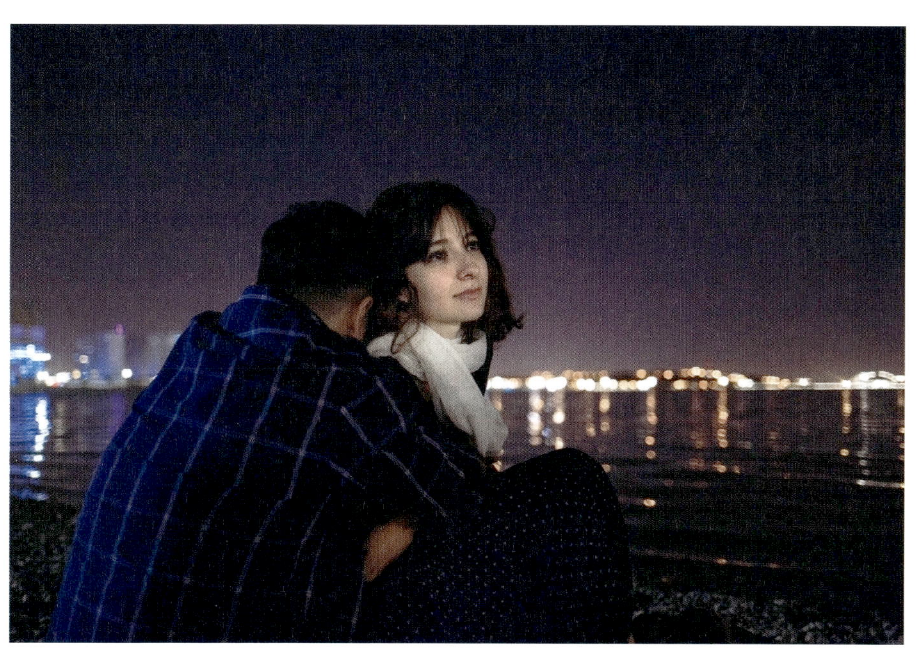

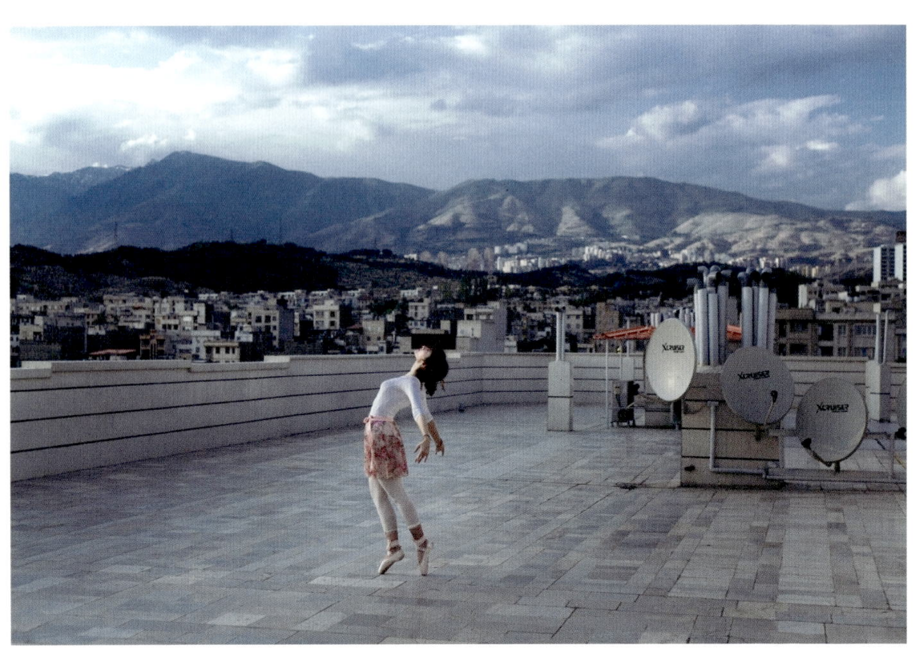

WILKO MEIBORG

SONG-MACHINE

34

In the last 60 years, a serious hype has developed in Indonesia around all kinds of songbirds. The love for these animals is deeply rooted in culture, but due to the enormous population growth it is becoming a problem for the birds, which are increasingly threatened by extinction in the wild. An expression of this love are competitions in which songbirds compete against each other. Wilko's project aims to question what we can learn about ourselves through this phenomenon.

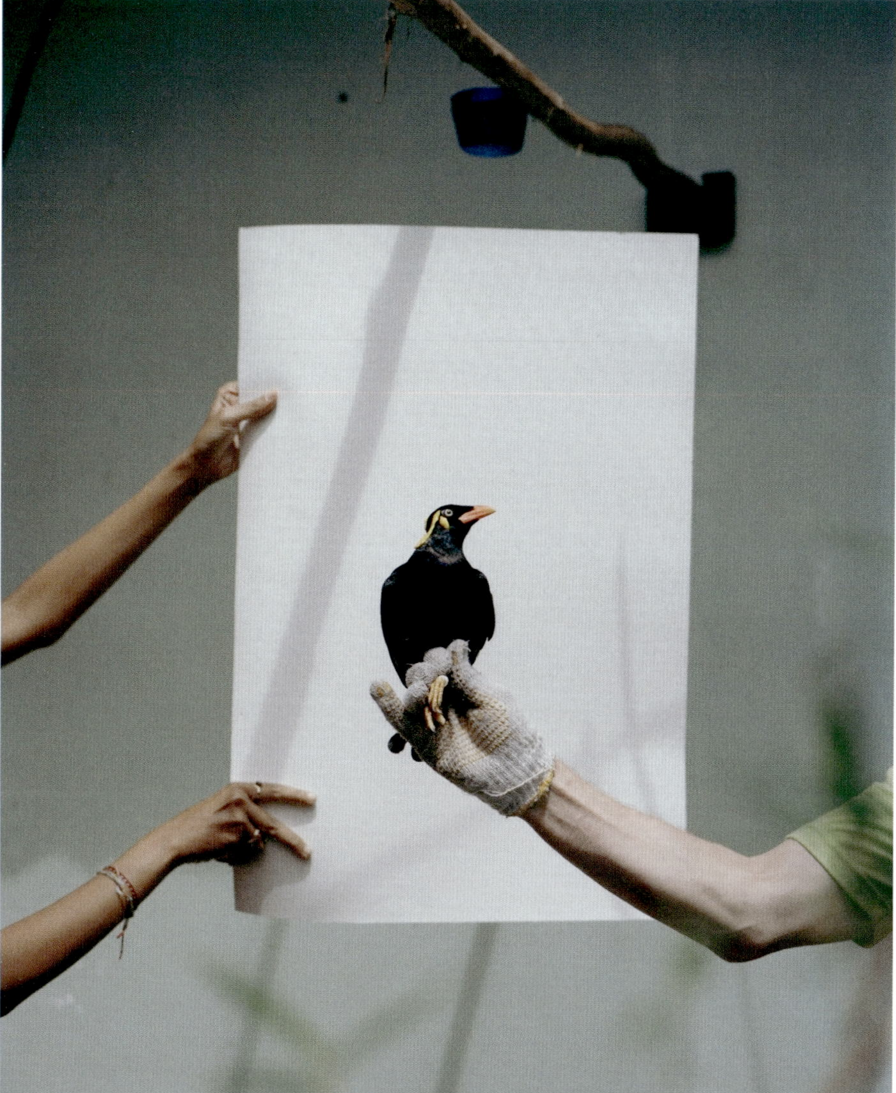

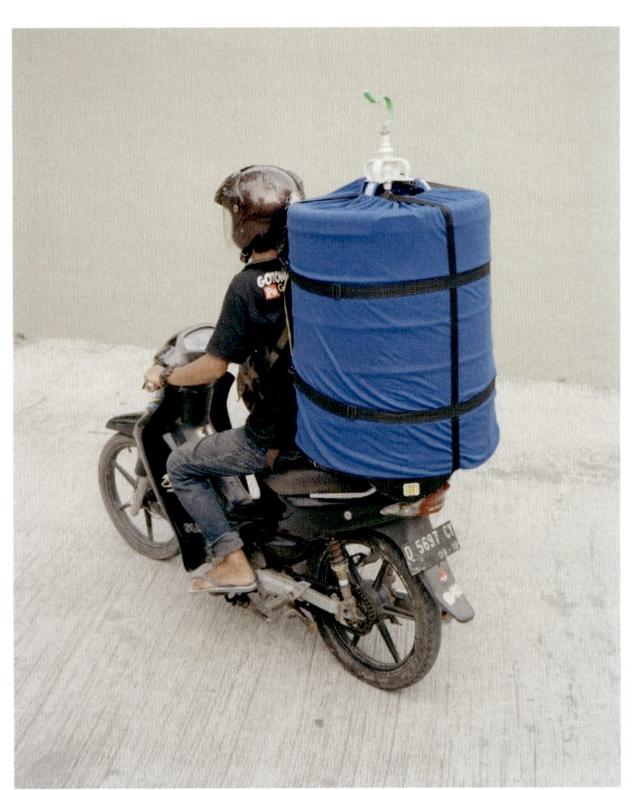
D 5697 CY

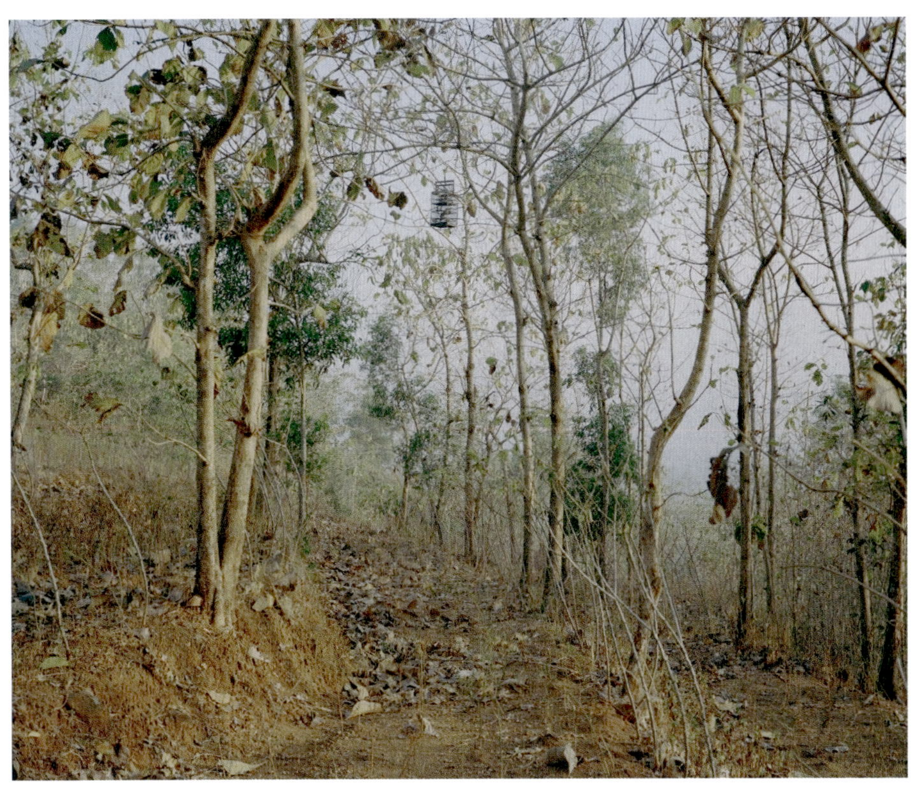

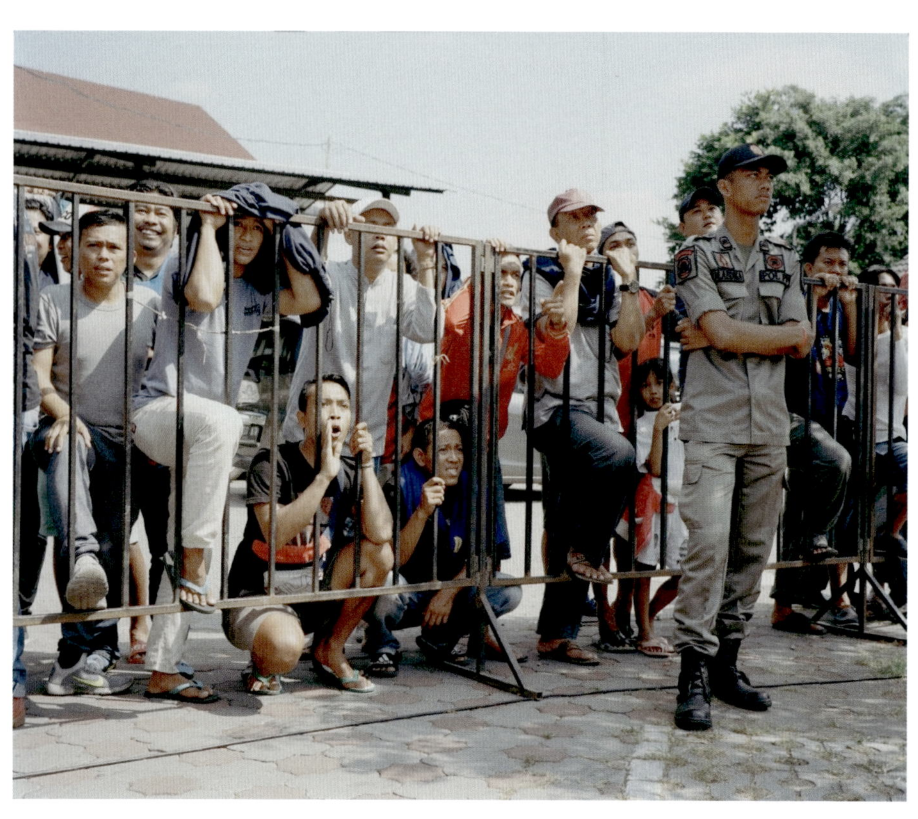

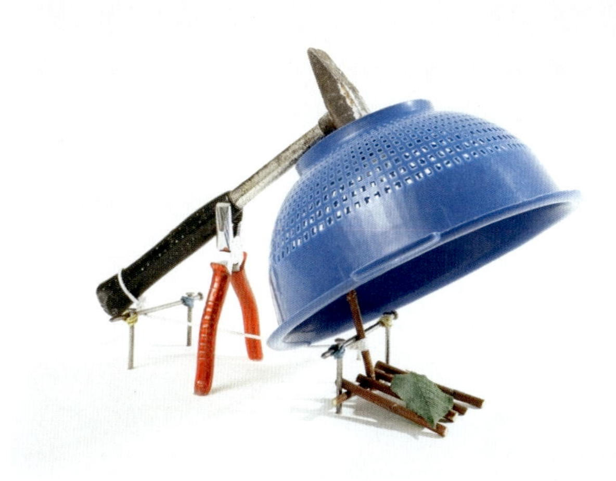

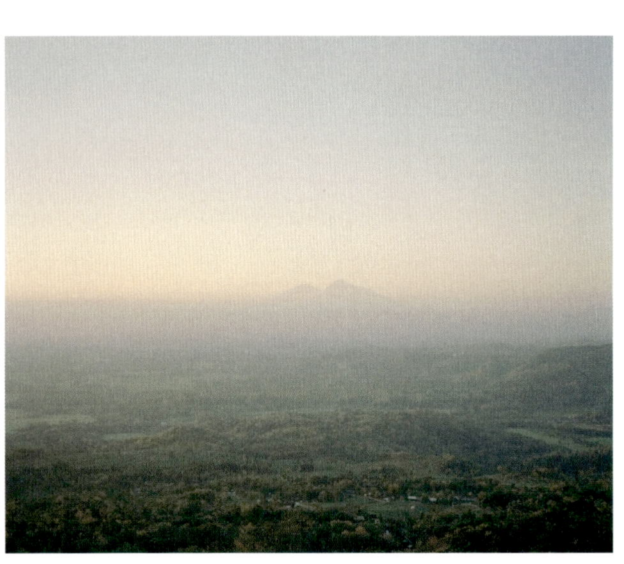

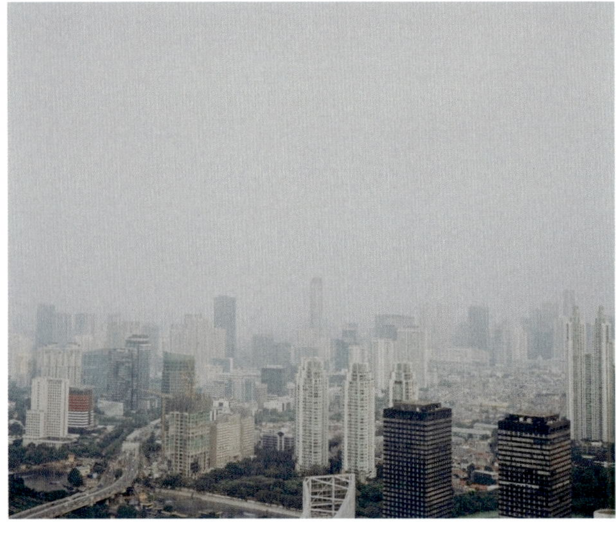

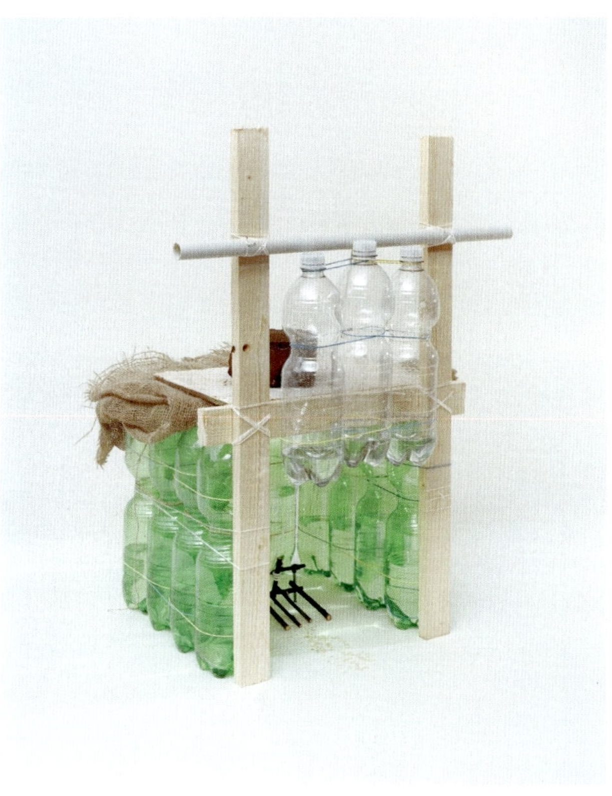

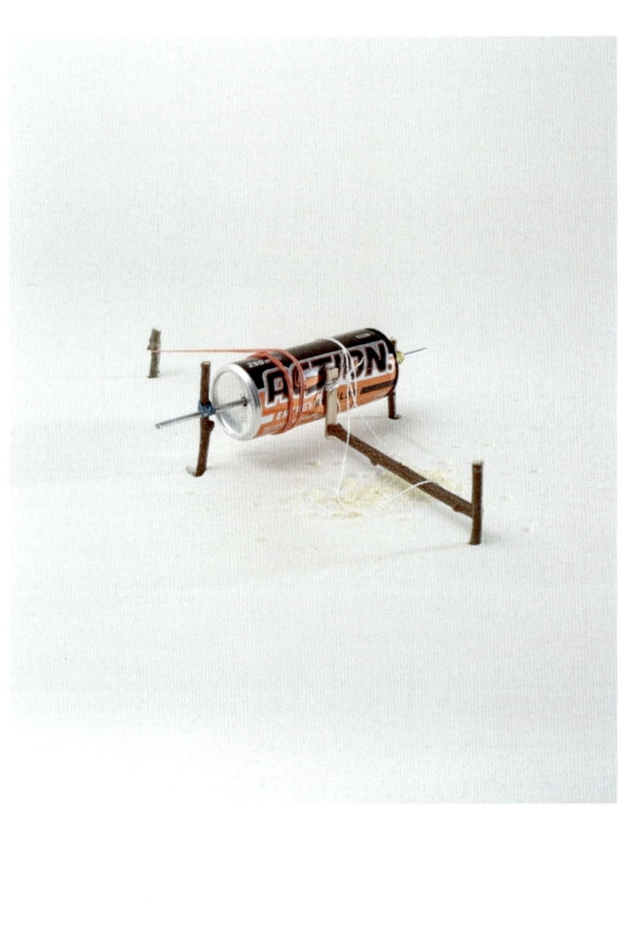

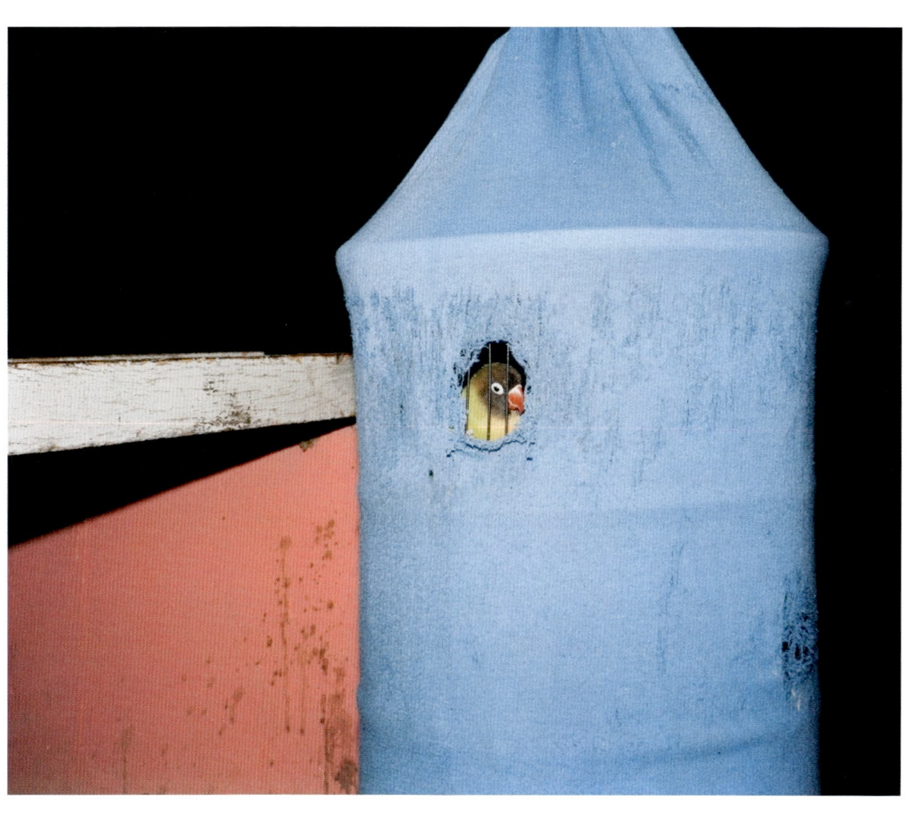

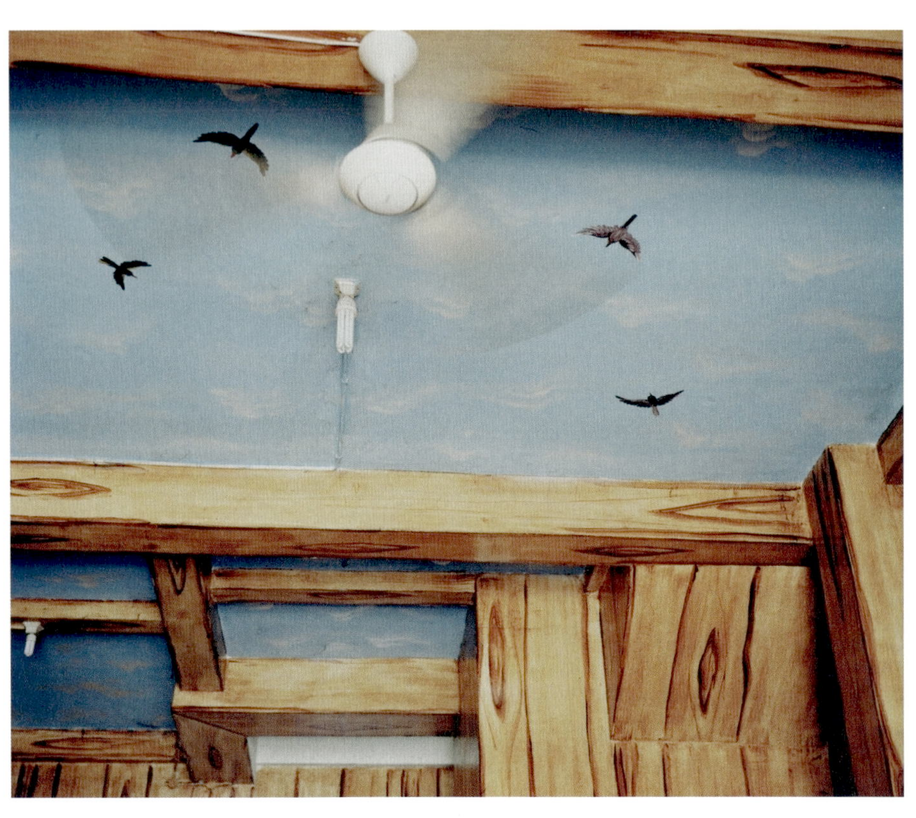

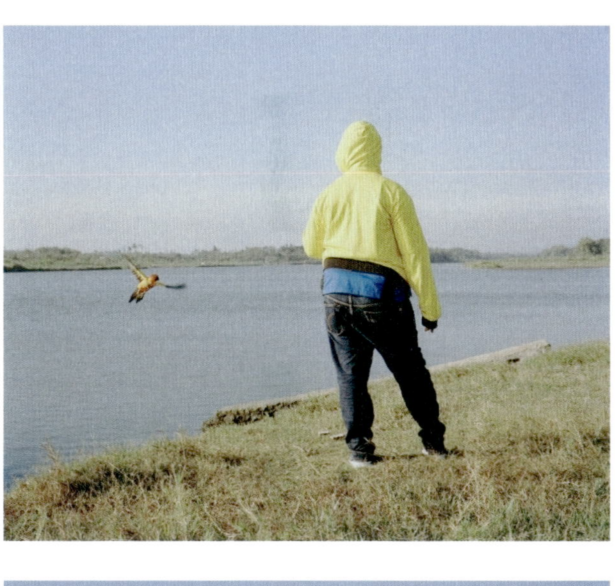

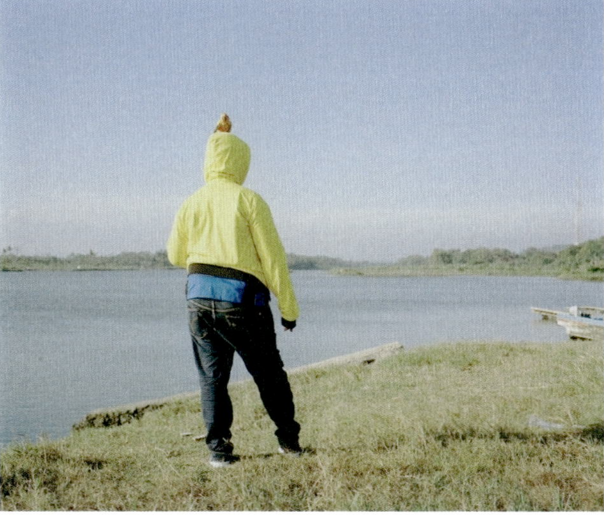

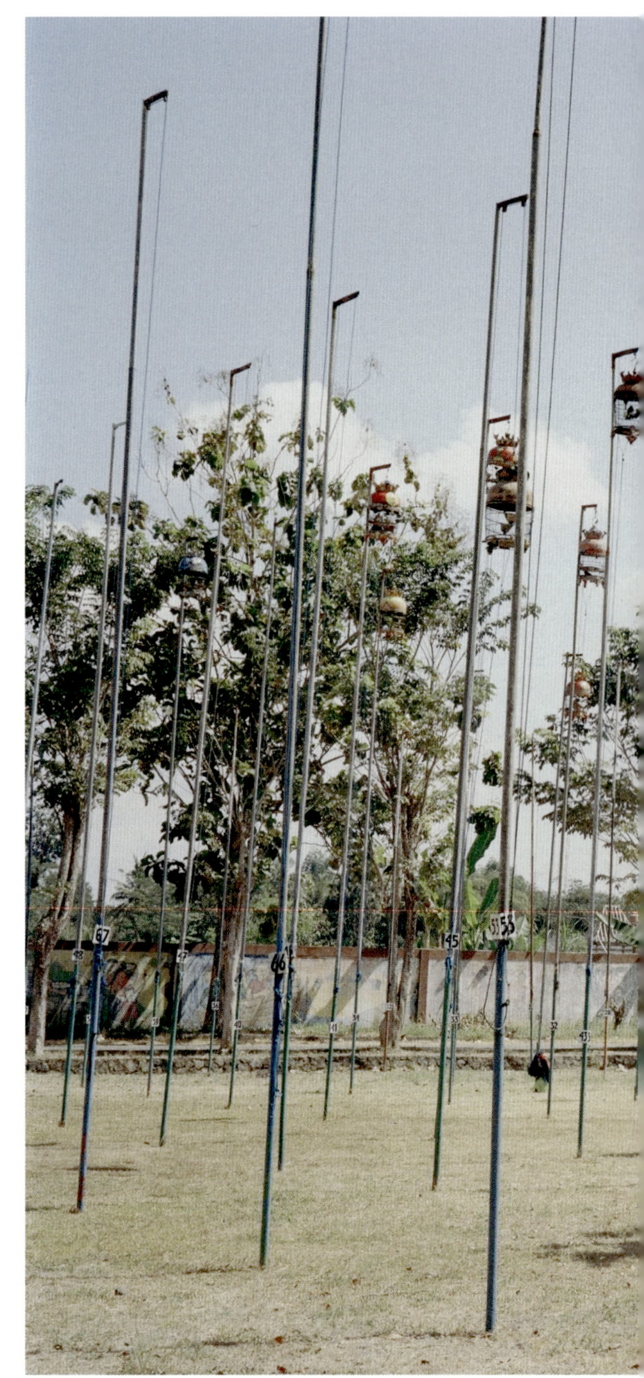
67
66
45

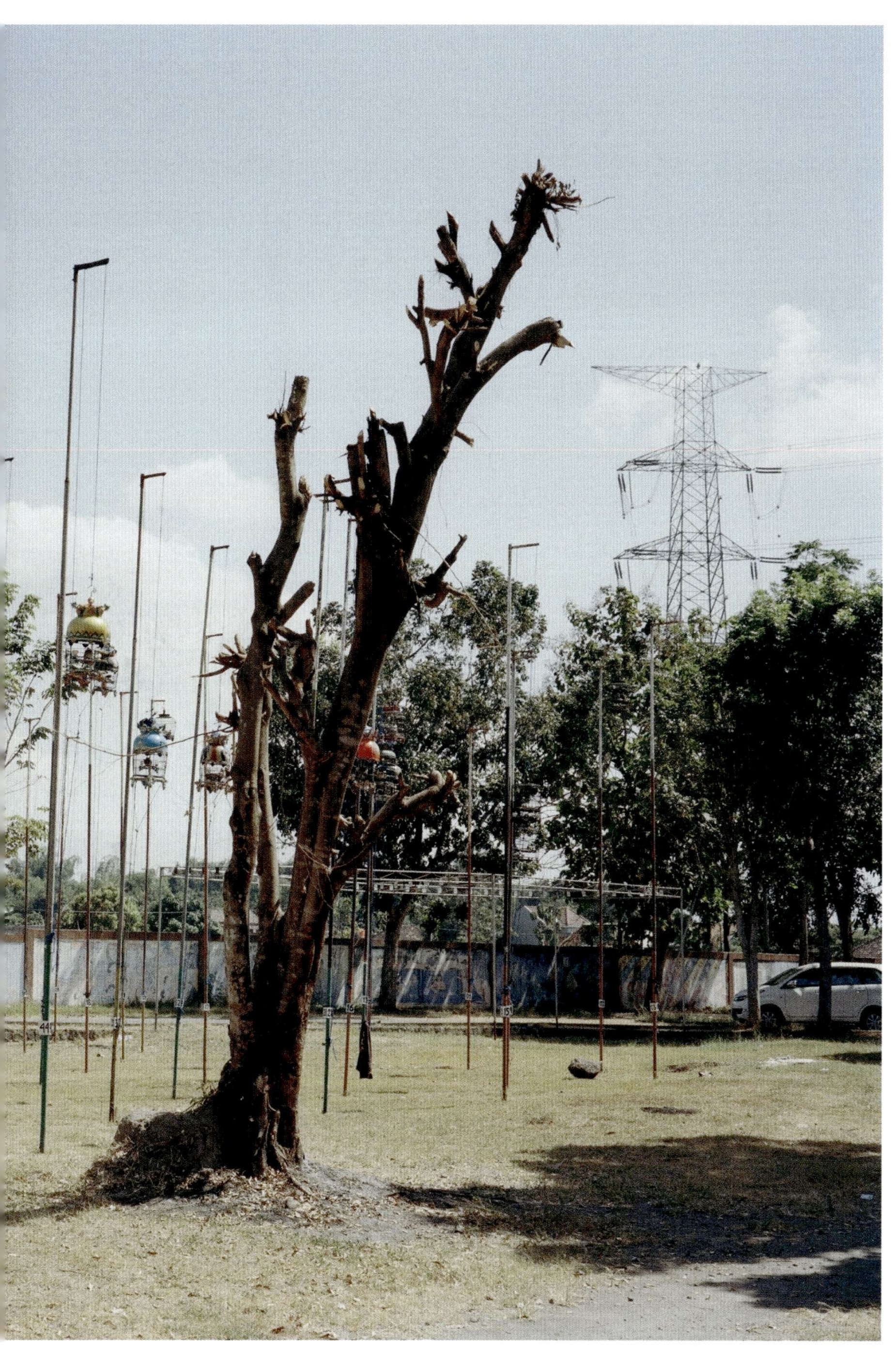

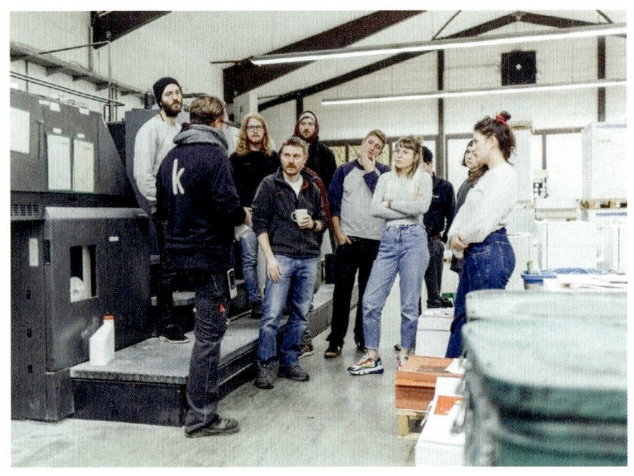

After further01's final printing file was finished, the work on the book wasn't. This left a lot of people thankless, at least in print. So we want to thank Kettler for giving us a group tour through their printing house and Integralis for showing us their bookbindery. Special thanks to the awesone lunch and tasty black tea. Thank you to Elke for hosting the packaging party and Atelier Amore for hosting the release party and exhibition. Thanks to all the fotobussis who contributed to the book by either putting stickers on the cover, wrapping it in print sheets, clearing your bedroom or garage to make space for a temporary warehouse, organizing the shipping, ..., without all of you we would have no book to work on and less friends to love.

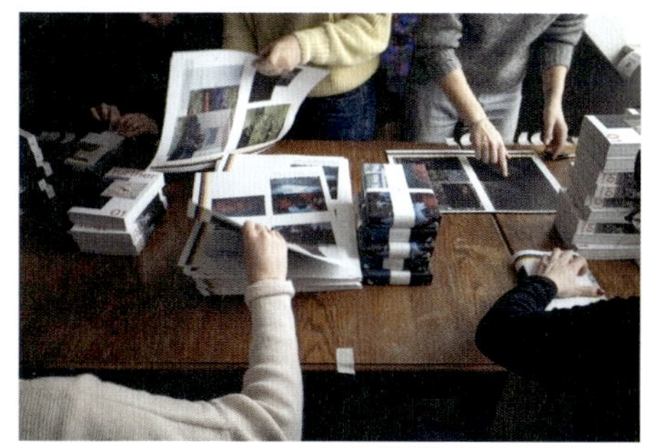

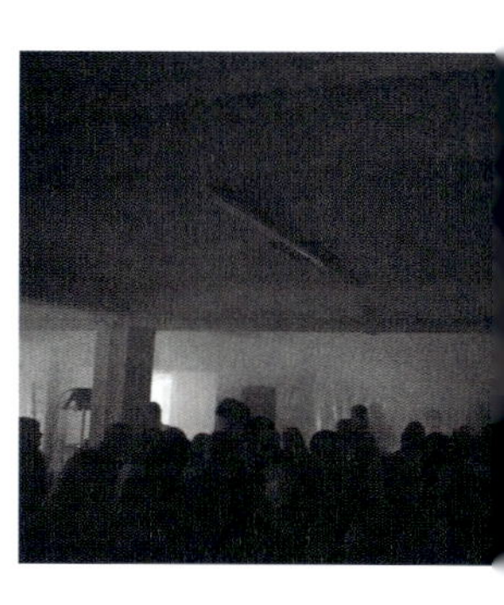

THANK YOU

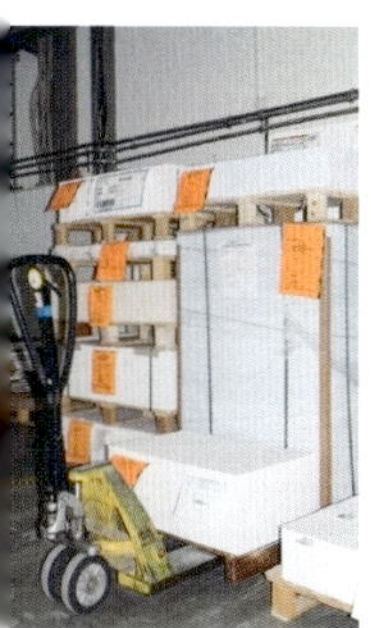

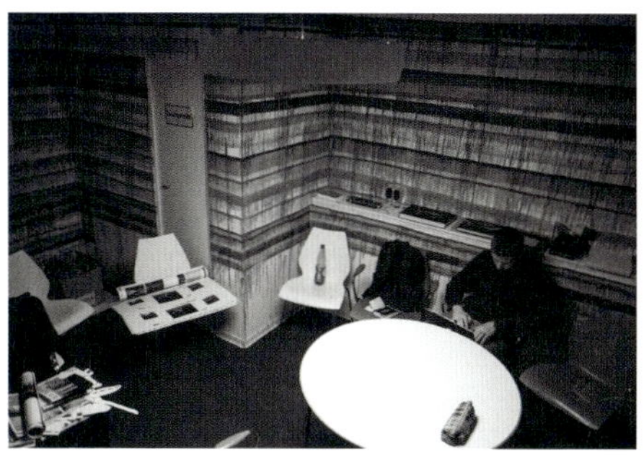

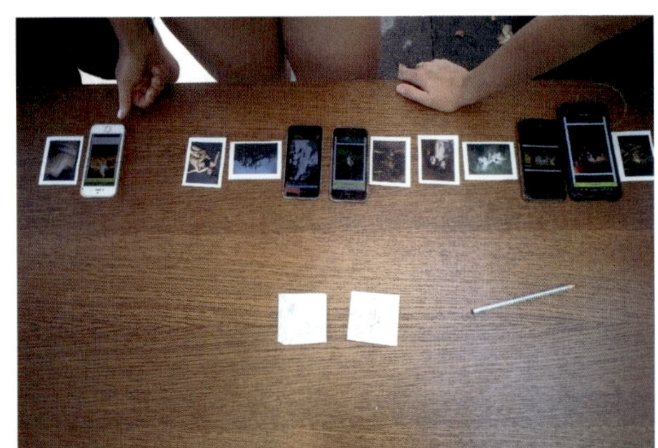

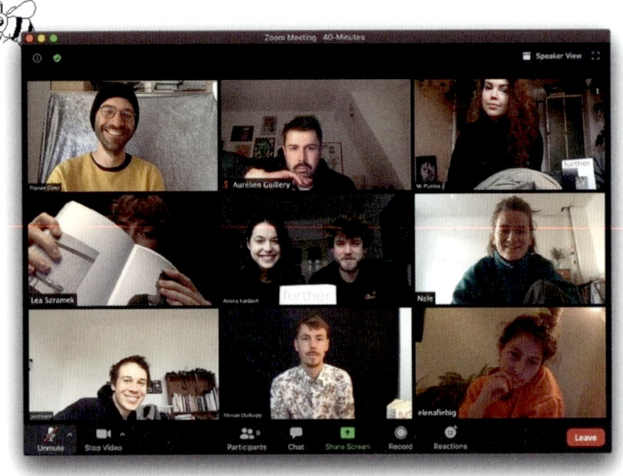
Zoom Meeting 40-Minutes
Speaker View
Aurélien Guillery
further
Lea Szramek
further
Nele
elenafiebig
Unmute
Stop Video
Participants
Chat
Share Screen
Record
Reactions
Leave

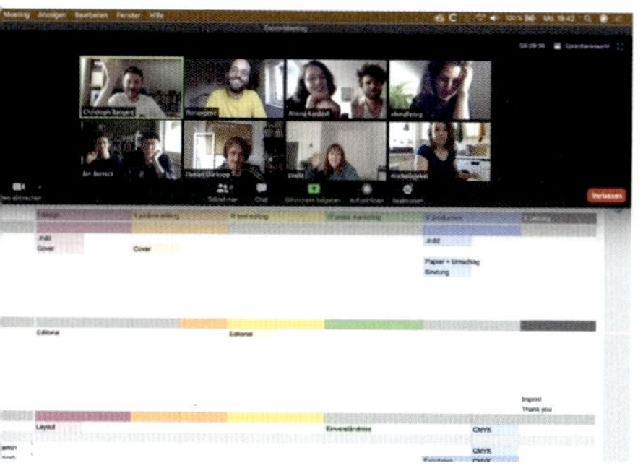

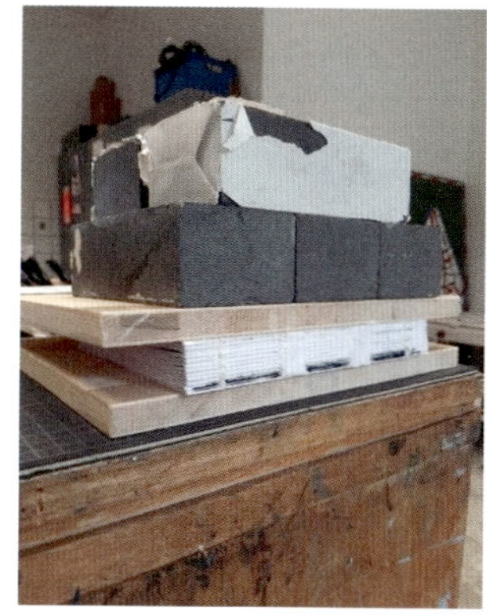

further 02 was made in roughly 52 hours of online meetings and one editing garden party in summer, as well as countless hours of individual work. We cumulated 62GB of data and 2.665 files. We used 24.248 words with 160.499 characters to communicate, mixed with 247 emojis (with our favorite being the bee). To keep this organized, we used 723 lines of
online spreadsheet
We had to mail eac
package during the
very urgent, otherw
pictures to edit. Th
weekly meetings w
than what followed
happy. further 02 w

THIS FREE ZOOM MEETING HAS ENDED

THANK YOU FOR CHOOSING ZOOM!

OK

but without hugs :(

IMPRINT

further 02 was made by Florian Dürkopp, Elena Fiebig, Florian Genz, Aurélien Guillery, Pia Henkel, Paula Hornickel, Michelle Jekel, Aliona Kardash, Nele Schulze, Lea Szramek, Magnus Terhorst and Lukas Zander of the fotobus Publication Team
with help from Christoph Bangert, Jan Borreck, Nils Heck, Josh Kern and Jule Wild

The book shows pictures by Eyad Abou Kasem, Paula de Abrantes, Carina Al-Hashemi, Britta Baumann, Sonja Baumeister, Felix Bernhard, Michael Braunschädel, Marvin Böhm, Nora Börding, Laurenz Bostedt, Lilly Dohmann, Leon Joshua Dreischulte, Domenic Driessen, Janick Entremont, Ronja Falkenbach, Jascha Fibich, Elena Fiebig, Jonas Freudenberger, Simon Gerlinger, Aurélien Guillery, Victor Hedwig, Taat Herzberg, Paula Hornickel, Luise Jakobi, Carsten Kalaschnikow, Ilkay Karakurt, Maren Katerbau, Jannis Keil, Jana Köhler, Mathis Körner, Juri Löchte, Vera Loitzsch, Pascal Mächtlen, Viola Maiwald, Jonathan Mahlendorf, Fiona Mentzel, Merle Meuleneers, Asli Oezcelik, Ola Rebisz, Amelie Sachs, Michael Schmidtmann, Ardelle Schneider, Marie Schwarze, Ole Spata, Torsten Spinti, Jan Staiger, Axel Javier Sulzbacher, Alex Telieps, Magnus Terhorst, Giulia Thinnes, Angelina Vernetti, Magdalena Vidovic, Jonas Völpel, Celia Wagner, Benjamin Zvonar, Florian Genz **as well as** Shirin Abedi, Katja Aßfalg, Jasper Bastian, Jan Borreck, Daniel Chatard,

Paper:
Sappi Atelier 260 g/m2
MagnoMatt 135 g/m2

Supplied by: IGEPA & inapa

Typefaces:
Unknown by Lukas Haider & Alexander Raffl
Moderat by Tightype

Production:
Druckerei Kettler, Bönen

Published by:
Verlag Kettler, Dortmund, www.verlag-kettler.de

ISBN: 978-3-86206-874-6
1st Edition ©2020 fotobus society, Verlag Kettler

Editors:
Florian Genz, Lea Szramek, Michelle Jekel, Magnus Terhorst, Aurélien Guillery, Elena Fiebig, Aliona Kardash, Florian Dürkopp

Printed and bound in Germany